1898

1898

THE BIRTH OF THE AMERICAN CENTURY

DAVID TRAXEL

ALFRED A. KNOPF   NEW YORK   1998

THIS IS A BORZOI BOOK
PUBLISHED BY ALFRED A. KNOPF, INC.

Copyright © 1998 by David Traxel
Published in the United States by Alfred A. Knopf, Inc., New York, and simultaneously
in Canada by Random House of Canada Limited, Toronto. Distributed by Random
House, Inc., New York. Simultaneously published in Great Britain by Viking,
a division of Penguin Books, Ltd., London.
www.randomhouse.com

Grateful acknowledgment is made to the University of Wisconsin Press for permission to
reprint excerpts from *Beatrice Webb's American Diary, 1898,* edited by David A. Shannon,
copyright © 1963. Reprinted by permission of the University of Wisconsin Press.

Library of Congress Cataloging-in-Publication Data
Traxel, David.
1898: the birth of the American century / David Traxel.—1st American ed.
p. cm.
Includes bibliographical references and index.
ISBN 0-679-45467-5
1. Eighteen ninety-eight, A.D. 2. United States—Civilization—1865–1918.
3. Spanish-American War, 1898.
I. Title.
E711.T73 1998
973.8'9—dc21 97-34370
CIP

JY '98

Manufactured in the United States of America
First American Edition

For Rosemary

Contents

List of Illustrations

Preface

This is a book about one of those rare years, such as 1846 and 1861, that have changed the course of American history. Great economic and social forces had been gathering strength for decades: men and women just reaching early middle age had grown to maturity while the United States was being transformed from an agricultural society guided by natural rhythms into an increasingly frenetic industrialized one ruled by clocks and stopwatches. By 1898, nature's nation, as it had always prided itself, appeared to have become a paragon of technological innovation and commercial power.

During these same few decades its population changed in composition from a chiefly Protestant Anglo-Saxon people to a polyglot amalgamation of all the world's races and creeds, while the gap between rich and poor widened alarmingly. Independence and individuality, qualities highly prized by Americans, came under attack from the giant corporations beginning to dominate the economy, enterprises that seemed to be interested only in turning citizens into consumers. All these enormous mutations occurred domestically while a perplexing and dangerously unstable world developed outside the country's borders. Powerful imperial nations arose, armed with modern weapons that seemed capable of conquering both space and time, turning the oceans that had long served as protective moats into potential highways for aggression. It was an uncertain time when anything seemed possible.

Young Americans in the 1890s saw such developments as both threats and opportunities. Their own nation was a confused mix of civilization and barbarism, of economic strength and military weakness, of patriotic unity and alienating diversity, but, even though harboring an angry sense of inferiority to Europe, they remained confident that the United States was the last best hope of mankind. Impatient with, yet in awe of, their elders, young males felt that new conditions required new approaches, and they were also driven by a fierce longing to match or surpass the glorious military achievements of their fathers in the Civil War. Their sisters and sweethearts aspired to prove their worth by correcting the world in their own manner.

As a result of these pressures and desires the nation would turn from a long history of isolation and preoccupation with its own affairs to active foreign involvement and the challenges of being a world power. During twelve months of rich confusion, wild contradiction, and violent change, the United States in 1898 advanced from being viewed as a country of sharp-dealing businessmen with a second-rate military and little international influence to acknowledgment as a respected member of the imperialists' club, alongside Great Britain, France, Japan, and Germany. It was the first and necessary step in making the twentieth century the American Century.

I have attempted to render a portrait of America in 1898, warts and all, that depicts its people as individuals, as men and women acting from a sense of personal freedom. In telling their stories, I have avoided any overarching theory or analytical approach that would make decisions and events seem orderly, predictable, and exclusively determined by large impersonal forces. Luck, contingency, and individual initiative also played their parts.

WRITING A BOOK of history entails large obligations that are a pleasure to acknowledge. Staff at the Joseph W. England Library were always ready with expert assistance. Philip Gerbino and Charles Gibley proved flexible and supportive, while William Walker demonstrated again his knowledge and appreciation of history as well as superb administrative skill. Alan Misher and Garnett McCoy also deserve recognition for their support of the humanities. Robert Harding and David Greenway's comments on several early chapters were a great help. Samuel McIlvain, Chris Scornavaca, and Tania Lee provided interesting material that found its way into the text. Robert McCracken Peck rendered support in numerous ways, including bringing a relevant lucky charm back from Ulan Bator. Marion Friedman, Sam Gugino, Mary Lee Keane, Caruso Kimballi, Lisa S. Lustgarten, Edward McIlvain, Joshua McIlvain, Amalie Rainey, Anne Ranck, Tony and Susan Scirica, Becky Sinkler, and Anne Taylor were always there when needed. The most needed of all, and the one without whose support this book could not have been written, is Rosemary Ranck.

I would also like to thank the Smithsonian Institution, the Fulbright Commission, the National Endowment for the Humanities, and the Camargo Foundation for grants that prepared me to understand, however imperfectly, the issues and events I have dealt with here. All faults of fact or interpretation, of course, remain solely my own.

1898

PROLOGUE

Hail thee, city born today,
Commercial monarch by the sea,
Whose throne is by the Hudson's way,
'Mid thousands' homesteads join'd to thee.

Opening of "Ode to Greater New York"

FREEZING RAIN HAD BEEN punishing the crowd for hours, but tens of thousands of people continued to jam their way into the streets, eager to celebrate New York's historic moment; at precisely midnight on this Saturday, just as the year 1898 was born, a colossal new city would come into being, instantly leaping from thirty-nine square miles to 320, raising its population of 2,000,000 to 3,400,000, and attaining the status of second-largest metropolis in the world as Brooklyn, Staten Island, Queens, Manhattan, and the Bronx lost their independence and became absorbed into Greater New York. Only London, center of a world-encircling empire, would be larger, and New Yorkers, who had voted this giant city into existence through a referendum, were confident they would soon catch up; they already took pride in having twice as many telephones as that city.

All afternoon New Year's Eve festivities had disrupted normal routine; in the financial district the saloons put out delicacies to accompany the champagne punches they "brewed . . . for all comers." The exchanges, perhaps under this bubbling inspiration, grew rowdy with "joyful horseplay," according to a *New York Times* reporter, who noted that the most lively of them was the Produce Exchange, where there were "the usual football

3

games, and some throwing of grain, flour, and dough. On such occasions the main effort is to cast the pigskin into the wheat 'pit.' This was more than successful, as on one rally of the players two balls were launched into the clamoring brokers."

At the old Brooklyn City Hall, now only to be seat of a borough, there was more an air of mourning; the "City of Churches" was to be self-governing no more. Ex-mayors held an "observance" of the change that filled the council chamber and was addressed by the pastor of the oldest local congregation, who spoke on the history of the area. Will Carleton then read his poem "The Passing of Brooklyn," which began:

> *Now while the bells of the steeples turn golden,*
> *Now as the year has waxed sacred and olden,*
> *And as the new century clearer and clearer*
> *Flashes its headlights another mile nearer*
>   *And moments are nigh*
> *When the fierce gongs and the steam trumpets*
>   *braying,*
> *Once more the triumphs of time are displaying,*
> *Why does a feeling of sadness surround us?*
> *As when the blade of bereavement has found us?*

As Mr. Carleton went on at some length to detail for his listeners their reasons for sadness as the speeding headlights of the new century drew nearer, a far different atmosphere filled the streets of Manhattan, in spite of the nasty weather. Umbrellas helped against the wet, although gusty wind made their shelter uncertain; many men sought more reliable protection and warmth in saloons, where, a journalist reported, "liquor flowed . . . in reality like water." Powerful searchlight beams crisscrossed dark clouds as elaborately decorated floats, the carriages of dignitaries, and numerous marching bands were organized into a parade at Union Square.

A decision to postpone was reversed, and right on schedule, at 10:15 p.m., the procession set out down Broadway. First came the grand marshal, Colonel George Moore Smith of the Sixty-ninth Regiment, with an escort of fourteen mounted policemen, then the band of the Seventh Regiment, then five open carriages containing a large Chicago delegation. The Chicago Democratic machine had earned this place of honor by helping Tammany Hall beat back a reform movement to win the recent mayoral election. Falling into line from the immediate side streets were marching units like the Robert Anderson Battery in their long gray coats and fire helmets, Veteran Firemen's Associations, rifle-carrying Irish Volunteers, German societies, United Italian societies, Hungarian societies, the Garde Lafayette, and bicycle clubs.

Floats called forth the greatest enthusiasm from the crowd. The fruit-trade float was a huge colorful cornucopia spilling forth a bountiful harvest; another advertised the Bijou Theater's production of *Uncle Tom's Cabin* with a depiction of a log shanty and a Southern plantation. The Tammany Hall political machine was represented by a giant tiger with electric lamps for eyes, flanked by pictures of Mayor Robert Van Wyck and of the Boss himself, Richard Croker. One favorite, no doubt because of the self-satisfaction it provided citizens lining the route, showed a gigantic figure of Liberty enlightening a world that was rising from a nest of fountains "all brilliantly lit by electricity." No reporter mentioned whether this allegorical figure of democracy came before or following the Tammany Hall predator, but it was an advertisement not just for the American political way but also for the new Siegal-Cooper department store and bore the invitation, "Meet me at the fountain," after an architectural detail of that commercial palace.

Broadway was crammed with more than the parade; there were impatiently clanging cablecars full of passengers along its eastern side that were backed up for blocks. All went well, however, until the lead sections reached the Broadway Central Hotel, near Bleecker Street, where there was a bottleneck. Horses already nervous from noise and excitement became difficult to control, and a team drawing a carriage full of Chicago politicians swerved in front of a rumbling cablecar, which startled them back toward the waiting ranks of marchers. A sudden explosion of fireworks then stampeded the team through the Seventh Regiment band and up onto the sidewalk, where they panicked, kicking and plunging violently, "throwing men and women in all directions" until Policeman O'Donohue of the West Forty-seventh Street Station caught the bridle of one and steered the team against a lamppost, "where they stuck fast." The injured were carried into the lobby of the hotel, and after some frantic minutes the parade reorganized and continued its march, leaving behind, gleaming on the wet pavement, a tuba and several smaller brasses now in two-dimensional form.

Ethnic singing societies had made their own short procession from the

Stadts Zeitung building to City Hall, each man carrying a tall staff to which was attached a varicolored paper lantern. As they marched and sang, the men rhythmically shifted the lanterns, providing a beautiful light-and-sound show that was overwhelmed by the weather, the noise, and the powerful electric displays all around them.

City Hall Plaza blazed with the national colors. Clusters of red, white, and blue lights were attached to fence posts around the park, and mounted on the Hall itself were two American flags, twenty feet by thirty, made up of thousands of tinted incandescent bulbs that through some miracle of technology made the banners appear to wave in the wind. Over the center of the front portico was an anchor thirty feet long, symbolizing New York's maritime trade, and at the ends of the structure were two giant representations of the Shield of the Republic. The surrounding buildings, every window crowded with onlookers, were illuminated, and on their roofs were mighty searchlights; all this brilliance reflected off the slick asphalt and the badges and brass buttons of the police, who stood shoulder to shoulder on the streets, keeping the crowds from the square.

Slowly, however, their ranks were pushed toward the park by the sheer numbers of people pressing forward to view the spectacle. Often the happy crowd sang along when one of the bands played a familiar tune, thousands of male and female voices echoing among the tall buildings. Everyone was in such good spirits, including the police, that even staggering drunks were only told to go home. "If they talked back the police men laughed," a journalist wrote in amazement. "Few arrests were made and those only by direction of Captains or Sergeants."

As the choral groups marched into place in front of City Hall, they began competing for a sterling silver cup, but the wind, the oompah bands, exploding firecrackers, and dazzlers made hearing, let alone judging, difficult for the celebrities who were to pick the purest assembly of voices. Ten gleaming trophies were being offered for categories besides singing, including best float, best bicycle company, best costume; competition in all of them was fierce as the stinging rain beat down.

The silver loving cups, the fireworks, some of the drinks, and even the fierce radiance of the lights had been provided for the public celebration by a tall, awkward, fabulously wealthy thirty-five-year-old Californian who had come to New York because it was the great national model of sophistication and style as well as the arena for success in America, especially in his chosen field of journalism. Locked in a fierce competition of his own, a circulation war with Joseph Pulitzer of the *World,* he craved any publicity that might give him an edge. "Putting out a newspaper without promotion is like winking at a girl in the dark," William Randolph Hearst believed, "well-intentioned but ineffective." Nothing involving the *Journal* or its city was going to be done in the dark if he could help it.

Some Manhattan civic leaders had initially resisted the idea of a celebration; one, unhappy over the successful referendum, had argued instead that a "funeral service" be held for old New York. Politicians had dithered and disagreed over the form an official ceremony should take, so Hearst, as private individual, had stepped in, raising money from a variety of rich metropolitan types, such as financier J. P. Morgan and Tammany boss Richard Croker, as well as reaching into his own bottomless pockets. The elaborate festivities were organized by *Journal* staff while under an enormous press of other work, which ranged from mounting a special Christmas dinner for five thousand *Journal* newsboys, many of them orphaned and living at the Roosevelt family–supported Newsboys' Lodging House, to sustaining Hearst's energetic crusade to start a war between the United States and Spain. The publisher himself was too shy to face such an enormous crowd, but watched all the festivities from the offices of his newspaper, which overlooked the square.

At ten minutes to midnight, the harbor contributed its part to the carnival with every ship, boat, and ferry pulling its steam whistle; more and more people crowded into the area around City Hall Park and the surrounding streets; choral groups shifted to "Auld Lang Syne" while bicyclists demonstrated their skill and daring by speeding up and down the hall's steps. But all this chaotic activity ceased and the crowd fell silent at the stroke of twelve, as the searchlights, buzzing with electricity, flooded the flagstaff mounted on the City Hall cupola in a bath of white, while the chimes of Old Trinity Church sounded in the background. At that very instant, the mayor of San Francisco, standing over three thousand miles away by the Golden Gate, pushed a button that sent an electric charge speeding through the line from the Pacific coast to this Atlantic maritime city, which then triggered a motor that shot the newly designed blue-and-white flag of Greater New York up the pole. Skyrockets streaked overhead, the cheers of a hundred thousand citizens resounded through the streets, and round after blank round was fired by a battery of artillery pieces drawn up by the Post Office, gunsmoke eddying and swirling through the choking crowd before rising in great billows to join the low clouds. The tremendous roar went on for fifteen minutes, "a saturation of light and sound" the *Times* called it, before snow started falling so fast that the mass atomized into thousands of individuals struggling homeward.

AND IN SUCH MANNER, to one degree or another, the New Year was heralded around the nation. Big cities held celebrations to match their size; small towns held their own, quieter observances. Adventuresome inhabitants took trains to the nearest metropolis if they desired more excitement.

San Francisco held a particularly noteworthy festival. Even as early as nine o'clock Pacific Time, when the mayor pushed his button sending a playful electric current racing across the country to raise the national symbol in New York, "All the town and his wife were out, bent upon having a good time." Citizens felt they had a victory to celebrate, since just a few days before they had elected a slate of "freeholders" to draft a new charter that might result in elimination of the corrupt political machine dominating city government. "The bosses, however," reported the *New York Times,* "are much annoyed at the result, and it is feared . . . that when the charter comes to a vote [ballot box] stuffing will be resorted to."

THERE WERE THE USUAL unusual events that the nation's journals made a point of reporting to entertain their audience: A couple in Missouri made the front pages by exchanging wedding vows over the telephone, a use of the instrument that William McKinley, as the first president to actually conduct the nation's business over the "wire," must surely have approved of. He had recently told a reporter that he thought this technological marvel was valuable primarily because it "is bringing us all closer together." Also in evidence on this Sunday morning were the traditional New Year admonitions and frettings by intellectuals. One running debate in the *New York Times* was over "A Burning Question in Literature"—whether the recent great increase in the number of books being published was an enrichment of civilization, or a "growing evil." Another article inquired, "Has New York Advanced in the Fine Arts?"

But of course not all was joy, ingenuous wonder, or intellectual pondering, as eager newspaper readers were quickly informed. One shocking incident occurred in Lonoke, Arkansas, when a mob attacked the store of Oscar Simonton, an African-American who had ignored warnings to leave town. As the mob broke down his door, Simonton escaped through a window. "No less than thirty shots were fired at him, three of which took effect, one in his left side and two in the thigh and shoulder." Badly wounded, he managed to escape to Little Rock, but the *New York Times* recalled that just a few months before, a Professor Hollingsworth, who had persisted in conducting a school in Lonoke for Negro children, had been found dead, hanging on a fence with sixty-nine bullet holes in his body.

Alcohol, as well as racism, was a constant source of problems in American society, and several national temperance efforts were launched on this first day of the new year. Even though the police of New York had been tolerant at the gala in City Hall Park, there were two or three hundred drunks arrested on the East Side alone, most singing in their defense the old refrain of "bin celebratin'." One, Patrick McLaughlin, who was charged with fighting because there were a number of large scratches on his face, claimed to have only been drinking.

"You say you were only drunk, and that you were not fighting," said the puzzled magistrate, "while the officer says you were fighting. How's that?"

Mr. McLaughlin felt he had a perfectly reasonable explanation: "Judge, you can see I wasn't fighting. Up our way when there's a fight, somebody gets hurt. I'm as sound as a dollar."

Either because he was charmed by the savage innocence of this defense or because it fit so amusingly into the prevailing stereotype of the Irish-American, the judge released Patrick McLaughlin without charges.

Disease still carried off the innocent, no matter how rich or how beautiful. Lucille Pulitzer, teenage daughter of one of the country's most powerful men, died on New Year's Eve at Chatwold, the family home in Bar Harbor, having suffered greatly for four months as a mysterious disease ravaged her body; Joseph Pulitzer had brought in the most prestigious physicians in the country, but, for all his wealth and influence, was unable in the end to do anything more effective than what the poorest parent of the poorest child might have done.

Accidents, too, were thick on newspaper pages, although here class was more of a determinant. Anyone might be run down by a stampeding horse or speeding bicycle, or burned in the frequent house fires, but it was the unprotected workplace, full of clanging, banging, smashing machines, that maimed and killed tens of thousands every year. Other dangers also awaited working men and women. In Lattimer, Pennsylvania, indictments were being prepared against deputy sheriffs who had gunned down dozens of miners during a strike in September of 1897, killing twenty.

Bessie Potter and Christopher Robert, along with many others, had not been able to bear the thought of living another day, let alone facing a new year. Women in this state of desperation seemed to prefer drinking carbolic acid, a particularly horrible way to die, while men usually favored a gun to the head. Both Potter and Robert left reporters, readers, and those who knew and loved them mystified as to why an attractive brunette of twenty-five ("The dead woman's feet and hands are small. She has a beautiful set of teeth, and her fingernails are well kept. The general appearance . . . was that of a person of refinement and scrupulously neat personal habits") and a wealthy builder would choose to end their lives.

As fascinating to the reading public as suicides was crime of all sorts, and there were a number of dramatic accounts of burglary, robbery, and murder, two of which were particularly troubling. Eli Shaw was jailed in Camden, New Jersey, accused of murdering both his mother and his grandmother. This was such a doubly intriguing but unthinkable crime that the trial would claim major attention all year. An outraged son of a mother decided to torment the accused at the start of the new year by sending him a bomb wrapped as a present. It fizzed when opened, then put out an acrid smoke; there was no explosion, but it left Shaw so terrified he could not sit still for days.

An incident on a Broadway cablecar involving a pickpocket caught by Patrolman Frederick Probst was also given a great amount of space. The criminal, who turned out to be a wanted member of the deadly Whyo Gang, put up a violent resistance, finally in desperation shoving a revolver against Probst's head and pulling the trigger. The gun misfired, but the fight continued for several blocks until other officers came to their com-rade's rescue, having to club the Whyo until he finally quit chewing on one of Probst's fingers. The truly shocking detail to a nation that relied on indi-vidual initiative was that of all the passengers on board the car, "Not one of them came to Probst's assistance." When the crook was safely in custody, however, a crowd gathered and began shouting, "Lynch him! Lynch him!"

But stories of potential rather than actual violence claimed the biggest headlines at the dawn of 1898, and they had to do with dangers outside the borders of the United States. A serious threat of war between the Great Powers had developed in both China and Africa, and these threats would never really disappear in the coming months, even while the United States itself was engaged in deadly combat. Great Britain, France, Russia, Ger-many, and Japan were all rivals for international empire, a Darwinian strug-gle that left Americans troubled about how to respond. Exactly where Kiao-Chau, Hai-Nan, and Fashoda were located was a mystery, but people understood the growing reliance of their economy on foreign markets that these imperial powers threatened to close. American businessmen were particularly fond of contemplating "the illimitable markets of China," but there were many other spots on the globe that also promised good profits.

The same technology that Americans were celebrating with telephone marriages and waving flags constructed from incandescent bulbs added to their unease as one new weapons development quickly followed another. Huge modern battleships were being built that could cross the once-protective waters of the Atlantic and Pacific in a matter of days, steel ships with powerful cannon capable of leveling cities from miles off shore; and recently the press had been full of stories about an exciting new craft that raised even more unsettling questions about how to defend the country. Torpedo boats were fast and small, yet reportedly armed with devices able to sink the largest dreadnoughts. As if to emphasize the country's unreadiness to meet a serious challenge like the one the European nations were presenting to one another, an editor of the *Times* sent a reporter to inspect the battle-scarred Civil War era "monitors" at the League Island Navy Yard. Though admittedly obsolete, a subhead proclaimed they were ALWAYS READY FOR SERVICE.

New weaponry was now often threateningly close to American cities in places like Haiti, where the Germans were making demands on the local government to pay compensation for supposed indignities visited on one of their citizens, and Cuba, where Spain was ruthlessly suppressing the populace's desire for independence, while blaming the United States for what success the rebels had enjoyed.

While contemplating geopolitical developments, some Americans began to feel not fear but the stirrings of resentment and ambition. Though relatively weak now, why shouldn't the country arm with modern weapons? Why refrain from the race for empire? The United States should take its rightful place on the world stage. What better way to protect itself than by projecting strength overseas? And how better to improve the world than by being a champion for good, ensuring the spread of liberty, democracy, Protestant Christianity, efficiency, and, certainly, "unrestricted commerce." It was time, a growing minority felt, for "the Eagle to spread its wings and scream."

Those wings, at least economically, were already spreading too wide for some European leaders, who had traditionally looked with scorn on the United States as a country with great resources and potential, but little real understanding of power. They saw this weakness as springing from a foolishly broad democratic system that produced leaders more concerned with mouthing abstract moral platitudes than with intelligently applying force and diplomacy. But even during the worldwide depression of the 1890s, which was just beginning to loosen its grip, American exports continued to flow abroad, causing Count Agenor Goluchowski, the Austrian foreign minister, to warn in the last weeks of 1897 against this threat from American energy and organizational talent:

> The disastrous war of competition which we meet with at every step and in every field of human activity, upon the part of countries beyond the seas, a contest which is now going on but which will become greater in the near future, calls for immediate and comprehensive resistance unless the nations of Europe are to be seriously crippled in their most vital interests and are willing to fall victim to a disease which will surely lead to their destruction. They must fight shoulder to shoulder against this common danger, and they must go into this contest armed with every weapon of defense that their resources afford.

FOR THE FIRST TIME in decades the White House was dark, and quiet, on New Year's Day, 1898. Normally there would have been a constant flow of flag-bedecked carriages delivering elegantly dressed ambassadors and attachés in full uniform to the main entrance, while a thick line of patient men, women, and children watched and waited for their turn to shake the hand of their president and offer best wishes for the coming year. This was a citizenry that felt a personal connection to government. The Executive Mansion, though structurally so rotted and weak that engineers had repeatedly warned its floors could not support such weight, was traditionally a welcoming venue to "all citizens who are sober, washed, and free of bodily advertising." But this year the White House was in mourning, large iron gates closed and locked, because William McKinley's eighty-seven-year-old mother had just died.

The president was an early riser, usually leaving his twin bed around six and, after shaving and washing, walking down the corridor to the Cabinet room, where he had appropriated one end of the large conference table as work space. There he went over papers and reports for a couple of hours before his invalid wife, Ida, made her way to the breakfast table, when he would hurry to be at her side. Ida McKinley's health had been broken by the deaths of their two young daughters many years before, and since those tragedies he had made her happiness his major concern. This devotion to his wife was well known, as had been the president's strong ties to his mother, and these loyalties were important wellsprings of his popularity with the American people. "In honoring your mother and your wife, you have honored womankind," one female supporter had pronounced during the election of 1896. Others, considering his unselfish honesty and old-fashioned sense of honor along with his domestic virtues, pronounced him a "Christian gentleman" or, using one of the favorite images of the time, "a medieval knight."

Though handsome in a virile "matinee idol" style, the president did not radiate charisma or any sort of sensual excitability; instead, his calm gray eyes and dignified presence gave the American people a reassuring perception of serene maturity and sober judgment. He had marked his rise to the dignity of his office with a new, fancier style of dress—white piqué waistcoats—and refused to allow the public to see him chewing the cigars that he always kept handy and that sometimes had stained his satin labels back in the days when he had been a congressman and then governor of Ohio. A man of regular habits, he was marked by a few startling eccentricities. One, born of supreme, though quiet, self-confidence was his style of shaving his fleshy, unlined face. Striding about a room, never even glancing at a mirror, he would often dictate correspondence to a secretary while taking rapid, dextrous strokes with a well-honed straight-edged razor.

A conservative Republican who believed in the cooperation of government and big business, McKinley had been sworn into office the previous March after winning a bitterly divisive campaign against William Jennings Bryan. His immediate goal had been to return prosperity to a nation devastated by the great depression that had begun in 1893. In the worst financial collapse in U.S. history to that time, banks and businesses had failed by the score; tens of thousands of farmers had declared bankruptcy; millions of workers had lost their jobs; and bloody pitched battles had been fought between striking union men and guards hired by corporations.

But now some of that class anger was receding, as gold from the huge Klondike strike of 1897 was flowing into the banks, providing a basis for credit and economic expansion. A different threat to public happiness had elbowed its way onto the nation's front pages, and this was causing the president great difficulty.

Spain's ruthless suppression of a revolt that had started in its colony of

Cuba in 1895 outraged the American people, who feared that they were passively allowing the same kind of large-scale atrocities to take place just off their shores that the Europeans had allowed the Turks to commit on the helpless Armenians just a few years before. Valeriano Weyler, the Spanish governor-general, had rounded up peasant farmers and unemployed sugar-plantation laborers from the countryside and confined them in what amounted to prison camps, *reconcentrados,* in order to deprive the rebels of their support. The result was a victory of sorts—these tactics had weakened the rebellion—but at tremendous human cost. Hundreds of thousands of men, women, and children had died of starvation and disease during confinement.

American newspapers had made a moral crusade of the story, both from genuine revulsion and from recognition that it was a circulation-builder. Increasingly, many citizens were willing to see the nation go on an actual military crusade to stop the horror that lay just ninety miles from the American shore. McKinley, who had risen from teenage private to twenty-two-year-old major during the Civil War while taking part in some of its bloodiest battles, was doing all he could to keep the United States at peace while trying to ameliorate conditions in Cuba.

Pressure was being applied to the Spanish government of Práxedas Mateo Sagasta, who had recently replaced the assassinated premier Antonio Cánovas del Castillo. Reforms had already been instituted: "Butcher" Weyler had been ordered home, and been succeeded as governor by General Ramón Blanco, who had orders to conduct more humane policies; a compromise program of political autonomy for Cuba went into effect on January 1. Although Spaniards, and especially the military, resented what they saw as unwarranted American interference, it increasingly looked as if war could be avoided, unless something unexpected happened.

Clara Barton, "Angel of the Battlefield" during the Civil War and founder of the American branch of the Red Cross, had met with the president the last week in December, seeking his advice on how to help; on New Year's Day she presided at the organizing of the Central Cuban Relief Committee in New York City. Now seventy-six years old, she had recently returned from months spent in the Ottoman Empire providing relief to Armenian survivors of the Turkish massacres. Barton was sure that her experience dealing with a government guilty of such great persecution would help her conduct an effective aid program in Cuba.

.   .   .

LESS OPTIMISTIC ABOUT a peaceful end to Cuban misery was the assistant secretary of the navy. Theodore Roosevelt was one of those who believed the United States needed a more aggressive foreign policy, and a strong military force to back it up. He had been responsible for two recent decisions that he thought would strengthen the country's position if the dispute with Spain worsened.

On January 1, Commodore George Dewey was rowed out to the cruiser *Olympia,* then riding at anchor in the harbor of Yokohama, Japan, to assume command of the U.S. navy's Asiatic Squadron. Roosevelt had engineered his selection because he believed Dewey to be an officer of fighting spirit, one who, in the event of war, would prove resourceful and independent enough to carry the day against the Spanish fleet guarding the Philippines, even though he and his ships were thousands of miles from a home base.

Closer to Washington, another naval officer was also preparing for action. For more than two weeks the battleship *Maine,* commanded by Captain Charles Sigsbee, had been waiting at the naval installation at Key West, just five hours' steaming from Havana. Out of sensitivity to Spanish feelings, no official American vessel had visited Cuban ports for three years, and even the routine exercises of the Atlantic Squadron had been moved north. Now, however, maneuvers had been scheduled for January in the Dry Tortugas just off the Florida coast, and the *Maine* was on semi-alert. Assistant Secretary Roosevelt had supported both renewed exercises and the presence of a capital ship in case Fitzhugh Lee, American consul-general in Havana, needed such support to protect American lives.

While waiting to be summoned, Captain Sigsbee was using his ship's steam launches to patrol against any filibustering expeditions that might try to sneak across the ninety miles to the island to deliver arms or other aid to Cuban rebels; nearly every day he and Fitzhugh Lee exchanged cables to ensure that telegraphic communication remained open. In case of potential trouble, a coded message would alert Sigsbee to build steam in the *Maine's* triple expansion engines, then a second one would order him to come quickly. The captain, proud of his huge, gleaming white battleship, felt able to meet any challenge, and in letters to his wife compared himself to the American world heavyweight champion "Fitz" Fitzsimmons.

Such a small, isolated base as Key West meant boring liberties for the "Jackies," or enlisted men, who spent what free time they had supporting their "baseball 9" in a league made up of teams representing individual ships. A cold spell dampened their spirits, as did meager rations, but even more disturbing to the crew was the *Maine*'s reputation as a "Jonah" or "Hoodoo" ship, the result of men having been swept overboard and drowned on earlier missions.

Some excitement and a lift to morale had been sparked during the holiday season, when Captain Sigsbee ordered the installation of a scintillating technological marvel for Key West along the same, if more moderate, lines that William Randolph Hearst provided for New York City. The *Maine* was "illuminated" with hundreds of electric lights strung fore and aft along the mastheads and funnels and encircling the superstructure decks. The local newspaper wrote it up as "One of the finest displays of electricity ever witnessed in the city."

A New Year's Eve event in Cuba was probably missed by most readers of the *New York Times* since it was reported in small type and buried at the bottom of an interior page. A "torpedo" or mine had exploded in Havana harbor, just off the floating dock, "but no damage was done."

CHAPTER 1

LAND OF CONTRASTS

*[The] United States stands out as preeminently the "Land of Contrasts"—
the land of stark, staring, and stimulating inconsistency; at once the home
of enlightenment and the happy hunting ground of the charlatan and the
quack; a land in which nothing happens but the unexpected; the home of
Hyperion, but no less the haunt of the satyr; always the land of promise, but
not invariably the land of performance; a land which may be bounded by
the aurora borealis, but which has also undeniable acquaintance with the
flames of the bottomless pit; a land which is laved at once by the rivers of
Paradise and the leaden waters of Acheron.*

James Muirhead

As HE WANDERED the United States compiling information for a traveler's
guidebook, the Englishman James Muirhead encountered such a bewil-
dering range of incongruities and paradoxes that he decided to also write a
more complete study, one that would not only describe but seek to account
for such enormous diversity within a single country. When published in
late 1898, the book bore the title *Land of Contrasts*—the only fitting one,
Muirhead thought.

One major contrast causing "extraordinary clashes" in the country was
that between youth and age, not just between generations but also
between the civilization of the Old World and a rawer continent still bearing the markings of frontier wilderness. By studying this uncomfortable
meeting of traditional and modern, foreign visitors often thought they
might be able to discern the heretofore hazy shape of what was to come,

the *"lendemain,"* or future, as the French intellectual Paul Bourget wrote, of civilization.

Americans were fascinated by these European reflections because they were similarly concerned with the divergent states of their society in 1898. Regions, classes, races, the two sexes, often seemed in such threatening disagreement that some feared the contrasts foreigners found so informative might be signs that, rather than opening to a bright future, their civilization was ending before it had a chance to flower. Both the severe economic depression following the Panic of 1893, and the recent presidential election had revealed divisions pitting labor against capital, farmers against city dwellers, and the Eastern states against the West and South.

That election had been won by William McKinley at least in part because his friend Mark Hanna, himself a wealthy businessman, had squeezed enormous sums of money out of terrified capitalists like J. P. Morgan, John D. Rockefeller, J. J. Hill, and hundreds of their fellows who were convinced that William Jennings Bryan's radical plan to adopt bimetallism, by which silver as well as gold coins would be struck and circulated, would dissolve the international credit of the United States, dismantle the industrial economy, and disperse their fortunes.

Bryan, the Democratic candidate (he was also nominated by the Populist Party), and his fervent supporters were moved by an almost religious conviction that the expansion of the money supply brought about by bimetallism would be the savior of the "little man"; it would, they believed, release him from "the cross of gold and the crown of thorns" that kept currency inflexibly tight and made the life of a debtor hell. And if such measures hindered the rush to an industrial "modern" way of life, all the better.

The thirty-six-year-old former congressman and newspaper editor was the greatest popular orator of the age, and as much an evangelist as he was a politician. "More than any one I have known," wrote the journalist Frederic Howe, "he represented the moralist in politics. He wanted to change men. He was a missionary; America was a missionary. . . . He was the *vox ex cathedra* of the Western self-righteous missionary mind." His platform not only demanded "the free and unlimited coinage of silver at the ratio of 16 to 1 for gold," and an income tax, but also pointed to monopolies, protective tariffs, and government interference in strikes, often with armed soldiers, as being ways the rich kept common people under their control. "The humblest citizen in all the land, when clad in the armor of a righteous cause," believed Bryan, "is stronger than all the hosts of error. I come to speak to you in defense of a cause as holy as the cause of liberty—the cause of humanity."

Hanna, however, fought back with the fabulous sum of twenty million dollars, using this war chest with exemplary skill to run the first lavishly financed presidential campaign. Republican orators like ex-President Benjamin Harrison, Speaker of the House Tom Reed, and the fiery Theodore Roosevelt had their expenses paid as they crisscrossed the country, while William McKinley presented himself as "above the fray" by staying at home to welcome thousands of the Party faithful, who made well-publicized pilgrimages, subsidized by the railroads, to his front porch, where they would be photographed with the candidate. Clever writers were hired to produce reams of books, pamphlets, position papers, and preset newspaper articles. When William Allen White, the young editor of the *Emporia* (Kansas) *Gazette,* wrote a powerful editorial entitled "What's Wrong With Kansas," which poured scorn on the simple-mindedness of Bryan's solutions to the economic problems of farmers, Hanna had five hundred thousand copies printed and distributed throughout agricultural regions. Theodore Roosevelt wrote a friend that "Hanna has advertised McKinley as if he were a patent medicine." The American national symbol was also claimed for the cause—red, white, and blue becoming the colors of the Republican campaign; when a young Bryan supporter tore a Party flag down at a McKinley rally and burned it, he was condemned for desecration of the national symbol.

Bryan, though possessed of little money, made his own contributions to modern campaigning by the aggressive, energetic pace he set. Traveling over eighteen thousand miles by train, shaking hands and talking to supporters until late in the night, he was a speaker of such rare eloquence that the baggage handlers on his "special" would rush the loading and unloading so they could then run to the rear car and hear him deliver his speech again, though they might have already listened to it more than a dozen times that day. Glorying in the title of the Great Commoner, he used Republican attacks on his lack of refinement and dignity to rally supporters and emphasize the differences between the good simple people who worked with their hands in field or factory and the overly sophisticated parasites who lived off them.

Labor leaders like Eugene Debs and Samuel Gompers endorsed the Democrat, but employers of many of Bryan's followers warned workers that if he was elected their factories would close, or the railroad be forced to cut back operations. Immigrants were appealed to by the Republicans with flyers in their own languages pointing out the serious cultural differences between their ways of life and those of the native sons in the Democratic camp.

The final vote of 7,000,000 for McKinley to 6,500,000 for Bryan also revealed the regional cleavages of the country. McKinley overwhelmingly carried the East, including every state east of the Mississippi and north of the Ohio, plus Kentucky and West Virginia, for 271 electoral votes; Bryan took the South and most of the states west of the Mississippi for 176. He was not discouraged, and would be the Democratic candidate again in 1900 and 1904.

AMERICAN FARMERS WERE more blessed than those in foreign nations because most of them owned their land instead of working, as peasants and tenants, for others. Since the end of the Civil War more new acreage had been cultivated than in all the country's history, but now this good earth was becoming less plentiful, although Cherokee lands in Oklahoma had just been "bought" from the Indians there and opened to eager home-steaders. Those who worked hard and saved could still make a living, as one young man in Iowa bragged, who was then quoted in *Harper's Weekly* in October of 1898. His parents had come to the state in the 1860s, just after he was born. "My father being a poor man and having a large family, we were early taught hard work. On the morning of my twenty-first birth-day my father informed me that from that time on I was my own man, and gave me the big gray team in the barn (without halter, bridle, or harness), saying, if I could not add to that in so good a country as this, he had no more to waste on me." The youth worked for wages on a neighbor's place until he earned enough to buy a set of harness and a yearling heifer, "and from that time to this I have never been without cattle." A year and a half later his brother came of age, and was given a team of bay horses. The two became partners, "leasing a piece of land which we got for the breaking of it. This ground produced sixty bushels of corn to the acre for our first crop, making over seven car loads of corn, for which we received thirty-five cents per bushel." The brothers then bought four hundred acres, paying off a heavy mortgage at eight percent, becoming, at least for a time, prosperous. The editor at *Harper's Weekly* thought one could "read the whole history of pioneer life in that farmer's story." Inspiring as history, perhaps, but at the beginning of 1898 the future looked less hopeful.

For the majority of farmers, no matter how diligently they labored in their fields, times were hard during the 1890s. As prices of basic commodities like corn, wheat, and cotton tumbled under the flood of new production, and freight rates charged by the railroads climbed, the burden of debt became heavier than ever before. Protests grew, leading to the founding of the Patrons of Husbandry (the Grange), Farmers' Alliances, and the Populist Party. These groups blamed their problems on the plutocrats and their new industrial order, which robbed the people of the fruits of their toil. Some of their anger was expressed in song:

> *My husband came from town last night*
> *Sad as a man could be,*
> *His wagon empty, cotton gone,*
> *And not a dime had he.*
>
> *Huzzah-Huzzah*
> *'Tis queer I do declare:*
> *We make the clothes for all the world,*
> *But few we have to wear.*

It was not only economic troubles that plagued farmers; Thomas Jefferson had called them "the chosen people of God, if ever He had a chosen people, whose breasts He has made His particular deposit for substantial and genuine virtue. . . ." Their wisdom, coming from contact with the earth and their "yeoman" independence, had been the ideal of the Republic for so long that they were having difficulty dealing with their new image as backward rubes, hayseeds, or country bumpkins, butt of the jokes of smooth-talking, unscrupulous city folk who mocked them as allegedly bereft of intelligence, sophistication, or any sense of fun. To the "people of the soil" cities, with their saloons, gambling halls, and masses of foreign people speaking strange tongues, seemed the source of much that was wrong with contemporary America, and these godless places were not only growing more powerful and influential but also luring away innocent country children with promises of easier money and a more stimulating way of life.

Sitting around the potbellied stove and within reach of the proverbial cracker barrel at a crossroads store was one way rural folk found stimulation and a sense of community. Here the farmer and his wife could see their neighbors and buy "necessaries" from the shelves and counters that

were customarily divided between dry goods on the right side and groceries, tobacco, quack nostrums, and well-known patent medicines on the
left—nostrums having secret ingredients, while to be "patented" required
some revelations. Scattered around the room would be stands or glass
cases for household goods like cutlery and glassware, as well as sundry
other items such as dyes, flavorings, tools, and, if the county wasn't dry,
whiskey. Even luxury articles, such as perfumes and wall clocks, might be
carried.

Credit was often extended until the crop was in and sold, and service
was personal. If you wanted some soda crackers, the clerk would reach into
the barrel or box and grab a serving, the rule being "one handful, one
nickel." Often, however, the owner would encourage trade by allowing customers engaged, say, in a game of checkers to help themselves to this staple
for free. Crackers were such an institution that jokes circulated around
them, like the one about the customer who complained that mice were living in the store's barrel, to which the owner replied, "That's impossible.
Mice could not possibly live in my cracker barrel because the cat sleeps
there every night."

But progress was reaching even into these small remote emporiums.
Competitive pressure was rising from catalogue merchants like Sears and
Montgomery Ward, and technology was beginning to affect even their
simplest wares. "Applied science is rapidly undermining the few scraps of
sentiment that are still associated with our daily life," lamented the *Agricultural Almanac* of 1898. "The scents that we fondly imagine to be dis-
tilled from the sweet breathing children of Flora are in reality extracts
from coal tar, and even worse. The raspberry flavor in our confectionery is
a product of benzol, with a name about thirty syllables in length; essence
of pineapple is just acetate of some dreadful hydrocarbon compound."

The independent small towns that provided whatever center the farmers
had outside their homes, churches, and the nearby store were also undergoing fundamental change as they lost their self-sufficiency and became
tied to a railroad culture. Farmers and country towns still made up three-
fifths of the country's population, and the journalist William Allen White
thought such communities formed the bedrock of American values.
Though conservative himself, like most of his neighbors, he found some of
the recent changes good, especially the beginnings of local advertising,
which freed newspaper publishers from being chained to their subscribers.
"A new drygoods store had come to town. It was buying page advertisements, putting on special sales. The hardware dealers were realizing that

advertising would bring results, so they told about their buggies, farm implements, kitchen gadgets and paint, in quarter-page and half-page lots. The newspaper business in country towns passed definitely in those latter years of the nineteenth century out of its character as beggar and black-mailer, and became one of the major industries of every little town."

White, though just turning thirty, had been able to obtain the three thousand dollars in financing to purchase the *Emporia Gazette* partly because of personal connections; he was known locally as an intelligent and honorable young man of good prospects. Wages were low in small towns—his reporters made around $9 a week—but so were costs. "A frying chicken cost fifteen cents, steak ten cents a pound . . . flour two dollars a hundred, sugar twenty pounds for a dollar." He liked the scale of the place, which allowed one to know fellow citizens almost too well, and appreciated the solid values and lack of extremes he found there. Entertainment was through groups of friends: there was an "old whist crowd," a "young danc-ing crowd," a "lodge crowd," and a "church social crowd." No matter what set one belonged to, activities took place in parlors during winter, on porches in the spring and fall, and yards in summer warmth. All their lives, but particularly the dance set's, were undoubtedly enhanced in 1898 by the introduction of a mass-produced version of Edison's "Improved Gramo-phone" that sold for only twenty dollars.

Even the violent aspects of rural communities seemed more personal, more on a human scale, than in the cities. In the spring of 1898, White, in a report on the results of a mayoral election in Emporia, indulged in some mean-spirited remarks about the defeated candidate, Colonel Luther Sev-ery. "In his defeat, I twisted a stick of scorn in his sore entrails. . . . I had no grudge against him. I was just a young smart aleck, and he was a man of seventy." By the following morning he had already forgotten the piece, and, meeting Severy on Main Street, he touched his hat and said, "Good morn-ing, Colonel." The next moment he was coming to, lying on his face in the muddy intersection, "and the old colonel was dancing around me waving a broken cane and men were trying to lead him away. Back of my ear was a bleeding welt which became a bump."

White felt no anger toward the old man, but rose grinning, rubbing the mud from his vest and trousers. He went back to his office, wrote an amus-ing description of the incident, and encountered his assailant on the street again the next day. "I saw his hand fluttering and quickly reached out to grab it. There we stood, he with tears in his eyes, and I tried to say quickly that I was sorry, then he said it, so we both said it—and it was all over. It was a case of temper with him and idle meanness with me, put into rather cutting and unjustified rhetoric. I think it taught me a lesson."

THE WEST AND MIDWEST were famous as the wellsprings of American optimism. States like Nebraska had endured the worst drought in their history during 1896 and 1897 while also suffering the pain of economic depression. Yet civic leaders of Omaha, inspired by the phenomenal success of Chicago's Columbian Exposition in the same year as the 1893 crash, still had confidence enough to consider hosting a World's Fair to display the victories of modern agriculture in turning the "Great American Desert" into productive cropland and to promote the industrialization and development of the Trans-Mississippi West, with the focus on their city as gateway to the region.

The idea was taken up enthusiastically by many local groups, including the Knights of Ak-Sar-Ben, a businessmen's association that appealed to its members with a secret initiation ceremony and other mysterious rituals, all of which were inspired by Washington Irving's account of the Spanish explorer Francisco Coronado's wanderings through their region centuries before in his quest for the Seven Golden Cities of Cíbola. The exotic-sounding Knights (Ak-Sar-Ben was a reversal of their state's name) did all they could to promote the exposition, including sponsoring a parade in late 1897. "Twenty floats designed and built in Omaha, at a cost of $20,000," bragged their souvenir program, "covered with living figures in superb costumes, escorted by mounted knights and ten bands, pass through three miles of streets illuminated by strings of incandescent lights, making the most beautiful fall festival in the United States." Most of the floats told the story of Coronado's quest for riches, but the final two carried tableaux entitled "Welcome Prosperity" and the "Trans-Mississippi Exposition." From the "porticos of the float devoted to the fair, muses representing Art, Science, and Literature tossed flowers to the throngs lining the streets."

To William Allen White this whole organizing effort showed the power of Anglo-Saxon democracy in the land west of the Great River, a place where "no . . . class lines are drawn. . . . In this Trans-Mississippi country there is no family of distinction. . . . Every tub stands on its own bottom, and if there is any caste, the spendthrift is the only outcast, and the dishonest debtor is the only man from whom the people flee as from the unclean.

"The chairman of one of the most important sub-committees was a telegraph messenger boy a generation ago. His friend on the right was a farm-hand then. The young man near the window was an office boy during the panic of seventy-three. One of his associates on the finance committee used to twist brakes out of Denver on a cattle train. . . . It was absolutely democratic. The men around the luncheon table made no pretensions to academic culture. Here and there was a college-bred man, but he had for-gotten who Phidias was, and the other men didn't care who he was."

But in spite of these common touches, there was resistance. Farmers who supported the Populist Party were suspicious of the fact that all the organizers but one were from the city of Omaha (population 150,000 and growing), and doubted that any benefits would come to country folk. "It seems to me," a Populist leader argued, "that with the present condition of our people it is damnable to ask for money for that Omaha show."

Backers of the exposition, however, were determined. "We shall not always have hard times; we are bound to have good harvests some day. By the time the exposition is ready the people will have money in their pockets to pay to see it; it will be a revelation to the world of what we have and an education to our own people. We know it will be a success; and we think we can pay expenses." Argument was made that it was the duty of Nebraska to help educate the young to the new world that was taking shape beyond American borders. "We are living in an age of surprises," the *Omaha World-Herald* argued, "and these great expositions broaden the minds of the people. Makes them respect each other's opinions. That is worth more to the next generation than much book learning." Promoters had a powerful ally in William Jennings Bryan, and they also followed the advice of a supporter to "commence a system of missionary efforts in the rural districts of this state," the "missionating" being conducted by Nebraska women's clubs.

The desire to advertise and to promote Progress in the West, to over-come the region's reputation for rude living and frontier barbarism, was a strong motivation, but the organizers also wanted to deal with a related concern very much on the minds of late nineteenth-century Americans: civilization. The idea of Progress came from Darwin's startling argument for the evolutionary development of men and animals, which had been deeply absorbed into American thought and life. To illustrate how far the country had "evolved," and to put the achievements of "civilization" in per-spective, while at the same time providing an attraction to lure Eastern tourists, it was decided to host "an extensive exhibit illustrative of the life, and customs and decline of the aboriginal inhabitants of the western hemi-

The Fifth Avenue chateau of John Jacob Astor in 1898. (*Museum of the City of New York. The Byron Collection*)

sphere." One backer argued: "This grand ethnological exhibit undoubtedly would be the last gathering of these tribes before the bronzed sons of the forests and plains, who have resisted the encroachments of the white man, are gathered to the happy hunting ground." Last gathering and also first, since it was proposed to invite tribes from all across America to this "Indian Congress." To help with the effort, the United States Congress was asked to provide one hundred thousand dollars.

The rest of the money for the fair was donated by the state, corporations, and individuals from all walks of life. Construction was started on the bluffs outside Omaha, and by early 1898 there were five thousand men turning corn fields into a magical vision of a city, designed by the architectural firm of Walker and Kimball.

·   ·   ·

A SENSE OF EQUALITY was hard to find in the cities. As profits from the growing industrial economy poured into these centers of investment capital, the contrast between wealth and urban poverty grew beyond what even the most pessimistic observer would have predicted just a generation before. While capitalists built enormous mansions that resembled Renaissance Italian villas or châteaux of the Loire Valley, millions of immigrants were crammed into tenement buildings that lacked basic comforts and all but the most rudimentary forms of sanitation.

But these millions had come from far worse conditions, living in rigidly hierarchical societies that often regarded them as little more than beasts of the field, cannon fodder, or worse. The enormous human fertility of Europe during the nineteenth century had produced an excess of the unwanted, to whom the United States seemed to offer refuge and opportunity. The major source of this immigration had now shifted from northern to southern and eastern Europe, which did not please native-born Americans, who had found the Catholic Irish an arduous enough challenge to assimilate. Now there were hundreds of thousands of newcomers, close to a million in 1898, arriving yearly who did not share their religion, their language, or their morals.

Strong backs were needed, however, to service the mines, railroads, and factories of the industrial economy, and recent arrivals often took the jobs, at lower wages, of Americans or earlier immigrants. Nativist movements to control or end immigration would have little success until the 1920s, but indignation was growing as "Old Stock Americans" saw their country, especially their cities, changing for what they were sure was the worse.

Newcomers paid little attention to these resentments, settling in places where there would be enough of their fellows to give at least an illusion of the old country and traditional culture. These were often not exclusive enclaves, but sections of a city where diverse ethnic groups would overlap; a German neighborhood would also be a Greek, Irish, Jewish, or Polish neighborhood as well. Few had skills or even enough English to get along outside their community, but machine production or brute toil required few specialists, and the men found work in factories or mines or as general laborers while their wives took jobs as domestics or seamstresses.

Stories of easy wealth circled the globe. "Now and then I had heard things about America," a bootblack named Rocco Corresca remembered, "that it was a far-off country where everybody was rich and that Italians went there and made plenty of money, so that they could return to Italy and live in pleasure ever after. One day I met a young man who pulled out a

handful of gold and told me he had made that in America in a few days."
The young man advised him on how to work his way across the ocean as a
stoker. Although Corresca had to labor hard after he arrived, he was for the
first time in his life able to regularly eat meat.

The huge, energetic cities stunned these country people as soon as they
came ashore. "New York astonished me by its size and magnificence,"
remembered a Greek immigrant from Sparta, "the buildings shooting up
like mountain peaks, the bridge hanging in the sky, the crowds of ships and
the elevated railways."

Lew Chew had heard the same stories in Canton, although he had also
been told how barbaric were the "red haired, green eyed foreign devils with
the hairy faces," who not only failed to worship their ancestors "but pre-
tended to be wiser than their fathers and grandfathers." Most shocking and
disgusting of all was the way they would walk the streets arm and arm with
their women. In Canton, women were allowed on the street only in the
evening, when they carried water jars to the wells. "Then if they met a man
they stood still, with their faces turned to the wall, while he looked the
other way when he passed them. A man who spoke to a woman on the
street in a Chinese village would be beaten, perhaps killed."

When Chew was sixteen, a fellow who had left the village in poverty
years before returned from America, purchasing "ground as large as four
city blocks and made a paradise of it." This convinced Chew that he would
like to go to the land of the "American wizards," who obviously had wealth
to spare. He must have made it into the country just before the Chinese
Exclusion Act of 1882 banned Chinese immigration. (One advance in 1898
brought to Chinese who had made it to these shores was a Supreme Court
ruling that overturned racial laws denying citizenship to immigrants' children who were born here.) Working as a servant, then laundryman, in the
mining regions of the West, Chew was able to save a good amount of
money, although there were difficulties. Some of the miners were "wild
men who carried revolvers and after drinking would come in to our place to
shoot and steal shirts. . . . One of these men hit his head hard against a flat
iron. . . ." Chew had to flee, moving to Chicago and opening a very successful laundry, then doing the same in Detroit. In 1897 he went home to
China, returning to the United States in 1898 to start another laundry in
Buffalo. But conditions had changed: technology in the form of steam-
cleaning equipment, combined with cheap immigrant labor from Europe,
robbed the occupation of much of its profit. Chew became a merchant.

Most newcomers wanted to become Americans, although they still retained strong ties to the home country. The Spartan mentioned above left his job in a bicycle factory and repatriated to Greece in 1897 to fight in the Greco-Turkish war of that year. He quickly returned to the United States the next year, became a citizen, and prospered. "I got down to business, worked hard and am worth about $50,000 to-day. I have fruit stores and confectionery stores." Most of his compatriots felt as he did: "They all think this is a fine country. Most of them are citizens. Only about ten per cent go home again, and of these many return to America, finding that they like their new home better than their old one."

Financial profit was not the sole reason for immigration, and this was especially true for Jews from eastern Europe who had faced prejudice and horrendous pogroms at the hands of their neighbors. "The only hope for the Jews in Russia is to become Jews out of Russia," wrote one Jewish intellectual, and by 1898 almost half a million, estimated to be one-third of the Jewish population of Europe, had moved to New York City alone.

Mary Antin, as she Anglicized her name, was born in Polotzk, Russia, where as a child she, and her community, had been mistreated by towns-people. "I accepted ill-usage from the Gentiles as one accepts the weather. The world was made in a certain way, and I had to live in it." Priests and governmental authorities encouraged the harassment, claiming that the Jews "used the blood of murdered Christian children at the Passover festival." She grew afraid of seeing the cross, and whenever she was in a Gentile house she tried to avoid looking at the icons. To protect herself, "I knew how to dodge and cringe and dissemble before I knew the names of the seasons."

As an excuse for their animosity, Christians said Jewish merchants and moneylenders "preyed upon them, and our shopkeepers gave false measure. People who want to defend the Jews ought never to deny this. Yes, I say, we cheated the Gentiles whenever we dared, because it was the only thing to do. . . . Is not that the code of war? Encamped in the midst of the enemy, we could practice no other. A Jew could hardly exist in business unless he developed a dual conscience, which allowed him to do to the Gentile what he would call a sin against a fellow Jew. Such spiritual deformities are self-explained in the step-children of the Czar."

All this changed for Mary at the age of twelve, when her family emigrated to Boston, Massachusetts. On arrival, she felt she had entered the Promised Land. "Everything was free, as we had heard in Russia. Light was free; the streets were as bright as a synagogue on a holy day. Music was free; we had been serenaded, to our gaping delight, by a brass band of many pieces." Even more wonderful was the promise of free education.

In Polotzk, there had been a ratio established of only ten Jews for every hundred Christians in the high school; at the university it was three to one hundred—this in spite of or because of the traditional Jewish dedication to learning. In the Old Country, within the rigid caste system of the Jewish community, "One qualification only could raise a man above his social level, and that was scholarship. . . . A poor scholar would be preferred in the marriage market to a rich ignoramus. In the phrase of our grandmothers, a boy stuffed with learning was worth more than a girl stuffed with bank notes."

The "apex of her personal contentment" was on the sunny September morning she first entered an American public school, and so began the process of education and assimilation. Here, of course, was another "contrast." Parents of all these ethnic groups, raised in the Old Country, speaking different languages or dialects, worshipping their God in rituals that had not changed for hundreds of years, and believing in tightly bound families ruled by a stern father, were now confronted with wildly different customs not only outside their homes but also inside, as their children took on American clothes, American speech, and, most disturbing of all, independent American ways.

CITY POLITICAL MACHINES, more than any other American institution, were concerned with the general welfare of immigrants, and ensured that they at least learned enough to become citizens who would vote the proper ticket. One of the centers of this education, as well as a hub of manly social life, was the neighborhood saloon.

By 1898, there were over 215,000 licensed liquor dealers in the country and another 50,000 "blind pigs," or unregulated bars. They ranged in style from quiet wood-paneled businessmen's retreats to German beergardens with brass bands, to workers' saloons, to noisome waterfront dives; only the increasingly influential temperance movement refused to see any distinctions, arguing that soda fountains would serve just as well to satisfy all healthy needs for socializing. So important were these havens for workers that unions often held their gatherings there; sixty-three of the sixty-nine unions in Buffalo, New York, for example, met for business in saloons.

Usually located on a corner for visibility, easy access was provided by swinging doors to "the long mahogany," or counter, fronted by its brass footrail and backed by a large mirror. Walls were decorated by chromolith-ographs of sports figures, such as John L. Sullivan, or heroic events, such as *Custer's Last Fight,* which was commissioned and distributed by the Budweiser Brewing Company, as well as reproductions of paintings of nude women, a particular favorite being Adolphe William Bouguereau's *Nymphs and Satyr.* Free newspapers, especially the racy *Police Gazette,* were provided for customers, along with the only free toilets available in cities. Beer was usually a nickel, while whiskey would demand ten or fifteen cents. "Men drank their whiskey straight," wrote the Chicago columnist George Ade; "to do otherwise would have been considered effeminate—followed by a chaser of water, milk, or buttermilk."

Behind the bar would be a cache of bonbons for sale, known as "wife pacifiers," for the workers' saloon was a man's world, although women and children would line up at the back door with buckets or "growlers" (pitch-ers) to fetch beer home for supper. "In the saloon, life was different," Jack London pointed out in *John Barleycorn.* "Men with great voices laughed great laughs, and there was an atmosphere of greatness." Rare was it for even the owner's wife, who had probably fixed the salty and thirst-inducing free lunch, to actually serve customers. "There is one profession that is closed to women in the United States," James Muirhead noted, "that of barmaid. That professional association of woman with man when he is apt to be in his most animal moods is firmly tabooed in America."

Serving as a working-class men's club, the bar also lent itself to politics, and bar owners—always informed on local issues and aware of who needed a job, a meal, or a roof over the head—became important cogs in the city machine. It is no wonder that Finley Peter Dunne placed his fictional social commentator Mr. Martin Dooley behind the bar of his own saloon on Chicago's Archey Road. What better location from which to view and comment on the vagaries of modern life? This was the year that Mr. Doo-ley's native shrewdness and hard common sense would be lifted from newspaper columns and published in hardcover, achieving such large sales as to make him a national figure.

Workers needed these havens now more than ever, feeling besieged by the forces of big capital and technological change. Bloody battles had been fought during the 1890s, particularly during the Homestead and Pullman strikes, for the right to unionize and earn a living wage. This violent year would see those struggles continued. Working-class women frequently took an active part in strike actions themselves, and more and more often had to seek employment outside the home to help support their families, although there were still strong prejudices against it.

People were fascinated by the development. Newspapers would frequently run and widely distribute stories like the one in January 1898 about Annie and Mary Wilson, two sisters who split rails and shaped wooden mine supports for the Spring Hill Coal Company near Wilmerding, Pennsylvania. "The work is not hard when you get used to it," one of the women told a reporter, "and then we can make more money . . . in one day than we could in a week working in a kitchen. What's the difference, so long as the work is honest, how one makes a living?" Local people regarded them as strange. They "all talk about us, but we don't care. . . . We are earning a good living and don't owe anyone a cent." There were, of course, few havens except their homes to which such women could retire after work.

ONE OTHER GROUP came seeking sanctuary in the cities, but found little solace there. African-Americans were fleeing the South in increasing numbers during the 1890s, driven out by successful white attempts, both through legislation and through violence, to deny them the ballot, economic independence, or even human dignity. Although Northern newspapers carried reports of lynchings, these seemed to be read more as aids to feeling superior to the benighted region than as calls to action. The Civil War had been fought, the slaves freed; now it was time to heal the wounds, reconcile the nation, get on with business. In 1896, in *Plessy v. Ferguson,* the Supreme Court had supported this sentiment: separate was fine as long as equal facilities were provided, but the nation needn't worry too much about defining, or defending, "equal."

Crowded into segregated areas that usually contained the worst of an already inadequate housing stock, these new urban arrivals found even fewer opportunities than the most alien and "outlandish" of foreign immigrants. Philadelphia was the closest large Northern city for many black refugees, who had been coming in large numbers even before the abolition of slavery, and by 1898 about forty thousand were living there. The Republican political machine that dominated "the Quaker City" took some interest in the welfare of these voters in return for their votes, but not much, and their lives were dominated by poverty, disease, and crime.

Brought to Philadelphia by reformers to study the "Negro problem" was the brilliant sociologist William Edward Burghardt Du Bois, an African-American in his late twenties who had grown up in Great Barrington,

Massachusetts, in a region relatively free of racial prejudice. Taking under-graduate degrees from Fisk University and Harvard, he then studied in Germany for two years before returning to Harvard for his Ph.D.

Du Bois immersed himself in the slum life of Philadelphia's Seventh Ward from August 1896 to January 1898, then wrote his study and shep-herded it through publication. During his investigation he encountered some resistance from residents of the neighborhood, for the sociologist was very much a child of New England: reserved, elegantly dressed in a suit with a starched white shirt, carrying a cane like a dude, and conducting himself with a formal, old-fashioned politeness. More than once people had complained to him, "Are we animals to be dissected and by an unknown Negro at that?" But rare was an outright refusal to cooperate, and Du Bois spent months walking the rough streets, knocking on strange doors, questioning every qualified subject.

It was obvious to him that the miserable condition of the Negroes in the Seventh Ward did not spring from their racial heredity but from the degra-dation of slavery which had left them ignorant and lacking in proper values. The most important factor of all was the deep-rooted prejudice of contem-porary society. In the mid-nineteenth century there had been successful black doctors, lawyers, and businessmen, while numerous black barbers had owned shops serving white patrons. African-American caterers had dominated their trade, and thereby "might have been said to rule the social world of Philadelphia through its stomach."

Some black caterers were still prominent, but had lost their primacy. Philadelphia society now looked to New York, Paris, and London for what was proper fashion—snapper soup seemed passé, as did hosting parties at home. Such elite needs were now being met by the same revolution sweep-ing through all American business, even catering—"the application of large capital," as Du Bois wrote. "It is the . . . development from the small to the large industry, from the house-industry to the concentrated industry, from the private dining-room to the palatial hotel. If the Negro caterers of Philadelphia had been white, some of them would have been put in charge of a large hotel, or would have become co-partners in some large restaurant business, for which capitalists furnished funds."

The sociologist thought that two related factors were complicating and impeding the rise of a solid black middle class: the successive waves of black newcomers from the South, who lacked the values and skills neces-sary for success, and the rising tide of European immigrants, who were preferred by native white employers and could blend into the larger society quickly. Some labor unions welcomed African-Americans, as the cigar-makers did in Philadelphia; others actually wrote the word "white" into qualifications for membership, partly from racial prejudice, partly in the "spirit of monopoly and the desire to keep wages up."

One of the few industrial concerns hiring Negroes in the Philadelphia area was the Midvale Steel Works in nearby Germantown, which possibly had decided to take this radical step at the suggestion of Frederick Winslow Taylor, who was becoming famous for his drive to make American business more efficient through time-and-motion studies. Workers, who started at $1.20 a day, were a mix of white and black, native-born and immigrant. "Our object in putting Negroes on the force," the manager said, "was twofold. First, we believed them to be good workmen; secondly, we thought they could be used to get over one difficulty we had experienced at Midvale, namely, the clannish spirit of the workmen and a tendency to form cliques." Foremen generally wished to have their gangs made up solely of members of their own ethnic group, but the managers decided to intermix the workers. Blacks proved hard workers, and "cliques" were weakened, which evidently also had the benefit to the company of weakening the union.

But Midvale was an exceptional plant; most of the blacks of Philadelphia, as in other large cities, faced a job market that disdained their best efforts and left them only the tasks forsaken by all who had better choices.

BOOKER T. WASHINGTON, who had been born a slave but through energy and intelligence won an education and became head of the Tuskeegee Institute in Alabama, was deep in the South, on the front lines of the fight over the African-American future. He argued that blacks should willingly accept their inferior social status until they were able to make economic gains, a position that later made him the target of forceful criticism by Du Bois.

"The wisest among my race," Washington said, "understand that the agitation of questions of social equality is the extremest folly, and that progress in the enjoyment of all the privileges that will come to us must be the result of severe and constant struggle rather than of artificial forcing. No race that has anything to contribute to the markets of the world is long in any degree ostracized." He also spoke against abandoning native Americans for the benefits of immigrant labor. Don't hire "those of foreign birth, and strange tongue and habits," he pleaded to white employers. "Cast down your bucket among those people who have, without strikes and labor wars, tilled your fields, cleared your forests, built your railroads and cities, and brought forth treasures from the bowels of the earth. . . . While doing this, you can be sure in the future, as in the past, that you and your families will be surrounded by the most patient, faithful, law-abiding and unresentful people that the world has seen . . . with a devotion that no foreigner can approach, ready to lay down our lives, if need be, in defense of yours, interlacing our industrial, commercial, civil and religious life with yours in a way that shall make the interest of both races one. In all things that are purely social we can be as separate as the fingers, yet one as the hand in all things essential to mutual progress."

COMPETITIVE STRIVING and jostling in the streets under conditions of poverty heightened by racial and ethnic suspicion often led to insults, rage, and violence between these varied peoples new to crowded city life. By 1898 crime, and especially the murder rate, in the United States had climbed several times beyond that of even the most undisciplined European countries, and reformers were frantically looking for ways to diffuse tensions and better conditions for the hard-pressed poor.

A vibrant popular culture provided some ease for the stresses and strains. The safety bicycle furnished fun and the opportunity to flee from city to countryside at a reasonable price—secondhand ones could be found for only twenty dollars. Edison's marvelous invention the Kinetoscope, which made pictures move, provided diversion, as did theaters presenting sentimental plays in Yiddish, Italian, German, and other languages. Bands played everything from John Philip Sousa to polkas to Ragtime in saloons and on the avenues.

One of the earliest Ragtime tunes, by Scott Joplin, gave some indication of the strained nature of American society during the 1890s, and the need for violent release. "The Great Crush Collision March" commemorated a stunt staged in Waco, Texas, on September 15, 1896, when two locomotives were positioned facing each other a mile or so apart on the same track. Steam pressure was built up and then both were set in motion with their throttles tied down for full speed. Tens of thousands had come to witness the grand event, and a number of these thrill-seekers were killed or maimed by the rain of shrapnel that resulted from the collision and subsequent explosion. That the attraction of this sort of barbarous entertainment was not limited to the wilder stretches of the West can be seen in the story told by a young woman about her father, the mild-mannered, genteel rector of an Episcopal church in New York City. During summers at Northeast Harbor, Maine, he would wander off to sit alone on the rocky shore, contemplating the mountains and sea. "There he would vanish into an unseen world to which he was sure we would all eventually go." But there were also other thoughts jostling their way into his reveries. "He told me confidentially that if he had unlimited money he would engage two locomotives and have them placed face to face on the track. At a given moment the engineers would start them and then cleverly jump off before the crash. Another favorite wish was to construct a house entirely of glass which he could demolish with a hammer."

Whole districts of cities were devoted to somewhat more peaceful if still exciting fun, such as Coney Island, which drew hordes of visitors to their Ferris wheels, waterslides, and Shoot-the-Chutes. Probably the most preferred of all entertainments was vaudeville, especially after development of its fast-paced "continuous show," which reflected the very tempo of the streets. "The vaudeville theatre," wrote a contemporary performer, "is an American invention. There is nothing like it anywhere else in the world. . . . [it] belongs to the era of the department store and the short story." Interspersed with acts by strongmen, acrobats, singers, tap dancers, and trained animals would be comedic sketches making fun of silly rich fops, country bumpkins, watermelon-stealing blacks, plus Italians, Jews, and other immigrants who made foolish observations in broken English. Though dealing in stereotypes, this public airing of prejudices seems to have helped soothe cultural misunderstandings, by depicting the common humanity recognizable under the exaggeration.

Probably the greatest spectacle of all took place outdoors, on the bustling boulevards of cities and big towns, places now made glorious under the miracle of electric lights. People would walk, stand, or sit for hours "watching the world go by," a constant flow of varied costumes, different sounds, diverse faces. Mary Antin remembered the freedom of Saturday nights in 1898 "when Bessie Finklestein called for me; and Bessie and I, with arms entwined, called for Sadie Rabinowitch; and Bessie and Sadie and I, still further entwined, called for Annie Reilly; and Bessie, etc., etc., inextricably wound up, marched up Broadway, and took possession of all we saw, heard, guessed, or desired. . . . Parading all abreast, as many as we were, only breaking ranks to let people pass . . . we continued on our promenade; loitering wherever a crowd gathered, or running for a block or so to cheer on the fire-engine or police ambulance." The fears of rural parents were justified; it was hard to keep children down on the farm once they had seen the excitement and glitter of city lights.

FOR ALL THE ANXIETY, the great majority of citizens were sure that problems would be aggressively faced up to and dealt with. America was not Europe, and legitimate worry was not despair. Although some poets, writers, and intellectuals tried to import the exquisite melancholy spirit of decadence at the end of the century, it did not find fertile ground. A popular response to arguments that life was boring and not worthwhile for the sensitive was Edmund Vance Cooke's satire entitled "Fin de Siècle," which was printed over and over again, then set to music and used in several shows:

> *This life's a hollow bubble*
>   *Don't you know?*
> *Just a painted piece of twoubble,*
>   *Don't you know?*
> *We come to earth to cwy,*
> *We gwow oldeh and we sigh,*
> *Oldeh still and then we die,*
>   *Don't you know?*
>
> *It is all a howwid mix,*
>   *Don't you know?*
> *Business, love and politics,*
>   *Don't you know? . . .*
>
> *Business, oh, that's beastly twade,*
>   *Don't you know?*
> *Something's lost or something's made,*
>   *Don't you know?*
> *And you wowwy, and you mope,*
> *And you hang youah highest hope*
> *On the pwice, pe'haps of soap,*
>   *Don't you know?*
>
> *Politics! oh, just a lawk,*
>   *Don't you know?*
> *Just a nightmaeh in the dawk,*
>   *Don't you know?*

You pe'spiah all day and night,
And afteh all the fight,
Why pe'haps the w'ong man's wight,
Don't you know?

Waving over all these entertainments, marching at the head of parades, flanking the altar in churches, and saluted from every orator's podium was the sacred symbol of unity that would surmount the diversities of American life: Old Glory. It was patriotism that would bring the nation together, all true Americans were certain, and be the almost religious instrument of assimilation. A loyal swelling affected every heart when viewing the flag, and every citizen would do his or her duty when called upon. This passion had been building through the decade, and when John Philip Sousa, son of a Portuguese immigrant, had composed the "Stars and Stripes" in 1897, the public rushed to play its stirring patriotic tune: Three hundred thousand dollars worth of sheet music had quickly been sold.

CHAPTER 2

THE ADVENTURE OF PROGRESS

I have seen America spread out fr'm th' Atlantic to th' Pacific, with a branch off iv the Standard Ile Comp'ny in ivry hamlet. I've seen th' shackles dropped fr'm th' slave, so's he cud be lynched in Ohio. . . . An' th' invintions,—th' steam-injine an' th' printin'-press an' th' cotton-gin an' the gin sour an' th' bicycle an' th' flyin'-machine an' th' nickel-in-the-slot machine an' th' Croker machine an' th' sody fountain an'—crownin' wur-ruk iv our civilization—the cash ray-gisther. What gr-reat advances has science made in my time. . . . War an' pest'lence an' famine have occurred . . . but I count thim light compared with th' binifits that have fallen to th' race since I come on th' earth.

Mr. Dooley

A "DELUGE OF WONDERS" was changing the world, one contemporary journalist wrote, and there seemed no end to the fertile ingenuity of American backyard tinkerers, trained engineers, and even college professors. Designated by public acclaim as the greatest of all these wizards was Thomas Alva Edison. Born in 1847, Edison from childhood had displayed a lively curiosity, dogged persistence, and stamina. He had received only a few months of formal education, but when he was nine years old his mother gave him an elementary text on physical science that inspired him to conduct all the experiments it described. This fascination with science, particularly chemistry, had to be temporarily put aside when he was twelve because his family's precarious financial situation required that he go to work.

Taking a job selling newspapers, candy, and fruit on a train that made a daily round trip between his home town of Port Huron, Michigan, and Detroit, Edison managed to convince the conductor to allow him to set up a small laboratory in the baggage car to continue his juvenile research. Unfortunately, one day a rough section of track caused the car to lurch wildly, knocking over a water jar full of phosphorus sticks. Exposed to air, the phosphorus ignited, setting the wooden floor of the car on fire. Edison and the conductor managed to put it out, but that was the end of these mobile experiments.

The boy had already become interested in telegraphy, partly through the way it had helped him make some extra income. In April 1862, he learned of the Battle of Shiloh while preparing for the return trip from Detroit, and convinced a telegrapher to send a brief bulletin to each operator along the line to be chalked up on the station bulletin board. Edison then took a thousand copies of the *Free Press* to sell rather than his usual two hundred. "When I got to the first station . . . the platform was crowded with men and women. After one look at the crowd I raised the price to ten cents. I sold 35 papers." The next station was even more crowded, so he demanded fifteen cents, then at Port Huron there were so many people that he yelled, "Twenty-five cents, gentlemen—I haven't enough to go around." This success convinced him that "the telegraph was just about the best thing going, for it was the notices on the bulletin that had done the trick. I determined at once to become a telegrapher."

As an itinerant operator, Edison traveled the country, studying the way the telegraph system and its equipment worked, with every spare moment spent tinkering and conducting experiments. Through such concentrated efforts he received his first patents at the age of twenty-two, for electro-mechanical improvements to the telegraph and a more efficient stock ticker. As with his selling of newspapers, Edison knew how to reap the most profit from his creations. Using the income they provided, he established a research laboratory, essentially an "invention factory," at Menlo Park, New Jersey, staffed with talented and ambitious young scientists and engineers. Edison and his team set about systematically searching for practical discoveries that could be immediately put into manufacture, promising "a minor invention every ten days and a big thing every six months or so." Amazingly, he was able to keep to this schedule for a while. Quickly came a carbon transmitter for the telephone, then, most famous and profitable of all, the phonograph.

A number of attempts had been made to develop an effective incandescent lightbulb, but none had proved satisfactory. Edison decided he would succeed, and he eventually did. "I have let other inventors get the start of me in the matter somewhat," he admitted to a reporter at the beginning of the quest, "because I have not given much attention to electric lights, but I believe I can catch up to them now."

"If you can make the electric light supply the place of gas, you can easily make a great fortune," the reporter pointed out.

"I don't care so much for a great fortune," Edison responded, "as I do for getting ahead of the other fellow."

The first part of the statement was obviously absurd, but required by the mores of late nineteenth-century American society: one could not admit to the love of Mammon. But the observation about getting ahead of the other fellow is even more revealing about what was encouraged—competition was healthy, the way society, not just the individual, grew stronger and more productive. Darwin's study of the process of natural selection proved that: only the fittest contender survived.

Competition Edison would have aplenty, particularly from George Westinghouse, another precocious youth, who had been awarded his first patent at the age of nineteen and then went on to build a fortune based on his invention of the railroad air brake and various other improvements to the rail system. Their battle to determine whether Edison's direct current or the alternating current backed by Westinghouse would become the source of power for America ended in a bitter defeat for the Wizard of Menlo Park. Generally, however, he was victorious in the endless legal wrangles he engaged in to protect his discoveries from those who infringed on his patents.

Edison was a natural hero for the age: born into poverty, denied a formal education, but achieving wealth and glory through perseverance, energy, and native ability while at the same time improving the world. He was a transition figure—both the archetype of the striving individual tinkerer and then a director of well-financed team research. By 1898, he was settled in new, state-of-the-art laboratories, working on, among other projects, inexpensive methods of separating iron ore from low-grade deposits, an electric automobile, and motion pictures. So confident were Americans that there was nothing this genius couldn't do that later in the year a science-fiction writer named Garrett P. Serviss would produce a story entitled "Edison's Conquest of Mars." He was providing an inspiring example for ambitious, practical-minded experimenters working in barns, toolsheds, and bicycle shops across the country.

THE SCIENTIFIC APPROACH of close observation, quantification, and experiment was being applied not only to learning how nature worked but also to studying the way humans labored at their jobs.

Here the pioneer was Frederick Winslow Taylor, who had possibly played a role in convincing the Midvale Steel Works in Germantown to take the radical step of hiring African-Americans. Raised a Quaker, Taylor appreciated the need people felt for individual fulfillment, but this acknowledgment was combined with an evangelical zeal to subordinate impractical personal desires to the needs of tight group organization. Only by such control could productivity be improved. "In the past," he wrote in *The Principles of Scientific Management*, "the man has been first; in the future the system must be first." Personal satisfaction would follow, since he believed an inefficient man was like "a bird that can sing and won't sing." Taylor was convinced that this was the path to a Golden Age when all tensions within American society would be dissolved. Rivalries between capital and labor, races, religions, sectional jealousy between East, West, and South would wash away in the bounty flowing from the new industrial cornucopia. Followers compared him to Jesus for the liberating effect he had on those who labored without thought or pride in what they did, labored essentially like brute animals. Workers, however, commonly saw him as the cold, profit-driven intellectual with a stopwatch who had taken joy from their labor, and who was trying to turn them into flesh-and-blood machines.

Taylor had begun as an engineer and an inventor, responsible for such important developments as the largest steam hammer ever built in this country, and a process, High Speed Steel, that enabled cutting tools in lathes to keep their edge longer and operate three times faster, tripling the output of machine shops. Eventually he would hold a hundred patents. But his greatest contribution to the new industrial economy came through his studies of the workplace.

In 1898, Taylor left Midvale to join the Bethlehem Steel Company. He was immediately struck by how irrationally the important task of shoveling was carried out, since each worker brought his personal shovel to the plant and used it for a wide variety of materials. "We would see a first-class shoveler go from shoveling rice coal with a load of 3 1/2 pounds to the shovel to handling ore from the Messaba Range, with 38 pounds to the shovel. Now, is 3 1/2 pounds the proper shovel load or is 38 pounds the proper shovel load? They cannot both be right. Under scientific management the answer to this question is not a matter of anyone's opinion; it is a question for accurate, careful, scientific investigation."

For five months he and his staff conducted that investigation through a plan he had devised:

First. Find, say 10 to 15 different men . . . who are especially skillful in doing the particular work to be analyzed.

Second: Study the exact series of elementary operations or motions which each of these men uses in doing the work which is being investigated, as well as the implement each man uses.

Third. Study with a stopwatch the time required to make each of these elementary movements and then select the quickest way of doing each element of work.

Fourth. Eliminate all false movements, slow movements, and useless movements.

Fifth. After doing away with all unnecessary movements, collect into one series the quickest and best movements, as well as the best implements.

This new method, involving that series of motions which can be made quickest and best, is then substituted in place of the 10 or 15 inferior series which were formerly in use.

The "science of shoveling" that resulted led to mockery from critics and strong resistance from workers, but it more than tripled productivity. Fifteen specifically designed shovels were needed to efficiently move various materials, and by constant experimentation even the most useful length of handles was determined. Just a few years later "140 men were doing the work formerly done by 600. The cost of handling material was cut in half, and the shovelers still employed were receiving a 60 percent increase in wages." Factories across the land began hiring "time and motion" experts to continue such advances.

A SEVERE BLIZZARD struck the Northeast on Wednesday, February 2, laying a deep mantle of snow across the countryside, stopping railroads, and forcing residents to either walk or take sleighs to move around the cities.

For some people the next few days were a chance to play. Schools were closed, and children built snowmen, rode their sleds down whatever open slopes they could find, and targeted icy missiles at one another or on the hats of passersby who did not look fit enough to run them to ground.

More profitable business was conducted by three men who met in the law offices of James B. Vredenburgh in Jersey City, New Jersey, on Thursday. Making their way through the immense snowdrifts was difficult, but they had persevered, coming together at noon to lay the foundation for peace in a war of biscuits that had started in 1890 and had now grown too costly to continue. New Jersey was particularly friendly to independent companies that wished to merge into large national corporations, and Vredenburgh was a specialist in arranging such matters, so it did not take long to go over the papers and then sign them, combining the American, the New York, and the United States baking enterprises into a dominant trust: the National Biscuit Company. As soon as the formalities were completed, a telegram was sent to Adolphus Green in Chicago, another lawyer expert in creating corporations.

NEW OR IMPROVED technologies after the Civil War, like electricity, railroads, and the telephone, had led to national markets that rewarded economies of scale. Whenever a new product was successfully introduced, however, dozens, sometimes hundreds, of entrepreneurs would start their own companies, flooding the market and driving down prices so that after a few years many would have gone bankrupt and the survivors would be barely holding on. Such cutthroat competition seemed so wasteful to men like John D. Rockefeller and Andrew Carnegie that they set out to establish their industries on what they considered a more rational basis. This led to fierce Darwinian battles to determine who would devour whom, the victors winning through ruthlessly cutting the cost of wages, materials, and transportation so they could buy the latest technologies to improve efficiency. Single-minded geniuses of organization grew to dominate industries like oil and steel, as well as the distribution of commodities like sugar, salt, and matches, ending the era of competition and establishing one of big business. Philip D. Armour, head of a giant meat-packing concern that bore his name, bragged, "Of course I have no other interest in life but my business . . . I do not love the money; what I do love is the getting of it, the making of it . . . I do not read, I do not take any part in politics . . . but in my counting-house, I am in my element."

A new form of business structure was devised that allowed directors to evade laws against monopoly by having a single board of trustees control the different corporations that made up a trust. When states and the federal government began taking regulatory action against trusts, another form, the holding company, was used to build huge empires by allowing one corporation to hold and control the stock of numerous others. The majority of stock in a desired company would be bought, instead of its total assets, meaning that for the cost of 51 percent in stock, 100 percent of what the company owned was the investor's. Another advantage was that this control could be achieved through the medium of the stock market, avoiding the messy, time-consuming negotiations with management that would otherwise have been necessary. New Jersey had blazed the trail on holding companies, becoming the preferred state in which large capitalists incorporated.

Bakeries had continued following traditional methods longer than most American businesses because products like bread, crackers, and cakes were perishable, so they needed to be made close to their customers. Most stages of the baking process were not yet mechanized, but continuously fired "reel" ovens were adopted, which raised productivity; train speed increased while the track network grew; and refrigerated railroad cars were improved. These helped bakers meet the changing requirements of their customers as men and women moved into cities and took jobs in factories and offices, leaving less time for home cooking. Inventors like James Henry Mitchell of Philadelphia began applying their fertile talents to the field, Mitchell alone developing a dough-sheeting machine, another that made sugar wafers, and several that helped speed cake production. The new reel ovens revolved dough through precisely calibrated temperature zones that made it possible to control quality better than ever before.

But such machines, just as in steel mills and railroad yards, were expensive, and required large-scale production to make them affordable. Regional bakers began to discuss ways of joining together, and in 1890 a number of firms in the Midwest became the American Biscuit & Manufacturing Company, while some in the Northeast formed the New York Biscuit Company. A short time later, bakeries in Ohio, Indiana, and Pennsylvania became the United States Baking Company.

The usual pattern of intense competition began as the two largest combinations, the American and the New York companies, brought more independent bakeries under their control and expanded into each other's territories, offering the public only slightly different styles of ladyfingers, cookies, oyster crackers, pretzels, and bread. Price therefore became important in gaining sales and driving the other group out of business. New York Biscuit had the advantage of being backed by the fortunes of Philip Armour and of George Pullman, builder of the Pullman railroad sleeper, and these men agreed in late 1895 to advance whatever funds were needed to win the war. Prices were immediately lowered by 25 percent across the board, putting New York's products on sale at below cost.

The American Biscuit Company could not match this discount, and it looked as if the only choice was to be absorbed, on poor terms, by their opponent. But then an event occurred, also reflective of the times, that reversed the situation. William Moore and his brother were major investors in New York Biscuit, and had been the legal brains behind its formation. They had as well played important roles in forming the Diamond Match Company. In that business, too, there had been an excess of competing firms that recognized the rationality of combining to control the market for matches, of which well over a billion a day were used. New machinery had been introduced that cut the sticks from wooden blocks, then dipped the heads and dried them in one operation.

Rumors of further productivity gains, and plans to build foreign plants that would allow Diamond to dominate not only the American but also the European match market, led to feverish speculation in the stock, pushing the price from $120 to $248 a share without a pause. Some of the energy fueling this rise came from the Moore brothers buying on margin while they continued to be heavily invested in the New York Biscuit Company. When, however, speculation went on too long without anything happening to back up the rumors of European expansion, the market in Diamond stock collapsed, bringing down with it the fortunes of many speculators, including the Moores.

Now it was the American Biscuit Company's turn to attack by cutting prices, and that caused their opponent's stock, which had already declined because of the Moore brothers' financial difficulties, to fall another twenty points. Major bloodletting seemed likely.

Frank O. Lowden, George Pullman's son-in-law and lawyer, was directed by Pullman to try to arrange something, and the resources of the Illinois Trust & Savings Bank of Chicago, owned by Philip Armour, were put at his disposal. Patiently using the intelligence and political skill, as well as the financial muscle, that later won him the governorship of Illinois, Lowden was able to convince the opposing sides that everyone would gain from merging into one major company.

As can be seen, lawyers were now important elements in making a business successful, a far different condition from the pioneer entrepreneurial age of just a generation earlier. Also new was the prominence that financiers had assumed: immense corporations need access to massive amounts of capital. Bankers like J. P. Morgan became national figures whose support was necessary for success. It was a sign of these new times that as soon as the lawyer Adolphus Green received the telegram from New Jersey announcing the formation of the National Biscuit Company, he made his way, through the deep drifts of yet another blizzard that had struck Chicago, to the banking offices of the Illinois Trust & Savings Bank, where the major investors had assembled to work out details of stock issuance and elect officers. They now had a company that merged 114 bakeries firing over 400 ovens and consumed 2,000,000 barrels of flour a year to put out 360,000,000 pounds of crackers.

But in spite of this capacity, success was not assured. "When the company drew its first breath," Adolphus Green later said, "we were watching anxiously to see whether it would live or not."

ONE DAY WHEN Thomas Edison and his secretary, A. O. Tate, were riding in an open carriage through the countryside, Edison pointed to a valley they were skirting that had a stream wandering through it. "Tate! See that valley?"

"Yes," the secretary replied, "it's a beautiful valley."

"Well, I'm going to make it more beautiful. I'm going to dot it with factories."

Here speaks the voice of progress and industry—but resistance to this ideal of the machine in the garden was already gaining strength by the end of the nineteenth century. Henry David Thoreau, Frederick Law Olmsted, and George Perkins Marsh had laid the groundwork with their writings on the importance of unspoiled nature to a full and healthy life. Even Thomas Edison's comment shows at least some sensitivity to this, since he desired to "dot" nature with his factories rather than to pave the whole bucolic scene.

Interest in preserving natural resources had steadily increased during the 1880s and 1890s as the destruction of forests, grasslands, rivers, and mountain slopes accelerated under the breakneck pace of the industrial age. The Adirondack mountains had been saved from clear-cutting, and the Yellowstone region made into the nation's first national park, while in

California the Sierra Club was founded in 1892 to save the Sierra Nevada mountains, particularly the jewel of Yosemite Valley. The overpowering drive of the times for profit and development meant that conservationists had to find solid economic arguments to support their goals. The Adirondacks had been set aside because businessmen in New York were convinced that extensive logging of the region could dry out the water sources for the Erie Canal and the Hudson River, important transportation routes that underlay their prosperity. Yellowstone was established with the political support of railroads hoping to profit from carrying tourists to its wonders and lodging them there. At first this alliance of the utilitarian-minded and the followers of Thoreau, Olmsted, and Marsh, who loved nature for itself, had worked well, but as development pressure increased, severe strains began to develop between these philosophies. In 1898, open warfare broke out between Gifford Pinchot and John Muir, the respective leaders of the two factions, for the soul of the movement.

Born into a wealthy family, Gifford Pinchot had traveled in Europe as a boy, attended Phillips Exeter Academy, then entered Yale University, where he engaged in campus religious work, played football for Walter Camp, and won awards for public speaking before graduating in 1885. Loving the out-of-doors, and at the urging of his conservationist father, who had been impressed with European forest management, he decided to become the first American to make his career in scientific forestry.

Eighteen months spent working with experts in Germany, such as Dr. Detrich Brandis, as well as attending the French silviculture school in Nancy, confirmed his decision to dedicate his life to forestry, although the libertinism of his French fellow students led him to contemplate starting a Christian mission there to set them on the proper path of virtue. On reflection, he decided that their dissoluteness had gone too far to permit rescue, and he returned home.

Pinchot now knew that trees should be regarded as a renewable crop like any other, and that if they were carefully harvested the soil need not erode nor streams dry up or be choked with silt. The challenge lay in convincing American farmers who, along with most of their fellow citizens, regarded the continent's resources as inexhaustible, and viewed trees as an impediment to be burned so the fertile earth underneath could be farmed. Although they did not deliberately burn forests, timber barons were no more enlightened, seeing in these vast tracts of wilderness only a source of profit to be ruthlessly exploited before moving on to the next virgin tract. "Cut and run" was their policy.

In order to prove the worth of the European practice of sustained yield, Pinchot accepted an offer to oversee Biltmore, the estate of George Vanderbilt in North Carolina. He wrote out a plan with three goals for this five-thousand-acre forest. "The first is profitable production, which will give the Forest direct utility. If this were absent, the existence of the Forest would be justified only as it lends beauty and interest to the Estate. Second, a nearly constant annual yield, which will give steady occupation to a trained force, allow a permanent organization, and make regular operations possible. Third, an improvement in the present very mediocre condition of the Forest, without which its future would be nearly hopeless." Local loggers were retrained to conduct selective cutting, sparing some mature trees for propagation and not touching the younger ones.

Pinchot recognized the importance of publicity, and wrote up his results in a pamphlet distributed at the exhibit on Biltmore that he mounted for the Chicago World's Fair in 1893. As his reputation grew, he became a consultant for landowners interested in improving the yield of their holdings without doing permanent harm to the larger environment. Later in the decade he served as secretary of the National Forest Commission as it conducted a study for the National Academy of Science on government forests; then, in 1898, at the age of thirty-two, he became head of the Division of Forestry within the Department of Agriculture, where he set about trying to institute a rational, scientific, and above all *practical* approach to the use of resources.

Born in Scotland in 1838, John Muir had grown up on a frontier farm in Wisconsin, where life was hard and schooling out of the question: "We were all made slaves through the vice of over-industry. . . . We were called in the morning at four o'clock and seldom got to bed before nine, making a broiling, seething day . . . seventeen hours long loaded with heavy work, while I was only a small stunted boy." The father's eccentric but rigid Calvinism, which taught that suffering and fortitude qualified one for heaven, combined with his equally fervent belief in corporal punishment, did not make conditions any easier for his eight children, of whom John was the third, and the oldest son.

Spurred on by whippings with a leather strap, Muir had learned much of the Old and New Testaments by heart, and he was often able to protect himself and his siblings when conditions threatened to grow too harsh by quoting apt passages, as when his father decided that henceforth they would all be vegetarians and the boy was able to point out that God had fed the Prophet Elijah on meat as well as on bread and vegetables in the wilderness. The only book allowed in the house was the Bible, but Muir used various stratagems to get around this dictum, and managed to convince his father to allow him to read in the morning as long as he was ready for labor at dawn.

Muir began rising at one o'clock in order to pore over borrowed books, and to tinker—designing and whittling into form various clocks, doorlocks, a self-adjusting windmill, and an automatic mechanism that would release feed to horses at any time desired. Neighbors encouraged the talented youth to enter some of these creations in the state fair at Madison, where he won a fifteen-dollar prize and the offer of a job in a machine shop. Even more important, he decided to apply for admittance to the University of Wisconsin: "With fear and trembling, overladen with ignorance," he called on the university's acting president, "and told him how far I had got on with my studies at home, and that I hadn't been to school since leaving Scotland at the age of eleven years, excepting one short term of a couple of months at a district school, because I could not be spared from the farm work."

Impressed with the young man's burning desire for an education, the acting president welcomed him to the world of learning. Muir managed to study for two and a half years at the university, spending less than a dollar a week by living on bread and milk. To allow maximum use of his time he designed and constructed a clock-bed which tilted at a designated hour and set him on his feet so that he only needed to take a step to the mechanical desk he had also made that automatically raised and opened, in order and at a set pace, the books he was going to read that day.

Muir was introduced to the beauty of the natural world through field trips and the writings of Henry David Thoreau, Ralph Waldo Emerson, Louis Agassiz, and Alexander von Humboldt. On his own, after almost losing an eye in an industrial accident, he began making long expeditions through untamed portions of the North American continent. It was while on a thousand-mile "botanizing" walk to the Gulf of Mexico that he decided from then on to be a pupil in the "University of the Wilderness" rather than in civilization, "which drives its victims in flocks, repressing the growth of individuality." He felt, inspired by Emerson, that there was "an essential love, overlying, underlying, pervading all things," but that humans, having misunderstood God's message, did not live in that spirit. "The world we are told, was made especially for man—a presumption not supported by all the facts. A numerous class of men are painfully astonished whenever they find anything . . . in all God's universe, which they cannot eat or render in some way what they call useful to themselves."

Instead, Muir believed, God had created every living thing in the world for the "happiness of each one of them" instead of just for mankind. "The universe would be incomplete without man; but it would also be incomplete without the smallest transmicroscopic creature that dwells beyond our conceitful eyes and knowledge." He traveled to California, and on arrival immediately headed for the Sierra Nevada where he lived for several years. As he ranged through these mountains he became aware of the destruction that loggers and shepherds were causing. Giant sequoias, the largest trees in the world and the most difficult to fell, were being dynamited, then rushed to mills for sawing, and enormous flocks of sheep "are driven to the mountain pastures every summer, and in order to make easy paths and to improve the pastures, running fires are set everywhere to burn off the old logs and underbrush. . . . Whether our loose jointed Government is really able or willing to do anything in the matter remains to be seen."

When the National Academy of Science formed the Forest Commission, Muir had been invited to become a member, but he had refused, serving instead as an *ex officio* advisor. In 1896 he had guided some of the commissioners, including Gifford Pinchot, through the devastation left behind by loggers, prospectors, sheep herders, cattle ranchers, and railroads after they had looted the public lands of the West. All agreed that something had to be done quickly to stop any further abuse, Muir and others believing that the army, which had done a splendid job of protecting Yellowstone National Park in its early years, should immediately be brought in to protect the forest reserves. Pinchot objected, wanting professional foresters to be in charge from the beginning, even if that caused a delay.

Muir and Pinchot became friends during this journey, and when the party reached the Grand Canyon the two men went off in freezing weather to camp on the south rim. "Muir was a storyteller in a million," Pinchot later wrote. "We made our beds of cedar boughs in a thick stand that kept the wind away, and there he talked till midnight. It was such an evening as I have never had before or since." But there were deep philosophical differences. Both agreed that the government had to begin the rational administration of the public domain; the problem was in defining rational. Muir wanted some land set aside to be preserved in an untouched state; Pinchot wanted resources managed so they would be more productive for a longer period of time. Muir argued for the intangible benefits that would flow to people from such protected areas, while Pinchot could only appreciate material gains that he felt would advance progress and civilization.

Since the conservation movement was under attack from loggers and other rapacious business interests, the two men and their respective followers tried to suppress their differences and cooperate, but the strains became too powerful in 1897. Muir and Pinchot encountered each other in Seattle, just after Pinchot had been quoted in the newspapers as saying that sheep should be allowed to graze in the forest reserves. Muir, who regarded sheep as "hooved locusts," asked Pinchot if he had been quoted correctly, and the forester admitted he had. Muir told him bluntly, "I don't want anything more to do with you. When we were in the Cascades last summer, you yourself stated that the sheep did a great deal of harm."

When Pinchot was chosen to head the Division of Forestry in 1898, he immediately started fighting to bring public forests managed by the Department of the Interior under his control at Agriculture, and to further organize the administration of natural resources. Pinchot was a talented bureaucratic maneuverer, and a gifted speaker who enjoyed appearing at public forums and arguing for his idea of scientific management. "Conservation," as he defined it, "is the foresighted utilization, preservation, and/or renewal of forests, waters, land, and minerals, for the greatest good of the greatest number for the longest time."

Muir may have been a wonderful raconteur by the warmth of a wilderness campfire, but he felt uncomfortable addressing large audiences. It was through writing that he was most effective in winning people to his point of view. In January and July of 1898, he wrote articles for the *Atlantic Monthly* attacking Pinchot's narrowly utilitarian approach to conservation and pointing out that the national parks were havens offering God's peace to animals and humans alike while a blind, ruthless destruction went on all around them. "Thousands of tired, nerve-shaken, over civilized people are beginning to find out that going to the mountains is going home; that wilderness is a necessity; and that mountain parks and reservations are useful not only as fountains of timber and irrigating rivers, but as fountains of life." Visit these parks with all their natural wonders, "And a multitude of still, small voices may be heard directing you to look through all this transient, shifting show of things called 'substantial' into the truly substantial, spiritual world whose forms, flesh and wood, rock and water, air and sunshine, only veil and conceal, and to learn that here is heaven and the dwelling-place of the angels." Because of Muir's articles the circulation of the *Atlantic* increased dramatically, and Muir became recognized as the national spokesman for preserving wilderness.

This battle has continued to be fought down to our own day between those who would set aside part of the dwindling wild areas and those who would exploit all the public lands, either through Pinchot's sustained yield principles or the quicker old-fashioned style. Both Pinchot and Muir were sincerely convinced they were right, and neither totally excluded the other's concerns from his thinking. By far the greater share of victories has gone to the utilitarian side, which was able to make strong economic arguments to win support for its policies. Pinchot hoped that opening the land to wider use would be a way of allowing common people to benefit from natural resources, not just lumber barons or monopolists. Like many Americans he feared that the big capitalists' and corporations' drive for profits, healthy up to a point, could acquire a power that excluded all other considerations. "No man," he was convinced, "can make his life what it ought to be by living it merely on a business basis. There are things higher than business."

AMERICANS HAVE ALWAYS loved speed—fleet horses, fast trains, the swift new torpedo boats. The vehicle of choice for people of the 1890s, one that delighted men and women alike, was the safety bicycle. How quickly, how gracefully that silent two-wheeled steed moved when the roads were good enough to allow proper pedaling, and how wonderful to be able to leave the cares of the city behind to go for a spin into the country, effortlessly moving through both time and space.

Much easier to learn to ride than its high-wheeled predecessor, the bicycle had undergone constant technological improvement during the decade. Ball bearings were developed for the wheels and gear brackets; frames were made of tubular steel; spoked wheels were introduced; and pneumatic rather than solid rubber tires were mounted. These advances lightened the machines to under twenty-five pounds, so most adults could physically handle them. The usual pattern of entrepreneurial competition then occurred: more than 250 companies began mass producing bicycles from interchangeable parts, with capital investments totaling over sixty million dollars. This led to overproduction, which lowered the price of new top-quality brands to less than $75, making them much cheaper and easier to maintain than a horse, which cost about $150 to buy and $25 a month to feed and stable. Installment plans also aided sales, and by 1898 there were around four million riders in the United States.

People used the "wheel" to commute to work, as well as for relaxation, and it helped open small-town life to broader influences. "On the bicycle

A Gibson girl and her beau rest during a bicycle ride in the country. From Charles Dana Gibson's *Sketches and Cartoons* (New York, 1898). (*Courtesy of the Free Library of Philadelphia*)

you could go where you pleased, fixing your own schedule," remembered an Ohioan of his youth. "It took you to 'the city' to attend a theater matinee and back home in time for the evening meal. Soon after I owned a bicycle I rode with two other boys the sixteen miles from our Ohio town to Dayton and, at a cost of fifty cents for a seat in the peanut gallery, saw Joseph Jefferson in *Rip Van Winkle,* the first good actor any of us had ever seen. That was *living*. Our horizons were broadening."

Amateur and professional racing circuits were popular, as were clubs for enthusiasts. Fiction writers and newspapers devoted much space to stories of bicycle derring-do. Theodore Roosevelt, when police commissioner of New York City, started a Bicycle Squad that quickly caught the public's attention. "The members . . . soon grew to show not only extraordinary proficiency on the wheel, but extraordinary daring," he wrote in his autobiography. "They frequently stopped runaways, wheeling alongside of them, and grasping the horses while going at full speed; and, what was even more remarkable, they managed not only to overtake but to jump into the vehicle and capture, on two or three different occasions, men who were guilty of reckless driving, and who fought violently in resisting arrest. They were picked men, being young and active, and any feat of daring which could be accomplished on the wheel they were certain to accomplish."

The bicycle helped break down the old-fashioned image of women as being weak and helpless, since they could ride one as easily as their beaux, and it was also a great aid to romance. A couple or a group of couples could wheel off, with the "cyclometer" supposedly acting as chaperon, for if they had truly cycled so far in, say, two hours, there had obviously been no time for hanky-panky. The weakness of this line of reasoning was pointed out in the humor magazine *Life* in August 1898, when a daughter tried to make that argument:

> *Her mother frowned. "My dear," she said,*
> *"Last night I chanced to see*
> *Your beau and you absorbed in talk*
> *Beneath a spreading tree."*
>
> *"And as you talked, he whirled your wheel*
> *Until the figures showed*
> *That you had traveled twenty miles*
> *Or more along the road."*
>
> *L'envoi*
> *Oh maidens fair and lovers true,*
> *If you would win your fight,*
> *Don't play your cyclometric game*
> *Unless you're out of sight.*

Bicycle clubs lobbied to improve the nation's notoriously bad roads, and enthusiasts wanted ever greater speed, thus preparing the way for the automobile.

Much early automobile development had taken place in Europe, but by the mid-1890s hundreds of Americans were tinkering with various ways of propelling carts and two- and three-wheel cycles. There were enough of these pioneers to support a trade magazine entitled *The Horseless Age,* although twenty million horses and mules were then laboring in the fields and streets of the nation. "A pleasing prospect it is," the magazine enthused, "that rises before us in contemplating this array of horseless

vehicles! From the gradual displacement of the horse in business and pleasure will come economy of time and practical money-saving. In cities and
town the noise and clatter of the streets will be reduced, a priceless boon
to the tired nerves of this overwrought generation. Then there is the
humanitarian aspect of the case. To spare the obedient beast, that since
the dawn of history has been man's drudge . . . will be a downright mercy.
On sanitary grounds too the banishing of horses from our city streets will
be a blessing. Streets will be cleaner, jams and blockades less likely to
occur, and accidents less frequent, for the horse is not so manageable as a
mechanical vehicle." Technological progress would bring efficiency, moral
improvement, and a cleaner, safer world.

Engineers and mechanics trained in the design and manufacture of
"wheels" were able to apply their knowledge to this new means of transportation as bicycle sales began to slump from their height in 1896. Entrepreneurs started producing light "steamers," which shared the ball
bearings, steel tubing, wire spokes, and air-filled tires of the bicycle. It was
the splendid machine tools developed in bicycle manufacturing that would
allow Americans to quickly dominate the international market for automobiles once the proper mechanical design evolved.

In 1898 the Stanley twins began selling steam cars to the public, as did
at least two other companies. At this time the Stanleys did not really know
or care how to run a modern business (they would start up again after the
turn of the century and last until 1925). They did no advertising, and in fact
closed their factory to visitors, adopting an air of mystery. The brothers
soon sold their patent rights to Amzi L. Barber, who had made a fortune
through manufacturing matches. This entrepreneur believed that if his car,
which he named the Locomobile, was built using modern production techniques it could be sold inexpensively to a mass market. For a few years he
managed to do just that.

Electricity was the marvel of the age, so it was only natural that other
innovators turned to it to power their designs. In early 1898 the mail-order
company Montgomery Ward had two electric horseless carriages custom-
made, for three thousand dollars each, as "advertising novelties" that were
sent, as was boasted in that year's catalogue, to "the smaller towns of the
Union so that those who might otherwise never see a horseless carriage
will have the opportunity." They were novelties instead of practicalities
because they lacked batteries capable of holding sustained charges, a challenge that Thomas Edison was trying to solve. There were, however, com-

panies in Chicago, Philadelphia, Boston, Cleveland, and Brooklyn manufacturing battery-driven cars, and at the electrical show held in Madison Square Garden in the fall four of them offered their creations. Two years later, at the first real automobile show in the United States, over a third of those exhibited were electric, although steamers still made up the majority.

Few of the steam and electric innovators could understand at first why anyone wasted their time working with "explosive" vehicles. As Colonel A. A. Pope, who had been the country's largest bicycle manufacturer before shifting to the production of electric vehicles, said with notable common sense, "You'll never get people to sit over an explosion."

There were good reasons, however, why mechanics like Alexander Winton, the Duryea brothers, and Henry Ford continued to experiment with the gasoline engine: it was light for the amount of power it produced, cheaper to manufacture and to operate than either steam or electric engines, and much more efficient in its use of fuel. As a contemporary magazine pointed out, the gasoline automobile had "developed more all-round good qualities than any other carriage. In spite of its clumsy and complicated mechanism, it does not get easily out of order. It will climb all ordinary hills; it will run through sand, mud or snow; it makes good speed over long distances—say, an average of fifteen miles an hour. . . . It carries gasoline enough for a 70-mile journey, and nearly any country store can replenish the supply."

The earliest practical gasoline engine in America had been developed by George Selden in the late 1870s, but he had trouble convincing anyone to finance his efforts. To a friend who was ready to invest five thousand dollars in the 1880s, he impulsively predicted, "Jim, you and I will live to see more carriages on Main Street run by motor than are now drawn by horses."

The friend, who was a hard-headed man of business, recoiled, telling him, "George, you are crazy, and I won't have anything to do with your scheme."

Selden persevered, improving his engine design and finally obtaining a patent in 1895, a patent he would later use to bedevil his competitors, demanding royalties on every gasoline motor produced until Henry Ford beat him in a lawsuit.

Ford, born on a Michigan farm in 1863, had in childhood shown a magical touch with anything mechanical, loving to take apart and reassemble watches or any other gadget he could place his hands on. In 1879, over the objections of his father, he became an apprentice in a machine shop in Detroit, repairing watches at night for extra income. Over the next nine years he became an expert mechanic and steam engineer, but his father, trying to lure him back to the life of the land, offered Henry forty acres of woodland to clear and farm. The son accepted, using the opportunity to marry his sweetheart. Then he set up a sawmill, sold the timber, and used the money to equip a workshop on the land, where he started to experiment with a little steam vehicle. Like so many American inventors, Ford was convinced that technology would liberate man from the burden of brute labor and offer a better way of life than that lived by his father's generation. After a few years struggling with this particular machine, he decided that in order to proceed with his work he needed to know more about electricity. The Fords moved back to Detroit, Henry taking a job as an engineer for the Edison Illuminating Company at forty-five dollars a month.

His work with steam had convinced him that gasoline engines offered a more likely route to success, and that is where he concentrated his efforts every evening after returning from his work at the powerhouse. Lean to the point of asceticism, the young man enjoyed unusual energy and stamina while being totally dedicated to his work. "We often wondered when Henry Ford slept," one of his neighbors remarked later, "because he was putting in long hours working [at the Edison plant] and when he went home at night he was always experimenting or reading." He usually did not labor alone in the little brick shed behind his rented house, but convinced a number of other skilled mechanics and craftsmen to help. This willingness and ability to bring others into a team effort would later help him build his empire.

Over the next six years what he built and rebuilt was the "quadricycle," which was propelled by a four-cycle motor with two cylinders, which managed to produce three to four horsepower. The body weighed only about 750 pounds, but could carry the driver and a passenger at speeds of around fifteen miles an hour. A young girl who was given a ride on the unusual beast never forgot "the peculiar sensation of what seemed to be a 'great speed' and the sense of bewilderment I felt when I first rode in this carriage which moved without a horse." The inventor found that crowds gathered wherever he went, and that American males were so confident of their own mechanical ingenuity that if he left the quadricycle alone for even a moment someone always climbed aboard and tried to run it. "Finally, I had to carry a chain and chain it to a lamp post whenever I left it anywhere." In addition, he had to endure mockery from his father, who thought it was foolish for a grown man to be playing with such a toy.

The Duryea brothers and Alexander Winton were also making progress. H. H. Kohlsaat, publisher of the Chicago *Times-Herald* and friend of President McKinley, sponsored the first American race for horseless carriages on Thanksgiving Day, 1895, the purpose being to determine if the machine was yet superior to the animal. A total of ten thousand dollars in prizes was offered to draw competitors. Conditions were made challenging by an early storm that dumped a foot of snow on the roads and temperatures that never managed to climb out of the thirties, but a Duryea gas buggy managed to average more than six miles an hour over the 52.4-mile course and took first prize, impressing newspaper readers with its toughness.

This race sparked national interest in automobiles, although for a year or two financiers remained unimpressed, and it wasn't until 1897 that a number of investors came knocking at workshop doors. Alexander Winton, based in Cleveland, managed to attract enough capital to organize the Winton Motor Carriage Company, and on March 24, 1898, made the first sale of an American gasoline-powered automobile built from a regular assembly process (the Duryeas had earlier sold some hand- or custom-made vehicles). Winton began advertising in technical magazines, evidently figuring that was where his customer base would be found. The first ad ran in the July 30, 1898, issue of *Scientific American,* displaying a small picture of his fourteen-hundred-pound phaeton. "Never gets 'winded' " the copy would claim in this series, or "Away with the whip!"

Henry Ford, who was now chief engineer at Edison Illuminating and making around nineteen hundred dollars a year, had financed his own work on the quadricycle. This put a severe strain on the family budget, especially after his son Edsel was born. Money was so tight, "It seemed as if we would never have any for ourselves," his wife Clara remembered. Another burden was the president of the local Edison powerplant, who regarded his tinkering as a ridiculous obsession. "My gas-engine experiments were not more popular with the president of the company than my first mechanical leanings were with my father," he wrote later. "It was not that my employer objected to experiments—only to experiments with a gas engine. I can still hear him say: 'Electricity, yes, that's the coming thing. But gas—no.' "

Thomas Alva Edison himself, whom Ford met at a company convention, thought differently. When told "There's a young fellow who's made a gas car," Edison had him come and sit close so he could ask detailed questions about the ignition and piston action. After Ford sketched some of his design on the back of a menu, Edison pounded his fist on the table, rattling the dishes. "Young man," he said, "that's the thing! You have it—the self-contained unit carrying its fuel with it! Keep at it!" These words from the most famous inventor in the world did help keep Ford on his search. He sold his quadricycle to a local man for two hundred dollars and began building improved, and more expensive, versions.

These machines impressed some of the businessmen who had been watching his progress, and in the November 1898 issue of *The Horseless Age* it was announced that "Henry Ford, of Detroit, Michigan . . . has built a number of gasoline vehicles which are said to have been successfully operated. He is reported to be financially supported by several prominent men of that city who intend to manufacture the Ford vehicle. From Mr. Ford himself no information can be gleaned regarding his vehicle or his plans for manufacture." This financial support allowed the start of production. Ford resigned from the Edison plant, and the Detroit Automobile Company was formed, manufacturing nineteen or twenty cars. But the firm was undercapitalized. Ford thought the cars built were too expensive for their questionable quality, and the public evidently agreed, for they did not sell very well. A strong, lightweight, dependable automobile, capable of releasing rural folk from the isolating tyranny of bad roads, is what he envisioned, but he could not convince his investors to finance the improvements needed. The company collapsed in 1900.

By that year dozens of entrepreneurs had plunged into the field, most of whom quickly went bankrupt. Those who survived began joining together and gobbling up competitors in the American way until only giants remained. They enjoyed for a while a seller's market as people began to accept the new contraption as a vehicle of liberation.

Ford, in the tradition of strive and succeed innovators like Edison, kept at his work, building racing cars and winning a national reputation as a competitive driver. The Ford Motor Company was founded in 1903 with twenty-eight thousand dollars in capital, locally raised, for he held a Midwestern farmer's suspicion of Wall Street and Eastern capitalists. This time Henry insisted on retaining control, so that his vehicles would have high standards and low prices. Constant experimentation went on during these early years, until he and his team developed a moving assembly line so efficient the company was able to mass-market the Model T for around four hundred dollars. To Ford, the enormous changes the automobile brought to people's lives proved that the American belief in progress through technology was not misplaced: "Machinery is accomplishing in the world what man has failed to do by preaching, propaganda, or the written word."

ANOTHER MACHINE THAT would change the world beyond recognition was under development in 1898, although it required of its advocates even greater courage and imagination than the automobile. Mankind's age-old dream of flying still seemed to most scientists just that, a fantasy for dreamers. "The example of the bird does not prove that man can fly," wrote the famous American mathematician and astronomer Simon Newcomb just two months before the Wright brothers made their successful first flight in 1903. "May not our mechanicians . . . be ultimately forced to admit that aerial flight is one of that great class of problems with which man can never cope, and give up all attempts to grapple with it? . . . Imagine the proud possessor of the airplane darting through the air at a speed of several hundred feet per second! How is he ever going to stop? . . . The construction of an aerial vehicle which could carry even a single man from place to place at pleasure requires the discovery of some new metal or some new force. Even with such a discovery we could not expect one to do more than carry its owner."

But Samuel Pierpont Langley, also an astronomer and chief of the Smithsonian Institution, had become fascinated by the challenges of flight during the 1890s. He first studied the work of foreign experimenters, and then, using his scientific training, he began investigating the role wind played. Wing surface and shape were obviously important, so he made a careful study of lifting ability based on Frisbee-like plates that he or an assistant twirled through the air. This allowed him to work out a formula for each square foot of wing needed to lift specific weights. A special steam engine was designed as a power source, and on May 6, 1896, his pilotless machine flew three thousand feet at Quantico, Virginia, the longest flight made by a heavier-than-air craft up to that time.

By 1898 his invention was capable of flights of up to one mile, although these would sometimes end with a nosedive into the Potomac. Langley put on some demonstrations that March in Washington, D.C., to which he invited Theodore Roosevelt, a friend he had met through the Cosmos Club. Roosevelt was then under tremendous pressure as assistant secretary of the navy, preparing his force for a possible conflict with Spain, but he took time to attend the demonstrations and was properly impressed. "The machine has worked," he wrote his boss, Secretary John Long. "It seems to me worth while for this Government to try whether it will not work on a large enough scale to be of use in the event of war." At his urging a board of scientifically trained officers was established that reported favorably on the "revolutionary" advantage such a machine would give to the nation's armed services.

Congress then allocated Langley fifty thousand dollars to improve his design. Confident that he would be the first to achieve manned flight, he proceeded slowly, carefully determining the amount of wing surface needed, the optimum size of the propeller, and the type of engine to use. Steam was abandoned as being too heavy, but a gasoline engine light and robust enough was also difficult to design. In 1903 his assistant and pilot, C. H. Manly, was able to build one that was capable of powering the big "tandem monoplane," which had two sets of wings, one behind the other. In September and December 1903 attempts were made to fly Langley's machine, which he named the *Aerodrome,* but on both occasions there were serious launch accidents. The inventor was ridiculed in the press; Simon Newcomb, after the first try, wrote that the whole endeavor was impossible; and the congressional appropriation ran out. Just nine days after the December failure, Wilbur Wright successfully took the craft he had built with his brother, Orville, aloft at Kill Devil Hills, near Kitty Hawk, North Carolina.

The Wright brothers were bicycle mechanics from Dayton, Ohio, who had become interested in flying in 1900. They studied the success and failures of other experimenters, especially Langley, and became friends with Octave Chanute, who had designed a series of gliders from 1896 to 1898 that he had flown on the shores of Lake Michigan.

With Chanute's help the brothers constructed their own gliders, which they periodically tested at Kill Devil Hills, where steady Atlantic winds gave the lift needed for longer and longer flights. Both developed into skilled glider pilots, and each successive machine became more sophisticated. In early 1903 they built a twelve-horsepower engine and conducted a thorough study of propellers, using a wind tunnel of their own design. Then on December 17, after waiting through days of bad weather, Wilbur made the first manned flight ever in a heavier-than-air machine—120 feet and 12 seconds long. "They did it! They did it," a local youth shouted that afternoon in the town of Kitty Hawk. "Damned if they didn't fly!"

CHAPTER 3

YOUTH AND NEW IDEAS

I had let career go hang, and was on the adventure-path again in quest of fortune. . . . True, the new territory was mostly barren; but its several hundred thousand square miles of frigidity at least gave breathing space to those who else would have suffocated at home.

Jack London in the Klondike

To be young in a growing world which was full of new ideas was stimulating and exciting. I loved it.

Nathalie Smith Dana

CIVILIZATION SEEMED A mixed blessing to many young middle-class men and women in early 1898. Advances in science and technology were all very well, and few questioned the idea of Progress—the view that the world was improving year by year was accepted as fact. But many chafed at the restrictions that traditional civilized behavior placed on them, and feared the great cleavages between rich and poor, finding particularly repugnant the obsession with excessive profit by American business and with comfort and luxury by the American people. They agreed with Gifford Pinchot that these desires were not worthy purposes—the great question was where to find better ones.

Men like Theodore Roosevelt, who would turn forty this year, feared that modern life was rotting the old American virtues out of their generation: softening their bodies, their character, and their willpower. One way these men responded was by taking up the modern form of chivalry established by their fathers, a knightly code that emphasized duty, honor, and a willingness to make sacrifices for a good cause. Such causes ideally involved defending the weak, especially women and children, but the code could also mean defending one's own reputation and sense of dignity. It was common for drugstores of the time to employ a specialist in the treatment of black eyes because so many men felt obliged to requite an insult with their fists. Desire for romantic associations, raising ordinary people above the humdrum modern reality of office and factory routine, spanned classes and geographical regions. A popular novel of 1898, entitled *When Knighthood Was In Flower*, was just one sign of this need for chivalrous excitement. The Knights of Ak-Sar-Ben, which added romance and solemn ritual to the lives of businessmen in Omaha, had counterparts everywhere.

Chastity before marriage was part of this code, although it was perhaps too often honored in the breach. Prostitution was rampant in the big cities, where there were well-organized red-light districts, and even in relatively small county centers like Lancaster, Pennsylvania, which reportedly had twenty-seven bordellos at the turn of the century. Middle- and upper-class women were put on a pedestal, and one of the justifications for prostitution was that it helped protect their virtue. Even so, there were many roving males, cads and bounders, who hoped to nudge them off their honored position by taking advantage of their innocence or naive curiosity. "Even in the daytime," remembered one young woman of this period, "if alone, I was followed by stray men." Nevertheless, an element in the appeal of popular public figures like Theodore Roosevelt and Richard Harding Davis, a journalist, war correspondent, and novelist, was their strict adherence to the standards of gentlemanly forbearance and purity.

This was a generation of men both inspired and burdened by the glory their fathers had won in the Civil War, a glory that was constantly being renewed, flaunted it often seemed, through speeches, Grand Army of the Republic parades, and books. There was resentment of their elders, as well, for often military leaders were too old-fashioned and stuck in their ways to adopt modern weapons, logistics, and tactics; older politicians did not understand the new conditions of the world, nor the need for America to play a greater role in ordering them. Also aggravating were the huge amounts paid out for Civil War pensions, often, it was claimed, to those who faked or lied about their service. Newspapers and magazines in 1898 would run exposés of such corrupt practices, and point out that the United States spent more on pensions than Germany, the most aggressively militaristic nation, spent on its armed services.

There was no denying, however, that older generation's achievements, or moral authority. In 1895, Oliver Wendell Holmes, Jr., who had been severely wounded three times during the Civil War and who would soon serve on the Supreme Court, gave an address to the Harvard graduating class that received wide attention. "War, when you are at it, is horrible and dull. It is only when time has passed that you see that its message was divine. . . . We need it in this time of individualistic negations. . . . We need it everywhere and at all times. . . . Out of heroism grows faith in the worth of heroism."

Individualistic negations seemed in constant evidence to the youths listening to Holmes' message: just look at how businessmen elevated the accumulation of wealth above charity, social harmony, justice, and even patriotism. They placed profits above honor, and politicians were no better, having become nothing more than handmaidens to the corporations that were growing larger and more powerful by the day, forming an "unholy alliance" that many of this impatient generation saw as undermining the foundations of the Republic.

But if Oliver Wendell Holmes was right, and only war would counter this selfish arrogance, where could its rigors and glories be found? How to win the moral prestige that their fathers had achieved by fighting and winning (or in the South's case losing) a great crusade? The United States, and indeed much of the Western world, had been at peace for decades, which meant that youth had grown up without the opportunity to hear shots fired in anger—while constantly hearing about epic battles that had decided great issues.

Some pride was taken that Stephen Crane, one of their own, was capable of producing what was widely recognized to be the best war novel ever written by an American—*The Red Badge of Courage*—without ever having been himself under fire. Based on interviews and other research, the book won Crane respect among literate journalists and editors when it was published in 1895. But, however vivid, it was still just a novel, an imitation. Young men wanted a real, if romantic, whiff of gunsmoke, blood, and steel; they wanted a chance to be their own heroes.

The one event offering an approximation of full-scale war was a struggle between Greece and Turkey that broke out in the spring of 1897, but which lasted only a short while. Reporters, including Stephen Crane and Richard Harding Davis, flocked from around the world to have the honor of covering it. So pent-up was the demand to be close to what was still thought of as chivalrous combat—Europeans too felt deprived, not having savored real bloodshed since the Franco-Prussian war of 1870–71—that million-aires steamed in their private yachts to the shores of Greece, then hired guides to take them to where battles were likely so they could hear the whistle of bullets and the roar of cannon, and attest later at dinner parties to the quiet heroism of the wounded and dying, who were expected to offer examples of stoic endurance that underscored the tragic cost of glory. Almost everyone arrived too late for real action, but that close brush whetted appetites.

American youth poured some of their energies into sports, particularly football, with an intensity that shocked even the English, who had their own passion for manly contests. The "swollen salaries of baseball players" were bad enough, thought the English visitor James Muirhead, but more shocking was the way even prestigious universities turned what should have been the pleasure of training for games into hard work in order to reap the "gate-money," or admission fees charged to see victorious football teams. It seemed too much like war, he reported, where "all was fair," and college players would deliberately try to hurt opposing stars to put them out of the game. The Frenchman Paul Bourget also found the game too violent: "The roughness with which they seize the bearer of the ball is impossible to imagine without having witnessed it." Even Mr. Dooley, Finley Peter Dunne's fictional Irish-American bartender who had seen it all, expressed shock at the behavior of football spectators in 1898. "Says wan crowd: 'Take an ax, an ax, an ax to thim. Hooroo, hooroo, hellabaloo. Christyan Bro-others!' an' th' other says, 'Hit thim, saw thim, gnaw thim, chaw thim, Saint Alo-ysius!'"

Competitive sports provided one of the means through which this generation of men defined themselves, and it would be to sports—football and baseball in particular—that they would turn for analogies to what they would later witness in combat.

Another area that offered opportunity to show toughness and grit was the Great West, which still held expanses of undeveloped country containing a rugged human population that was refreshingly close to barbarism. But even here enthusiasm was given a desperate edge by the speed with which wild lands were disappearing, by government clerks who had declared the frontier ended after the census of 1890, and by the historian Frederick Jackson Turner, who had mourned that its influence was now at an end. Young men were drawn like filings to a magnet by its challenging dangers, just as it drew their fathers' capital by the profitable, if risky, investments it offered. Crane had gone there, and Roosevelt, and Richard

Harding Davis, Owen Wister, Frederic Remington—legions of the restless and adventurous. There were ranches, mines, bandits, cowboys, and Indians, as well as vast forests, huge rocky mountains, and ice fields as endless as its deserts, all offering an exotic but authentic world fascinatingly different from the city.

In 1897 and 1898 the place that drew hardy souls was the Yukon, where great deposits of gold had been discovered. Jack London was one among thousands who sought freedom in the frozen region, where he was gathering material for his first successful stories. Another writer who rushed up to this "last frontier" was Hamlin Garland, who eagerly sought the dangers and discomforts of life around the Klondike River: "I believed that I was about to see and take part in a most picturesque and impressive movement across the wilderness. I believed it to be the last march of the kind which could ever come in America, so rapidly were the wild places being settled up." Included among his reasons was a desire to flee the frustrating concerns of modern life. "I wished to return to the wilderness also, to forget books and theories of art and social problems, and come again face to face with the great free spaces of woods and skies and streams." If this generation of men was going to be caught between an overrefined civilization and barbarous disorder, it would welcome the rough challenge of taming the disorder. That challenge would be one of the great motivations for the war these men fought and the imperialism that followed it.

One of the stances reinforced for young Americans by the adventures they experienced or read about in the West was traditional American directness—the "go straight at 'em" approach—and an impatience with subtlety or any sort of complexity that was not purely mechanical. They loved to take apart a bicycle or a rifle, just as their sons would later make a hobby of disassembling flivvers, but they did not see other realms of life, especially those having to do with the human heart, as warranting such close attention. The masculine ideal also called for calmness under stress, no matter how extreme, and a self-control so firm that not a tremor showed on the face or a quiver in the finger. It is no wonder that poker was the card game of choice.

Art, or at least Fine Art, was held in suspicion, although they could appreciate the bold colors and dramatic verve of a Frederic Remington painting. Such a work, after all, usually told a story, and a damned good one, too, about courage, duty, and sacrifice. But "readily accessible" painters were rare enough that aesthetic satisfaction had to be found elsewhere. "Speaking of American art," wrote W. A. Rogers in *Harper's Weekly,*

"it has shown itself in the past few years in an unexpected direction. Foreigners usually tell us that it is impossible for art to flourish here in these
days, because this is the age and the country of invention and mechanics.
But . . . any intelligent observer can find art in its highest form in the work
of our best mechanical engineers. You have only to contrast the tawdriness
of the little locomotives of a few years back, ornamented with brass-work
to hide their inherent ugliness, with the severely simple yet elegant lines of
the great passenger engines of to-day, to see how the mechanical engineer
has added to economy of power that highest element of Greek art, perfect
proportion." Rogers reported that the best American inventors "studied the
proportions and forms of animals and plants" to find the strongest and
most economical shapes, and one of these industrial designers told him
that his ideal was to get a machine to look as though "it had naturally grown
that way."

INCREASINGLY, it was Theodore Roosevelt who was, with his intelligence,
energy, and willpower, regarded as the shining star of this generation. His
whole demeanor promised seriousness instead of cynicism, and moral purpose rather than frivolity. The young Englishwoman Beatrice Webb, who
visited the United States in 1898 with her husband, Sydney, to study urban
problems, thought he was the most remarkable man she met that year, and
gave a perceptive description of him. He was "a short thick-set, bullet-
headed man with an extraordinarily expressive face, all his features move
when he speaks. The dark, shaggy eyebrows, the keen grey eyes and the
powerful jaw—all combine in a series of grimaces as he gesticulates his
words. He has abundance of ready wit, splendid fighting courage and a
thorough knowledge of the world he lives in. Perhaps it is the deliberately
sought out rough and tumble of his past life that has lent to his outward
address a slight vulgarity. He has the loudness and hearty egotism of the
man who has shouldered his way through life."

The energy, fighting courage, and hearty egotism attracted both men
and women to his support, and he had a particular charm for journalists,
who admired his colorfulness and integrity. The politically ambitious Roosevelt was, in turn, already savvy enough about public relations to cultivate
their attentions. William Allen White's reaction to this charismatic figure
can be seen as fairly typical. When the Kansas newspaperman met him in
1897, he was suddenly awakened "to the new time that was to be" and felt
"afire with the splendor of the personality that I had met." The two men

had lunch together and talked over the political situation in the country. "I had never known such a man as he, and never shall again. He overcame me . . . he poured into my heart such visions, such ideals, such hopes, such a new attitude toward life and patriotism and the meaning of things, as I had never dreamed men had." Many young men were convinced that if given the chance he, and they, could tame this strange new world of technology and concentration of wealth, and bring the growing economic and political chaos, both in this country and in the world, under control—inaugurating "the new time that was to be." The future, the twentieth century, they were sure, would then belong to the United States.

Roosevelt's background as well as his personality and experience made him the perfect spokesman for his generation. His father, who gained a national reputation for good works, belonged to a wealthy Old Dutch family in New York, but his mother was a Bulloch from a plantation-owning clan in Georgia. Theodore passed his early childhood years during the Civil War, in a household uncomfortably reflective of the great political and cultural differences between the two clashing regions of the divided nation—his mother's two brothers were naval heroes on the enemy side. The senior Roosevelt, however, did not serve in the Union armed forces, instead hiring a substitute. This left his son, as it did other young men in similar situations, such as Richard Harding Davis and Stephen Crane, with a burning need to prove himself in combat.

Roosevelt was a frail child, suffering from asthma and poor eyesight, who became a passionate reader and writer. Reading was more important to these middle-class children than it had been for any earlier generation in American history, and they took many of their guiding principles from their childhood magazines and books as well as their elders. "I was nervous and timid," he remembered later in life. "Yet from reading of the people I admired—ranging from the soldiers of Valley Forge, and Morgan's riflemen, to the heroes of my favorite stories—and from hearing of the feats performed by my Southern forefathers and kinsfolk . . . I felt a great admiration for men who were fearless and who could hold their own in the world, and I had a great desire to be like them." He found that if he followed the example of these heroes and *acted* unafraid, all fear disappeared.

The study of animals and plants also fascinated Roosevelt, spurring the budding naturalist to roam the Long Island countryside with magnifying glass, butterfly net, or hunting rifle in hand, building strength in his legs and lungs. But this wasn't enough. His father constructed a gymnasium in the house stocked with dumbbells, horizontal bars, and a punching bag, telling him: "You have the mind but not the body, and without help of the body the mind cannot go as far as it should. You must *make* your body. It is hard drudgery to make one's body, but I know you will do it."

Theodore worked hard at this dreary business and then, after being tormented by bullies once too often, took up boxing and jujitsu to better defend himself, going on to box competitively at Harvard, where his father advised him to "Take care of your morals first, your health next, and finally your studies." He grew into an energetic youth, with a store of curiosity about the world and abounding self-confidence. Like many young men, he was a "dude," wearing gloves and a silk hat, and sporting a gold-headed cane. All these furnishings, along with strict standards of personal cleanliness, helped to define him as different from the ordinary mortals walking the streets. One of the particularly strong desires of "dudes" was to mark themselves off from big-city businessmen, who dressed uniformly in conservative black suits. These adventurous youths found little romance in the ledger book.

After graduation from Harvard, and early marriage, he attended Columbia Law School briefly, but found the prevailing morality unattractive. "The *caveat emptor* side of the law, like the *caveat emptor* side of business, seemed to me repellent; it did not make for social fair dealing." Roosevelt made himself conspicuous with the impertinent questions he would ask his professors. Why *should* the "buyer beware"? Why couldn't laws be written that would protect both buyer and seller from unfair practices? He seems to have developed a particular distaste for lawyers who made a specialty of defending corporations engaged in "sharp practices."

Roosevelt decided that a better way to improve this disappointing world was to enter politics, for which he drew criticism from some members of the family and their friends. Didn't he realize politics was a low affair, populated by louts, ruffians, and corrupt hacks, not to mention Irishmen? Even more difficult was the challenge of convincing the Republican political machine that such an elegant dude was sincere and tough enough to stick the game to the end. Nevertheless, he persevered, hanging around Party headquarters until he overcame what Bret Harte called "the defective moral quality of being a stranger." First elected to the New York assembly at the age of twenty-three, he served three terms, and was closely identified with the small but active reform element. The work was satisfying, but "if conscientiously done, very harassing."

This difficult but happy and fulfilling way of life ended abruptly in 1884, when both his mother and his wife died within hours of each other in his home in New York City. Grief-stricken, he fled to the West. "He did not want anybody to sympathize with him," a fellow assemblyman noted. "He hiked away to the wilderness to get away from the world. . . . He went out there a broken-hearted man." In the Badlands of the Dakotas, Roosevelt ranched, hunted, and grieved. "It was still the Wild West in those days," Roosevelt wrote, "the Far West, the West of Owen Wister's stories and Frederic Remington's drawings, the West of the Indian and the buffalo-hunter, the soldier and the cow-puncher." Here he had to prove himself anew. Cowboys looked with suspicion on a "four-eyes," and almost fell out of their saddles with astonishment when he would call across the dust and swirl of a roundup, "Hasten forward quickly there," as if he were still strutting around the playing fields of Harvard. But he soon won their respect, and before returning to the East for good he had learned to run an open-range ranch, knocked out a gun-pointing bully in a bar, and tracked down and brought to justice several outlaws. He then wrote popular books about the history of the region, as well as his own experiences there, that helped smooth somewhat the cultural divide between what was seen as the effete East and the wild and woolly West.

By 1898, Roosevelt had remarried, was a father, and had run unsuccessfully for mayor of New York. While a member of the national Civil Service Commission, which was usually regarded as a harmless backwater, he had so impatiently pushed for reform as to inspire President Benjamin Harrison's observation that Roosevelt "wanted to put an end to all the evil in the world between sunrise and sunset." He had then served as an active and demanding police commissioner of his native city before, with a great deal of political maneuvering, he managed to get appointed assistant secretary of the navy. There he dedicated himself to correcting what he regarded as mistaken defense policies of the past. His actions in 1898 were going to make his national reputation—by August he would be the most famous and talked-about man in the country—and lead directly to the presidency three years later.

THE SISTERS AND SWEETHEARTS of young middle-class men in 1898 chafed even more than they did at the restrictions of outmoded custom. "The atmosphere of change had its effect upon the minds of young people," recalled Nathalie Dana, member of a well-off New York family, who turned twenty years old in 1898, "and as I grew older I began to question social customs." Those included everything from the "chaotic" house interiors favored by their parents to the requirement that women keep silent before the opinions of men and use every proper opportunity to hunt for a wealthy husband. In this vein, Mrs. Constance Carey Harrison, an older well-known writer, published a book in 1898 for the "Ladies' Home Journal Girls' Library," entitled *The Well-Bred Girl in Society.* Advising her readers that at balls and parties, "The occasion becomes an universal exchange, a market in which wares are offered and accepted or passed by for whatever is more attractive to the seeker," Mrs. Harrison reminded them of an important element in their charm: "the truth is the average man prefers mental repose rather than mental titillation in the companionship of women."

And if one did not desire to be on the market, or be a source of repose? The opportunities that middle-class American women enjoyed, though comparatively limited, amazed visiting European observers, every one of whom felt required to include a chapter on her. "The American woman has never learned to play second fiddle," wrote Muirhead in *America, the Land of Contrasts,* noting that there were eighty "lady doctors" in Boston and twenty-five female lawyers in Chicago. "There are numbers of women dentists, barbers, and livery-stable keepers . . . a railway pointswoman in Georgia; and one of the regular steamers on Lake Champlain, when I was there, was successfully steered by a pilot in petticoats." 1898 was also the year that the California Perfume Company, shocking many, initiated the use of women as door-to-door sales agents.

An unprecedented change had taken place with the coming of the bicycle, which destroyed the myth of feminine fragility, and the daringly split skirt that was required to ride it. Most young men now thought women should take an active role in life, though still within limits. Artist Charles Dana Gibson, through drawings in books and magazines, created the Gibson Girl, one of the icons of the age. Usually shown with a tennis racket, golf club, or some other sporting equipment, she became the model for many young women. The writer Richard Harding Davis, in stories and novels that were often illustrated by his friend Gibson, wrote of athletic and intelligent heroines who helped their men and themselves out of dangerous spots. These works of fiction were often set in exotic climes, where brave young Americans defeated bandits, revolutionaries, or evil dictators while still remaining proper ladies and gentlemen.

Of course, novels and a few new job opportunities don't tell the full story. Poor women often had to work for their families to survive, and this fact added to the pressure on middle-class women not to take up paying jobs, since their making money would imply that their fathers or husbands were unable to earn enough to support them, and they would also be taking income from those who needed it most. Against great resistance from their elders, young women began attending secondary schools and even college, but once graduated found few outlets for their talents, still confronting the traditional view that "man does, woman is."

Nonetheless, a New Woman was increasingly recognized in society. Not content to be merely an accompaniment to male lives, she was struggling for true independence. The sociologist, writer, lecturer, poet, and suffragette Charlotte Perkins Gilman, author of the short story "The Yellow Wallpaper," about a woman driven mad by the constrained role that society and her husband imposed on her, was at the height of her powers in 1898, publishing the monumental, and witty, *Women and Economics: A Study of the Economic Relation Between Men and Women as a Factor in Social Evolution.* (She wrote in the book that the Gibson Girl, in contrast to the average woman, was "braver, stronger, more healthful and skillful and able and free, more human in all ways.")

Gilman believed women should have equal access to the satisfactions of education and career, and that a society denying them these rights was damaging itself. One way to free women to pursue their interests would be to relieve them of the burdens of homemaking. Cleaning, washing, and cooking should be taken care of communally, with central kitchens under the supervision of scientifically trained dietitians. She thought that a good beginning toward restructuring society was being made through the growing women's club movement, "the most important sociological phenomenon of the century . . . marking . . . the first timid steps toward social organization of these so long unsocialized members of our race. . . . Now the whole country is budding into women's clubs. The clubs are uniting and federating by towns, States, nations; there are even world organizations. The sense of human unity is growing daily among women." Also the sense of being able to express themselves intellectually. Nathalie Dana's Aunt Lydia researched and delivered papers to her club, although "mental activity was considered questionable for women, as thinking was supposed to be unladylike."

Newspapers seemed to consider it so. They frequently ran stories mocking the pretensions of women seeking "unity" or intellectuality. The *New York Times* told of "pretty" Mamie Frey, the only woman watchmaker in Chicago: "She is acknowledged to be an expert, but women . . . prefer to trust their timepieces to a mechanic of the other sex. That's why she is unhappy." Another story making the rounds reported a meeting of a woman's club in a Western city that was discussing the future of American international relations when a Chinese merchant showed up with colorful samples of his silk goods. All important debating points were said to be forgotten in the excited rush to peruse and purchase.

And yet, for all the charges of frivolity, women were expected to be the "civilizing" force in morals and in appreciation of the arts. Believed to be both more righteous and more sensitive than men, women were supposed to find their satisfactions in those areas. One great moral arena was the fight against alcohol, seen as the cause of family violence, poverty, disorder, and vice. Although the Woman's Christian Temperance Union was only intermittently effective in gaining legislation to outlaw drinking during the 1890s, Frances Willard used her great organizing gifts to increase membership to over 150,000 and she also extended its concerns to broader questions of women's rights, including suffrage. After her death in February 1898, the WCTU narrowed its focus, pulling back from these progressive interests, becoming truly formidable, in alliance with the Anti-Saloon League and the Prohibition Party, in the first two decades of the twentieth century, when they were able to have the Eighteenth Amendment passed, along with the Volstead Act enforcing it.

Mothers were honored as the guardians of their sons' virtue, and they took to the task with energetic seriousness. Douglas MacArthur's mother, for example, installed herself in a nearby apartment while he attended West Point so she could continue her maternal guidance, and Franklin Delano Roosevelt's fulfilled her duty for decades, even moving into the White House, where she would eavesdrop on his telephone calls, after her son was elected president. But Mama was also often a best friend and confidante, as with Theodore Roosevelt, Richard Harding Davis, and numerous other loyal sons. *Dear Mother* was the title of a well-received book, published after the turn of the century, that consisted of loving letters written by young men to their mothers.

Moral concern spilled over into the arts. It was unthinkable to patronize painters, sculptors, or writers who dared too realistic a presentation of what was seen as the "indelicate" or sordid side of mankind. This, in spite of a national longing for American achievements in the arts to match those in other fields, blocked or delayed the maturity of the writers and artists of the 1890s, a group that the literary historian Larzer Ziff calls a "lost generation." Stephen Crane's *Maggie: A Girl of the Streets* was just one of a number of works excoriated for its depiction of low life. Kate Chopin's bold novel *The Awakening,* written in 1898, explored the sexual flowering of a married woman with two children who initiates adulterous affairs before drowning herself in despair over the lack of self-fulfillment in her life. Although it sold well, Chopin's work was viewed as being in bad taste, too redolent of feminine discontent and sensuality, and therefore not welcome in respectable homes. Even established literary figures, such as Henry James and Mark Twain, felt driven to find more welcoming environments in Europe, James moving in 1898 to England and Twain taking up residence in Vienna.

Europe provided the great model for achievement, paradoxically because there artists were seriously addressing "unclean things." But most of those Americans interested in art ignored as best they could exponents of base realism such as Emile Zola, and preferred lighter works, painters and writers who pursued noble abstractions like "beauty" and "truth." An English writer of genius did enjoy a revival in 1898. There is, announced a writer in the *New York Times,* "a veritable Jane Austen renaissance." At least part of that renewed interest came through a general longing for a society as stable as the one she depicted so well, and admiration of the model Austen provided of how proper young women should behave.

European classical music was followed avidly by a small cultivated audience, one great debate centering on Wagner's worthiness to be included in the canon with the beloved, airy Italians. "Wagner's operas were new," one fan remembered, "they were a revelation to some people and repelled others." Mark Twain was fond of quoting the humorist Bill Nye's remark about Wagner. "I have been told that Wagner's music is better than it sounds." Arthur Whiting, with the Kneisel Quartet, introduced the music of Brahms to this country during the late 1890s, but acceptance was slow and reluctant. The German's compositions were thought too obscure and pompous.

One lively American talent did debut in New York in the spring of 1898. Isadora Duncan was a twenty-year-old Californian who had developed a new "interpretive" form of dance based on nature, what she understood of the ancient Greeks, and a belief in the sacredness of the human form. Barefoot, wearing flowing white robes, she performed graceful solos to music by Mendelssohn and Chopin that would revolutionize the dance world. But New York that year found her more sensational than serious. It was only after achieving success in London, Paris, and Berlin that her genius would be recognized in her native land.

Second-rate European painters such as Meissonier, Fortuny, or others of the French Salon were preferred to American talents like Winslow Homer, regarded as an illustrator, and Thomas Eakins, who was too gloomy and a rumored degenerate. Robert Henri, John Sloan, and their circle of realist painters, who were just moving to New York City, would have a brief period of popularity after the turn of the century before losing out to another, more modern, wave of Europeans.

One way to deal with this European dominance was to join it. Artists, musicians, and writers would often study or live for years in France, England, Germany, or Italy. Architects and painters usually went to Paris, sculptors to Rome, musicians and singers to Germany. Occasionally, to help bookings, a singer, conductor, or instrumentalist's name would be changed to something a bit more exotic, sporting an extra vowel or two. Europe also provided more important inspiration. In 1898 the National Institute of Arts and Letters was founded to "foster, assist and sustain an interest in literature, music and the fine arts." Its European model was the Académie Française, and its hope was to provide a voice for the serious working artist in America. Within two years, it boasted 250 members.

EDUCATION WAS THOUGHT to be unhealthy for young women, on the grounds that its cerebral challenges strained their abilities and even wore them out physically. Nathalie Dana's parents would not allow her to attend Bryn Mawr because a cousin had died after graduation, "although her death was caused by typhoid fever and occurred a whole year after she had left college." Weeping until Father was driven mad or gave in was a technique frequently used, but Dana decided instead to take up art, traveling to Germany to study music.

Those women who did attend college were often unable to find fitting employment for their hard-won skills, but one area that increasingly welcomed women was social work among immigrants and other poor suffering in the cities, especially the two million children under the age of sixteen who were toiling in factories, mills, and machine shops.

This call to moral action fit perfectly with the great spirit of idealism that swept through Protestant America in the latter part of the nineteenth century, resulting in extensive foreign missionary work as well as uplifting endeavors at home—including the founding in 1898 of the Gideon Bible Society by two traveling salesmen who wanted to help spread the Good Word. "The object of the Gideons," they announced, "will be to recognize the Christian traveling men of the world, to encourage one another in the Master's work . . . to improve every opportunity for the betterment of the lives of our fellow-travelers, business men and others, with whom we may come in contact; scattering the seeds all along the pathway for Christ." This idealism was also reflected in the popularity of utopian novels, such as Edward Bellamy's *Looking Backward,* which pictured a halcyon future of general leisure, abundant goods, and safe, beautiful cities—if only caring people would bring kindness and order to a chaotic present. Charlotte Perkins Gilman, like many another young American, noted in her diary a strong desire to accomplish during her life "the utmost attainable advance of the human race."

As the Darwinian revolution kept shaking the foundations of Protestantism, and the new industrial system led to bloody struggles between labor and capital, a religious movement called the Social Gospel arose that tried to reform society by following Christ's teachings. Books and pamphlets with titles such as *In His Steps: What Would Jesus Do?* sold millions of copies, inspiring young men and women to dedicate themselves to good works in the hope of establishing God's kingdom on earth.

Jane Addams and Ellen Gates Starr established the model social settlement center, Hull House in Chicago, "as an experimental effort to aid in the solution of the social and industrial problems which are engendered by the modern conditions of life in a great city." Jane Addams went on to explain that they had three motivations in what they were doing: "first, the desire to interpret democracy in social terms; secondly, the impulse beating at the very source of our lives, urging us to aid in the race progress; and, thirdly, the Christian movement toward humanitarianism." Here, too, was a chance for an adventurous life different from the ordinary. Robert Archey Woods titled a book about his personal experiences in the crusade *The City Wilderness.*

Hull House combined a nursery, kindergarten, playground, and housing for unmarried working women, while also sponsoring ethnic festivals and offering classes that would help assimilate immigrants. Its greatest success as a social center was with women and children, for men were reluctant to give up their saloons. From experience, Addams learned that little could be done unless local laws were changed, so she and her allies began a campaign against boss rule, fighting for laws that would eradicate child labor, reduce the hours women were made to work, require all children to attend school, improve job safety, and recognize labor unions. Women's suffrage was advocated because reformers were confident that women, the great moral force in American life, would provide the votes necessary to pass progressive legislation.

There were over eighty such settlement houses in 1898, and by 1910 there would be more than four hundred in cities and towns around the country, trying to bring reform to local government and improve the lives of slum dwellers.

Other young men and women looked abroad for their own ways to extend democracy, aid progress, and do good works.

CUBA HAD FIRST rebelled in 1868, at a time Spain itself was suffering political turmoil. That Ten Years' War for independence had been suppressed, but at great cost to both the mother country and the people of the island. In 1895 the embers flared anew, and this time caught in the Cuban countryside with more strength. There had been little economic recovery there even after the coming of peace; too many sugar mills had been destroyed, and there was not enough capital to rebuild and modernize production. Economic hard times were even more severe during the depression that started in 1893, and after the United States imposed a higher tariff on sugar the next year to protect domestic growers, tens of thousands of additional workers lost their livelihoods, barely subsisting on what they could grow on their own patches of land.

The resulting misery had again led to unrest, but this time there was an important new factor: Cubans who had fled to the United States during the earlier uprising, but had never given up their revolutionary purpose, were now eager to play an active role in supporting the revolution. The leader of these dedicated patriots was the lawyer José Julian Martí, who was based in New York but traveled tirelessly from city to city visiting Cuban exile communities, raising money for the cause, and organizing his Cuban Revolutionary Party.

Americans were sympathetic to the idea of independence for Cuba, and not just because of their traditional support for colonial peoples fighting for liberty against oppressive monarchies. There was a long history of interest in the island that lay less than a hundred miles south of Florida, including a strong desire by pre–Civil War Southerners to purchase Cuba as a new slave territory. Northern victory had ended that dream, but the United States had come close to conflict with Spain over Cuba during the Ten Years' War, when in 1873 the *Virginius,* a ship flying the American flag and carrying some American passengers as well as others of various nationalities, had been captured in international waters by a Spanish warship and taken to the city of Santiago de Cuba.

The local governor, who knew that the *Virginius* had been intending to land arms and recruits for the insurgents, called a summary court-martial, condemned all the crew and passengers to death as "pirates," and immediately ordered the executions—shooting, then decapitating them—and had their heads displayed on pikes. Because of the remoteness of Santiago, on the southeast coast, it was a while before word got out, or the Spanish government's orders to stop could reach the governor. Over fifty men were massacred, including the American captain, Joseph Fry.

War drums in the United States began beating immediately, and the secretary of state, Hamilton Fish, called the act "brutal, barbarous, and an outrage upon the age." Anti-Spanish demonstrations were held in New York and other cities, and war fever rose so high that the American fleet was ordered to assemble at Key West. But President Grant and Secretary Fish did not want war, nor were they in a good position to fight one, since there was no American fleet capable of carrying out offensive actions against even a second-rate power such as Spain. In the end, the Spanish government defused the crisis by apologizing for any disrespect to the Stars and Stripes and paying a large indemnity to the families of the victims.

Recognizing that conditions were ripe for another attempt at independence, José Martí returned clandestinely to Cuba in 1895. He had proven himself a brilliant organizer, speaker, writer, and fundraiser, and was the moral center of the independence movement. It was perhaps foolish for such an untrained, unsoldierly intellectual to take to the field, but he, like many other men in the nineteenth century, was driven by the demands of honor, believing that it would be hypocritical to live as "one who preached the need of dying without . . . risking his own life." He was killed in battle soon after his arrival, but, as he had planned, there were many others to carry on the struggle both in the haven of the United States and in the dangerous tropic lushness of Cuba.

The field commander of the insurgency was General Máximo Gómez y Báez, more seasoned than old at seventy-two, and as tough as saddle leather. While fighting in the Ten Years' War, he had realized that the major theater of a successful insurgency would have to be the rich western provinces of Havana, Pinar del Río, and Matanzas. He focused his attacks in the west, conducting a classic guerrilla campaign—ambushing Spanish units, running from set battles, harassing outposts, and burning sugar plantations and mills to reduce the economic value of Cuba to her colonial master. "The chains of Cuba have been forged by her own richness," he announced, "and it is precisely this which I propose to do away with soon." Guerrilla warfare made for a messy and savage struggle.

The Spanish were unable to effectively counter these tactics until the ruthless *reconcentrado* policy was developed by General Valeriano Weyler y Nicolau, nicknamed "The Butcher" by the American press. The rural population was ordered to move into fortified towns, and the countryside was stripped of crops, cattle, and anything else useful to the rebels. With the peasants in these camps, the rebels would be deprived of food, recruits, and intelligence. In order to further limit their mobility, Weyler reintroduced and expanded the *trocha* system used during the Ten Years' War. These were trenches that cut across the entire width of the island in two places; once completed, with their supporting forts, artillery, barbed wire, and land mines, they were impassable. The forces of the insurgents were thus divided, their support in the countryside diminished, their areas of operations reduced, and Weyler was confident they could now be dealt with.

AMERICAN REPORTERS HAVE always been quick on the scene of a good story, and were early on this one. The Cuban Junta, which served as a kind of government-in-exile for the rebels, maintained a press office on lower Broadway in New York that pushed its revolutionary point of view and furnished many stories emphasizing Spanish cruelty and intransigence, but the major newspapers and press syndicates began sending their own people to the island from the very beginning of the insurrection in 1895.

The national newspaper scene in the 1890s was fiercely competitive, and in New York City, with fifteen dailies and approximately thirty weeklies, it was particularly ferocious. New printing technology, which allowed large press runs, was expensive to buy, and the advertising needed to pay off these costs depended on large circulation, circulation that had to be won from competitors through political partisanship, lurid headlines, sensational stories, and "scoops."

Or at least that is how the two most powerful and competitive publishers of the day saw it. Joseph Pulitzer was a Hungarian Jewish immigrant, born in 1847, who from early youth wanted to be a soldier, an opportunity denied him in his native land because of anti-Semitism. The Civil War gave him his chance; he served in the Union cavalry, then settled in St.

Louis and took up journalism, learning the rudiments of the trade first on a German-language paper before gaining control of the *Post-Dispatch*. New York was the great arena, however, and there were also some unpleasant developments in St. Louis after a Democratic politician was shot dead in the office of the paper's managing editor, so in 1883 he bought the *New York World* from financier Jay Gould, who had been unable to make it profitable. Pulitzer quickly turned the publication around, promising and delivering a paper that was "not only cheap but bright, not only bright but large, not only large but truly Democratic—devoted more to the news of the New than the Old World—that will expose all fraud and sham, fight all public evils and abuses—that will serve and battle for the people with earnest sincerity." Part of that battle was conducted through thrilling headlines such as "ALL FOR A WOMAN'S LOVE," "A BRIDE BUT NOT A WIFE," "LITTLE LOTTA'S LOVERS," and, after almost four hundred children died during a heat wave, "HOW BABIES ARE BAKED."

By 1898, Pulitzer had built a fortune on his gift for mixing the sensational and the sentimental, a style he did not invent but developed and elaborated from earlier models. Success, however, came at a tremendous cost; he had destroyed his health through the physical and mental strain of overwork. Almost completely blind, he was also plagued by a hypersensitivity to noise, so that he was forced to spend much of his life in soundproof rooms. Then, at the start of the year, his teenage daughter's death intensified his pain. All this personal unhappiness led Pulitzer several times to give up the day-to-day management of the *World,* but he found it impossible to surrender the excitement and challenge of putting out the paper for long—especially since he was now faced with the greatest challenge of all.

William Randolph Hearst had been expelled from Harvard for presenting various professors with ornate chamber pots that sported their names across the porcelain receiving bowl, but working on the Harvard *Lampoon* had sparked an interest in journalism and he had spent the next year as a cub reporter for Pulitzer's *World.* He then went home to San Francisco and asked his father, a rough-and-ready miner who had struck it rich on the Comstock Load, to give him that city's *Examiner.* The elder Hearst had earlier acquired the paper as part of a successful political effort to have himself appointed a United States senator, but it was a money-loser. Willie convinced the old man that he could turn it into a money-maker, and, using Joseph Pulitzer's methods along with his own gift for picking talented writers, such as Ambrose Bierce, he quickly did.

Drawn to the great metropolis of New York like so many others of his generation, Hearst bought the *New York Journal* in 1895, using some of the $7,500,000 that his mother had given him when she sold the portion of the Anaconda Copper Mining Company she had inherited at his father's death. Soon he was battling Pulitzer on his own ground, not just by imitating the *World*'s style, but even to the point of hiring away the older man's most prized editors and reporters. One of the innovations Pulitzer had pioneered was a single-panel Sunday cartoon called "Hogan's Alley," which featured a street urchin nicknamed the "Yellow Kid" after the bright splash of color (possible because of the expensive new presses) that decorated his robe. The Kid and his tenement buddies were used to mock the pretensions of upper-crust New York life, and the cartoon was a very popular feature, so popular that when Hearst added insult to injury by hiring away the original artist, R. F. Outcault, Pulitzer responded by having the painter and illustrator George B. Luks continue the panel for the *World*. Thus there were two competing "Yellow Kids" and a new name for the Pulitzer-Hearst approach to the news—"yellow journalism." William Randolph Hearst liked to think of what he did as "journalism that acts," meaning that it was not enough to simply report the news; if necessary the publisher should direct his reporters and editors to take a hand in fighting for a good cause.

Although the other successful New York papers were not as sensational as the *World* or the *Journal,* the style had spread across the country so widely that a contemporary researcher estimated in 1898 that around one half of the newspapers in the twenty-six major cities he studied were "yellow" in approach. It was a consummate style to entertain and inform an audience of the imperfectly literate and barely educated.

Fires, murders, and scandals could take such a readership only so far, however, and it was with great enthusiasm that the yellow press took up the cause of the Cuban *insurrectos.* They printed without question the very questionable reports coming from what one disillusioned reporter called "the war news factories" located in Cuban exile communities in Florida and New York, and avoided reporting the burning and pillaging committed by rebel columns.

The stories their own correspondents provided were often not any more accurate than those provided by the Junta press offices. One reason was the constant need for sensational news to report, but some of the exaggeration came from the difficulty these men had in understanding the different kind of conflict that was actually being fought. The Civil War was the only example they knew of armed struggle: massed ranks of men, supported by cavalry, firing as they advanced upon the other side. They could not imagine a successful campaign that involved the hit-and-run tactics of a guerrilla force. Most journalists were sure that if there was fighting it had to be large scale, with cavalry charges, set-piece battles, heroic derring-do, waving flags, and gentlemanly demeanor under fire. If reality was unwilling to provide such inspiring moral lessons, then the human imagination was encouraged to step in and touch up the narrative a bit.

The themes of this touching up, and often making up, took various forms, but stories about women provided opportunities for particularly moving copy because of the great value placed on the civilizing role of feminine virtue in the United States. There were reports of innocent female victims—"WEYLER THROWS NUNS INTO PRISON. BUTCHER WAGES BRUTAL WARFARE ON HELPLESS WOMEN," was one *Journal* headline—but also favored were descriptions of women warriors who fought on the side of the rebels. A thrilling account in Hearst's *Journal* told of a cavalry troop of Amazons who raided Spanish lines, fought ferociously with machetes, then tended the enemy wounded with motherly solicitude.

But Hearst's greatest story of oppressed womanhood appeared during the last half of 1897, when he took up the cause of Evangelina Cisneros, who had been jailed on charges of trying to rescue her rebel father from a Spanish prison on the island. Stories of this innocent girl's sufferings in jail were kept constantly before the public, and a "Women's Noble Appeal for Miss Cisneros" was launched, encouraging women to appeal directly to the Queen Regent of Spain for mercy; a petition drive gathered thousands of signatures of Americans asking for the maiden's release, at the head of which appeared the name of President McKinley's mother. Then on October 8 came the most stirring news of all. Evangelina, with the help of a Hearst-organized team, had escaped. She and her rescuers made their way to the United States, where enormous rallies were held in her honor. At the one in Washington, D.C., she was introduced to President McKinley before a cheering crowd of tens of thousands. The "Journalism That Acts" had acted, and not for the last time.

To counter the hype, exaggeration, and outright lies of the yellow press, there were dailies that did their best to report accurately what was happening in Cuba. In New York alone Whitelaw Reid's *Tribune,* James Gordon Bennett's *Herald,* Edward Lawrence Godkin's *Evening Post,* and Adolph Ochs' *Times* were more or less traditional in their approach to the news. They probably were even more influential than the yellow press in creating the public's outrage and sense that something had to be done; people took seriously what these papers had to say, and the scale of the Spanish atrocities was undeniable.

Even at these respectable newspapers fundamental changes were taking place. The editor, often nationally known and a political power through his reputation for wisdom and genteel morals, had always been the bright star of the journalistic firmament. Now his independence was being undercut by both the business office, with its increased demands for profit to pay for the new technology, and by the once lowly reporter, who was demanding and getting a byline and, consequently, fame. As the contemporary journalist Irvin Cobb put it, "The time of the Great Editor had waned and faded, the time of the Great Reporter succeeded it."

This change had begun a decade earlier when a new type of individual began entering the field. Reporters had always been viewed as bohemian at best, and otherwise as ne'er-do-wells, fly-by-nights, and, especially, drunkards. But during the late 1880s and early 1890s young middle-class men with college experience, a desire for knowledge of the wider world, and some sophistication signed on.

Stephen Bonsal, for example, had studied in Germany before becoming a war correspondent at the age of twenty, covering in 1885 the war between Bulgaria and Serbia. By 1898 he had labored as a city reporter in the United States as well as having traveled the more remote and dangerous parts of the globe, working mainly for the *Herald* but also occasionally serving as a State Department official. Poultney Bigelow, son of a diplomat, had attended school in Germany with Kaiser Wilhelm, and had ranged the world covering news for American and British papers. Arthur Brisbane, son of a founder of the Fourierist Utopian commune of Brook Farm, had been educated in France, then made a splash in journalism by covering the Jack the Ripper murders in London. John Bass, Frederick Palmer, and many others fit this new pattern. They were drawn by desire for adventure, the excitement of big-city life or foreign lands, the possibility of renown through their byline, and increasingly good salaries. Another benefit was the social mobility the profession offered—the chance to rub elbows with street toughs at a Bowery Bar in early afternoon and attend a society gala in the evening, with stops in between to interview politicians, policemen, visiting dignitaries from Omaha or Paris, and confidence men.

The great emblem of youthful American journalism during the 1890s was Richard Harding Davis, who was born to the profession in 1864, since his father, Clark, became theater critic and managing editor of the

Philadelphia Inquirer and his mother, Rebecca, was not only a celebrated short-story writer but also a commentator for New York newspapers and national magazines. Davis attended Lehigh University, where he paid more attention to sports than scholarship, flunking out in 1883. His parents were not enthusiastic about his decision to become a reporter because of the general disrepute in which the trade was held (editors and commentators were of a higher order), but Davis persevered and was soon recognized as one of the most gifted writers of the younger generation. Football games, tenement fires, bunco steerers and confidence men, cops, heiresses, royalty, or foreign wars were delineated and explained in clear, concise language that used familiar images his readers could appreciate. But his fame did not rest on these achievements alone. For one thing, he was handsome in a square-jawed, manly way that both men and women found attractive; Charles Dana Gibson based the appearance of his "Gibson Man" on Davis, and the "Gibson Girl" owed some of her character to the heroines of the short stories and novels he also wrote, to great profit and acclaim.

Some of these stories caught the glory and excitement of the New Journalism and spread its glamor to the public: "Gallegher" told of a young newspaper copyboy who captures a murderer, and "The Reporter Who Made Himself King" described the frenetic adventures of Albert Gordon as he spent his first day on "one of the innumerable Greatest New York Dailies" covering New York; "He had left Yale when his last living relative died and had taken the morning train for New York. . . . He arrived at the office at noon, and was sent . . . to Spuyten Duyvil, where a train had been wrecked and everyone of consequence to suburban New York killed. One of the old reporters hurried him to the office again with his 'copy,' and after he had delivered that, he was sent to the tombs to talk French to a man in Murderers' Row . . . at eight, he covered a flower show in Madison Square Garden; and at eleven was sent over the Brooklyn Bridge in a cab to watch a fire and make guesses at the losses to the insurance companies."

Hearst had approached Davis in 1895, just after buying the *Journal,* and asked him to cover the Thanksgiving Day football match between Yale and Princeton. The publisher hoped to gain some acceptability by hiring such a well-known writer, but Davis wasn't interested. When Hearst told him to name his price, Davis facetiously replied, "Five hundred dollars," figuring that would be the end of the matter, but Hearst immediately agreed and made the most of the resulting publicity so that the edition of that day's *Journal* sold out.

Davis reluctantly took other freelance assignments from Hearst, although he did not respect the man or his type of journalism. Still, the Californian did pay well, and Davis was confident that he could wrest guarantees of good behavior from him. Irresistible was an offer of three thousand dollars, plus expenses, to spend a month with Gómez and his rebels in Cuba in late 1896. Unfortunately, little went as planned, and the escapade ended with Hearst misrepresenting a story Davis had written about the search of an upper-class Cuban woman on board an American ship in Havana harbor. Hearst had Frederic Remington illustrate the scene for the front page with leering Spanish officers surrounding a naked girl, under a headline: "DOES OUR FLAG PROTECT WOMEN? INDIGNITIES PRACTISED BY SPANISH OFFICIALS ON BOARD AMERICAN VESSELS." Public response was tremendous; cries for war in defense of both feminine and national honor rang out, and sales of the edition, to Hearst's delight, set a record of close to a million copies. Then Pulitzer's *World* investigated, and in a front-page story reported that the young woman had been searched by a matron, not Spanish officers.

Davis had been angry when he saw the misleading illustration, but he was furious and humiliated by the *World* story. It was true that he had not been absolutely clear about who had done the searching, but he felt his wording indicated that it had not been male Spaniards. Feeling that he had been taken advantage of, he swore never to work for Hearst again.

The suffering Davis witnessed in Cuba turned him from a moderate on the question of American intervention into an active proponent, just as it changed so many others who traveled there. He made a public demand, heard more and more often as tensions rose, that the United States become a visible presence in Havana, "where there should have been an American man-of-war these past six months."

CHAPTER 4

HUMANITY AND SELF-INTEREST

I would regard a war with Spain from two viewpoints: First, the advisability on the ground both of humanity and self-interest of interfering on behalf of the Cubans, and of taking one more step toward the complete freeing of America from European domination; second, the benefit done to our people by giving them something to think of which isn't material gain.

Theodore Roosevelt

A FRENCH OFFICER visiting an American warship in the 1880s was reported to have exclaimed nostalgically at her guns, *"Ah! Capitaine, les vieux canons!"* This cultivation of the antique occurred because for the first two decades after the Civil War the United States had been indifferent to the world as its attention was absorbed by the tremendous changes affecting agriculture, finance, industry, and the country's very social structure itself. But as exports of wheat, corn, coal, and steel became more important to the economy, and European empires continued to grow and threaten these interesting foreign markets, the need for the country to be able to project overseas power became evident, at least to some.

In 1889 the United States and Germany had nearly come to blows over competing territorial claims in the Samoan Islands, and when a naval officer, Lieutenant Carlin, was feted in San Francisco for the heroic handling of his ship during a cyclone in the same region, he used the occasion to point out his service's needs: "Gentlemen—it's very good of you to give me this dinner and to tell me all these pretty things, but what I want you to

87

understand—that fact is—what we want and what we ought to get at once is a navy—more ships—lots of 'em."

By 1891, the navy was receiving larger allocations and modern steel vessels were being built, but another crisis that year showed there was still far to go. During a period of political unrest and anti-American feeling in Chile, a mob attacked American sailors on shore leave in Valparaiso, killing two and seriously wounding seventeen others. At first President Harrison took a hard line, but had to reconsider when the American fleet turned out to be weaker than the Chilean, and panic spread when it was rumored that the Chileans might raid the West Coast. A compromise was struck—Chile paid an indemnity—and the crisis passed. But the humiliation lingered, and politicians in favor of expanding the navy used the affair to explain that the United States needed to spend more, and quickly modernize the fleet.

Added impetus was given to the argument by a series of confrontations between Britain and the United States, the most serious over the boundary between Venezuela and the British colony of Guiana in 1895–96. When gold was discovered in the disputed region, Britain tried to bully the Venezuelans into backing down from their claims. The United States stepped in to protect a fellow-American republic under the Monroe Doctrine, and also to protect its own interests. More and more Americans felt threatened by the growing empires of Europe, and saw in Britain's actions an attempt to expand its territories in South America because the other powers were blocking British expansion in Africa and China. Richard Olney, secretary of state, informed the British that "today the United States is practically sovereign on this continent, and its fiat is law upon the subjects to which it confines its interposition." Olney went on to explain that his country was not going to knuckle under to threats: "Why? . . . It is because, in addition to all other grounds, its infinite resources combined with its isolated position render it master of the situation and practically invulnerable as against any or all other powers." The Eagle was beginning to spread its wings and scream, though perhaps a bit prematurely.

When the British did not seem to take the American position seriously, President Cleveland began rattling his saber, telling Congress, and the world, that the United States alone would determine the proper boundary line of Venezuela–Guiana and ensure that Britain respected it. For a while war looked possible, and fleets were beginning to rendezvous before cooler heads prevailed. The business community in the United States did not want a war, especially with the economy as fragile as it was; at the same time the British had their attention forcefully drawn to the ambitions of

Imperial Germany when the kaiser sent a telegram to President Paul Kruger that seemed to offer aid to the Boer South African Republic in any struggle against English aggression. Queen Victoria's government realized that the growing strength of America would make for a valuable ally.

There was also a new factor. Over the previous fifteen years the United States had started celebrating its Anglo-Saxon heritage. Writers trying to explain the surge of the industrial revolution and imperialism argued that these developments, along with democracy, had come from deep racial roots in the Anglo-Saxon peoples—who were naturally adventurous, inventive, and cooperative, and who so hated disorder that they were going to bring the whole array of barbaric or degenerate cultures in the world to a new level of civilization by taking on the burden of ruling them. That a great deal of the chaos, backwardness, and intolerance manifest in American and English history had to be ignored in order to reach these conclusions did not present an insurmountable challenge. Now, in the interest of a common Anglo-Saxon progress, a new understanding was being struck with the country's old colonial master. But this understanding would hold only as long as Britain paid proper respect to the younger nation, abandoning its arrogant attitude of superiority.

MUCH IN INTERNATIONAL relations seemed new and unsettled during the 1890s because of the aggressive competition for colonial possessions. Helping to understand the forces at work was a tall, lean, bald-headed naval officer with a nose like a hawk's beak. Alfred Thayer Mahan was more an intellectual than an effective commander of ships and men, and that was a saving grace in a career that had given him more frustration than satisfaction. In *The Influence of Sea Power Upon History,* published in 1890, he presented a theory, based on his study of European wars from 1660 to 1783, that had all the strength and charm of its simplicity: a nation's military and commercial power directly related to control of the sea lanes. In the thick volume he explored the intricate relationships of trade, geography, war, and technology to effective power. It was one of those books, perfectly matched to the needs of its time, that changes the world.

In Britain, greatest sea power of the nineteenth century, people thought the book brilliantly explained the strategic reasons why they were now the strongest economy of the nineteenth century: Her Majesty's Government gave Mahan a medal, while Oxford and Cambridge awarded him honorary degrees. The Germans, coming late to the imperial race, were eager to make up for lost time and had begun to challenge other European powers for colonies, while also eyeing the United States as a potential rival. They took the book's lessons seriously. Kaiser Wilhelm told an American friend, "It is on board all my ships and constantly quoted by my captains and officers," and admitted that he too was trying to "learn it by heart."

Mahan sparked a lively domestic debate during the 1890s about the direction the United States should take. Should the Republic continue to heed George Washington's warning to avoid foreign entanglements, or did it need to expand to meet the challenges of the age? Mahan argued that as an industrializing economy of great efficiency, the nation would soon produce more than could be absorbed by the home market. Other modern nations were facing the same dilemma, and the competition for foreign markets would be won by those with the greatest sea power, that is, those with large modern fleets of armored, big-gunned battleships and cruisers that could rely on overseas coaling stations to project their might around the world. In 1897, Mahan studied the place of the country in this new and dangerous environment in *The Interest of America in Sea Power, Present and Future.* "Whether they will or no," the naval officer contended, "Americans must now begin to look outward."

One of the most fervent supporters of Mahan's point of view was Theodore Roosevelt, who reviewed *The Influence of Sea Power* enthusiastically for the *Atlantic Monthly.* Roosevelt had written a definitive history, *The Naval War of 1812,* at the age of twenty-two, and this book, it turned out, had influenced Mahan's theorizing. The men became close friends and allies in the struggle to fund a new, powerful navy. So fervent had been Roosevelt's proselytizing that it had almost cost him the appointment as assistant secretary of the navy. "I hope he has no preconceived plans which he would wish to drive through the moment he got in," McKinley told Senator Henry Cabot Lodge when the senator came to argue his friend's qualifications for the post. To another Roosevelt supporter the president expressed reservations about his aggressive personality: "I want peace, and I am told that your friend Theodore—whom I know only slightly—is always getting into rows with everybody. I am afraid he is too pugnacious."

McKinley had overcome his doubts, as well as the resistance of party bosses who feared that the young man was also too aggressive a reformer. John D. Long, who was appointed secretary of the navy, had his own reservations about the firebrand: "If he becomes Assistant Secretary of the Navy he will dominate the Department within six months!" But after meeting him, he had to agree, "Best man for the job."

Long was a poetry-writing lawyer who had served three times as governor of Massachusetts before being elected to Congress. A gentle, generous, and charming man, he had retired from his law practice after an attack of "nervous prostration," or a breakdown, but felt well enough to handle the cabinet post when asked for help by his good friend McKinley. He knew nothing of naval matters, nor did he intend to learn; it was traditional in America then to think that anyone of accomplishment in this great democracy could handle just about any government post without specialized skills. Besides, there were plenty of naval officers on his staff to help with the details. "What is the need," he confided to his journal, "of my making a dropsical tub of any lobe of my brain when I have right at hand a man possessed with more knowledge than I could acquire?"

Roosevelt and Long got on well together, the younger man making an effort to be loyal, subordinate, and agreeable while eagerly taking on the duties of his superior when Long, who hated the heat of Washington, felt the need to retire to the New England freshness of his farm at Hingham Bay, Massachusetts. As "hot-weather secretary," Roosevelt was able to put some of his own ideas and projects into operation during the summer months of 1897, in spite of meeting resistance on a number of points.

The American navy had four battleships of the first class in 1898, and two of the second, and although there were five first-class battleships under construction, they were far from completion. Congress had set the price for their armor plate so low that no provider could be found, and work on three of the behemoths had stopped as a result. Still, the illusion persisted that since the ships had been authorized, the navy was continuing to grow in strength. The assistant secretary was disgusted with this fantasy and proposed that six more battleships be built, plus six more heavy cruisers and seventy-five of the new torpedo boats, whose speed and maneuverability, he thought, might make them the deadliest force of the future. Of one point he was certain—there was no luxurious plenitude of time to prepare for trouble. It took years of hard labor to build one of the new armored ships, and a war could be fought and lost before even those already in the yards were finished; there was also a severe shortage of ammunition and weapons, ranging from rifles to twelve-inch cannons.

Roosevelt, of course, was not alone in believing that the country needed a strong navy to meet the challenges offered by Germany, England, Japan, Spain, and other countries, and that to be really effective such a navy required coaling stations abroad, which meant that the United States needed to expand beyond its current borders. The exclusive Washington

Metropolitan Club provided a convenient place for people of like mind to meet and discuss Mahan's ideas, and the political strategy necessary to implement them.

A particular friend was Leonard Wood, whom Roosevelt had met only after becoming assistant secretary of the navy, but with whom he formed an immediate close bond based on their shared ideas and a common love of physical challenges. Wood was like a hero out of a Richard Harding Davis short story in the way he combined, according to Roosevelt, "the qualities of entire manliness with entire uprightness and cleanliness of character." An army surgeon, he had taken part in the arduous campaigns that General Nelson Miles had conducted against the Apaches, where he had gained a reputation as one of the few white men who had the endurance and hardihood to match the Indians being pursued, and his qualities of leadership had resulted in his being put in command of fighting men, although he was only a surgeon. Courage under hostile fire had won him the Medal of Honor, which Roosevelt regarded as "the most coveted of distinctions."

The two friends spent as much time as possible in the outdoors, in the warm weather taking long walks through the rough, undeveloped country-side surrounding the capital, on colder days kicking a football in a vacant lot, and during the rare periods of snow using skis or snow skates that had been sent to Roosevelt from Canada. The subject of their discussions was always the same topic—the possibility of war with Spain. "We both felt very strongly that such a war would be as righteous as it would be advanta-geous to the honor and the interests of the nation." They were both deter-mined that if war came they were not going to stay in the safe environs of Washington, but head for the action.

FOR ALL OF President McKinley's optimistic feelings that the new govern-ment in Spain would be able to meet American demands, there were numerous factors standing in the way. The mother country had itself suf-fered from revolution and political instability during the previous decades; the monarchy had been restored only in 1876, and the first new king, Alfonso XII, had died in 1885. Maria Cristina, of the Austrian royal house, was serving in 1898 as regent for her twelve-year-old son, Alfonso XIII, but there was a rival claimant living in exile, Don Carlos, who enjoyed strong domestic backing and was waiting patiently for any false step. General Weyler, who had returned to Spain after being relieved of his duties in

Cuba, was being cultivated by all the discontented factions, but for the moment held back from committing himself to a coup d'état, although he did let it be known that had he been given but a bit more time he would have crushed the insurrection. Prime Minister Práxedes Sagasta and Maria Cristina knew they could go only so far before igniting popular unrest that would be used by their enemies. The Spanish people would not stand for any outright grant of independence, to either Cuba or the other colonial jewel with an active insurgent movement, the Philippines.

Even the granting of autonomy enraged Spanish conservatives. *Peninsulares,* or native-born Spaniards, were to be excluded from the island's autonomous government, which they regarded as radical and likely to legislate against Spanish economic interests. There was also the humiliation of Spain being dictated to by the immature, upstart republic to the north of Cuba, a nation held to be without honor, morals, or proper religion, a nation consisting of meddling Yankees responsible for the recall of their hero Valeriano Weyler, and, many Loyalists were sure, for the undeserved successes of the rebels. The "Ultra-Loyalists," as they called themselves, were convinced that their interests, their profits, their favored status, even the honor of the army, were on a bargaining table from which they were excluded. Conspiracies began to breed.

The Cuban insurgents, for their part, refused the autonomy that the Spanish government offered them with the New Year, regarding it as too little too late. "Independence or death" was their position, which extended even to the fighting units in the island's jungles. General Máximo Gómez y Báez announced that anyone advocating the autonomy proposal would be shot. At this stage of the struggle, with the United States day by day becoming more involved in their cause, insurgent leaders realized they had nothing to gain by compromising with the Spanish. *Cuba libre* was the only cheer allowed.

An American who understood the difficulties of the situation was Fitzhugh Lee, U.S. consul-general in Havana. One of the famous Virginia Lees, he was nephew to Robert E. and had served as a general of Confederate cavalry during the Civil War; though now a bit too stout to ride a horse into battle, he had kept the flowing mustache and *élan* of a cavalryman. After serving as Democratic governor of Virginia and a United States congressman, he had been appointed consul by President Cleveland, although the president had begun to distrust Lee's judgment by the end of his term. William McKinley had evidently kept him in office for political reasons; it helped to have a Democrat in such a critical place.

In December 1897, rumors had reached Lee of a plot by *peninsulares* and other Ultra-Loyalists against Americans on the island, and he urged, not for the first time, that a warship be stationed in Havana harbor, ready to protect American citizens. On this occasion, the administration took his request seriously, partly from increasing concern about the dangers of the situation, but also because German warships had recently been too active in the Caribbean. In 1897 they had held naval maneuvers in the region, practicing exercises based on a possible war with the United States. Now they were dictating humiliating terms to Haiti in a confrontation over what the Germans claimed was an insult to their national honor, and also hanging about the Danish West Indies and Cuba as if there were truth to the reports about their government buying those colonial possessions from their European masters. If these islands, or any other New World possessions, were going to change hands, the United States wanted to make it absolutely clear that they were not passing to another European power. "I doubt if those Spaniards can really pacify Cuba," Theodore Roosevelt wrote to Lieutenant-Commander W. W. Kimball, a naval strategist, "and if the insurrection goes on much longer I don't see how we can help interfering. Germany is the power with whom I look forward to serious difficulty." And he warned Secretary Long, "Germany shows a tendency to stretch out for colonial possessions which may at any moment cause a conflict with us." Roosevelt had the *Maine* waiting in Key West, ready to respond to a coded two-part request for assistance from General Lee.

WEDNESDAY MORNING, January 12, was when the rioting started. Governor-General Blanco, suspecting that trouble was being planned, had stationed additional soldiers and police at the Havana bullring—bullrings being where popular uprisings often began in the mother country—and perhaps because of those precautions the instigators instead used the streets of the capital, with crowds shouting, "Long live Weyler! Long live Spain! Down with autonomy! Death to Blanco!" Newspapers that had supported the government's autonomy program and criticized General Weyler had their offices wrecked, their printing presses disabled, and their staffs beaten. The leaders of the riot were Spanish military officers, and an American newspaperman noted a "fraternal spirit" between them and the police. "It was a political demonstration of the Army against autonomy and it served its purpose. Three or four score of the officers who participated . . .

were placed under military arrest, but they were never punished . . . and they were returned to their commands."

Fitzhugh Lee telegraphed the preliminary part of his code to Key West when the rioting flared again toward evening, then went back into the streets to try to gauge the situation. There was more trouble in the night and the next day; armed guards were stationed to protect the governmental palace and the American consulate. Lee kept Washington informed of developments in a series of cables: "Uncertainty exists whether Blanco can control situation. If demonstrated he cannot maintain order, preserve life, and keep the peace, or if Americans and their interests are in danger, ships must be sent, and to that end should be prepared to move promptly. Excitement and uncertainty predominate everywhere." But Lee, at least, kept calm; there was no second telegram to Captain Sigsbee requesting the *Maine*.

CERTAINLY LESS THAN CALM was Theodore Roosevelt. American newspapers saw the riots as proof that the new Spanish policy had failed and that Americans in Cuba were endangered; the assistant secretary agreed with them, and immediately visited his chief to discuss what should be done, not just in terms of ships and men, but apropos his own plans for resigning if war came, and fighting in the front lines.

Long was both amused and irritated, telling the thirty-nine-year-old Roosevelt that he took things too earnestly, and teasing him about wanting to get in a "bushwhacking fight" with Cuban mosquitos. "The funny part of it all is," the secretary confided to his diary that evening, "that he actually takes the thing seriously . . . he bores me with plans of naval and military movement, and the necessity of having some scheme to attack arranged for instant execution in case of an emergency. By tomorrow he will have got half a dozen heads of bureaus together and have spoiled twenty pages of good writing paper, and lain awake half the night . . ."

Roosevelt must have worked through the night rather than lain awake, for the next morning he had his "twenty pages" ready in an effort to convince Long to overcome his boredom. "I feel, sir, that I ought to bring to your attention the very serious consequences . . . if we should drift into a war with Spain and suddenly find ourselves obliged to begin it without preparation. . . . Certain things should be done at once if there is any reasonable chance of trouble with Spain during the next six months." These

The U.S.S. *Maine* enters Havana harbor on the morning of January 25, 1898. (*Courtesy of the U.S. Naval Historical Center*)

"things" included concentrating the scattered warships of the navy at strategic points so they would be ready to impose a blockade on Cuba and the Philippines, reinforcing Dewey's Asiatic Squadron, and assembling "a flying squadron composed of powerful ships of speed and great coal capacity" that could attack the coastal cities of Spain. Roosevelt ended with a recommendation that all haste be used in acquiring more coal, men, and ammunition.

The report had some of the desired effect, and Long did order small redeployments of the fleet, though nothing to the extent that his worried assistant had recommended.

JUST AFTER THE RIOTS in Havana, some newspapers reported that the *Maine* was on its way there to protect American lives and property, but it was not until January 24 that the battleship was ordered to Cuba, and those orders were given only after a great deal of debate, changes of mind, and diplomatic maneuvering. The administration talked to the Spanish ambassador, Enrique Dupuy de Lôme, about sending an American ship to Havana on a "friendly visit," but Dupuy had warned against doing so, saying that his government would see such an act as unwarranted interference and perhaps the first step toward intervention.

McKinley, however, felt that something had to be done, given the unstable conditions in the island's capital. Also, there were four German warships in the Caribbean in January 1898, and American officials besides Theodore Roosevelt had begun wondering just what the kaiser had in mind. Two German naval vessels were soon due in Havana harbor, and this possibly played a role in the decision to send the *Maine*. Fitzhugh Lee advised strongly against the deployment, and was sure that the last word in the matter would be his. The battleship's arrival surprised everyone.

Spanish officials were angry at the unexpected visit, but observed all the correct formalities. Dignified and polite visits were exchanged between naval officers, the proper salutes made, and Lee was able to cable to Washington, "Ship quietly arrived, 11 A.M. to-day; no demonstrations so far." Nor were there to be any in the days to come. Lee and Sigsbee both thought the intimidating presence of the *Maine* was responsible for the calm in Havana, not realizing that as a precaution the Spanish government had placed under house arrest the most active supporters of Weyler and the Ultra-Loyalists.

PRESIDENT McKINLEY felt great satisfaction with the way things had transpired. At a formal diplomatic dinner in the White House on January 26, the evening after the *Maine*'s arrival, he made a special effort to put the Spanish ambassador at ease.

Señor Dupuy was known for his personal dignity and reserve, and the energy with which he had served the interests of his country, but he had suffered great aggravation during his three years in Washington. Personally a member of the conservative faction and a follower of the assassinated prime minister Cánovas, he was not pleased with the way Sagasta's liberal government had bowed to American demands to recall General Weyler and install an "autonomous" Cuban regime. He was particularly unhappy with the decision to send, over his protests, a warship to Havana, a resentment that the president tried to soften.

Grand White House banquets of the time were served in the only large space available, the corridor. After the table was cleared, the gentlemen would retire to the state dining room for coffee, cigars, and conversation. On this occasion McKinley made a point of inviting Dupuy, who was dressed in "a uniform glittering with gold braid and decorations," to sit with him at a small table, along with the ambassadors of Germany, Britain, and France. Before these important dignitaries the president said to Dupuy, "I see that we have only good news," then went on to praise Dupuy's understanding of the American political situation, and assured him that "you have no occasion to be other than satisfied and confident."

Pleased as the ambassador was to be so complimented, it did not warm his heart to McKinley or change his negative opinion of the man or his policies. Being a diplomat, he smiled, bowed, and kept his personal feelings to himself, to be shared only with his closest confidants.

Don José Canalejas, a good friend of Enrique Dupuy de Lôme, was a politician as well as editor of *El Heraldo,* one of Spain's most influential newspapers. He had journeyed to the United States and Cuba late in 1897 in an attempt to understand the difficulties his country was facing, and had been in Havana when the *Maine* arrived. Since the situation had remained calm, Canalejas decided a week later that it was time to return to Spain. While his private secretary was packing his papers, Gustavo Escoto, a Cuban friend of the secretary's, stopped by. Escoto, a secret agent of the Junta, offered to help the secretary gather up all the material, keeping his eye open for anything interesting. When Escoto spotted a letter from Dupuy de Lôme to Canalejas, he waited until the secretary wasn't looking and slipped it into his own pocket.

The efficiency of the Cuban network in the United States was then demonstrated. The document was quickly spirited to Washington, while copies were sent around the nation. On February 9, Horatio Rubens, the Junta's legal counsel, and John J. McCook, a well-known Republican lawyer who was a firm believer in their cause, met with Assistant Secretary of State William Day to give him the handwritten letter, which contained passages revealing the lack of sincerity in Spanish promises to honor Cuban autonomy, together with rude personal remarks about William McKinley.

That same morning the *New York Journal* ran a huge headline across its front page: "THE WORST INSULT TO THE UNITED STATES IN ITS HISTORY." Then in slightly smaller-size print: "Spain's Minister Calls President McKinley a 'Low Politician Catering to the Rabble.'" Underneath was reproduced a facsimile of the letter Dupuy de Lôme had written to José Canalejas, along with a translation that read in part: "Besides the natural and inevitable coarseness with which he repeats all that the press and public opinion of Spain have said of Weyler, it shows once more that McKinley is weak and catering to the rabble and, beside, a low politician who desires to leave a door open to himself and to stand well with the jingoes of his party." The ambassador then went on to imply that Cuban "autonomy" was a charade to fool the American people into removing their pressure on Spain.

The resulting uproar shook both nations. Enrique Dupuy de Lôme admitted writing the letter and resigned before the United States could request his recall; Spain apologized for the diplomat's indiscretions, but did so slowly and grudgingly, as if recognizing that, no matter what it did, this event had reignited popular outrage over conditions in Cuba. Three resolutions proposing recognition of Cuba as an independent republic were present in the Senate the week after the letter was published, and there were signs across the country that McKinley and those closest to him who resisted war were beginning to lose control even of the Republican Party on the issue. As a friend of Secretary Long wrote from Boston a few days after the letter was published: "The jingo members of Congress and vile unscrupulous, jingo, yellow journals have so wrought up and stirred popular feeling that we seem to be slanting on the verge of a war with Spain with all its terrible consequences."

THE WEEKS IN HAVANA had gone fairly well for Captain Sigsbee and the *Maine*. The exchanges of visits with Spanish officials, though not warm, were punctiliously correct; Acting Governor-General Parrada, after personally admiring the battleship, sent as a present a case of fine sherry, and Captain Sigsbee reciprocated with a copy of his book *Deep Sea Sounding and Dredging*. As a particular mark of courtesy, the captain and Fitzhugh Lee had been allowed to attend the bullfights, although that exotic experience had been marred by a handbill passed around the crowd by dissident Spanish officers calling on their compatriots to resist the insulting presence of the "Yankee Pigs," and ending:

**Death to the Americans! Death to autonomy!
Long live Spain! Long live Weyler!**

By early February, however, much of the hostility had passed, and the threat to American citizens had diminished so much that Washington considered withdrawing the *Maine*. New Orleans had invited the ship for

Mardi Gras on the seventeenth, and the Navy Department, worried that the longer the ship was at Havana the greater the chance of an outbreak of yellow fever, was ready to send her to the festival.

Fitzhugh Lee and Charles Sigsbee, however, wanted the battleship to stay or, if withdrawn, to be replaced by another, large and powerful enough to dominate the harbor and remind the Spanish that the United States was no longer a naval weakling; as Lee put it, the ship should serve "as object lesson and to counteract Spanish opinion of our Navy." Yellow fever would not be a problem until the rainy season began in April, he reminded his superiors, arguing, "We are masters of the situation now and I would not disturb or alter it." As the two responsible men on the scene, their arguments were persuasive; the *Maine* would stay.

But neither Lee nor Sigsbee was completely at ease, and the *Maine* was kept at an extraordinary level of alert. All visitors had to have an escort; a quarter watch was kept during the night; sentries were fully armed; ammunition was kept by the six-inch and rapid-fire guns; a head of steam was maintained so that the turrets could swing to counter any assault; the men were drilled every day. They even continued "gun-pointing" practice, using a boat steaming to various parts of the harbor as a target, although great care was taken to ensure that the guns never pointed toward the Spanish men-of-war.

The captain did entertain the few Spanish and Cuban officials he could lure aboard, and also various Americans who were in Havana. Clara Barton and her staff enjoyed their visit. "Captain Sigsbee's launch courteously came for us, his officers received us; his crew, strong, ruddy and bright, went through their drill for our entertainment, and the lunch at those polished tables, the glittering china and cut glass, with the social guests around, will remain ever in my memory."

ALTHOUGH THE *MAINE* was kept from attending the New Orleans Mardi Gras, Havana celebrated a similar pre-Lenten festival. On the second night of Carnival, February 15, revelers wearing colorful masks and costumes danced through the port city's streets and cafés, filling the tropic air with music and laughter, everyone trying to enjoy as much self-indulgence as possible before the necessity of self-denial.

Clara Barton, never one for such frivolous pursuits, was in her room overlooking the harbor, laboring with an assistant on paperwork. She paused once by the window and looked out at the pale shape of the *Maine* as it swung at its mooring, remembering her visit to the battleship a few days before and how healthy and energetic the officers and men had been.

Other Americans mingled freely in the heat and happy chaos of Carnival. George Bronson Rea was having dinner with Harry and Frances Scovel in a café by the Parque Central. Rea and Scovel were journalists known for the risks they took in covering the insurgency, traveling through all parts of the island, on both sides of the line. But the two men held differing views on the struggle. Rea, correspondent for the *New York Herald,* was one of the rare reporters who defended the Spanish against charges of having committed deliberate atrocities, although even he had to admit the tragedies of the *reconcentrado* policy. His book *Facts and Fakes About Cuba* had attempted to counter some of the more colorful distortions put out by the Junta and repeated in the yellow press.

Scovel, on the other hand, had spent six months in the jungles with Máximo Gómez, writing so favorably of the general's cause in Pulitzer's *World* that he had been expelled from the island. Slipping back, he was caught again by Spanish troops as he was trying to cable his story, and thrown into jail. The *World* had immediately launched a successful publicity campaign to free its correspondent, enlisting civic groups and politicians along with other correspondents and publishers.

As the trio now sat at their table, surrounded by the happy rhythms of Carnival, they noticed that their crystal wine glasses were vibrating.

Another journalist abroad in the festive night was Walter Scott Meriwether, a veteran of ten years as an officer in the navy, who now used his expertise to cover naval matters for the *New York Herald.* This evening, as he did every evening at nine o'clock if there was no news, he had gone to the cable office at the governmental palace and sent a one-word message: "Tranquilo." Afterwards, as he stopped on the palace's steps to light a cigar, he caught sight of the white hull of the *Maine* glowing in the harbor between the Spanish warship *Alfonso XII* and the recently arrived commercial steamer *City of Washington.* He felt, as he stood there drawing on his Havana, a quick surge of pride in the beauty and power of the battlewagon.

On board the *City of Washington,* two other Americans, Sigmond Rothschild and Louis Wertheimer, also appreciated their view of the long white form of the ship. They had watched earlier as a group of sailors had danced on her starboard gangway to the music of an accordion, then they had retired to the smoking room. At 9:30 Rothschild suggested that they go to the stern to take another look at the *Maine.* Both were involved in the tobacco trade, and probably sympathized with the effort to stop the fighting in Cuba; "We're well protected here," Rothschild said to Wertheimer, "under the guns of the United States."

By 9:30 most of the officers and sailors on board were already in their hammocks or preparing to turn in. Only the men on watch and the armed sentries pacing the deck would have been able to hear the faint sounds of Carnival wafting over the water, sounds that had been answered a half hour earlier by the bugle notes of Marine Corporal Newton sounding taps.

Captain Sigsbee was in his cabin struggling with a letter to his wife. "I laid down my pen to listen to the notes of the bugle, which were singularly beautiful in the oppressive stillness of the night. Newton, who was rather given to fanciful effects, was evidently doing his best. During his pauses the echoes floated back to the ship with singular distinctness, repeating the strains of the bugle fully and exactly." As the melancholy notes died away, Sigsbee reluctantly returned to his letter. He had just discovered in a long-unused jacket a message to his wife that one of her best friends had entrusted to him, and he was having a hard time finding the words to explain how he could have forgotten to mail it to her.

High thin clouds had dimmed the sky by 9:40 that night, so that only the brightest stars shone through. Lieutenant John Hood, officer of the watch, sat on the port side of the *Maine* with his feet up on the rail, watching, probably with some longing, the lights of the city. Near him sat Lieutenant Blandin. Neither officer seems to have been particularly alert, although a small boat had been spotted nearby earlier in the evening.

As John Hood watched the lights of Havana, he felt a tremendous shuddering begin under the forward part of the ship. "I instantly turned my head . . . there was a second explosion. I saw the whole starboard side of the deck and everything above it as far as the aft end of the superstructure spring up into the air with all kinds of objects in it—a regular craterlike performance with flames and everything else coming up." He leaped for cover, then ran aft.

Blandin heard a "dull sullen" roar, then a sharp explosion. "A perfect train of missiles of all description, from huge pieces of cement to blocks of wood, steel railings, and fragments of gratings" fell on the deck; a chunk of cement struck him on the head and sent him sprawling. He jumped up immediately and started after Hood, who had just had his hat knocked off by a piece of flying debris. Blandin called to him, afraid that the other officer was dazed by shock and about to jump overboard in panic, but "he answered that he was running to the poop to help lower the boats."

Rothschild, still standing at the stern railing of the *City of Washington,* "heard a shot like a cannon shot. It made me look toward the *Maine*. I saw the bow rise a little. After a few seconds there came a terrible mass of fire and explosion, a black mass. Then we heard a noise of falling material. It didn't take a minute until the bow went down. There was a cry 'Help! Lord God save us! Help! Help!' The cry did not last a minute or two." A huge column of flame and gray smoke shot upward to a height of 150 feet, then spread out into a rolling canopy "which overhung the *Maine,* and from which descended a rain of fragments of ship and of bodies, some pieces falling half a mile" from the mooring.

Clara Barton and her assistant were working when the table began shaking under their hands and "the great glass door opening on to the veranda, facing the sea, blew open; everything in the room was in motion or out of place." They, like Lieutenant Hood, Rothschild, and other witnesses, described a volcanic explosion. "The deafening roar was such a burst of thunder as perhaps one never heard before. And off to the right, out over the bay, the air was filled with a blaze of light, and this in turn filled with black specks like huge specters flying in all directions. Then it faded away, the bells rang, the whistles blew, and voices in the street were heard for a moment; then all was quiet again."

Walter Scott Meriwether was just stepping through the door of a café when the blast hit. "The city shook to a terrific explosion. Amid a shower of falling plaster every light in the place went out, as did every other electric light in the city." People kept calling, "What is it" What is it?" A man in the darkness yelled that the arsenal across the bay had blown up, but as a squadron of cavalry went by at a gallop, a tall Englishman told Meriwether that it must have been the *Maine.*

Seconds after George Rea and the Scovels had noticed their wine glasses vibrating, the café was hit by the shock wave; windows blew in, people dove under tables, the costumed revelers in the Parque Central ran. The correspondents rushed to the broken windows of the café and watched the harbor blaze "with an intense light, and above it could be seen innumerable colored lights resembling rockets." They made sure that Frances Scovel was all right before hailing a carriage to take them to the waterfront. People seemed divided as to what action to take. Some, fearing that the noise signaled the beginning of another riot, sought the haven of their own doorways, others ran to the customs dock to discover what had happened.

Rea and Scovel shoved their way through the excited crowd and told the guard at the gate that they were officers off the *Maine,* a ploy that many other journalists would use in the days ahead to gain access to forbidden places, a ploy that would lead to rumors that most of the ship's officers had been ashore at the time of the explosion.

On the dock they found Colonel José Paglieri, chief of the Havana police, already in a boat. Paglieri was an old nemesis of Harry Scovel, having arrested him more than once, but he willingly allowed the Americans to join him. The oarsmen were frightened, and as they rowed near the fiery hulk, with ammunition exploding about their heads, they began to lose their interest in getting any closer. "The colonel beat one of them with his cane," Rea reported. "I whacked the other with a rope's end, until they concluded to proceed."

The nearer they came, the more complete appeared the destruction. "The scene as it unfolded itself to our vision was terrible in its significance," Rea continued. "Great masses of twisted and bent iron plates and beams were thrown up in confusion amidships; the bow had disappeared; the foremast and smoke stacks had fallen; and to add to the horror and danger, the mass of wreckage amidships was on fire, and at frequent intervals a loud report, followed by the whistling sound of fragments flying through the air, marked the explosion of a six-pound shell."

The scene was lit only by the "red glare of flames" dancing on the black water until the beam of a searchlight swept across their part of the harbor, revealing that they were surrounded by dismembered bodies. "Great God!" Scovel gasped, "They are all gone! This is the work of a torpedo, and marks the beginning of the end."

CAPTAIN SIGSBEE had struggled for half an hour before he finally had his apology finished. At 9:40 he was just slipping it into an envelope when his world blew apart.

Darkness, smoke, and a moment of panic after the tremendous rending crash of the explosion made the captain experience "the instinct of self-preservation," but "this was immediately dominated by the habit of command." The ship was sinking to port, and he went up the now-slanting deck to the shattered portholes of the starboard side, thinking to escape through one of them, but on second thought that sort of scrambling exit seemed unworthy of his dignity. He made his way back down and through to the passageway, where he had a violent collision in the darkness with another man. It turned out to be Marine Private William Anthony, his cabin orderly, who reported that the ship had been blown up and was sinking. Together the men made their way through blackness to the deck, where Sigsbee found his officers.

Thinking the *Maine* had been attacked, and that he heard cheers from the shore, possibly a sign that boarding parties were organizing to capture what remained, he ordered that sentries be posted, ready to repel the enemy. Then, unable to comprehend the scope of the disaster, he stood on the starboard siderail of the poop deck and tried to make sense of what he saw, while Father John Chidwick, the ship's chaplain, stood nearby calling to the men to say the name of Jesus, and shouting the ritual words of absolution over and over again.

The most terrible damage had taken place in the foremost part of the ship, where the two explosions had originated. That was where the enlisted men's quarters were located, and few of them survived. Most were killed outright as they slept in their hammocks, but some were alive long enough to be tangled in the wreckage and drowned while calling for rescue. Others managed to work free, but were so badly burned or injured that they did not live long.

Boats from the Spanish cruiser *Alfonso XII* and the American steamer *City of Washington* were searching desperately for survivors in spite of the exploding ammunition. "They bent their oars at the slightest sign of human life afloat," Harry Scovel reported about the Spaniards, "and their officers worked like mad."

Captain Sigsbee was having a hard time orienting himself. The ship seemed to have been smashed, then twisted back upon itself. "One of the smoke-stacks was lying in the water on the starboard side. Although it was almost directly under me, I had not at first identified it." He could dimly see white forms floating on the water, and hear faint cries for help, so he ordered that boats be lowered, although it turned out that only three of the ship's thirteen were still serviceable. All the fire-fighting equipment had also been destroyed, and gradually the realization dawned that there was not much more that could be done: the *Maine* was beyond saving. When Lieutenant-Commander Wainwright, his executive officer, whispered to him that the forward magazine of ten-inch shells might have fallen into the still-blazing fire, Sigsbee reluctantly gave the order to abandon ship. She had sunk so far that all the men had to do was step directly from the deck into a boat. The captain made a point of being the last to leave: "There was favorable comment later in the press because I left last. It is a fact that I was the last to leave, which was only proper; that is to say, it would have been improper otherwise; but virtually all left last."

Rea and Scovel were impressed by the captain's calmness as he stood on the deck of the *City of Washington* among several dozen of his wounded men. "Captain Sigsbee bears the calamity like an American officer and a gentleman," Scovel wrote. "He was not even outwardly ruffled by the awful calamity. He received the Spanish chief of police as calmly as though his quarterdeck were not a wreck and his men mangled and drowned."

Sigsbee spent some time with his wounded sailors, then stayed for a while watching the exploding rounds of ammunition arching over his old ship, as if he still could not believe that the disaster had happened. Finally he went into the captain's cabin to quickly pencil a telegram to the secretary of the navy reporting the disaster. He gave the message to Rea to send, then took it back to hastily add a few lines about the Spanish officers who were arriving to express their sympathies.

American reporters were already jamming the telegraph office, but Rea waved the official messages and he and Scovel were allowed to go to the head of the line. Although everyone was impatient, they all knew that it was unlikely Spanish censors would allow any of the straight news stories to be sent that night. Scovel, however, had acquired from a Cuban friend a blank form already bearing the censor's stamp and had been carrying it for several weeks for just such an important story; soon after Sigsbee's report went off, Scovel's followed.

CHAPTER 5

WAR FEVER

There are many things worse than war. It may be that the United States is to become the Knight Errant of the world. War with Spain may put her in a position to demand civil and religious liberty for the oppressed of every nation and of every clime.

Charles C. McCabe
Methodist bishop

I have been through one war; I have seen the dead piled up, and I do not want to see another.

William McKinley to Leonard Wood

"IT WAS ALMOST impossible to believe that it could be true, or that it was not a wild and vivid dream." Secretary of the Navy John Long had been awakened from a sound sleep by his daughter, who was returning from a ball, at 1:30 a.m. and given the telegram that had just been delivered by a Western Union messenger boy. "As my eyes went over and over the letters, I seemed to see between the lines the harbor at Havana, lying under the shadow of night, suddenly rift with a column of fire and startled with the thunder of the explosion of the noble battleship." Whatever hopes he had of being lost in an evil dream were quickly dashed; he immediately sent orders for lighthouse tenders to be rushed to Havana, and for the president to be awakened. Long, the quiet soul from Massachusetts, then girded himself to deal with the deluge of reporters and dispatches that he knew would be descending on him.

President McKinley, roused from his own comfortable sleep, also had trouble absorbing the news. Pacing the floor, he kept repeating to himself, "The *Maine* blown up! The *Maine* blown up!"

F. J. HILGERT, the Associated Press man in Cuba, had managed to get a brief cable out before the censors shut down the line. At 2:10 a.m. the *New York World's* office was galvanized by the news, and within an hour had an edition on the streets with a four-column headline: "U.S.S. *MAINE* BLOWN UP IN HAVANA HARBOR." There was also a four-column engraving of the ship that had been in the files, and a story about her reputation as a "Jonah" or "Hoodoo" ship. Scovel's cable arrived soon after and was incorporated into later editions with the headline "WORLD STAFF CORRESPONDENT CABLES IT IS NOT KNOWN WHETHER EXPLOSION OCCURRED ON OR UNDER THE *MAINE*."

Pulitzer's *World* had scored a "beat," but William Randolph Hearst and his *Journal* were not far behind. Hearst had gone home before news of the disaster arrived, so the night editor immediately telephoned him. Hearst asked what else was on the front page.

"Only the other big news," was the answer.

"There is not any other big news," Hearst said. "Please spread the story all over the page. This means war!"

There was not much information in the early stories, but through the headlines and the details emphasized there was already a slant being given to the event. The *World's* first headline, given above, is an example: by using "blown" instead of "blows" the act is presented as deliberate; in the second the implication is that a submarine mine might have destroyed the ship. Both the *World* and *Journal* began their coverage of the story with implications of Spanish treachery that were to become more overt in the coming days.

PRESIDENT MCKINLEY AND Secretary Long met for breakfast at nine o'clock to discuss the most recent dispatches; at a full cabinet meeting later in the morning it was decided the official position would be that, until and unless the board of inquiry found differently, the destruction of the *Maine* was the result of an accident. The president, impressing everyone with his composure, called for calm and self-restraint, and promised, Long noted in his diary, "that the public would know the real truth as soon as he did himself, and until then he asked for a suspension of judgment."

Other responsible voices joined in the call; even Captain Sigsbee, in the shock and horror of the immediate aftermath, had had the presence of mind to ask in his telegram that "public opinion" be suspended until the true cause had been ascertained, adding the line about Spanish officers coming to express their sympathies in a deliberate effort to "strengthen the quieting effect" of the cable.

McKinley told Senator Charles Fairbanks of Indiana, "I don't propose to be swept off my feet by the catastrophe. My duty is plain. We must learn the truth and endeavor, if possible, to fix the responsibility. The country can afford to withhold its judgment and not strike an avenging blow until the truth is known. The Administration will go on preparing for war, but still hoping to avert it. It will not be plunged into war until it is ready for it."

But many were being swept by their anger into making a quick judgment: "The *Maine* was sunk by an act of dirty treachery by the Spaniards, I believe," Theodore Roosevelt wrote a fellow member of Harvard's Porcellian Club on February 16, but he expressed these feelings just to close friends, being careful to use only the word "accident" in public dealings. In addition, he was trying to gird himself to face potential tragedies at home; both his wife, Edith, and his eldest son, Ted, were suffering from severe illnesses. In 1884, when both his mother and his first wife, Alice, had died within hours of each other, he had run from room to room trying to comfort them; now it seemed that such a tragedy might be repeating itself. Roosevelt's way of dealing with such stress was to be even more active and focused.

The Navy Department became a hive of frenetic activity as the nation's unreadiness for war became obvious. The loss of the *Maine* had reduced the nation's fleet to only seven modern armored warships, and one of the most powerful of those, the battleship *Oregon,* was on the West Coast. Agents began searching for ships in Europe that could strengthen the American force, only to find that Spanish agents were frequently bidding against them; private American vessels—yachts, merchant steamers, tugboats—were available, but often at outrageous prices the owners thought they could demand, given the national need. "Some men, at cost to their own purses, helped us freely and with efficiency," Roosevelt later recalled; "others treated the affair as an ordinary business transaction; and yet others endeavored, at some given crisis when our need was great, to sell us inferior vessels at exorbitant prices, and used every pressure through Senators and Congressmen, to accomplish their ends."

Charles R. Flint, one of the men with a freighter to sell, left a record of his transactions with the assistant secretary of the navy, "a young man at the very peak of his truly tremendous physical and mental energy," who was also at this particular moment a young man with no time to spare. He impressed Flint by already knowing all the important details about the *Nictheroy* when they met:

"What is the price?" he asked.

"Half a million dollars."

"I will take her," Roosevelt snapped.

"Good," Flint said. "I shall write you a letter—"

"Don't bother me with a letter. I haven't time to read it."

"We eventually did have a formal contract," Flint wrote, "dictated by Mr. Roosevelt. It was one of the most concise and at the same time one of the cleverest contracts I have ever seen. He made it a condition that the vessel should be delivered under her own steam at a specific point and within a specific period. In one sentence he thus covered all that might have been set forth in pages and pages of specifications. For the vessel *had* to be in first-class condition to make the time scheduled in the contract! Mr. Roosevelt always had that faculty of looking through details to the result to be obtained."

Roosevelt now lived at the office most of the time, although both his wife and his son Ted were still seriously ill. On the morning of Friday, February 25, Edith was so feverish that, afraid she was going to die, he summoned the famed Sir William Osler from Johns Hopkins Medical School in Baltimore to attend to her. Then, propelled by duty, he went off to the Navy Department.

John Long had been unable to sleep much since his nightmarish awakening in the predawn hours of the sixteenth, and his body had been afflicted with aches and pains that could be relieved only by "mechanical massage" applied to his stomach and legs by an unusual electric-powered machine under the command of a Washington osteopath. Feeling a need for the attentions of this technological wonder, Long took the afternoon off on the twenty-fifth to hobble first to the osteopath, then to his corn doctor. The burdens of office were left on the well-braced shoulders of Theodore Roosevelt, who knew exactly what needed doing.

First a cable to Commodore Dewey ordering him to assemble the Asiatic Squadron in Hong Kong and prepare it for offensive operations in the Philippine Islands "in the event" of a declaration of war with Spain; then orders to "Keep full of coal" to other squadron commanders around the world and an authorization for navy coal-buyers to obtain all they could; rendezvous points for scattered ships were named; ammunition in war-sized quantities was ordered; guns necessary to convert yachts and commercial steamers to warships were commanded to be taken out of storage; requests were made to both houses of Congress to pass bills authorizing the recruitment of enough sailors to man an expanded battle fleet. A very busy afternoon, and a satisfying one.

After he had completed his labors, the assistant secretary stopped by to see his chief at home, who was resting so comfortably that the younger man must have decided not to worry him with too detailed an account of what he had accomplished. When John Long came into his office the next morning he was shocked, "because during my short absence I find that Roosevelt, in his precipitate way, has come very near causing more of an explosion than happened to the *Maine* . . . the very devil seemed to possess him yesterday afternoon." Nevertheless, however precipitate, none of the orders was countermanded, although the secretary decided never to leave Roosevelt in charge again.

On top of all these trials of his office, the secretary of the navy had to bear the brunt of aggressive press questioning about the sinking; "the newspaper men cluster like bees around me," he complained to his diary. He recognized the honorable mission of the press to gather information for the public, and he had great respect for a number of individual reporters. "Some of these newspaper men are men of excellent ability and good address. . . . Some of them are of great adroitness in obtaining what they want; some are of great ability in their comprehension and digestion of matters of public interest." More aggravating were the irresponsible ones who caused "disquietude . . . by sensational newspaper articles."

It was probably the *World* and the *Journal* that he had most in mind as causing the "disquietude." They had started with headlines implying Spanish treachery, and these increased in vehemence as the days went on. On February 17 the *Journal* ran a banner headline announcing: "DESTRUCTION OF THE WARSHIP MAINE WAS THE WORK OF AN ENEMY." The *Evening Journal* claimed: "WAR! SURE! MAINE DESTROYED BY SPANISH," and added as a bold lie, "This Proved Absolutely by Discovery of the TORPEDO HOLE." Hearst offered a "$50,000 Reward for the Detection of the

Maine Outrage," and began sneering at President McKinley's calmness: "WILL ANYTHING MAKE HIM FIGHT?" was the headline over one such story.

The *World* was only a bit slower in using similar headlines, although Pulitzer's people attacked Hearst and the *Journal* for running "reckless war scares" and "manufactured news," which James Gordon Bennett's *Herald* joined in criticizing. Hearst ran a front-page response charging that Bennett, who lived in Europe, had lost touch, and that Pulitzer, who had been born in Hungary, "came to this country too late in life to absorb the spirit of American institutions or the temper of the American people. Men of this type are unfitted, by their environment, to gauge the force and trend of public sentiment in the United States. Their habit of mind is European; their instincts anti-American." No matter how self-righteously Pulitzer and Hearst attacked each other, the result was an enormous leap in circulation for both men's papers, with Pulitzer's *World* selling five million copies in a week, and Hearst's *Journal* managing over one million on one record day.

More affecting than the lurid headlines were the horror stories coming out of the hospitals sheltering the survivors. Walter Scott Meriwether, who had cabled "Tranquilo" at nine o'clock the night of February 15, was one of the first to reach the wards a few hours later. Through the early morning, he watched as stretcher after stretcher was carried in with burned and maimed sailors. "Men that I took by the hand and with the best voice I could command spoke cheerful words to are this morning dead or will be helpless cripples for the rest of their lives." One man was having his face bandaged by Spanish doctors who were being particularly gentle with him. "There is something in my eyes," he told them. "Wait and let me open them." But both his eyes were gone. "At the end of the ward," reported Meriwether, "was a lusty marine crying, 'for God's sake, let me die!'"

Clara Barton had rushed "to the Spanish hospital, San Ambrosia, to find thirty to forty wounded. . . . Their wounds were all over them. . . . The hair and beards singed, showing that the burns were from fire and not steam. . . . Both men and officers are very reticent as to the cause, but all declare it could not have been the result of an internal explosion."

Rituals were used to help the American people in their angry mourning. At dawn the day after the explosion a small crowd watched as the flag in front of the White House was raised, then lowered halfway down the pole; Sigsbee had the same ceremony performed over the *Maine*, with Old Glory flying from the wreckage that rose above the foul harbor water. At the Navy Department, a group gathered around a model of the battleship, watching as the glass case was opened so its tiny ensign also could be placed at half mast.

In Chicago, Sol Bloom heard the news early in the morning of the sixteenth. Burning with patriotic anger, he jotted down a rough draft of a song of tribute to the dead and injured sailors while riding on a streetcar to his job as manager of the music section at Rothschild's department store. There he turned the notes over to his able staff to finish, firing them up with references to Bunker Hill, Bull Run, and Gettysburg. That night "The Heroes Who Sank with the *Maine*" was performed at the Haymarket Theater, and the audience responded by standing on their chairs, cheering and demanding encore after encore.

The Naval Court of Inquiry was formed and began its deliberations. The Spanish government had asked for a joint investigation of the sinking, but Theodore Roosevelt had vigorously opposed the idea, writing to a close friend that "I myself doubt whether it will be possible to tell definitely how the disaster occurred by an investigation; still it may be possible, and it may be that we could do it as well in conjunction with the Spaniards as alone. But I am sure we never could convince the people-at-large of this fact. There is of course a very large body of public opinion to the effect that we some time ago reached the limit of forbearance in our conduct toward the Spaniards, and this public opinion is already very restless, and might easily be persuaded to turn hostile to the administration."

This political argument may have decided the issue; McKinley and his advisers agreed that the United States would conduct its own investigation, but would assist the Spanish in their independent study, if asked.

Captain William Thomas Sampson was named president of the court of inquiry. Commander of the battleship *Iowa,* Sampson had wide experience and expertise in explosives; the rest of his board was equally strong in professional skills. The hearings began, with all members and witnesses sworn to strict confidentiality, on Monday morning February 21 in Havana harbor, aboard the American lighthouse tender *Mangrove,* with Captain Charles Sigsbee called as the first to testify.

Sigsbee, McKinley, and Long, among others, had appealed for patience and a withholding of judgment until the investigation had run its course. Business leaders were also calling for self-restraint, fearing that the shaky economic recovery from 1893 could not survive a plunge into war. Grenville Mellen Dodge, railroad magnate and Civil War general, wrote to the president of his fear that events might fly out of control. "Other nations would be brought into it and then no one could underestimate the great distress and destruction that would come upon our country." Many Protestant, Jewish, and Catholic religious leaders quickly lent their voices to the cause of peace. An Episcopalian rector in Washington condemned "wild clamors for blood, blood, blood," and Rabbi Joseph Stolz of Chicago spoke against "savages" who wanted war. Jules Cambon, the French ambassador, wrote Paris, "In nearly all the churches pastors have given pacific sermons; this is especially noteworthy because there is in the passions aroused against Spain something of old Huguenot and Puritan hatreds." Perhaps in reaction to this rise of ancient fervors, some Irish and Italian priests began to say that it would be sinful for American Catholics to join a war against Spanish Catholics.

But in spite of all these respectable voices calling for peace, the public's war fever was rising. There were a few clerics who spoke for immediate action, such as the Episcopal clergyman in Indiana who wanted "to make Spanish the prevailing language of hell," but the passions seemed to gather force more from popular sentiment and the stories in the press than from leaders. The historian Ernest May has described emotional excess feeding upon itself as at a tent-meeting revival, with theater audiences cheering, stamping, and weeping at the playing of "The Star-Spangled Banner" as patriotic zeal swept the nation. One knowledgeable observer who was opposed to the frenzy described how strong it was even in the backwoods of central Missouri: "everything is war talk up in our part of the country, and patriotism is oozing out of every boy who is old enough to pack feed to the pigs."

The Reverend Washington Gladden, one of the founders of the Social Gospel movement, was sure that it was a selfless desire to help humanity that was behind the excitement. "To break in pieces the oppressor, to lift from a whole population the heavy hand of the spoiler, to lead in light and liberty, peace and plenty—is there any better work than this for the great nations of the earth?" The United States would fight "not for territory or empire or national honor, but for the redress of wrongs not our own, for the establishment of peace and justice in the earth. . . . Perhaps this experience may awaken in us that enthusiasm of humanity by which life is purified. In saving others we may save ourselves."

Ominously, much of the bellicosity was beginning to be directed against President McKinley. The restlessness and depleted forbearance that Theodore Roosevelt described in February had by the end of March become widespread, shared, though still discreetly, by Roosevelt himself, who in his increasing frustration with the president's slowness to act, told friends that McKinley had "no more backbone than a chocolate eclair." Others, with less to lose, were more public in their criticism; McKinley was hanged in effigy in Colorado and Virginia, his picture was hissed in New York theaters, offensive letters began arriving at Republican politicians' offices. Secretary Long received this advice from one correspondent, "If we wer in Spaines place and they in ours they would wipe us of the map as regards the Maine it was a planed plot and De Lome is at the bottom of it . . . the people are indignent wake up the president people in general will not stand it much Longer."

As a politician famous for an uncanny ability to read the feelings of his people, McKinley was fully aware of how unpopular he was becoming. Ambassador Stewart Woodford in Madrid was kept busy trying to effect some acceptable change in Spain's policy toward Cuba, but he continued to meet strong resistance. The queen and her government refused to recognize the legitimacy of Cuban demands for independence, or even that the Cuban people themselves were successfully fighting for freedom. Woodford wrote the president that "all Spain has been educated to believe that all help to the insurrection comes from us and that the rebellion only lives because of our sympathy and assistance." It seemed unlikely to the diplomat that this attitude could be changed, and he also doubted that the government would be able to show much more flexibility on Cuba for fear that any meaningful accommodation would result in toppling the Restoration of 1875. "They prefer the chances of war, with the certain loss of Cuba, to the overthrow of the Dynasty. They know that we want peace, if we can get such justice for Cuba and such protection of American interests as will make peace permanent and prevent this old Cuban question from [continual] resurrection."

In early March, Assistant Secretary of State Day met informally with the new Spanish ambassador, and warned him that unless his country ended the *reconcentrado* policy, announced an armistice, and accepted American arbitration over the struggle in Cuba, the crisis between their countries could go beyond anyone's control.

To put even more pressure on Spain, McKinley just a few days later submitted and pushed through Congress the "Fifty-Million-Dollar Bill," an unprecedented allowance of power to the executive branch, which allocated that amount "for the National defense and for each and every purpose connected therewith to be expended at the discretion of the President." McKinley also began investigating other possibilities, including buying Cuba outright or putting it under the protective care of the United

States, as Britain had done to Egypt, but nothing came of them. The purchase plan died when it became obvious that Congress would not vote money for such a commercial transaction, an inglorious resolution smacking of the bazaar, and Woodford reported that Queen Maria Cristina, though briefly tempted, would abdicate before agreeing to something so dishonorable.

The "Fifty-Million-Dollar Bill" did, however, focus Spanish attention. "It has not excited the Spaniards," Woodford reported with great satisfaction, "it has stunned them. To appropriate fifty millions out of the money in the Treasury, without borrowing a cent, demonstrates wealth and power." Unfortunately it also encouraged the Cuban rebels to refuse to compromise and to continue to hold out for complete independence, while the Spanish hoped even more fervently for help from other European powers. This was a danger that the administration fully recognized. When McKinley made his argument for the fifty million dollars he had warned that the Spanish government might find powerful European allies to take their side: "Who knows where this war will lead us; it may be more than war with Spain."

Although the president viewed the allocation as a peace measure that could be used to pressure Spain, the American people saw it as evidence that the nation was threatened and war inevitable. Hearst had his *Journal* run a huge celebratory headline: "FOR WAR! $50,000,000!" Joseph Wheeler, ex-Confederate cavalry leader and present member of the House of Representatives from Alabama, shook the chamber with a Rebel yell to celebrate this turn toward action. War fever continued to mount nationally, and was given added heat when one of McKinley's strongest conservative supporters, Senator Redfield Proctor of Vermont, reported in horrifying detail his recent investigatory trip to Cuba, his calm delivery adding to the shock and anger with which his words were received.

"It is not peace nor is it war," is how he described the condition of the countryside. "It is desolation and distress, misery and starvation." The reconcentration camps were "virtually prison yards," where women and children were forced at gunpoint to live in filth and despair. "Torn from their homes, with foul earth, foul air, foul water, and foul food or none, what wonder that one-half have died and that one-quarter of the living are so diseased that they can not be saved? A form of dropsy is a common disorder resulting from these conditions. Little children are still walking about with arms and chest terribly emaciated, eyes swollen, and abdomen bloated to three times the natural size. The physicians say these cases are hopeless." Before Weyler had issued his orders to round these farmers up, they were "independent and self-supporting," now they were "dropping dead" across most of the country.

The chamber listened in silence as Proctor then went on dispassionately, "I went to Cuba with a strong conviction that the picture had been overdrawn; that a few cases of starvation and suffering had inspired and stimulated the press correspondents, and that they had given free play to a strong, natural, and highly cultivated imagination. . . . I could not believe that out of a population of 1,600,000, two hundred thousand had died within these Spanish forts . . . within a few months past." America had to do something to stay true to her own values. "To me the strongest appeal is not the barbarity practiced by Weyler nor the loss of the *Maine,* if our worst fears should prove true . . . but the spectacle of a million and a half of people . . . struggling for freedom and deliverance from the worst misgovernment of which I ever had knowledge. . . . I merely speak of the symptoms as I saw them, but do not undertake to prescribe. Such remedial steps as may be required may safely be left to an American President and the American people."

The American people, at least, were increasingly sure what steps to take. The fact that a senator so conservative and previously uncommitted was now saying that action was necessary and justifiable on the grounds of "undiluted humanitarianism" helped shift more citizens to the side of intervention. Even the business interests, although most were still resistant, began to split. The *Wall Street Journal* wrote that the speech "converted a great many people in Wall Street who have heretofore taken the ground that the United States had no business to interfere in a revolution on Spanish soil." The anti-war faction was furious. Maine Republican Thomas "Czar" Reed, speaker of the House of Representatives and fierce opponent of intervention, reportedly said, referring to the marble quarries that were the source of Proctor's wealth, "Proctor's position might have been expected. A war will make a large market for gravestones."

By the middle of March relations between Spain and the United States had grown so strained that the secretary of the navy decided, probably with urging from his assistant, that the battleship *Oregon* should be summoned from the West Coast to make the sixteen thousand-mile voyage to the East.

Newly built and based in San Francisco, the *Oregon* was one of the most powerful warships in the world. Heavily armored, she carried four thirteen-inch guns, eight eight-inch, and four six-inch, each of which could penetrate thick steel armor at a range of two miles. There were also twenty six-pound rapid-fire guns, a couple of Gatlings, and a half dozen torpedo tubes.

Although the battleship was driven by the most modern twin-screw, triple-expansion engines and was famous for her speed, it did not seem possible that she would be able to make the long voyage in time to be of help if war was declared. Still, her power could tip the balance and the attempt had to be made. She steamed through the Golden Gate on March 19, loaded with coal and ammunition.

THE PRESIDENT HAD KEPT the negotiations with Spain focused on the Cuban situation and separate from the destruction of the *Maine,* wanting to be an honest mediator and to avoid any hint that revenge was part of his concern. But no one could really ignore the investigation working behind closed doors in Key West and Havana while divers continued to work the wreck, bringing more bodies to the surface every day and searching for evidence of what had happened. Some members of the public were sure that if the assistant secretary of the navy were handling the inquiry, conclusions would be reached quickly. "Teddy Roosevelt," a passenger on an electric tram in New York was heard to say, "is capable of going down to Havana, and going down in a diving-bell himself to see whether she was stove in or stove out."

One of the first points the court of inquiry had to determine was the number of explosions. Some witnesses, such as Captain Sigsbee and Executive Officer Wainwright, who had been inside the stern of the ship, had only felt one, but most of the others, including those on land or on nearby ships, had definitely seen or felt two. Methodically the board then went through possible causes, eliminating one by one the internal dangers— such as spontaneous coal combustion, accidental explosion of cannon shells, or a boiler bursting—questioning experts in ship design and explosives, as well as examining the evidence brought up by the divers feeling their way through the blackness of the wreck. As board members studied the data, word began to seep out indicating the direction the inquiry was taking.

The press was in such a competitive frenzy to discover the cause of the explosion that even before the naval board had been appointed, the *World,* the *Journal,* and the *Herald* had crews of divers at the wreck. Spanish authorities quickly put a stop to this journalistic endeavor, although the *Evening Journal* cloaked itself in the mantle of patriotic concern: "Vultures now hover over the wreck of the *Maine,* picking to pieces the portions of the bodies of American sailors which rise to the surface. Spain, by refusing to permit the *Evening Journal's* divers to search the wreck and rescue the bodies, occupies the position of protecting these foul birds."

The greatest challenge for journalists was prying the findings of the Naval Court of Inquiry out of the locked canvas bag by which they were sent to Washington, guarded by four armed navy officers. Their train arrived at 9:35 on the night of Thursday, March 24, with Lieutenant John Hood, who had been on the deck at the time of the *Maine's* explosion, having the honor of carrying the twenty-pound report. When the waiting crowd of reporters and onlookers spotted them there was a shout, and a surge that pressed too close to Lieutenant Hood, who reached for his gun. This brought a clearing of the path to the hackstand, and the bag with its guardians was quickly on its way, followed by five cabloads of reporters.

Copies of the report were made at the White House, and when not being used by the president and his advisers, they were locked in a safe. The report was not to be presented to Congress until Monday. Somehow, though, the Associated Press was able to gain access to a draft. Papers hit the newsstands on Monday morning carrying an accurate summary of the evidence and judgment: "the loss of the *Maine* was not in any respect due to fault or neglect on the part of any of the officers or members of the crew of said vessel"; instead, "the *Maine* was destroyed by the explosion of a submarine mine which caused the partial explosion of two or more of her forward magazines. The court has been unable to obtain evidence fixing the responsibility for the destruction of the *Maine* upon any person or persons." The Spanish published the results of their own inquiry at about the same time, although no one paid much attention. They declared it an accident, probably caused by spontaneous combustion of coal in one of the storage areas near an ammunition bunker.

War seemed inevitable now, but McKinley kept trying to convince the Spanish government to make concessions dramatic enough to disarm the jingos: close the *reconcentrado* camps, implement an armistice that would be guaranteed until October 1, and while that was in effect Cuban self-government could be established. When the Spanish asked for specifics about the kind of "self-government," the Americans made their demands plain: "Full self-government would mean Cuban independence." Prime Minister Sagasta asked for more time, but there was no such luxury.

Spanish attempts to put together a coalition of allies had met with sympathy from Austria, Germany, and France. Kaiser Wilhelm II of Germany, proud upholder of the view that monarchy was the only proper form of government, had been particularly eager to help for months before the crisis came to a head. "Shall we other monarchs look on placidly as a brave colleague of ours has her land and probably too—through Cuba's loss—her throne torn from her?" Wilhelm disliked the upstart republic across the seas and was sensitive to the stress the German economy was feeling from American competition. But his advisers pointed out the importance of the American market for German trade, and the danger of becoming involved as an ally of Spain when there was so much competition for imperial advantage in the Far East and Africa.

Other powers recognized the dangerously growing strength of the United States; the French ambassador to Madrid wrote his ministry that a war would be "almost as prejudicial to the interests of Europe as to Spain." They were well aware of the threat American competition posed to their economies; this year would see American steel companies outproduce those of Germany, Great Britain, and France. But no one country was willing to take the lead in organizing European resistance.

President McKinley was nearing the end of his endurance. His trusted secretary, George Cortelyou, had noticed the change in mid-March. "He appeared to me careworn, did not look well, and his eyes had a far-away, deep-set expression in them." By the end of the month he was resorting to the use of narcotics in a vain attempt to sleep. "His face had grown seamed and haggard, with sunken, darkly circled eyes. He jumped at every sound. His manner was exceedingly quiet." Tormented by the suffering war would bring, he confided to his physician Leonard Wood his fear of again seeing bodies piled high.

Those around him marveled at his stoicism, but it was not iron-clad. On the evening of March 30, the violoncellist Leo Stern gave a recital at the White House, and McKinley took the opportunity to talk privately to his friend H. H. Kohlsaat, publisher of the *Chicago Times-Herald*. Leaving his wife and guests in the Blue Room listening to the recital, the president took Kohlsaat into the Red Room and the two men settled on a large crimson-brocade sofa. McKinley sat with his elbows on his knees, his head in his hands.

"I have been through a trying period," he told Kohlsaat. "Mrs. McKinley has been in poorer health than usual. It seems to me I have not slept over three hours a night for over two weeks. Congress is trying to drive us into war with Spain. The Spanish fleet is in Cuban waters, and we haven't enough ammunition on the Atlantic seacoast to fire a salute." The president then broke down, "and cried like a boy of thirteen."

Congress was threatening to break away; even Republicans were beginning to bolt under the goading of a public set on war. An important Republican senator shook his fists at Assistant Secretary of State William Day: "Day, by —, don't your President know where the war-declaring power is lodged? Tell him by —, that if he doesn't do something Congress will exercise the power." Vice-President Garrett Augustus Hobart warned McKinley that he could not hold the Senate back much longer.

The House of Representatives was also beginning to run free. When Thomas Reed of Maine was urged by ex-Governor Levi Morton of New York to "dissuade" the members from taking the warpath, Reed sarcastically told reporters, "Dissuade them! Dissuade them! The Governor is too good. He might as well ask me to stand out in the middle of a Kansas waste and dissuade a cyclone." Elihu Root, a leading light of the New York bar, wrote his friend Roosevelt, "I sympathize with McKinley . . .; but . . . if the administration does not turn its face toward the front and lead instead of being pushed, it seems to me it will be rolled over and crushed and the Republican party with it."

In the streets crowds were chanting:

> Remember the *Maine*!
> To Hell with Spain!

The president waited until Fitzhugh Lee and other American citizens left Havana on Easter Sunday, April 10, then sent his message to Congress the next day, asking for authority to intervene in Cuba. In simple and direct language he summarized the history of his negotiations, and stated the justification for armed intervention, a justification that included the "barbarities, bloodshed, starvation, and horrible miseries" that the Cuban people were still suffering, as well as the injuries done to American commerce, trade, and business. There was, too, the "enormous expense" the government had been forced to bear to stop filibustering, protect its citizens, and maintain a "semiwar footing with a nation with which we are at peace." There should be no recognition of "the so-called Cuban Republic" because it might place the United States under later obligations. He asked for authorization to intervene with whatever "military and naval forces as may be necessary."

During the debate that followed, Congress came close to recognizing the Cuban republic, and they did adopt the Teller amendment. Proposed by Senator Henry M. Teller, Democrat from Colorado, it specified that "the United States hereby disclaims any disposition or intention to exercise sovereignty, jurisdiction, or control over [Cuba] except for the pacification thereof, and asserts its determination when that is accomplished to leave the government and control of the island to its people." This statement was pointed to proudly as proving the disinterested, humanitarian goals of the country, but others criticized it as meaning that once the fighting was over the United States would take no responsibility for stability on the island. Newspaper publisher Whitelaw Reid expressed worries that many later believed came true: "I hope they [the Cubans] prove more orderly and less likely to plunge into civil strife and brigandage than has been expected. If the result of our efforts is merely to establish a second Hayti nearer our own coast, it will be so pitiful an outcome from a great opportunity."

The debates became more emotional as the various resolutions passed back and forth from chamber to chamber, attended by excited spectators. "The scene upon the floor of the House resembled a political convention," one observer wrote. "A half hundred of the Representatives gathered in the lobby in the rear of the hall and awoke the echoes with patriotic songs. 'The Battle Hymn of the Republic' was sung by General Henderson of Iowa, 'Dixie' and other songs were sung, led by some of the ex-Confederates, and then in tremendous volume the corridors rang with an improvisation: 'Hang General Weyler to a Sour Apple Tree as We Go Marching On.' . . . Soldiers bivouacking about the camp-fires in the enemy's front could not have been more enthusiastic."

Backed by this ardent spirit, the joint resolution allowing for intervention passed on April 19, with 42 senators voting yea and 35 nay, and the house vote 310 against 6. It was signed by the president just before noon the next day. There was still some hope on his part that the Spanish would accede to the American demand for Cuban independence, but Sagasta knew that to do so would bring down not just his government, but the monarchy itself. As an American resident in the country wrote, "Everyone here expects war, and the lower classes ardently desire it." The "intelligent classes" were fatalistic, preferring war to dishonor, even if war ended in defeat. On April 21, Spain broke diplomatic relations with the United States, and two days later it declared war.

.   .   .

"THE INTERESTS OF the country changed in a few weeks," wrote William Allen White. "The change was not an outward one. Trains ran on their scheduled time. Business men hurried to business. The wheel at the cistern was not broken; but there was a new motive guiding it. The public mind ceased wishing for prosperity; it began longing for victory at arms." It was as if the whole country had suddenly sprouted fields of red, white, and blue. "The Yankee," White claimed, "did not gather in hoarse-voiced mobs. He did not lose time from his work. A minute or two with a bulletin board at noon, and another over the newspaper before supper and before breakfast, were lost—but that was all. . . . The only way the poor dumb, stoical brute of a Yankee could show the patriotism that filled his swelling heart was by the spectacle of the flags. In April, everywhere over this good, fair land, flags were flying."

THE UNITED STATES had already taken action in anticipation of war: on April 21 the navy laid a blockade on the north coast of Cuba. Secretary Long and Theodore Roosevelt also argued that Commodore Dewey should descend on the Philippines as quickly as possible, but they ran into strong resistance from President McKinley, who did not agree to give the order until Sunday, April 24.

While such orders were given, still to be dealt with were the same problems that had been bedeviling war preparations for months: how to quickly reverse years of neglect of the military and naval forces. Theodore Roosevelt justly bragged to his diary: "Long is at last awake . . . I have the Navy in good shape." But he had also written a critique of the situation that the army faced under Secretary of War Russell Alger and Commander-in-Chief Nelson Miles: "Alger has no force whatsoever . . . Miles is a brave peacock. They both told me they could put 100,000 men in Tampa in 24 hours! The folly, the lack of preparation, are almost inconceivable."

There was more at fault here, of course, than the vain fantasies of two old men; the Congress of the United States had decided long before that there was no need for a strong military; many citizens, in fact, regarded such a force as a threat to the free institutions of the nation. Defeat would be terrible, but so might the fruits of victory. Moorfield Storey, a Bostonian who later became a leader of the anti-imperialist effort, warned that "in the intoxication of such a success, we should reach out for fresh territory, and to our present difficulties would be added an agitation for the annexation of new regions which, unfit to govern themselves, would govern us. We should be fairly launched upon a policy of military aggression, of territorial expansion, of standing armies and growing navies, which is inconsistent with the continuance of our institutions. God grant that such calamities are not in store for us."

Fear of a calamitous victory was not tormenting too many souls in Washington in April of 1898. Most government officials were all too aware of the country's weakness as they tried to ready their departments for war. Alger and Miles were not even sure where to start, although a good place would have been with the outmoded and haphazard organization of their department. There were obvious needs, however, that could be immediately addressed. With a standing army of only 26,000 men and just over 2,000 officers, most of them scattered around posts in the West, the nation called on its two traditional manpower sources: volunteers and the militia, or National Guard. On April 23, President McKinley issued a call for 125,000 volunteers. The immediate rush for the improvised recruiting offices proved that there would be no difficulty in putting men in the field; arming and equipping them would be another matter.

And where was this equipment to come from? How was it to be distributed? Congress had authorized the Fifty-Million-Dollar Bill in early March, but McKinley had sincerely meant that as a peace ploy to convince Spain to come to terms, not as the first step in preparing the country for hostilities. The president had never informed either the Navy or War Departments of his possible plans if war occurred, nor had he given directions on how to use the newly voted funds. As it was, the army received only a small part of the money, and it was not allowed to use any of it for purchasing modern arms, smokeless powder, horses and mules, or any other necessities for fighting. Even if the War Department had been a model of efficiency, the result of quintupling the size of the army without having warehoused the proper amount of uniforms, weapons, food, tents, and other myriad needs would have spelled chaos; instead, it was a disaster.

But other, more immediate, disasters were feared to be in the works. In late April news suddenly swept the nation that a Spanish fleet under Admiral Pascual Cervera y Topete had left the Cape Verde Islands off Africa heading west. To many Americans that could only mean that the fleet would raid the undefended American East Coast. Panic took hold of those who just a week before had been celebrating the new martial spirit in the land. The *New York Times* reported that society matrons were not going to open their summer houses until the threat was removed. Influential people began demanding that warships be stationed near their houses along the shore. A Georgia congressman wanted one to protect Jekyll Island, on the grounds that certain millionaires had their winter homes there.

Roosevelt was both amused and outraged by the hubbub. "Our people had for decades scoffed at the thought of making ready for possible war. Now, when it was too late, they not only backed every measure . . . that offered a chance of supplying a need that ought to have been met before, but they also fell into a condition of panic apprehension as to what the foe might do." He found the anxiety embarrassing: "So many of the business men of the city of Boston took their securities inland to Worcester that the safe deposit companies . . . proved unable to take care of them. In my own neighborhood on Long Island clauses were gravely put into leases to the effect that if the property were destroyed by the Spaniards the lease should lapse."

So great was the political pressure that Roosevelt was forced to do something to satisfy it. He ordered one of the antique Civil War monitors, those that the *New York Times* had written about on New Year's Day, stationed as token protection for a coastal city: "the fact that [it] would not have been a formidable foe to any antagonist of . . . more modern construction than the galleys of Alcibiades seemed to disturb nobody."

It was not, Roosevelt thought, the way to begin a war that was going to demand sacrifice, fortitude, and valor.

ONE NAVAL OFFICER who possessed an abundance of fortitude and valor was uncertain whether he should take part in the struggle.

Robert Peary was the only child of a young widow, one of those American mothers who felt it was her duty to guide her son through life. When Robert decided to enter Bowdoin College in Brunswick, Maine, his mother announced that she would move there with him, and when her brothers and other members of the family criticized the idea, arguing that a boy should be able to escape from his "mother's apron strings," she adamantly replied, "I am going to college!" None of this seemed to bother the youth himself; he graduated from Bowdoin with a degree in civil engineering in 1877, and four years later became an officer in the United States navy.

A member of the same ambitious generation as Roosevelt, Peary decided early in his naval career to make his mark in exploration. He also shared Roosevelt's keen understanding of the importance of public relations as well as his delight in overcoming physical challenges, so he fixed on what was considered an impossible exploit: journeying to the North Pole. He promised America to "nail the Stars and Stripes to the Pole." "I have put my whole life effort," he wrote later, "to accomplish something which seemed to me to be worth doing, because it had the great attraction of being a clean, manly proposition."

Peary served his apprenticeship under Eskimos, then mastered Arctic survival techniques by leading expeditions in northern Greenland, exploration work for which he was awarded the American Geographical Society's Cullom medal in 1897, and the Royal Geographical Society's Patron's Gold Medal the next year. He was confident that the only real barriers to his success were lack of funds and the United States navy. A financial crisis was temporarily averted when rich supporters promised him enough money to launch a new attempt; the navy was more of a problem. For years, believing his goal unattainable and jealous of his growing fame, that service had resisted giving him authorization for expeditions, although European Arctic explorers were almost always military or naval men who had the full support of their governments. It was only through the efforts of influential American businessmen and politicians that he was finally able in 1897 to gain a five-year leave to continue his quest.

In January 1898 he announced his strategy. He would set out that July in a vessel powerful enough to drive far to the north through summer ice, then sledge on when winter came. If he failed, he would stay in the north and try again the next year, and the year after that if need be, and so on until the Pole was conquered. But when the *Maine* was destroyed on February 15 he considered giving up his leave and rejoining the navy for the war he was sure would come. On reflection, however, the explorer decided that this struggle would probably not last long enough for his expertise in civil engineering to be much help. Adding to his unwillingness to stay around was news that a Norwegian expedition would be traveling in the same region he planned to use as a base. Could they have designs to beat him?

CHAPTER 6

THE GLORIOUS FIRST OF MAY

Dewey or Dooley, 'tis all the same. We dhrop a letter here and there . . . but we're th' same breed iv fightin' men. Georgy has th' thraits iv th' fam'ly.

Mr. Dooley

Success always makes success look easy.

George Dewey

"I'VE LOOKED IN HIS EYES," Theodore Roosevelt said when forced to defend his choice of George Dewey for command of the Asiatic Squadron. "He's a fighter." But more than a hawklike gleam had attracted the assistant secretary of the navy. Dewey also seemed an officer who did what was necessary without worrying about "red-tape minds," or the risk of damaging his career. The two men had become friends through the Metropolitan Club, gone horseback-riding often, and shared with each other their ideas about the necessity for American expansion. Dewey was particularly concerned about the navy's need for overseas bases.

In late September 1897, while John Long was on vacation in Massachusetts and Theodore Roosevelt was acting secretary, a letter from Senator William Chandler had arrived at the navy office recommending that Commodore John Howell be appointed to command the Asiatic Squadron. Roosevelt had decided he wanted Dewey in the post, and felt that although Howell was an officer "of the respectable, commonplace type," he was not the sort who "would act without referring things back to the home authorities." He unsuccessfully asked Senator Chandler to change his mind, argu-

ing that Howell was "irresolute and . . . extremely afraid of responsibility."
The Asia command, being halfway around the world and thousands of
miles from a home base, was so important and challenging that only an
aggressively independent commander would do. If the crisis with Spain
developed into war, as Roosevelt fully expected it would, then the
squadron would, under great logistical difficulties, be expected to attack
the Philippines to tie down Spanish forces there.

Quick action was necessary, since Long was returning the next day, and
Roosevelt suspected that the secretary, too, favored Howell. Dewey was
immediately summoned. "I want you to go," Roosevelt told him. "You are
the man who will be equal to the emergency if one arises." Then he asked
bluntly, "Do you know any Senators?"

The commodore replied that Redfield Proctor of Vermont was an old
family friend. Roosevelt, aware that McKinley respected Proctor, urged
him to make use of that friendship. At Dewey's request the senator from
Vermont called at the White House that afternoon, while Roosevelt pocketed Chandler's recommendation until the issue was decided. McKinley
listened closely, then agreed to take care of it "right away." Senator Proctor,
however, wise in the ways of politicians and knowing that the decision
could not be put off, pushed a pad of paper across the desk and said,
"Here, write it down, Mr. President." The result was that Secretary Long,
to his intense irritation, returned from vacation to find a letter from the
president requesting that Dewey be given the command.

Roosevelt had read his man's gaze correctly. Dewey had been something
of an undersized hellion in his youth, testing himself against nature by
swimming in the Winooski River at flood stage and brawling with the other
boys in Montpelier, Vermont, where he had grown up. His mother had died
when he was only five years old, and he had been raised by a stern but supportive father. In the best New England tradition there was to be no frivolity, and self-discipline was expected. Attending a stage show with his
father, young George laughed so hard at the comedian that "I fairly lost
control of myself, and my father made me leave the theatre." Nevertheless,
there were strong bonds of respect and affection between father and son.
"To my father's influence in my early training, I owe primarily all that I have
accomplished. . . . From him I inherited a vigorous constitution and an
active temperament. . . . He was one of those natural leaders to whom men
turn for unbiased advice. His ideas of right and wrong were very fixed."

Self-restraint in Victorian America had many qualifiers, the demands of
honor being one. While attending the naval academy at Annapolis, Dewey

was insulted by another cadet and fell back on what he called the "fistic arbitration of grievances" to settle the issue. "I did not lose a second and, springing around the table, I went for him and beat him under the table until we were separated." When called before the commanding officer, Dewey explained that the fellow had "called me a name . . . which no man can hear without redress." The officer agreed, and the other cadet was disciplined.

After graduation in 1858, Dewey served an apprenticeship at sea under the veterans of the War of 1812; he received his own baptism of fire in April 1862, when Admiral David Farragut led a flotilla of Union ships through stiff and bloody resistance to capture New Orleans. Later Dewey survived having a ship shot from beneath him while trying to run past the Confederate strong point at Port Hudson on the Mississippi; on another ship a shell exploded on the quarterdeck, killing the captain and four other officers, but leaving Dewey unscathed. Through all these violent experiences, the young officer had kept his eye on his commander, in whom he found a model: "Farragut has always been my ideal of the Naval Officer, urbane, decisive, indomitable. Valuable as the training of Annapolis was, it was poor schooling beside that of serving under Farragut in time of war." Whenever he faced a crisis, Dewey would ask himself, "What would Farragut do?"

The long postwar years of congressional neglect were difficult for Dewey to observe, as obsolete American ships deteriorated and foreign nations built new, technologically sophisticated, and heavily armored navies. Dewey took command of the *Pensacola*, a Civil War relic, in 1885, and noted that "there was not a fourth-rate British cruiser of modern build that could not easily have kept out of range of her battery, torn her to pieces and set her on fire." Not only England, but even Italy, Chile, and Brazil could boast of navies superior to the U.S. fleet. But George Dewey, unlike many fellow officers who resigned in discouragement, stuck to his career and was able to play a role in modernizing the navy once its obvious weakness became too embarrassing for an ambitious nation to bear.

Sixty years old when he took command of the Asiatic Squadron in the harbor of Nagasaki, Japan, he was below average height, at about five feet six, but compensated for that with dapper, well-cut white uniforms, a large gray handlebar mustache, and an air of quiet authority. He had earned a reputation with sailors for being a strict but fair disciplinarian, and with his peers for careful preparation and personal initiative in everything he did.

The squadron was painted in dazzling white and buff, with all brass polished, and every obscure corner in spotless condition: the American navy was famous for the cleanliness of its ships. Unfortunately, under this sparkling veneer the force itself was less than formidable when compared to the squadrons of the European powers.

Competition for pieces of China had unsettled the established relationships in the Far East. Germany's grab of the region of Kiaochow and subsequent control of Shantung province, Britain's occupation of Weihai, the Russian fortification of Port Arthur, and the growing strength of Japan, resulting from that nation's victory over China in 1894, perhaps meant that a dismemberment of the great prize was beginning, and none could afford to be left out. "Affairs are very unsettled here," Dewey wrote his son George. "The Germans, English and Russians and Japanese are playing a big game of bluff since it remains to be seen who will take the pot." Sometimes the bluff looked as if it might be called, and when a Russian naval squadron arrived at Port Arthur, he wrote: "Things look decidedly squally . . . and I should not be surprised to see a general war at any time." He had no doubts about what was at stake, writing his son that the tension centered on gaining favorable access to the markets of the Far East.

Like all Americans, including the very active missionary societies, Dewey felt that the United States had far more to offer the ancient cultures of Asia than did the European powers. There was no push for territory, except enough perhaps for a small naval base, or drive for political dominance; the goal instead was to keep the door to international trade open, with free access for all nations, especially to the Chinese market. Along with trade, there would be lessons taught about individual liberty, democracy, and personal initiative.

Japan offered a good example of what could be accomplished. Commodore Matthew Perry had forced that reclusive kingdom to "open" itself to contact with the West in 1854, during Dewey's first year in the Naval Academy. Now, as Dewey looked around the prosperous, modernizing nation, he saw proof of the benefits America could bring to the East. The emperor granted the new commander of the American Asiatic Squadron an audience, and Dewey came away impressed. It seemed to him that "Of all the changes which the world has seen in the last century, none has been so phenomenal as that so splendidly accomplished by Japan since the memorable visit of Commodore Perry."

As both Roosevelt and Senator Proctor had known, the energetic commander-in-chief was not one to sit waiting for orders from Washington. Tensions with Spain were mounting during early February, not diminishing, and Dewey decided that the *Olympia* would be better positioned at Hong Kong. The flagship left on February 11, and when it arrived at the new British colony six days later, Dewey found the harbor filled with men-of-war, and rumors about the *Maine*. The next day brought official confirmation from Long: "*Maine* destroyed at Havana February 15 by accident. Half-mast all colors until further notice."

While this news understandably gave a certain tautness to American routine, there was also tension between the other powers, which Dewey had noticed on his arrival, sensing "a feeling of restlessness and uncertainty in the air," a restlessness that grew even stronger after a German flotilla made its appearance in the harbor. British and American sailors saw themselves as Anglo-Saxon allies against a common enemy, and brawls became so frequent that the British governor of Hong Kong issued an order: since the Germans "belonged to a friendly nation and were guests at a friendly port," they should be treated as such.

A story making the rounds of the harbor illustrates the problem. A German and a Briton were drinking when the German proposed a toast to the kaiser, and the Englishman politely agreed. Then the German raised his glass again.

"To the Emperor," he shouted, and drank.

"What about the Queen?" asked the Englishman.

"To the Emperor," shouted the German, draining another glass.

"Well," responded the Englishman, "if you won't drink to the Queen, then up comes your Emperor," and he stuck his fingers down the German's throat.

This distrust reached higher than waterfront saloons. One of the ranking German officers was the kaiser's brother, Prince Henry of Prussia, a rear-admiral though not yet forty. Dewey found him personally charming, but there were several awkward occurrences that the commodore suspected might be deliberate insults to America, and, as he wrote later, "expressive of an attitude not altogether uncommon at that time with some European powers."

On one occasion, a group of German sailors paid a visit to the *Olympia*, and while on board one of them was recognized by the officer of the deck as a deserter from the American navy. Since he now belonged to the crew of a German man-of-war, he was not arrested, but the Americans later asked that he be surrendered to them, a request that met with a flat refusal. That a deserter would feel safe in coming aboard the flagship seemed like an intentional affront directed by his commanders.

Later, at a festive dinner given aboard Prince Henry's flagship, the *Deutschland,* Dewey felt that there were other deliberate offenses to the honor and dignity of the United States, such as toasting President McKinley last in a round devoted to national leaders, and then misplaying the American anthem. Feeling that these incidents could not be overlooked, he left the party early and issued an order forbidding his officers to attend any of the subsequent entertainments given in Prince Henry's honor. This caused the German prince to reconsider his actions and apologize, and he and Dewey began exchanging visits again, perhaps testing each other through frank discussions about the changing political situation in both the Caribbean and the Far East. At one point, while they were enjoying cigars and glasses of Liebfraumilch on board the *Deutschland,* Prince Henry warned his guest that "The powers will never allow the United States to annex Cuba."

"We do not wish to annex Cuba," Dewey assured him, "but we cannot suffer the horrible condition of affairs which exists at present in that island at our very doors to continue, and we are bound to put a stop to it." At another informal meeting, the prince wondered what the Americans wanted for themselves out of the maneuvering for advantage in Asia. "And what are you after? What does your country want?"

"Oh," Dewey teasingly answered, echoing the German response to criticism of their taking Kiaochow, "we need only a bay."

But for all the dangerous competition among the major powers, the immediate threat to America involved Spain, and Dewey knew that if war broke out between the two nations, his job would be to attack the Philippines. To be successful in such an attack he needed both coal to fire his ships' boilers and ammunition. Here was undeniable evidence that America's ability to project its power or protect its interests was severely limited by lack of overseas bases. If war was declared, the neutral nations, including even the friendly British authorities at Hong Kong, would have to follow international law and forbid use of their ports and territorial waters. Over and over, he would lament the handicap of being seven thousand miles from a home base.

Dewey had immediately set about buying all the coal available locally, but modern warships burned it in prodigious quantities—his own flagship *Olympia* had a voracious appetite for the stuff—and Hong Kong harbor was now filled with modern warships. The only solution he, and Washington, could find was for him to use the international cable to buy a load of coal in England, as well as the collier, the *Nanshan,* that it was shipped on.

He later bought another freighter, the *Zafiro,* to carry supplies for his flotilla.

Ammunition was an even greater problem than coal. None of his ships had even their normal peacetime allotment, and the secretary of the navy didn't seem to recognize the seriousness of the shortage, just as he failed to take other important issues seriously. Dewey contacted Assistant Secretary Roosevelt and he managed to have some shells loaded on the gunboat *Concord,* which was sent to augment the Asiatic Squadron in late February. A larger amount was shipped separately to Honolulu, where it was to be taken on board the *Baltimore,* a cruiser ordered to join Dewey in March. But even with these emergency shipments the squadron would have its ammunition bunkers only sixty percent filled.

Then came the historic set of orders directing the whole squadron to join the *Olympia* at Hong Kong, where it would be only six hundred miles from Manila. This was just one of the slew of commands that Theodore Roosevelt sent winging around the world while John Long visited his chiropractor and corn doctor on February 25. The *Olympia,* which had been due to return home, was ordered to stay, and new ships were assigned to the Pacific, though the most powerful were kept at home for the Caribbean and defense of the Atlantic coast. The speedy Revenue Service cutter *Hugh McCulloch,* which had just been launched a few months before in Philadelphia, was diverted from an around-the-world break-in cruise and joined Dewey on April 17, while the *Raleigh* was sent from the Mediterranean Squadron. As each addition to the squadron arrived, it was hauled, inspected, repaired, and made ready for combat.

As soon as Dewey had reached Asia, he had initiated an intelligence service, having his officers, dressed in mufti, boarding steamers posing as traveling businessmen curious about commercial possibilities in the Philippines, or hanging around the repair yards asking questions. In this way he learned that the Spanish squadron, though boasting more ships than his own, was in poor condition and contained many "lame ducks" that were well known in the Hong Kong repair docks.

More dangerous intelligence-gathering was the work of a mysterious businessman, his name lost to us, who made frequent trips to the archipelago, and of the resident consul in Manila, Oscar F. Williams, whose effectiveness was limited by his lack of naval expertise and by the tight surveillance he was kept under. "Two or more spies watch me constantly and my clerk is the son of a Spanish colonel. At times, I suspect the key to my consulate and its safe are in the possession of persons who have no right to them and that my office has been visited." But the consul was brave, resourceful, and well connected with local officials. He was able to gather information about the Spanish defenses that indicated weaknesses in both matériel and morale.

A growing insurgency in the islands was a development which Dewey was required to handle carefully. Suppressed in 1896, it was now gathering strength again, and looking to outside powers for help. "War exists," Williams had reported to the State Department in March, "battles are of almost daily occurrence, ambulances bring in many wounded, and the hospitals are full. Prisoners are brought here and shot without trial, and Manila is under martial law." To the commodore he wrote, enthusiastically and misleadingly, "Daily the cry arises, 'If the U.S. or Great Britain would only take these islands, how happy we would be. Why cannot the U.S. take us? Our islands are the gems of the ocean. The United States now takes half our export. They need an eastern home for their fleet such as the British have in Hong Kong.' " The commodore couldn't have agreed more about the need for a "home" for his squadron; the challenges of his preparations for war reminded him of that every day. But he had been given no clear directions about how much or what kind of support to give to the insurgent leadership. Through the American consul in Singapore, Dewey did open communications with Emilio Aguinaldo, the rebel leader who had been exiled by Spanish colonial authorities.

The course of events was accelerating by mid-April, and the commodore decided that it was time to cover the gleaming white hulls of his ships with greenish-gray paint, to remove some of the interior woodwork that could catch fire during combat, and have all ships' bottoms cleaned for speed. None of the hulls of the American ships was armored, although some, like the *Olympia,* were "protected," which meant that they had armored decks. Shields for the gun crews would have to be improvised from iron and canvas, and heavy steel chain would later be looped as protective cover for important but vulnerable equipment such as ammunition hoists.

The greatest worry of all for the commodore was the *Baltimore,* which carried the essential resupply of ammunition. Would it arrive before the squadron had to leave Hong Kong for neutral waters? Would attacking the Spanish fleet without the shells or the added firepower of the cruiser lead to disaster?

Opinion among the international experts in Hong Kong was that the Americans did not have much chance for success, with or without the *Baltimore* and its cargo, and that they would meet with certain destruction.

The colony's newspapers reported that the forts at Manila were too strong, that the mines at the entrance to the bay, combined with the Spanish fleet, made victory impossible. Several Chinese members of the crew of the *Olympia,* some who had served for years, deserted. At the Hong Kong Club no one would bet, even at heavy odds, on the success of the venture, and, during a farewell party given for the Americans, the British hosts had lamented: "A fine set of fellows, but unhappily we shall never see them again."

Dewey, confident in the power of his ships and the skill of his men, thought he knew better, but it was with relief that the *Baltimore* was sighted on April 22. As soon as the cruiser was anchored, lighters were at her side to unload the ammunition. Then the ship was hauled, its bottom scraped, the hull painted dull gray, and her bunkers filled with coal. None of this was done a moment too soon, for as she slid down the rails into the water the British governor sent a formal letter to Dewey requiring him to leave the harbor. War had been declared between Spain and the United States, and the laws of neutrality, which ordained that no "warlike stores" or coal could be brought aboard his ships, were to be strictly enforced. The squadron must leave Hong Kong waters within forty-eight hours.

Dewey had expected this, and sent six of his ships thirty miles down the coast to Mirs Bay, where he had improvised a base. This was Chinese territory, but he knew that China was too unorganized and weak to enforce its neutrality. Before leaving, he saw Prince Henry again, who said, "Well, Commodore, good luck. I may send some ships to Manila—to see that you behave."

"I should be delighted to have you do so, Your Highness," Dewey responded. "But permit me to caution you to keep your ships from between my guns and the enemy."

As the *Olympia, Baltimore,* and *Raleigh* steamed out of Hong Kong Harbor on Monday morning, British sailors lined the railings of their ships paying silent respect; convalescents on the hospital hulk were not under such tight discipline and gave a hearty round of applause as the ships passed. American residents of the city followed the flagship in small boats, blowing the steam whistles and shouting their good wishes until the *Olympia* swung out to sea; then they gave three cheers for the Stars and Stripes.

Dewey spent the next two days at Mirs Bay, assembling his fleet, distributing ammunition, and drilling his crew in target practice until the message he had been waiting for arrived from Hong Kong: "Proceed at once to Philippine Islands. Commence operations particularly against the Spanish fleet. You must capture vessels or destroy. Use utmost endeavor." On April 27, the commodore ordered his fleet to sea on one of the most important voyages in American history, a voyage that committed the country to an involvement in Asia which would stretch through the twentieth century.

There were 1,456 officers and men aboard the nine ships, and three reporters, who managed to join the expedition at the last minute. One of these journalists was an ex-naval officer named Joseph Stickney, who would become, as many reporters did during this unusual war, a combatant. The two others, John T. McCutcheon and E. W. Harden, had been accompanying the *Hugh McCulloch* on its around-the-world cruise, and Dewey reluctantly allowed them to stay with the Revenue Service cutter as long as they promised not to cable any information about his plans or movements. This was an arrangement McCutcheon scrupulously adhered to; unfortunately, Harden was less responsible. He managed to sneak a dispatch back to Hong Kong that was wired to the New York *World,* which then immediately published not only last-minute intelligence that Dewey had received about Spanish defenses and plans, but also the exact time and date that the fleet was to set sail for Manila.

The Americans used every moment to prepare for battle. The men had valor aplenty—Dewey was sure of that—but valor in modern warfare was not enough. It was "management and efficiency," just as in business, he wrote later, that made the difference between mastery or defeat in contemporary warfare. Yet along with exercising the big guns and fire-and-damage-control rehearsal, he also had his crews practice with sabers and small arms. Dewey, the man who had been trained by veterans of the War of 1812, "those heroes of the old sailing-frigates and ships of the line" as he remembered them, now was training young men who would be combat leaders in the Second World War. He was leaving little to chance, including, perhaps even hoping for, the need to board the enemy's ships and fight hand to hand. That would be a story for the nation to savor in these modern times, when machines killed at long distance.

Whatever the hopes, the battle of Manila Bay was fought modern fashion, and at a distance of five to six thousand yards. The Spanish did not take advantage of their superior knowledge of local waters to scatter and force the Americans to hunt them down, but instead anchored off Cavite, their naval base near Manila, in the hope that land-based cannon would provide protection for their aged fleet. On Sunday morning, May 1, that is where Dewey found them.

The Spanish opened fire first, but with such a wild fusillade that it was seen as a sign of panic. "Evidently the Spaniards are already rattled," Dewey said to one of his officers. He ignored the preliminary enemy salvo while steaming closer, following his hero Farragut's tactic of holding fire until sure of a target, then pouring it on. Finally he leaned over the railing of the *Olympia* and uttered the phrase that, slightly modified, would become a national byword for calmness under pressure: "You may fire when you are ready, Gridley."

The Spanish proved brave, but poorly equipped and inefficient at using what weapons they possessed. For five hours the Americans steamed back and forth exchanging fire with their enemy. At the end of that short span all the Spanish ships were burning or aground and 380 Spaniards were dead or wounded, while the only American casualties were eight sailors wounded.

The heat built up inside the ships was tremendous, with the engine rooms reaching over 150 degrees. Stokers, ammunition carriers, and gun crews had progressively stripped until some were wearing only shoes. On the *Raleigh,* a lieutenant had gone below to check on the ammunition gang and found them dressed in cut-off pieces of gunny sack, dancing a hula as they passed the powder and shells and singing a song he had never heard before: "There'll Be a Hot Time in the Old Town Tonight." Now all these grimy naked men raced on deck to cheer one another until they were hoarse. When one officer, covered in smoke stains and soot like everyone else, tried to clean himself after the battle, he was stopped by another officer: "No, don't wash your hands; no one is allowed to wash his hands. We don't go into battle every day, and we are not going to wipe off any of the smoke and dirt."

Lieutenant C. G. Calkins, an aide to Dewey, took pride in reporting that the Chinese members of the crew also "showed no fear in action and could bear comparison with any other race for cool industry and cheerful curiosity." George Dewey made a similar observation in his autobiography, perhaps hoping to counter some of the anti-Chinese prejudice in America, but when he later attempted to have some of these men admitted as immigrants, permission was denied.

That afternoon Dewey opened communications with Captain-General Don Basilio Augustín Davila. One of his requests was to use the Manila telegraph equipment to inform Washington of his victory, and when this was refused, he ordered the *Zafiro* to fish up the cable and cut it. Dewey was now on his own; the only way to contact the outside world was by sending a ship to Hong Kong to use the telegraph, and the bureaucrats in Washington would have even more difficulty in reaching him, a situation that did not dismay the commodore.

There was much still to do. His ships had to be repaired and the Spanish wounded looked after. Manila could be taken, but could not be held until American troops arrived, and he did not know what naval resources the Spanish still possessed in the islands—there were rumors of torpedo boats hiding in shallow coves, just waiting to strike at the unwary enemy. And what if, as likely, Spain sent another fleet, more modern and better led, to win back the islands?

Discreet encouragement was given to the insurgents, along with a certain amount of war-making matériel, so they could continue to pick away at the Spanish army positions ringing the capital. An immediate blockade was placed around Manila Bay to choke off the city, and all entering commercial shipping was diverted, unless it was a collier, in which case the coal was purchased for use by the fleet.

Within a few days of the victory a British warship appeared; then a French cruiser came visiting, followed by the *Itsukushima* from Japan. This was not unexpected, since the commander-in-chief understood that there would be a natural curiosity about what the Americans had achieved in the Philippines. But then the German warships began to arrive, coming into port one by one and refusing to defer to American requests to identify themselves or abide by the rules of the blockade. This was a problem Dewey would have to address over the coming weeks, along with his many others.

THE LAST THE WORLD had seen of the American Asiatic Squadron was a smudge of smoke as the ships steamed over the horizon and into the China Sea. On May 1 the Spanish government received a series of disjointed cables from the Philippines claiming that the Americans had appeared before Manila but had been driven off with heavy losses. These reports had been passed on to the international press. But then, late that same day, came a cable from the captain-general of the islands bragging that the defenders had obliged the enemy, with heavy losses, to maneuver repeatedly . . . "Our fleet, considering the enemy's superiority, naturally suffered severe loss. . . . There was considerable loss of life."

There was some initial confusion about where, exactly, all this had taken place. Even President McKinley had to rush to a globe, admitting, "I could not have told where those darned islands were within 2,000 miles." Once the problem of location was settled, the admission of a "severe loss" for the Spanish was encouragement enough for American newspapers to run headlines declaring a great victory, and the country began an excited, but temporary, celebration—crowding around newspaper offices for the latest bulletins, setting off fireworks, listening to bands play patriotic tunes. Women appeared in the streets wearing semimilitary costumes to go with the music. "One wore a blue gown with a buff stripe down each side of her skirt like the stripe on a cavalry man's trousers, a zouave jacket caught with gold frogs, which, thrown open, revealed a red, white, and blue striped waist beneath; her headgear was a campaign hat with crossed sabers over the top of the band. Another woman wore a blue gown with gold braid down the side of the skirt and a cocked hat like that of an admiral."

But after this first thrilling hint of great events, there was no more solid news, although that didn't stop William Randolph Hearst's *Journal,* and a few others, from inventing some to lend interest to their front pages. As more days passed without further word, the suspense grew. What had happened? What did "heavy loss" mean with regard to the Americans? Had Dewey lost the whole Asiatic Squadron in a desperate gamble? Or had the commodore won the battle, but at such cost that it would be a Pyrrhic victory? Why had he made no report? The headlines now began to reflect great nervousness, and fears of disaster.

DEWEY WAS TOTALLY absorbed in securing his position, as well as writing his official after-battle report, so it wasn't until Thursday, May 5, that he was ready to send his dispatches to Hong Kong. Three very impatient reporters also went along on the forty-eight-hour voyage of the *Hugh McCulloch,* each trying to figure out how to scoop the other two. Dewey had made them promise that his report would be filed first, but after that the order of precedence was up to them.

The informal contest set up a lively race to the cable office once they arrived, but it ended in a tie. Harden prevailed, however, by waiting until his rivals left after sending their stories. He then dispatched a shorter report to his newspaper, the New York *World,* giving the essentials of the battle, sending this one at the "urgent" rate of $9.90 a word instead of the press rate of $1.15 that McCutcheon and Stickney had used. Since Dewey's official report was in cipher, and therefore had to be double-checked for accuracy through repetition at each relay station, Harden managed to beat everyone by six or seven hours. A *World* reporter was able to rush to the White House before dawn on May 7 and convince a guard to awaken the president, who when told the news gave a "sigh of relief."

So great had been the tension and fear of severe losses that when the official news came that there were no Americans killed and only eight wounded in winning such a tremendous victory the nation went wild with enthusiasm, an enthusiasm that, ironically, was given added force by the very calmness Dewey was thought to have displayed. The New York *Journal* hosted a celebration in Union Square with a band, fireworks, and a hundred thousand guests. Dozens of Dewey songs immediately filled the vaudeville halls and saloons; hats, canes, jugs, plates, and silk scarves—anything that could be made to bear his mustachioed likeness—sold as fast as they could be manufactured; blacksmiths scrawled "Deweyville" over their doors to advertise their strength; "Dewey Did It, Didn't He?" was chalked on board fences along country roads; prints imaginatively recreating the battle sprouted on barroom walls, where, the denizens asserted, they improved the taste of the liquor. Mr. Dooley was moved to claim common lineage, and the newspapers were filled with proud effusions by journalists, politicians, and poets. A friend wrote to the commodore, "All the children born on the first of May are being named 'Dewey' by their parents," and there was a movement to make that date "Dewey Day."

The naval hero played another, less direct, role in children's lives, of which he was never aware. On the evening of May 7, L. Frank Baum was sitting in his Chicago parlor telling a bedtime story to his children and their friends about a Scarecrow who wished for brains and a Tin Woodman who longed for a heart. As he paused for a moment, Tweety Robbins, a young girl who lived down the street, asked:

"Oh, please, Mr. Baum! Where did the Scarecrow and the Tin Woodman live?"

Baum had not given any thought to the matter, but as he looked up his eyes were drawn to that evening's WAR EXTRA edition of the *Chicago Journal,* which declared the news of Dewey's victory in enormous headlines, and then just past the paper he noticed the bottom drawer of his filing cabinet, which was marked O–Z.

"Why," he said, grinning at the eager children, "the Scarecrow and the Tin Woodman, and the Cowardly Lion and the great Wizard, all lived in the marvelous Land of Oz!"

In New York, the filmmaker J. Stuart Blackton was frustrated by his distance from Manila Bay. Blackton was a pioneer newsreel producer, concentrating on crime and accidents in the big city. At the start of the war he had made a short entitled *Tearing Down the American Flag*, the first-ever propaganda film. When word came of the far-off victory, Blackton and his partner, Albert E. Smith, quickly bought sets of photographs of both the Spanish and American fleets, cut out the ships and mounted them on blocks of wood, then floated these armadas in a container holding an inch of water. Pinches of gunpowder were set off periodically on chosen vessels as the "action" was filmed frame by frame. The two men soon had a salable newsreel.

Scholars were also caught up in celebrating the new national hero. Princeton, Harvard, Yale, and the University of Pennsylvania conferred honorary degrees on Dewey, Penn showing an acute sensitivity to symbols: the certificate was sent to Manila in an exquisite box of Pennsylvania oak that was then wrapped in a large silk American flag, with a box of Vermont pine enclosing the whole.

In true democratic fashion, all of this popular hysteria found support among the politicians, who also wanted to share in the glory. President McKinley promoted Dewey to rear-admiral; Congress authorized a special bronze medal to be awarded to all the men who served with him and ordered Tiffany's to create a jeweled sword to be presented to the newly minted admiral in honor of the victory. And, also true to American tradition, there were proposals that Dewey should run for the presidency, some serious and some made in good humor, as when Senator Redfield Proctor teasingly wrote McKinley reminding him who had recommended Dewey to command the Asiatic Squadron: "There is no better man in discretion and safe judgment. We may run him against you for President. He would make a good one."

WHEN PRESIDENT MCKINLEY had issued his call for 125,000 volunteers he had included a special provision for three regiments "to be composed exclusively of frontiersmen possessing special qualifications as horsemen and marksmen." Secretary of War Russell Alger knew who the natural leader of such a novel military formation should be: a Republican politician of great promise who had proven himself as both horseman and marksman by ranching and hunting along the old frontier, who possessed boundless energy and the ability to lead men. The colonelcy of the First United States Volunteer Cavalry was immediately offered to Theodore Roosevelt, who demurred, but only because of his lack of experience in "military work," which might delay things so much that he and his outfit could miss the war. "I was wise enough to tell the Secretary that while I believed I could learn to command the regiment in a month . . . it was just this very month which I could not afford to spare." He proposed instead that he be appointed lieutenant-colonel, and that Leonard Wood, who knew well the bureaucratic ways of the army, become colonel of the regiment. And so it was done, although it was obvious to everyone before long that, as far as the public was concerned, this colorful outfit really belonged to Theodore Roosevelt.

Wood immediately began battling the chaotic distribution system and the red tape–obsessed bureau chiefs of the War Department to obtain uniforms, tents, horse gear, revolvers, rifles, and ammunition. The distribution system was only part of the problem. The various offices within the department were frequently headed by men Roosevelt described as "elderly incompetents," often someone who had been a gallant second lieutenant in the Civil War, but who had by now degenerated into a time-server. Being turned down by one administrator for making an "irregular" requisition, Roosevelt persisted, finally going over the man's head to have it approved by Secretary Alger himself. When he presented the signed order, the man threw himself back in his chair and exclaimed worriedly, "Oh, dear! I had this office running in such good shape—and then along came the war and upset everything!"

Leonard Wood, from his combat experiences in the Indian wars, understood the importance of using smokeless powder, an advantage Congress had long overlooked; though invented in the United States, it was not manufactured anywhere in the country. But again some of the Civil War veterans resisted. "One fine old fellow," Roosevelt remembered, "did his best to persuade us to take black powder rifles, explaining with paternal indulgence that no one yet really knew just what smokeless powder might do, and that there was a good deal to be said in favor of having smoke to conceal us from the enemy."

Thanks to the up-to-date knowledge and political influence of Roosevelt and Wood, the First Volunteer Cavalry was to be issued the modern .30 caliber, 5-shot magazine-fed Krag-Jorgensen carbine, the same arm used by the Regulars. All the other volunteer and National Guard outfits were equipped with old single-shot .45 caliber Springfield rifles using charcoal powder, which would later cost them dearly in combat. Another advantage of having the modern weapons was that it allowed Wood's Volunteers to be brigaded with the Regulars, and that meant they would be much more likely to see combat.

Leonard Wood set up headquarters at San Antonio, Texas, which was chosen as training base for the regiment because it was rich with horses and near the Gulf ports where embarkation for Cuba was bound to take place. Roosevelt stayed for several weeks at the Navy Department dealing with current matters and wrapping things up, while continuing to energize John Long, and telegraphing his well-placed railroad friends to make sure that once military officials approved requisitions for carbines, saddles, and other equipment from armories and storehouses there would be no delay in their transit to his troopers; he also put whatever spare time he had to good use saying his goodbyes to wife and children. All were healthy now, but even he must have felt some unease in leaving a growing family for the dangers of war.

Editorial writers, family, close friends, and Secretary Long all thought Roosevelt was making a terrible mistake in resigning to fight in the front lines. The *New York Sun* recognized "the instinctive glowing chivalry of his nature," but thought the nation would be better served if he stayed at his desk "organizing war." The writer Henry Adams thought he must have lost his mind. "What on earth is this report of Roosevelt's resignation? Is his wife dead? Has he quarreled with everybody? Is he quite mad?" Another friend, Winthrop Chanler, had a similar reaction: "I really think he is going mad . . . Roosevelt is wild to fight and hack and hew . . . of course this ends his political career. Even Cabot [Lodge] says this." Secretary Long, who had always looked upon his assistant with fond bewilderment, recorded his reflections about him in his diary: "He has been of great use; a man of unbounded energy and force, and thoroughly honest. . . . He has lost his head to this unutterable folly of deserting the post where he is of most service and running off to ride a horse and, probably, brush mosquitoes from his neck on the Florida sands. His heart is right, and he means well, but it is one of those cases of aberration—desertion—vainglory; of which he is utterly unaware. He thinks he is following his highest ideal, whereas, in fact, as without exception every one of his friends advises him, he is acting like a fool." But then Long stopped to consider, adding, "And, yet, how absurd all this will sound if, by some turn of fortune, he should accomplish some great thing and strike a very high mark."

Acting like a fool, perhaps, but for the man himself, as with the Cuban revolutionary José Martí and innumerable others who regarded themselves as men of honor, the issue was simple: He had preached the need for this war and, war having come, it would not be right to leave the dangerous fighting to others. "I know perfectly well that one is never able to analyze with entire accuracy all of one's motives. But . . . I have always intended to act up to my preachings if occasion arose. Now the occasion has arisen, and I ought to meet it." As for the opposition of his wife and his best friend, Henry Cabot Lodge, this was, he had earlier told President McKinley, "the one case" where he would ignore their advice or desires.

WILLIAM MCKINLEY, although he had resisted the idea of armed struggle with Spain, recognized that the surge of patriotic feeling could be used to finally end the sectional bitterness of the Civil War. Fitzhugh Lee, the ex–Confederate general who had led the last cavalry charge of that conflict at Farmville, Virginia, was now sixty-three and had lost his dashing figure, but his two years as consul in Havana had given him a good understanding of Cuba. His appointment as a major-general of volunteers made some military sense.

Appointment of Joseph "Fighting Joe" Wheeler to the same rank was more on political grounds, although he too was a graduate of West Point and had made a name for himself as a leader of Confederate cavalry, achieving the rank of lieutenant-general by the age of twenty-eight. Serving as a Democratic congressman from Alabama, he had become chairman of the House Ways and Means Committee, and it was he who had given the Rebel yell when Congress had approved the Fifty-Million-Dollar Bill. Now sixty-one years old, his white hair and beard and slight build made him look like a frail old man.

The president told him he was going to appoint fifteen new major-generals, and wanted him to be one of them.

"I am too old," Wheeler said.

"There must be a high officer from the South," McKinley argued. "There must be a symbol that the old days are gone. You are needed."

Wheeler accepted the commission.

THE STATE MILITIAS were also excited by this chance to serve the nation, but there were complications. They were under the control of the respective state governors, who were loath to surrender this source of political patronage to the national government, wanting to retain the power of nam-

"Cuba Reconciling the North and the South" (*Courtesy of the Library of Congress, photo by Fritz Guerin*)

ing the higher-ranking militia officers. The rank and file, used to electing their junior officers, also had hesitations about serving under regular army leadership, as a member of the House of Representatives pointed out in the chamber: "There is hardly a man on this floor who has not received letters from his constituents stating that they would be glad to volunteer, glad to fight for their country, if they can be officered by their home men. They want to know their officers and be officered by men who have been raised and who have lived among them."

Although part of this feeling came from genuine desire to be among "home men" whom they trusted, it also reflected a general hostility to the idea of a standing army, symbolized by the professional graduate of the military academy at West Point. A member of a Brooklyn National Guard unit spoke for many: "One of the reasons that we would not go willingly into the Regular Army is that we would have to serve under West-Pointers. For a self-respecting American of good family to serve as a private, corporal, or sergeant under a West Point lieutenant or captain is entirely out of the question. West-Pointers have seen fit to introduce a class feeling—no, I will go farther and say a caste feeling—between ourselves and non-commissioned officers and privates that is unpleasant in the extreme. . . . To fight for my country as a volunteer in the regiment that I love would be a glorious pleasure, but to serve in the Regular Army and do chores for some West-Pointer—well, I would rather be excused."

The trouble with this democratic sense of equality was that the resulting National Guard units were not military but social organizations. As William Allen White observed, they were trained only to "precede the fire company and follow the Grand Army squad in the processions on Memorial Day and the Fourth of July." The discipline and training of Regular officers was needed simply to keep them from being massacred in combat, not to speak of their becoming effective soldiers.

RECRUITING POSTS HAD magically appeared across the nation, often in empty storefronts strategically placed next to saloons, windows decorated with pictures of the *Maine* both before and after the explosion, and staffed by the local ward leader or ambitious fellows from the *Social Register*. It was the latest manifestation of a system that went back to the beginnings of war in American society: if you could recruit a platoon you became the lieutenant, a company gained a captaincy, if a regiment the men called you colonel, and you probably had a future in politics. The country was full of would-be officers and men of all classes eager to enlist for the crusade against Spain.

In Philadelphia, the grandson of wealthy financier Jay Cook resisted all entreaties from father and grandfather to stay home; he rushed to sign up, as did numerous other sons of privilege all across the country, including John Jacob Astor, reputed to be the richest man in the world.

One impatient middle-class recruit was Charles Post, who left his position as staff artist on Hearst's *Journal* to sign on with the Seventy-first New York in return for thirteen dollars a month in pay and all the hardtack biscuits he could manage to get his teeth into. At camp he learned to rise at five a.m. to the musical alarm of forty drums, twelve fifes, and twelve bugles, to march in ranks, to perform the manual of arms, and, if he didn't know how already, to drink whiskey—which flowed more easily through the camp than the piped water. "Every man had at least a brown-bottle pint at all times, which could be replenished by the newsboy bootleggers, or those of a higher category who dealt only in quarts and cases. Not to have a bottle of whiskey was simply open confession of abject poverty or poor bringing up."

Charlie Post also learned that, for all the reputed romance of soldiering, there were certain practical skills a man needed in order to survive—such as complimenting the cook no matter how bad the fare (he never had to do kitchen police), and learning how to compensate for army incompetence. He watched as Captain Malcolm Rafferty forcibly broke into a string of freight cars containing his regiment's food and equipment, necessities that were entangled in red tape. "He became, in Army law, no better than a common burglar and bandit, looter of the sacred supplies. . . . Thus we continued to eat, and official Washington gritted its teeth in formal, quintuplicate frustration."

ROOSEVELT FINALLY ARRIVED in San Antonio on the morning of May 15, his train pulling into the station where the regiment's brass band was playing its only tune, "There'll Be a Hot Time in the Old Town Tonight," a crowd of troopers waiting for him under a sign that read "This Way to Camp of Roosevelt's Rough Riders." There had been a great deal of play with alliterative nicknames—"Teddy's Terrors," "Teddy's Cowboy Contingent," and so on—before the press, knowing whom the public identified with the regiment, had adopted this one. At first it had been resisted, Roosevelt complaining to the *New York Times* that this was not "to be a hippodrome affair," but once "Generals of Division and Brigade began to write in formal communications about our regiment as the 'Rough Riders,' we adopted the term ourselves."

Although the congressional authorization had explicitly stated that the regiment should be raised in the unincorporated frontier regions of Arizona, New Mexico, Oklahoma, and the Indian Territory, Roosevelt saw this as a chance to build a military formation that would demonstrate that Americans could work together no matter what their background, class, geographical section, religion, education, or, within limits, race: a very model for the nation.

Some recruits came from elite colleges, but what Roosevelt looked for were men "in whose veins the blood stirred with the same impulse which once sent the Vikings over sea." They needed to share "the same temper" as the frontiersmen in the outfit—that is, they had to be men of action. There were athletes from Yale, Princeton, and Columbia, such as Jack Greenway, Horace Devereux, and Hamilton Fish, but also some New York policemen who had served under Roosevelt when he was police commissioner there, and Italian, Jewish, English, and Australian immigrant volunteers.

Many of the additions, however, were privileged bluebloods, and Roosevelt made sure all understood that they were to uncomplainingly pull their share of the dirty jobs. "I warned them that work that was merely irksome and disagreeable must be faced as readily as work that was dangerous." These Easterners not only added a certain sophisticated tone to the outfit but also brought more practical benefits. Woodbury Kane, William Tiffany, and some of the other New Yorkers had bought out of their own pockets two of the new Colt machine-guns.

The majority of the men were less polished, however—some of them very rough indeed—and Roosevelt was sure that "In all the world there could be no better material for soldiers than that afforded by these grim hunters of the mountains, these wild rough riders of the plains." Formed by the wilderness frontier that still existed to some extent in the Four Territories, they were unusually skillful with rifles, pistols, and horses, and hardened to the difficulties of outdoor life. They also offered living proof that the frontier, which had formed such a fundamental part of the American character, wasn't completely gone, no matter what government census clerks and historians claimed.

Some of the older Western recruits, who became captains and lieutenants, had taken part in campaigns against the Apache, Ute, and Cheyenne; others had been sheriffs or marshals in the most violent towns of the region. Most had killed men, and many bore scars from bullets, knives, and arrows. The younger recruits would benefit from the seasoning of these mature veterans of violence, although they too often bore the marks of personal combat, and a number of them had signed on using *noms de guerre* because of embarrassing encounters with the law. Some were white, some were Hispanic, some were Indian—most of whom came from the Cherokee, Chickasaw, Choctaw, and Creek tribes. Roosevelt was thrilled to discover among them names like Colbert and Adair, familiar to him from his study of frontier history.

These Americans shared the same traditional distaste for military discipline that marked their fellow-recruits to the National Guard or other volunteer units. Roosevelt remembered that one spokesman for this prejudice showed up at Colonel Wood's tent after twenty-four hours in camp and announced, "Well, Colonel, I want to shake hands and say we're with you. We didn't know how we would like you fellars at first; but you're all right, and you know your business, and you mean business, and you can count on us every time!"

In the heat, wind, dust, and mosquitos of Texas, Roosevelt set about melding this odd collection of volunteers into a disciplined fighting force, while Wood gave most of his attention to the maddening paperwork challenge of procuring their necessary equipment. The lieutenant-colonel had talked to the commander of one of the other "cowboy" volunteer cavalry outfits while still in Washington, asking him what his plans were for training his men, and the fellow had replied that all he was going to do was "give each of the boys two revolvers and a lariat, and then just turn them loose." Even without Wood, Roosevelt would have known better. He had his own men run through the basic drills first on foot, then, once the men had learned the rudiments, on horseback. There were some problems with the half-broken mounts that had just recently been rounded up on the plains, but they were solved by expedients like giving the horse "two tremendous twists, first to one side and then to the other, as it bolted, with the result that, invariably, at the second bound its legs crossed and over it went with a smash, the rider taking the somersault with unmoved equanimity."

The training went well, as did the bonding that was one of its desired results. Part of this growth of trust in one another came through the crude joking that American males have always used to deflate pretension and overcome differences, joking that includes the awarding of nicknames. "A brave but fastidious member of a well-known Eastern club," remembered Roosevelt, "who was serving in the ranks, was christened 'Tough Ike'; and his bunkie, the man who shared his shelter-tent, who was a decidedly rough cowpuncher, gradually acquired the name of 'The Dude.' . . . A huge red-headed Irishman was named 'Sheeny Solomon.' A young Jew who developed into one of the best fighters in the regiment accepted, with entire equanimity, the name of 'Pork-chop.' "

Perhaps the bonding took too strong a hold with Roosevelt, who fell in love with his outfit to a point that threatened discipline. After one particularly hot afternoon drill that left everyone choked with dust, the lieutenant-colonel halted his command at an outdoor resort called Riverside Park. Ordering them to dismount, he then shouted, "The men can go in and drink all the beer they want, which I will pay for." One trooper recalled that "Nectar never tasted as good as that beer."

The commanding officer, however, was not amused.

Leonard Wood and Roosevelt made an unusually effective team, with Wood concentrating on getting the Rough Riders properly equipped and Roosevelt guiding their training. The publicity Roosevelt received caused no problems. But Wood held strong ideas about what constituted proper military discipline, and over dinner that night he let his subordinate know "that, of course, an officer who would go out with a large batch of men and drink with them was quite unfit to hold a commission." The reprimand cast a pall over the rest of the meal, but after taking time to consider the point Roosevelt showed up at the colonel's tent. "I wish to say, sir, that I agree with what you said. I consider myself the damndest ass within ten miles of the camp. Good night."

Roosevelt certainly understood the need for traditional military discipline, but he was also a charismatic politician who knew other ways of getting men to do what he wanted. As one who never doubted his own ability to lead, and make men obey, he did not feel the need to follow all the proper forms quite so closely as regular army officers did. This would not be the last time he caused offense to the punctilious.

The men had at first been a bit wary of the Easterner. They had the Westerner's prejudice against a "four-eyes," and found his unfailing courtesy peculiar. (One remembered "he was polite almost to the extent of making one uneasy," although they were touched by his caring enough to memorize the name of every one of the thousand men in the regiment.) Roosevelt's unself-conscious habit of barking cavalry commands at thin air was startling, until they realized he was just practicing so that he could execute them properly, and they recognized his natural gift for leadership. As Edmund Morris put it, "Wood often asked advice, but seldom information;

Roosevelt asked information, but never advice." The soldiers respected Colonel Wood, who was nicknamed "Old Poker Face," but they soon regarded "Teddy" with the same affection he held for them.

The officer's mess was a particular pleasure for Roosevelt; the "tone . . . was very high" and marked by "a certain simple manliness. . . . During our entire time of service, I never heard in the officer's mess a foul story or a foul word; and though there was an occasional hard swearing in moments of emergency, yet even this was the exception." Some of the younger officers particularly impressed him. Jack Greenway had been a football and baseball star at Yale, and David Goodrich had been captain of the Harvard crew; both won commissions at San Antonio because of their intelligence, hard work, and toughness.

The skills of riding in formation and skirmishing quickly showed the rewards of intense training; less obvious were the rewards of discipline. Every night a good portion of the enlisted ranks would steal off to the rowdy pleasures of San Antonio, and sometimes serious trouble would ensue. In spite of whatever irritation some citizens might be feeling about this carousing, the city fathers decided to give an outdoor concert in honor of men likely to face combat soon. Professor Carl Beck, the German bandmaster (every city with any pretension to culture had one in the 1890s), included as a special tribute a piece entitled "Cavalry Charge" and for dramatic effect positioned a small saluting cannon in a safe place.

The Rough Riders became caught up in the spirit of the music, and at the first cannon shot one of the men shouted, "Help him out, boys!" Pistols were pulled, and a fusillade fired into the air. In the resulting chaos of screams, hurrahs, whoops, and gunshots the officers present tried to restore order, the electricity went out, and a number of troopers used the cover of darkness to sneak off to town to continue the celebration.

"I was in the Franco-Prussian War," the bandmaster proclaimed later, "and saw some hot times, but I was about as uneasy last night as I ever was in battle."

The lesson Colonel Wood was drawing from observation of his unconventional cavalry was also making him uneasy: "If we don't get them to Cuba quickly to fight Spaniards," he wrote his wife, "there is great danger that they'll be fighting one another." When, a couple of days later, a cable arrived from Washington, "Old Poker Face" was watched by everyone in the command tent as he read it. He turned and looked at Roosevelt; then the two men were "hugging each other like schoolboys, while war-whoops resounded through the camp." They were off to war.

There had been much worry in Washington over the reception troop trains might meet in the Old Confederacy, but the Rough Riders were grandly welcomed. At station after station in the small towns, local people gathered to cheer the troops. "They brought us flowers," Roosevelt recalled, "they brought us watermelons and other fruits, and sometimes jugs and pails of milk . . . the young girls drove down in bevies, arrayed in their finery, to wave flags in farewell to the troopers and to beg cartridges and buttons as mementos. Everywhere we saw the Stars and Stripes, and everywhere we were told . . . by grizzled ex-Confederates that they had never dreamed in the bygone days of bitterness to greet the old flag as they now were greeting it, and to send their sons, as now they were sending them, to fight and die under it." There had been tremendous newspaper publicity about the regiment, and several of the New York bluebloods, like Woodbury Kane and Hamilton Fish, had become national celebrities in such demand at the station stops that some of the cowboys began standing in for them. Even their popularity, however, paled in comparison to the requests for "Teddy," a nickname Roosevelt detested but would respond to from the public.

In spite of all this good spirit, it was a hard trip marred by missed connections, poor fodder for the animals, and little food for the men. At the stops, Roosevelt would be frenetically busy trying to set things in order, but on the swaying train he read Demolins' *Supériorité des Anglo-Saxons,* meditating on how his current experiences provided an ironic illustration of its message. "M. Demolins, in giving the reasons why the English-speaking peoples are superior to those of Continental Europe, lays much stress upon the way in which 'militarism' deadens the power of individual initiative, the soldier being trained to complete suppression of individual will, while his faculties become atrophied in consequence of his being merely a cog in a vast and perfectly ordered machine. I can assure . . . [him] . . . that American 'militarism' . . . has points of difference from the militarism of Continental Europe. The battalion chief of a newly raised American regiment, when striving to get into a war which the American people have undertaken with buoyant and light-hearted indifference to detail, has positively unlimited opportunity for the display of 'individual initiative,' and is in no danger whatever either of suffering from unhealthy suppression of personal will, or of finding his faculties of self-help numbed by becoming a cog in a gigantic and smooth-running machine."

As if the War Department were seeking to further develop the colonel's and lieutenant-colonel's powers of initiative, they stepped off the trains on

June 2 to find a "perfect welter of confusion." There was such a jam of freight cars that the railroad could not get them within six miles of Tampa itself, and although this was the base for the largest expedition ever to sail from American shores, no one seemed in command. Nor did anyone know where they were to camp, or drill, or even to draw food or water. Wood and Roosevelt bought food for the men out of their own pockets, commandeered some wagons to carry equipment, and set off across the sandy wastes to find a site to pitch their tents.

CHAPTER 7

WAITING FOR ORDERS

Th' ordhers fr'm Washin'ton is perfectly comprehinsible to a jackass, but they don't mane annything to a poor, foolish man.

Mr. Dooley

As DAWN APPROACHED, Lieutenant Maurer stopped trying to slip through the barrier; instead a ladder was found and propped against the Arch of the States, which enclosed the main gate. While Ensign Ewing McCormack held the ladder steady, the lieutenant, clutching a small ax, climbed resolutely up the face of the structure. By the time a guard was able to make out a dark shape against the white of the arch, it was too late; the first naked figure was within reach. Taking deliberate aim, Maurer swung her hatchet with full force against the statue, sending a large part of it smashing to the earth.

Guards now came running, and Lieutenant Dorothy Maurer of the Salvation Army was coaxed down from her perch, still clutching the telltale instrument of crime; both she and Ensign McCormack were arrested for malicious mischief. But there were no regrets, since it had been done for a noble cause. When challenged by a reporter at the police station, Maurer replied firmly, "I knew that I was doing right. It is our duty as Salvationists to go into the very depths of hell if necessary to save souls. We go into the dives of cities to raise the sinners out of the mire. Never in any place have I seen anything so disgraceful as those statues, even in Chicago, where I lived. It was not for myself, but for thousands of young people that I decided to destroy the statues. I tried to get into the grounds last night, but

154

failed. If I had not been disturbed I would have chopped every statue in pieces."

Lieutenant Maurer, of course, was not a serious threat to the Trans-Mississippi Exposition—war was. When it became obvious that there would be a declaration against Spain, some faint hearts in Nebraska thought the fair would have to be canceled or postponed. A local newspaper wrote, "Everybody thinks of war, talks of war and dreams of war in these times." Who would travel to Omaha with worries about kinfolk and the country riding on their backs? Wouldn't the newspapers be too crowded with news of the fighting, and depressing lists of casualties, to give any promotional space to the exhibition? And Congress, beset with greater immediate needs for government money, was balking at funding the Indian Congress, expected to be the biggest draw of the whole exposition.

But others pushed ahead with irrepressible optimism, the very definition of a Western booster; "The war with Spain isn't going to last forever!" went their argument. "And a little thing like a war with Spain isn't going to distract the American people from a big thing like the Trans-Mississippi Exposition." It opened on the designated day of June 1 with President McKinley demonstrating again the powers of technology, pushing a button at his desk in the White House that sent a charge along Western Union telegraph wires to start the fair's power plant running.

Twenty thousand visitors came crowding through the Arch of the States onto the elaborately landscaped grounds, oohing and ahing at the fountains and huge, many-columned buildings that spread around the half-mile-long lagoon called the Grand Canal. Just as at the Chicago Columbia Exhibition of 1893, the fantasy was that of a classical city: gleaming white, spaciously laid out, monumental staircases leading to porticos, with carvings and statues, more than a few of them nude, also decorating roofs and facades. Overlooking all from the golden-domed government building was a gigantic figure of "Liberty Enlightening the World," from whose torch shone a powerful searchlight at night.

So large was the fair, and so filled with fascinating objects, that it took more than one or two visits for people to understand what they were seeing.

A journalist overheard a "worthy country dame" enthusing to a friend:

"There is one building," she said, "it's jest beautiful; and the statues on it look lovely 'gainst the sky—"

"What building?" her friend asked.

"Why, I dunno 'zactly the name, it's 'bout the middle. On the lagoon.

Maybe it's the Agriculture; no, I guess it's the Manufactures. It's 'bout the middle. And the statues, they're ahead of everything!"

"What are they—what are they doing?"

"Well, now, I really didn't notice; but it's a man driving—I *guess* he's a-driving; and some folks trying to stop him—maybe's a runaway!"

Most visitors were paying closer attention to the statues. As the *Omaha World-Herald* gratefully pointed out, "had it not been for Lieutenant Dorothy's little escapade . . . thousands of people would never have thought of looking at the little nude Cupids and the females clad in Mother Eve's fig-leaf costumes." As it was, one of the most publicized and popular exhibits was a painting of a young girl posing for an art class in Paris. Within a few hours of the exposition's opening, over a thousand people paid admission for the risqué thrill of viewing it.

More serious displays were also popular. All nineteen states of the Trans-Mississippi region as well as the three territories sponsored exhibits, plus twelve states from the East. A particular success was the Minnesota "cottage" of hewn logs that featured details of life in a northwoods camp, with traps, skins, and guns on the walls; states balking at the expense of building their own exhibit could place their products in the "theme" halls: Agricultural, Apiary, Mines and Mining, Manufacturing, and the Dairy building, where busts of Admiral George Dewey and William Jennings Bryan, sculpted from large blocks of butter by Mrs. Caroline Brooks, were proudly on display. Oregon bragged of its timber resources, showing off one piece of fir ninety feet long and four feet square; Los Angeles County provided such an abundance of fruit that one writer admitted it "would of itself crowd the average county fair entirely out of showing. All the California fruits—raisins, dates, oranges, peaches, plums, grapes, cherries, apples, pears, melons—appear to grow to perfection in this county."

Attracting great interest was Mines and Mining, with exhibits, including a miniature gold mine, proving "the extraordinary diversity as well as the colossal amount of wealth of the Trans-Mississippi states underground." Just passing quickly through the building in a rickshaw or wheeled chair provided a tantalizing "spectacle of wealth." One could also cruise the Grand Canal in a gondola manned by white-clad sailors, although a jarring note was the huge snorting and puffing swan, flying an American flag from its tail, that wandered among the graceful black shapes of the gondolas, leaving "an odor of naphtha in its track."

Providing other spectacles was the Midway. There were thrilling wild animal acts (one lion was billed as having slain five trainers in five years);

Miss Ita Moluki, a hula-hula dancer; a free ride in one of the electric battery-powered automobiles that the Montgomery Ward catalogue company had bought as a novelty earlier in the year; and Thomas Alva Edison's "Wargraph," showed pictures of the battle of Manila and the shelling of Fort Matanzas, Cuba. A native of that island was Chiquita, "The Living Doll," a 26-inch midget from Havana; there were also vivid patriotic cycloramas of the Civil War, and the destruction of the *Maine*. A local judge had caused some trouble for the "Streets of Cairo" section by forbidding the "dance du ventre" or "any dance of an immoral character or anything subversive of good morals." But, though tamer and more "decent" than the Chicago fair's original, which had introduced America to Little Egypt's belly dance, the Midway offered excitement enough for an editor of the *South Omaha Stockman*:

> We saw the Casino, took in the chamber of horrors at the Moorish temple, took seltzer and lemon at the German village . . . shot the chutes until our hair turned gray . . . yelled ourselves hoarse at the Mexican bull fight in the Wild West show, tore around the curves on the Scenic railway until our dickeys, ties and heads were all awry, wondered at the marvelous exhibition of the Flying Lady . . . got the farthest above terra firma in the Giant See-Saw we ever expect to be, slid down the shoot the shoots at lightning speed and got out without a drop of water on us . . . saw the fall of Babylon pictured in a work of art, heard the roar of cannon at the bombardment of Matanzas . . . and even tried McVicker's Haunted Swing.

The West would gain from the exhibition more than just entertainment. The beautiful buildings would inspire a generation of village carpenters, Alice French believed, although they might "go wild at first, and there will be queer things in Southern and Western architecture. But the end will justify his quest for beauty. The time is coming when Americans of all classes will be a beauty-loving people. They will love it with some of the ardor which they now spend on the getting of money. Then our art will be the expression of no copied raptures or borrowed ideals, but of the yearning and the needs and the hopes of our own soul."

Classical design and sense of order were proof, an enthusiastic William Allen White thought, that here too, out on the windswept plains, was "Anglo-Saxon" civilization of a high order. "The temples that stand there are erected to appease the gods of the latter days, the gods of machinery, electricity, the liberal arts, and all their kith and kin. . . . At the very least the miracle of this Omaha Exposition, rising in what but yesterday seemed one of the earth's waste places, should strengthen the faith of Anglo-Saxons in the potency of their race and its institutions. . . . This civilization is not crumbling." It was Democracy that had provided the energy to build all this, and "Democracy may hold in its essence the vital element which may spread beauty over the world as widely as Democracy has spread commerce. . . . It is not phantasmagoria to imagine that when Democracy has conquered all the continents it can subdue, and the islands of the eastern and western seas, it will spend its energy making these domains things of beauty."

Fear of the cost of such conquests may help explain the extraordinary popularity of a morbid attraction called "Cabaret de la Mort." A reporter from the *Omaha World-Herald* admitted that while "the idea of drinking and eating off of coffins and being served by pretty widows was not fascinating, the reality was far from being horrible. A monk guides the way into the infernal region. . . . St. Peter was on guard at the gate. . . . After climbing the golden stairs of a beautiful grotto of gold, radiant under brilliant electric effects . . . [it] left an impression long to be remembered." Women were particularly drawn to the "Cabaret," making up six thousand of the eight thousand people who attended it during its first nine days.

"THIS WAS," Richard Harding Davis wrote, "the rocking chair period of the war. It was an army of occupation, but it occupied the piazza of a big hotel." That was the Tampa Bay Hotel, part of which served as the command headquarters of the army. A five-story pile of bricks that had been given an exotic "Moorish" look with silver minarets and arabesques over the doors and windows, it had been built in 1891 by Henry Plant, who had great hopes for Tampa as a railroad terminus. So great were these hopes that his pleasure palace spread over six acres of lush gardens, sporting peacocks as well as a golf course and an indoor swimming pool; its halls and five hundred rooms were decorated with over a million dollars' worth of tapestries, furniture, and sculpture imported from Europe.

Less impressive was the town and the surrounding barren expanse of palmetto, scrub pine, and brush. "A city composed of derelict houses and drifting in an ocean of sand," is how one reporter described it, "a dreary city where the sand has swept the paint from the houses, and where sand swamps the sidewalks and creeps into the doors and windows." It was in this sea of sand that the troops had to pitch their tents, eat their food, and, if they were lucky enough to have responsible officers, train.

The government was having trouble deciding what to do. Initial caution had given way after Dewey's astonishing victory to more ambitious plans. Tampa had been chosen when a limited invasion of Cuba, involving only ten thousand troops, had been envisioned; now in early June there were twenty-five thousand men milling about the area, and more on the way. Only two single-track railroads serviced Tampa, and then one single-track railway ran the nine miles between the city and Port Tampa, where there was only one wharf to load equipment and troops onto ships.

The logistics were a nightmare. Railroad sidings for fifty miles inland were jammed with freight cars, and the officials in charge of loading those cars had neglected to note their contents on invoices or on their exteriors. Officers had to break into them and rummage for weapons, ammunition, uniforms, canned goods; even the breeches of artillery pieces had been lost in the jumble. "No words can paint the confusion," Theodore Roosevelt lamented to his diary after the Rough Riders' arrival, "No *head;* a break-down of both the railroad and military system of the country." Optimistic dates of departure for the expedition would be set, then postponed.

In nominal charge of this chaotic mess was Major-General William Rufus Shafter. Shafter had been a hero in his youth, having won the Medal of Honor during the Civil War, and was reputed to possess a quick mind. But whatever talents the man could boast were now housed in an ungainly, and decidedly unheroic, body. Weighing somewhere around three hundred pounds, the general was so limited in mobility that one of his officers observed he "couldn't walk two miles in an hour, just beastly obese." Jour-nalists watching him try to heave his bulk up the grand stairway at the Tampa Bay Hotel were not impressed, nor were these young men charmed by his coarse manners and lack of recognition of their importance. He seemed proof to them of the sins of the seniority system as well as of their seniors in general.

Weighing just as heavily on Shafter as his excess pounds was his lack of experience in handling large masses of men and material. Although this failing was true of almost all the general officers, for the army had been just as starved of allocations for equipment, men, and manuevers as the navy, Shafter did nothing to compensate for the unfamiliarity of the task before him. Little was done to bring order out of chaos; clear lines of authority were not drawn to help his officers understand their tasks; and he often seemed befuddled by the sheer number of important details needing his attention. There was no clearly understood plan of operations to guide the staff.

Well over a hundred journalists crowded the scene, all of them searching for stories and mainly playing positive angles. Everyone, from foreign military attachés to the most cynical of journalists, was impressed with the regular army soldiers. The artist Frederic Remington, who was to both write about and draw the war, was struck by the stern, strong faces of the older officers. Size impressed one British reporter: "The men of the regular army seemed to grow in stature as you looked at them. At the first glance they were fine men, but after you had met a strapping fellow at every turn, at every moment of the day for a week, a conviction of their great size and strength had been beaten into your head by reiteration." Richard Harding Davis agreed, but added that they also knew their profession, being "as fine a looking body of soldiers as can be seen in any of the continental regiments. . . . Whether it was . . . artillerymen firing imaginary shrapnel at imaginary foes, or the doughboys in skirmish line among the roots of the palmettoes, or at guard mounting, or the cavalrymen swimming their horses, with both horse and man entirely stripped for action, the discipline was so good that it obtruded itself; and the manner in which each man handled his horse or musket, and especially himself, made you proud that they were American soldiers, and desperately sorry there were so few of them."

So few of them compared to the ragtag regiments of volunteers. Visiting the camps of green recruits from Florida, Michigan, Alabama, and Ohio gathered together under the command of General Fitzhugh Lee, Davis was depressed by their shortage of proper equipment. But even more alarming was the lack of common sense, evident everywhere. What uniforms and shoes they possessed "are dangerous to health and comfort" because they were poorly designed for the tropics and shoddily made by contractors interested only in a quick buck. The spirit of the men was excellent, but would spirit be enough? A colonel of the Florida contingent told Davis that a third of his men had never fired a gun. Their camps were organized with little regard for health, without proper drainage and with the latrines and refuse dumps sited to windward. When Davis pointed out all the unnecessary discomforts that the volunteers were suffering a Michigan colonel, who was a politician in civilian life, waved the criticism off. "Oh, well," he said, "they'll learn. It will be a good lesson for them." This seemed to be the only kind of lesson that would be offered; one commanding officer didn't have his men practice skirmishing because the terrain around his camp was too rough and uneven with roots, rocks, and hollows, all the difficult irregularities of a straggling pine grove, as if he expected Cuba to be as smooth as Main Street during the Fourth of July parade. Davis found a generational reason for the ineptitude: "I am pretty tired of . . . incompetent warriors. Those who know are too old to care, and those who know and care are too young to have authority."

Davis had a hard time deciding what to do about the blunders he saw. "I cannot decide whether to write anything about it or not," he confessed to his family. "I cannot see where it could do any good, for it is the system that is wrong—the whole volunteer system, I mean." In spite of his qualms, he ended up publishing a fierce attack on the incompetence of the officers of volunteer regiments, urging the president to appoint regular army officers to command positions in them. Davis was the first correspondent to deal seriously with these dangerous conditions, but even he ignored the more alarming incompetencies of the War Department. When Poultney Bigelow wrote such an exposé for *Harper's Weekly,* Davis, who detested Bigelow, attacked him for providing moral aid to the enemy, concluding his criticism, "That some official action will be taken in regard to this article is generally believed. Every one knows that mistakes have been made and that the condition of the volunteers is bad, but this is no time to print news of such a nature, and it is certainly not the time now, or later, to print reckless and untrue statements concerning our regular army." Davis defended his own article by explaining that he had complained only of errors that could be remedied, while Bigelow had both lied and broadened the attack. "There's lots to be written after the war is over but we're such a happy go lucky people that it won't matter."

AMONG THE MALE journalists were two women, Mrs. Kathleen Blake Watkins, who wrote for the *Toronto Mail and Express,* and Anna Northend Benjamin, a freelance writer for magazines such as *Harper's Weekly.* Though diligent and ambitious, they received less than a warm welcome from the military or their brothers of the press. Women had worked on newspapers for years, and some, like Nellie Bly, had achieved a measure of fame. Both Hearst and Pulitzer had used women reporters in Havana earlier in the year, but now the nation was at war, and these women were trying to be war correspondents, the most exciting, glamorous, best-paying position of journalism. The presence of female reporters was seen as an affront, if not to the men's sense of importance, then to their sincere desire to protect womankind from the unseemliness of real life. Even the gifted editor Arthur Brisbane, who believed himself something of an advocate for women's rights, felt the female reporters were pushing things too far. "Every beautiful newspaperwoman declared that of all mankind she was best adapted to enter Havana in disguise, interview Blanco, get his views on the war and on the enterprise of her newspaper, and return unscathed," he wrote. "Many tears were shed and much deep, indignant breathing was done by those heroic female reporters because no important newspaper would allow women to risk their lives even for the sake of news-getting."

Though patronized by the other correspondents, Watkins and Benjamin quickly showed that they were not to be taken lightly; both dug out previously untold stories, made important connections with informed officers, and ended up impressing the doubters. As one said about Kathleen Watkins, "By gosh, for a five-card draw she's hot stuff. There's steam comes out of her boots all the time, and the whole Chicago fire brigade couldn't put her out. The woman's special in the game with both feet. She's one of the boys." Watkins told her fellow journalists that she was not content to cover just Tampa. "I know what you think. You think it ridiculous my being here, you are laughing at my wanting to go; that's the worst of being a woman. But just let me tell you, I'm going through to Cuba, and not all the old generals in the old army are going to stop me." The generals tried, but didn't succeed; both Kathleen Watkins and Anna Benjamin managed to reach the island.

THE PRESS WAS fascinated by at least one volunteer outfit that was believed to be as good as the Regulars. The Rough Riders joined with other cavalry regiments to put on a special show of their horsemanship and new military skills up on Tampa Heights, the sandy pine-covered flats just inland from the sea; Richard Harding Davis escorted Edith Roosevelt, who had come down from Washington to bid her husband farewell, and several foreign military attachés to watch. "It was a wonderful sight to see two thousand of these men advancing through the palmettoes, the red and white guidons fluttering at the fore, and the horses sweeping onward in a succession of waves, as though they were being driven forward by the wind." As homage to their knightly ancestry there was a charge of one half against the other, and a mock battle with swords cutting gleaming curves in bright sunshine, the colorful Rough Riders using exotic Cuban machetes rather than the government-issue saber.

Davis recognized that, for all its glory redolent of chivalry, this scene of charging, swirling horsemen was of the past. "There will be few such chances again to see a brigade of cavalry advancing through a forest of palms in a line two miles long, and breaking up into skirmishes and Cossack outposts, with one troop at a trot and another at a walk, and others tearing, cheering through the undergrowth, their steel swords flashing over their heads and the steel horse-shoes flashing underfoot."

Davis was more of a prophet than he knew; just a few hours after taking part in this splendid spectacle, Wood and Roosevelt were informed that, because of lack of space on the transports, Shafter had decided that the Rough Riders, as well as the other cavalry units, would not be taking their horses to Cuba. Almost immediately a wit started calling the regiment Wood's Weary Walkers.

ENLISTED MEN DID NOT have access to the comforts of the Tampa Bay Hotel, and for many of them life in the out-of-doors was difficult. A hapless recruit from New York managed to encounter most of the possible miseries on his very first day in camp, where, Kathleen Watkins reported, he was "bitten by mosquitoes, stung by a tarantula, had a touch of malaria, ran his bayonet into his hand, sat down on a giant ants' nest, trod on an alligator, found a snake in his boot, and said he felt like a dirty deuce in a new deck."

Decks, new and old, were important for passing what free time they had. Poker was a favorite with most, and Mexican Monte came a close second with Westerners. But a new game had been learned from the black teamsters and the men of the Ninth and Tenth Cavalry, the only African-American cavalry regiments: craps. None of the white Northerners had seen it before they arrived in Florida, but after watching the players "bending in close groups over a poncho or blanket in the shade of a wagon and hoarsely cajoling the dice," they took it up so enthusiastically that, Charles Post of the Seventy-first New York continues, "before we embarked from Tampa, even the soda-water counters and ice-cream stands just beyond camp had a layout chalked on a poncho, with a soldier running the crap bank."

Places like Last Chance Street in Port Tampa served as their luxury resorts, with black women cooking delicious fried chicken over little clay stoves, and tent-saloons with a canvas awning in front sheltering a bar made of a couple of planks laid between barrels. These were tended by men wearing collarless white shirts who served only whiskey with a beer chaser, whiskey for getting there quicker, beer to help cool a parched throat. Crowds of soldiers, for many of whom this really was the last chance, waded through the hot, deep sand of the street eyeing the women standing behind each bartender, women who were willing to step into the tent for a price. The most popular attraction was a raw-lumber structure disguised behind a sign that read "Restaurant," where men waited in line until one of the doors would open and a woman's arm appear and beckon.

Post and his buddies had been fascinated by their ride through the South, although they were surprised when their train had been deliberately shunted around Richmond, the old capital of the Confederacy, because the government was unsure what their reception would be, given the resentment still lingering from the Civil War. But as the Seventy-first New York moved through this new, strange landscape, stopping in the welcoming small towns, it became more and more obvious that patriotic fever was as strong here as it was in the North. Few of these Northerners had ever traveled far from home, and they were charmed by the differences and the graciousness of the local folks.

Less charming was the racism they found once they reached their base. Black troopers of the Ninth Cavalry, as well-disciplined Regulars, had been appointed Provost Guard, which meant they acted as military police, rounding up drunks and those without passes in town. This shocked the people of Lakeland, near the preliminary training post for the Seventy-first before the outfit was moved thirty miles east to Tampa.

The local sheriff asked Post a question about New York City that had been preying on his mind. "Well, d'ya ever have niggra cops rounding you up an' throwin' you in the jug—like here?" He went on to say, "Well, it's sort of disturbin' to the folks around here to see niggras arrestin' you white folk."

Post tried to convince him that in the army it was the authority of the uniform and insignia of rank that mattered, not who wore it.

But the sheriff wasn't buying any such argument. "It ain't natural. . . . Yes, it shore don't seem right for a niggra on a horse to be herdin' up white folks, even if they is in the Army." And he told Post that if he, or any other white soldier, wanted to punch one of "these black bastards on a horse" and needed help, "I'm tellin' you jest you holler for it an' you'll be gettin' aplenty quicker'n scat. Us folk is with you boys every time."

THE TARGET OF THE American invasion of Cuba had changed several times, but now it seemed certain that Admiral Pascual Cervera y Topete's fleet had taken refuge in the port city of Santiago de Cuba on the southeast coast of the island, where it continued to pose a threat. If it somehow slipped out and evaded the American blockade it could create havoc on the East Coast, or on an invasion fleet. A courageous attempt by volunteers, led by Lieutenant Richmond P. Hobson, to sink an old collier across a narrow part of the port's twisting channel had failed; Admiral William Thomas Sampson then bombarded the defenses of the city on the morning of June 6, causing great damage, but he cabled Washington that same day: "If 10,000 men were here, city and fleet would be ours within forty-eight hours. Every consideration demands immediate army movement. If delayed, city will be defended more strongly by guns taken from the fleet."

President McKinley was already impatient; having gone to war reluctantly, he wanted it ended as quickly as possible. This eagerness explains some of the chaos of the first two months of the war effort. Efficiency of preparations did not matter as much as quickly putting an army in the field to threaten Spain's vulnerable colonies in the Caribbean and western Pacific because such a force would pressure the mother country to sue for peace. And if Cervera's fleet could be destroyed, captured, or securely bottled up in Santiago, then Spain would have lost the power to wage offensive warfare; the Atlantic coastal cities would be safe and Cuba and Puerto Rico could be plucked at leisure.

Loading of supplies had continued through the first week of June, but slowly, partly because of the sheer number of freight cars jammed into the yards, some of which started being held as far away as Charleston, South Carolina, to free up some space. The telegrams from Washington became more and more impatient and caustic, asking why, with thousands of men available, the cars couldn't be unloaded faster. But there was another source of delay: the two rival railroad companies that owned the only routes into Tampa were fighting over who would control this incredibly profitable government business. The Plant System, founded by the same entrepreneur who built the Moorish hotel, owned the one track running into Port Tampa, and this group refused to let the competitor's trains pass over it until Shafter threatened to take the system under military control.

The fact that much had been loaded at all was due to the dedicated officers and men who worked through the nights sorting ammunition, rations, and equipment and forming them into packets that could be issued to the troops. As this activity went on it was discovered that there was not as much space on the ships as had been thought. Already the cavalry units had been told that they could not bring their horses, but the Rough Riders were then informed that only eight of their twelve troops could take part in the expedition.

This was an even greater blow than the loss of the horses. Wood and Roosevelt, as they announced the decisions on who was to go or stay, had to endure the sight of men inconsolably weeping as they argued why they should not be left behind. One of the captains chosen to go was Maximilian Luna, commander of Troop F, from New Mexico. "The Captain's people," Roosevelt explained, "had been on the banks of the Rio Grande before my forefathers came to the mouth of the Hudson or Wood's landed at Plymouth; and he made the plea that it was his right to go as a representative of his race, for he was the only man of pure Spanish blood who bore a commission in the army, and he demanded the privilege of proving that his people were as loyal Americans as any others."

In the early evening of June 7 General Shafter received a series of peremptory telegrams from his superiors demanding that he finish final loading of his ships and sail for Cuba immediately, even if only with a force of ten thousand men "as you are needed at destination at once." It was explained that "Sampson says he had practically reduced fortifications, and only awaits your arrival to occupy Santiago." If the situation in Cuba was that favorable, then it wouldn't be too dangerous to leave equipment and men behind, ran the argument. Shafter agreed, wiring Alger, "I expect to have 834 officers, 16,154 men on transports by daylight, and will sail at that hour." Then the commanding general put the word out to the regiments: get on the ships or be left in camp.

That knowledge, no matter the exact language, swept through the sandy camps like a hot wind, beginning a rush that turned into, as one writer says, a "slow motion stampede." If M. Demolins, the French writer on Anglo-Saxon initiative, had been able to witness the frantic scramble for trains and ships, he would have felt all his philosophy vindicated. The Rough Riders were able to cover the nine miles of sand and swamp that separated Tampa from Port Tampa only by seizing a coal train that was passing in the wrong direction and forcing the crew to steam it backwards along the single track. Charles Post, whose own outfit solved its transportation problem by capturing another regiment's train at the points of their bayonets, had just hopped a freight car. "There came a waving and halloing far up the track. A train was approaching, and in the open door of a boxcar was Teddy, Colonel Theodore Roosevelt, grinning as his car passed our lines of flatcars [on a siding]. His khaki uniform looked as if he had slept in it—as it always did. He wore the polka-dot blue bandanna that was the hallmark of the Rough Riders. The rest of our army wore red bandannas."

Confusion was greatest on the pier. Roosevelt and Wood, after frantic searching through "this swarming ant-heap of humanity" for someone in charge, finally heard that the *Yucatan,* which was still waiting in mid-channel, had been assigned to three regiments, including theirs. Wood jumped in a launch, went out, and brought the ship in while Roosevelt "ran at full speed" to the train and double-quicked the Rough Riders back as the *Yucatan* came to the quay, arriving just in time "to hold her against the Second Regulars and the Seventy-first, who had arrived a little too late, being a shade less ready than we were in the matter of individual initiative." Roosevelt listened to a "good deal of expostulation," but his final argument was conclusive: "Well," he said with a toothy smile, "we seem to have it." The Seventy-first evidently did not consider using bayonets against the Rough Riders as they had to seize the train, but instead marched off to find another vessel less strongly held.

After dispatching work parties to bring aboard the regiment's gear, Roosevelt was leaning on the *Yucatan's* railing surveying his field of recent victory when he spotted Albert Smith and Jim Blackton standing in some confusion by an enormous tripod and camera. Having filmed the Seventy-first New York entraining for Tampa, they had decided to follow the regiment through the campaign. Now they were at the ship assigned, but the Seventy-first was not.

The curious Rough Rider called to them, "What are you men up to?"

"We are the Vitagraph Company, Colonel Roosevelt, and we are going to Cuba to take moving pictures of the war."

Before they fully understood what was happening, Smith and Blackton were being escorted up the gangplank while a beaming lieutenant-colonel told them, "I can't take care of a regiment, but I might be able to handle two more." As Smith commented later, Roosevelt's "zeal for publicity was alive and roaring."

Dabney Royster of Tennessee, one of the young boys who had been more or less adopted by the Rough Riders, managed, probably with their help, to sneak himself, a .22 caliber rifle, and three boxes of ammunition on board the *Yucatan.* The lad's desire to be under fire was undoubtedly lauded by the officers, but when discovered he was put ashore with his weaponry, weeping bitterly. Elsewhere on the transports there were other underage youths who were more successfully hidden.

Finally, it seemed, the time to go to war had come. As if to serve as a reminder of what accompanied the glory, a large shipment of gleaming, newly varnished coffins arrived on the dock and were stacked there for contemplation. The first-loaded ships set off down the channel; at four thirty in the afternoon General Shafter heaved himself aboard the *Seguranca,* and immediately sent a dispatch boat to order all the transports to return and anchor as close to the wharf as possible. Rumors were soon jumping from ship to ship that Cervera had managed to escape from Santiago, and that Spanish cruisers had been sighted just off Port Tampa.

Six days of miserable discomfort followed, the overloaded transports anchored just a short way out in the channel, with the men packed like sardines, no fresh meat or vegetables available or any way to cook the only rations available: "horrible stuff called 'canned fresh beef,' Roosevelt remembered. "At the best it was stringy and tasteless; at the worst it was nauseating. Not one-fourth of it was ever eaten at all, even when the men became very hungry."

LAST CHANCE STREET was put to the torch. "From the deck," wrote Charles Post, "we watched the burning of that sandy street in Tampa, that street of bartender-and-girl tents, together with the greater blaze made by the raw wood 'Restaurant.' How it started, no one knew. Perhaps . . . it had been started by angry soldiers. Perhaps by an overturned lamp in some brawl. The little tents flared quickly and were gone like the puffed-out candles on a birthday cake. But the 'Restaurant' blazed and burned in the night breeze like an irritated torch."

That no one knew the cause on board the transports, nor even about the fire itself very far from Tampa, shows the effectiveness of military censorship. Two black regiments, perhaps in response to rumors of white volunteers mistreating a young African-American boy, attacked the buildings along Last Chance Street, firing their guns, destroying the tent saloons, and raping the prostitutes. The Provost Guard and Tampa police, unable to control the situation, called in the Second Georgia Volunteer Infantry, a white regiment, and by daybreak the riot was quelled, at the cost of twenty-seven black troopers and several whites hospitalized.

THOUSANDS OF MEN suffered through sweltering heat during the wasted days swinging at anchor. Finally the navy was able to establish that the reported sighting had been an illusion: there were no Spanish ships at large. On June 14 the fleet began to move down Tampa Bay toward the open sea.

Charles Post and the Seventy-first had found berths on board the *Vigilancia,* another of the stubby, single-stack coastal steamers that were all the army, coming late to the ship-chartering competition, had been able to hire to carry its troops. On board were the same inadequate rations, disgusting water, and high spirits that could be found throughout the fleet. Over the weeks of training and enduring such hardships, these men too had learned to trust one another, bonding into a solid unit—and giving each other nicknames. Post was "Four-eyes," or "Doc," since he wore glasses. Time they passed as best they could, some carving skulls and crossbones or Cuban flags on their pipes, some reading or playing cards, others trying to guess if their destination was San Juan, Puerto Rico, or Santiago de Cuba, but the most popular activity, on every ship, was singing the songs that had been an important part of their social education—"Comrades," "Little Annie Rooney," "Sweet Marie," "Bill Bailey," "I Don't Like No Cheap Man," and dozens of others, including, of course, "Hot Time in the Old Town Tonight"—songs, Post recalled, that were "bawdy, some tender with easy sentiment, and some rather rugged." Each man had memorized every word; "Not to know the popular songs of the day, whether one could sing or not, was the mark of an illiterate."

Although there was no room on board the *Yucatan* for drill or skirmishing, Wood and Roosevelt kept the officers and men studying tactics. Many of the Rough Riders, being from the Great Plains, had never seen the ocean and were enthralled by the watery expanse in which they found themselves. One couldn't believe it was undrinkable, until he tried it; another, "who had never . . . before seen any water more extensive than the headstream of the Rio Grande," complained to a friend when a gust of wind caught him unawares, "Oh-oh, Jim! Ma hat blew into the creek!"

The former assistant secretary of the navy kept a professional eye on the naval escort, which had been greatly strengthened after the scare. He had always been fascinated by "the frail, venomous-looking torpedo boats," which were ordinarily towed, but once a "strange ship steamed up too close, and instantly the nearest torpedo boat was slipped like a greyhound from the leash, and sped across the water toward it; but the stranger proved harmless, and the swift, delicate, death-fraught craft returned again."

The foreign military and naval attachés aboard the *Seguranca* also had their eyes on these "death-fraught craft," and would then turn and regard the loose, informal collection of lighted transports that sometimes stretched for twenty miles across the startling blue of the Caribbean. A British navy officer was amazed at Shafter's lack of concern about torpedo boats. "Had any of these made an attack on the fleet spread over an enormous area, each ship a blaze of lights and with bands playing at times, a smart Spanish officer could not have failed to inflict a very serious loss." John Black Atkins, a British journalist, shared the surprise, as he wrote after the war: "Perhaps no nation but Spain would have allowed us a passage unmolested. Every night the fleet straggled over some fifteen miles of sea. . . . If only the Spaniards had launched the most ill-devised engine of destruction from the coast against our fragile walls. One expected it of them so keenly that one almost repented their negligence."

Roosevelt didn't worry about such dangers, enjoying the beauty of the voyage and feeling confident and proud of the undertaking. "Today we are steaming southward through a sapphire sea, wind-rippled, under an almost cloudless sky," he wrote his wife one day out. "Last evening we stood up on the bridge and watched the red sun sink and lights blaze up on the ships, for miles ahead and astern, while the band played piece after piece, from 'The Star Spangled Banner,' at which we all rose and stood uncovered, to 'The Girl I Left Behind Me.' But it is a great historical expedition, and I thrill to feel that I am part of it. If we fail, of course we share the fate of all who do fail, but if we are allowed to succeed (for we certainly shall succeed, if allowed) we have scored the first great triumph in what will be a world movement." A movement toward democracy and liberty under the tutelage of a country now stepping from its traditional isolation onto the world stage.

Death had already begun to make its appearance in the slow-moving convoy as horses and mules brought along for use in pack trains succumbed, their carcasses thrown overboard to float beside the steamers. As journalist Stephen Bonsal pointed out, "Evidently the plan pursued of loading the horses into the stifling holds of the ships a week before sailing is not proving a very great success."

And so the six-day voyage passed—the men half-starved, drinking rancid water, and singing their favorite songs under a cloudless tropic sky—the music drifting from ship to ship across a beautiful azure sea strewn with the bloated corpses of horses and mules.

CHAPTER 8

THE REAL THING

"But to get the real thing!" cried Vernall, the war-correspondent. "It seems impossible! It is because war is neither magnificent nor squalid: it is simply life, and an expression of life can always evade us. We can never tell life, one to another, although sometimes we think we can."

Stephen Crane

We hoped, and we feared: and we hoped we would not fear.

Private Charles Post

All men who feel any power of joy in battle know what it is like when the wolf rises in the heart.

Colonel Theodore Roosevelt

THE OREGON HAD SET a record steaming from California down the west coast of South America and through the Strait of Magellan. Off Brazil, a lone figure on a small sailboat named the *Spray* sighted its powerful form speeding north. Captain Joshua Slocum, completing the first solo voyage ever made around the world, saw "first a mast with the Stars and Stripes floating from it, rising astern as if poked up out of the sea, and then rapidly appearing on the horizon, like a citadel, the *Oregon!*" Slocum, so long at sea, learned that his country was at war with Spain. "Let us," Slocum signaled back, "keep together for mutual protection," but the great ship sped on, leaving the lone sailor with nightmares of giant yellow enemy flags looming over his frail craft.

The *Oregon* arrived in the Caribbean in time to help bottle up the Spanish fleet in Santiago de Cuba's harbor. This was seen as such a great achievement of American technology and naval skill that it was widely celebrated in song and doggerel, but although the battleship's thirteen-inch guns were a welcome addition to the fleet, the real importance of the voyage was the lesson it taught about defense needs. What if a more modern and efficient foe had engaged Admiral Sampson's force before the *Oregon* or any other ship from the West Coast had arrived? It finally seemed imperative that the U.S. build, and control, a canal through the Isthmus of Panama.

AMERICANS AND SPANIARDS had been fighting in the rugged Cuban countryside even before the armada left Port Tampa. On June 10, several hundred men of the First Marine Battalion landed near Guantánamo Bay to build a coaling station that would save the blockading ships the eight-hundred-mile trip to Key West, and almost at once came under attack.

Stephen Crane covered the landing, impressed by the steel blue of the sea contrasting with the palm fronds that turned to "crimson feathers" by the light of campfires, and by the spirit of the Marines, who were singing "Hot Time in the Old Town" as they went about their work. When the fighting started, however, he spent his time "lying flat and feeling the hot hiss of the bullets trying to cut my hair. For the moment I was no longer a cynic. I was a child who, in a fit of ignorance, had jumped into the vat of war."

Some of Crane's journalist friends who had missed the action pleaded with him the next day to write a dispatch for Joseph Pulitzer's *World,* the newspaper paying him to cover the war. "He was an artist from crown to heel," one wrote, "temperamental, undisciplined in the narrow sense of the word . . . contemptuous of mere news getting; thinking of his World connection as a convenient aid rather than as one imposing sharp and instant responsibility upon him." He dictated some pages to these responsible pressmen, then returned to the Marines to study the far more important story he saw in these fights, stories involving the complicated themes of cowardice and bravery he had addressed in *The Red Badge of Courage.* Additional journalistic accounts would be flung at the *World,* and then Crane would rework these pieces, slightly fictionalizing them, for more serious publication after the war.

The faces of men under pressure fascinated him as he watched to see if they would "betray" any sense of emotion. Especially interesting were those of the signalers, who had to stand up and "wigwag" flags during the day and lanterns at night to direct the *Marblehead*'s supporting fire. "I could lie near and watch the face of the signalman, illumined as it was by the yellow shine of lantern light, and the absence of excitement, fright, or any emotion at all on his countenance, was something to astonish all theories out of one's mind. The face was in every instance merely that of a man intent upon his business, the business of wigwagging into the gulf of night where a light on the *Marblehead* was seen to move slowly."

At least once the commander of the battalion, Colonel Huntington, came and stood beside the signalman, much to the horror of his staff. "At sight of the lights, the Spaniards performed as usual. They drove enough bullets into that immediate vicinity to kill all the marines in the corps.

" 'Colonel,' his lieutenant cried, 'won't you step down, sir?'

" 'Why, I guess not,' the Colonel replied, 'I am in no more danger than the man.' "

Crane accompanied a combined Marine and Cuban attack on a Spanish position. "Contrary to the Cubans, the bronze faces of the Americans were not stolid at all. One could note the prevalence of a curious expression— something dreamy, the symbol of minds striving to tear aside the screen of the future and perhaps expose the ambush of death. It was not fear in the least. It was simply a moment in the lives of men who have staked themselves and have come to wonder which wins—red or black."

He was considering his own courage and countenance as much as he was those of the men around him, for he was not just an onlooker during the fight. A shortage of Marine officers inspired Captain Elliot to ask the novelist to serve, in effect, as a junior officer, and Crane agreed. Elliot later commended him to Colonel Huntington, reporting that he had been of material aid during the action, carrying messages to fire volleys and maneuver to the different company commanders.

Others would also notice and comment on Crane's courage during the campaign, but he admitted to fear. When obeying one of Captain Elliot's orders, he acted "as jaunty as a real soldier, while all the time my heart was in my boots and I was cursing the day that saw me landed on the shores of the tragic isle." What he was exhibiting was self-control; what he felt it proved was "that I had inherited histrionic abilities." The other men also hid what was being suffered, showing only "quiet, composed faces. . . . They were not old soldiers; they were mainly recruits, but many of them betrayed all the emotion and merely the emotion that one sees in the face of a man earnestly at work . . . terribly hard at work; red-faced, sweating, gasping toilers."

THE NAVY, STRETCHED to its limit by the need to keep men and vessels on continuous high alert in case Admiral Cervera tried to sortie from his harbor refuge, had been impatiently awaiting the arrival of army reinforcements. At night three of the largest ships, the *Iowa, Oregon,* and *Massachusetts,* would come in close and take turns of two hours each, playing their searchlights on the narrow entrance, their guns leveled and ready. Admiral Sampson had considered trying to force his way in to destroy the Spanish fleet; but the stone forts, armed with a mix of antique smoothbore cannon and modern breech-loaders, were sited on towering cliffs above the tightly twisting channel. Most dangerous, however, were the electrical mines strewn across the channel that would be triggered from shore. The sooner army troops landed and captured the forts the better.

Most of those cramped aboard the transports must have felt the same desire for action. When finally, on the morning of Monday, June 20, the fleet swung west around a headland and it became obvious that Santiago de Cuba was the destination, troops spontaneously cheered. They were less jubilant when they came ashore two days later.

Shafter decided to ignore the navy's request that he assault the forts guarding the bay in front of Santiago, and instead planned to swing around behind them and capture the less well-defended city. The Cuban general Calixto García Íñiguez advised him to land his force at the village of Daiquiri, where only a few hundred of the twelve thousand Spanish troops in the region would be found.

Reveille was at 3:30 a.m. on June 22; the men dressed, dark shadows speaking only in whispers. Photographer Burr McIntosh remembered this near-silence of Americans preparing to assault a hostile shore as "one of the most impressive moments I . . . ever felt." Constricted in the holds crowded with tiers of bunks, the soldiers began strapping on their horse-collar blanket rolls, bulging haversacks, full canteens, and ammunition belts. By the time each had grabbed his rifle and clumsily climbed the long ladders to the deck, dawn had made visible the broader outline of the coast and the dangerous heights dominating the strand, especially one towering cone-shaped hill crowned with a blockhouse; the village and iron works were burning, having been set afire by the Spanish. A huge iron ore–loading pier and a smaller wooden dock were untouched.

With great difficulty the first troops were loaded into wildly tossing small boats, which were towed by steam launches toward the high surf crashing on a long arc of beach, but then they were halted while the navy bombardment belatedly started. Flames from the burning buildings and the shells exploding on the heights above the beach provided an entertaining spectacle for those leaning on the rails of the ships, and the bands began playing "The Star-Spangled Banner," "Yankee Doodle," and "Hot Time . . ." but as the men sang along they changed the words to ". . . in Old Cuba Tonight."

Especially interesting to onlookers, because it was an experimental and technologically complex craft, was the dynamite cruiser *Vesuvius*, which gently fired gun-cotton charges by compressed air from three immobile pipes protruding from her deck. Almost every square foot of her hull was filled with compression equipment, and the vessel itself had to be pointed at the target. "One might," Charles Post remembered, "by watching carefully, see the faint haze at the muzzles of the pipes as she fired and the compressed air was released. Then after a pause there would come a blast from the jungled hills beyond. It was like a blast from a quarry and a whole section of the hill would be torn off; the dynamite shells were very effective. The whole problem lay in landing on the target—to aim a ship is a problem in itself."

Those who had been loaded into the crazily jumping boats before the bombardment began were not as amused as, one by one, they became seasick, vomiting over the gunwales or, if jammed in the middle, using the bilges, disgusting the Jackies at the tillers. Everyone was happy to finally get ashore, although the same wild disorder marking the departure from Port Tampa was soon evident in the rush to reach land. "We did the landing," Theodore Roosevelt observed, "as we had done everything else—that is, in a scramble, each commander shifting for himself." Leonard Wood was also dismayed, writing to his wife, "You can hardly imagine the awful confusion and lack of system which meets us on every hand in this business," although he recognized, as so many did, the incredible luck that seemed to accompany the Americans. "Somehow everything seems to go in a happy-go-lucky way."

Most of the young men felt this turmoil as a personal, and national, humiliation, but it was really the same churning, deadly chaos created whenever Americans did something new, from opening a frontier to manufacturing bicycles, to fighting their first overseas war. Individual initiative, competitive drive, and the organization of cooperating groups were expected to somehow, over time, bring order and efficiency. In this war, of course, there was little time, and great human as well as monetary waste.

One of the first actions of the Rough Riders ashore was to raise Old Glory on the high, blockhouse-dominated hill behind the beach. When the soldiers and sailors spotted it, all bedlam broke loose. Malcolm McDowell, a reporter for the *Chicago Record,* looked up when he heard "a whooping-hurrah blast from the deep-toned whistle of the *Mattewan* and a wild jubilant yell from the soldiers." Other ships began blowing their whistles and sirens as they saw the flag, and waves of cheers echoed off the heights. "A quarter of an hour of whistle shrieks, cheers, yells, drum flares, bugle calls and patriotic songs were sent up. . . . Then the noise ceased, and out of it came the strains of the 'Star Spangled Banner' from the regimental band on the *Mattewan.* The soldiers ashore and the soldiers afloat were quiet until the brasses became silent, and then three full-lunged hurrahs crashed against the hill, and the salute to the flag was complete."

Amazingly, for all the chaos of an unrehearsed landing of green troops on a dangerous shore, by nightfall there were six thousand American soldiers in tents or gathered around campfires, with the loss of only two Tenth Cavalry troopers, who drowned when their boat overturned. Why the Spanish had pulled their soldiers out instead of rushing in reinforcements to defend Daiquiri is hard to understand. From the protection of the elaborate system of rifle pits and blockhouses it would have been possible to both resist an attack by Cuban insurgents and turn the clumsy landing into a massacre. Theodore Roosevelt noted, "The country would have offered very great difficulties to an attacking force had there been resistance. It was little but a mass of rugged and precipitous hills, covered for the most part by dense jungle. Five hundred resolute men could have prevented the disembarkation at very little cost to themselves."

At Daiquiri, however, the only enemies the Americans had to fight were heavy rain, swarms of mosquitos, and the eerie land crabs, which went rustling through the brush in such a way as to sound like Spanish cutthroats: the relative calm of darkness would be shattered by spooked sentries blazing away at the noisy intruders, often starting company-sized fire fights. One infantryman remembered: "The fight lasted all night long and [they] almost drove us from our position outnumbered as we were dozens to one in the darkness and ceaseless rain. . . . To be awakened from a doze of exhaustion by soaking rain, with land crabs clinging to one's ears, nose and hands and creeping all over the body, is not soothing to the nerves."

The next day most of the landing operation moved seven miles west to the fishing village of Siboney, better protected from wind and surf than Daiquiri, and on the way to Santiago.

Concern that the constantly retreating Spaniards would prove too scarce to furnish a real war drove everyone to outpourings of competitive energy. "From the moment that the first soldier landed on Cuban soil," noted the journalist Stephen Bonsal, "there were not wanting evidences of a very natural, but none the less deplorable rivalry between the officers and men of the several divisions composing the army corps, for the honor of striking the first blow at the enemy."

The most aggressive senior officer was Joseph Wheeler, late of Congress and now commander of the Cavalry Division, which was made up of both African-American and white Regular units, plus the Rough Riders. Roosevelt had always respected him as "the gallant old Confederate cavalry commander," and the diminutive sixty-two-year-old man now won new regard as an aggressive "game-cock" when he personally reconnoitered the terrain on the way to Santiago, discovered where the enemy stood, and started pushing his division toward them. He had not won the nickname "Fighting Joe" during the Civil War for sitting around a campfire.

No word of this movement had appeared in Shafter's orders, but the big general was still aboard the *Seguranca,* already feeling the effects of tropical heat. Wheeler, as the only other major-general, was ranking officer ashore, and he was determined, by God, that the glory of first blood was going to be his. But there were also legitimate military reasons for haste.

Earlier in the day Cuban insurgents had fought a skirmish with entrenched Spaniards just three miles up the road toward Santiago, and this was the area Wheeler had studied from horseback. Two trails joined there, forming a V that marked the beginning of the pass over the coastal mountains that would have to be captured if the march to the city was to continue. Quick action was essential, Wheeler believed, before the Spaniards, already estimated at around two thousand and with two Krupp cannon, strengthened their fortifications or brought in reinforcements.

Regulars were ordered up the larger of the two trails, called Camino Real, or "Royal Highway," along the valley floor; Wood and the Rough Riders were to follow the narrower one, shorter but more difficult, that ran along a high ridge less than a mile to the west. The columns were to meet at the V and discover if the Spaniards had continued to retreat toward the city or were going to fight.

Leonard Wood looked worn and haggard as the Rough Riders set off early the next morning, but Roosevelt, a reporter noted, was as "lively as a chipmunk." One of his horses had been drowned in the disembarkation, but he was mounted on the other, Little Texas, and wore, perhaps as tribute to the romance of knightly chivalry, his saber; as a realistic counter to the burdens of poor eyesight, he put several extra pairs of glasses in his saddle bags, and one in his hat. He was not going to be denied combat through faulty vision.

On the morning of the twenty-fourth, Wood and Roosevelt led their column along the narrow jungle trail just behind the scouts. As these first American soldiers ever to confront a jungle made their way deeper and deeper into its mysteries, the light became a muted green. Roosevelt found it "very beautiful . . . a delight to see the strange trees, the splendid royal palms and a tree . . . covered with a mass of brilliant scarlet flowers," and he was also delighted by the lovely call of wood doves in the labyrinthine depths of the canopy. Others, especially cowboys from the open plains, felt oppressed by the humid heat of all this unfamiliar luxuriance. "The jungle had a kind of hot, sullen beauty," one young trooper recalled. "We had the feeling that it resented our intrusion—that, if we penetrated too far, it would rise up in anger, and smother us."

These men had quickly freed themselves of anything they felt an encumbrance. The sight of all this discarded matériel and lack of route discipline horrified Stephen Crane. Arriving at Siboney just in time to see the tail end of the column slowly disappearing over the crown of a hill, the writer had pushed his frail body to catch up. After a while he passed "a few stragglers, men down with heat, prone and breathing heavily"; then he was right up with the column. "I know nothing about war, of course, and pretend nothing, but I have been enabled from time to time to see brush fighting, and I want to say here plainly that the behavior of these Rough Riders while marching through the woods shook me with terror as I have never before been shaken." Having just been with the Marines, he knew that the Spanish had learned the lessons of guerrilla fighting from the Cubans, "and they are going to use against us the tactics which the Cubans have used so successfully against them. The marines at Guantanamo have learned it. The Indian-fighting regulars know it anyhow, but this regiment of volunteers knew nothing but their own superb courage. They wound along this narrow winding path, babbling joyously, arguing, recounting, and laughing; making more noise than a train going through a tunnel."

Just past seven, at a place where the trail began to descend, scouts reported that signs showed the Spaniards were near. The order to fill magazines followed, and the men fell quiet, perhaps contemplating the fact that their new Krag rifles had been issued too late for anyone to have tested them, and wondering if they were good enough for the work at hand. They stood or lay by the side of the track, fanning themselves with their hats, chewing the long blades of Cuban grass, waiting. "Damn," one of them said. "Wouldn't a glass of cold beer taste good?"

Crane grew even more nervous as he heard "from hillock to hillock the beautiful coo of the Cuban wood dove—ah, the wood dove! the Spanish-guerrilla wood dove which had presaged the death of gallant marines." He mentioned this to some of the nearby men, but they told him that the Spaniards used no such signal. "I don't know how they knew."

Roosevelt noticed a cut strand of barbed wire to the left of the trail. "My God!" he said. "This wire has been cut today."

"What makes you think so?" reporter Edward Marshall asked.

"The end is bright, and there has been enough dew, even since sunrise, to put a light rust on it."

Suddenly Mauser rifle bullets sang through the air. A z-z-z-z-z-eu sound, which began low, rose to shrillness, then dropped to a moan that stopped abruptly, is how Edward Marshall described it, adding that it was a "nasty, malicious little noise, like the soul of a very petty and mean person turned into sound." To Roosevelt, they made a "rustling sound" like "ripping silk." The effects were immediate and deadly; in minutes a number of men were hit. Edward Marshall noted, "Every one went down in a lump without cries, without jumping in the air, without throwing up hands. . . . There is much that is awe-inspiring about the death of soldiers on the battlefield . . . the man lives, he is strong, he is vital, every muscle in him is at its fullest tension when, suddenly, 'chug' he is dead. That 'chug' of the bullets striking flesh is nearly always plainly audible."

The troops tried to spread out in skirmish formation, but the thick jungle growth made that difficult. In a few minutes they were out of touch with one another, hearing their comrades crashing through brush and breathing heavily, but unable to see anything. The Spanish were using smokeless powder, and the fact that this unseen enemy was killing men presented a very severe test for raw troops. As a first-time commander in combat, even the normally decisive Roosevelt was having self-doubts. "It was most confusing country and I had an awful time trying to get into the fight and trying to do what was right when in it; and all the while I was thinking that I was the only man who did not know what I was about, and that all the others did—whereas, as I found out later, pretty much every-body else was as much in the dark as I was."

Leonard Wood, grazed on the wrist when his gold cufflink was shot off, was so cool under the heavy fire that he won a new nickname, "Old Ice-box," although he did get irritated when a wounded trooper started cursing. "Stop that swearing," he ordered. "I don't want to hear any cursing today." Roosevelt remembered him striding along the path during the hot opening fusillade, leading his horse and growling, "Don't swear—shoot," the men laughing appreciatively, calmed by his example.

They needed to stay calm as the fight became messy and uncertain. At one point the Spanish in front of Roosevelt seemed to flee, and he wasn't sure what that meant in terms of the general skirmish. "I was never more puzzled to know what to do." He could not pull his force back toward Wood because the Spanish might then counterattack through the gap. "On the other hand, it did not seem to me that I had been doing enough fighting to justify my existence, and there was obviously fighting going on to the left." Through his mind kept running a refrain from a fox-hunting song: "Here's to every friend who struggled to the end."

Roosevelt plunged along the jungle trail, tripping on his ridiculous cav-alry saber as he ran, taking along two orderlies in case he had to send back for the men.

DOWN IN THE VALLEY, along the Camino Real, the Regulars were also engaged in a sharp firefight, which became so intense Joe Wheeler had to admit that he could not remember any heavier "musketry" from the Civil War. Resistance was so strong that he reluctantly sent for reinforcements for both his men and the Rough Riders.

As these fresh troops rushed up the trails they began meeting the wounded, their uniforms glistening with fresh blood.

"G'wan up—get there—they need you," one urged. Another offered a warning: "You can't see 'em."

"How'd you get yours?" Charles Post asked a man whose trouser leg was soaked in blood.

"Damn near stepped on the sonofabitch," the fellow answered angrily, "then he got me. But I got him. I got mine. Now you go an' git yours."

Richard Harding Davis, who had been with the Rough Riders from the beginning of the fight, noticed that "A tall gaunt young man with a cross on his arm was just coming back up the trail. His head was bent, and by some surgeon's trick he was advancing rapidly with great strides, and at the same time carrying a wounded man much heavier than himself across his shoulders. As I stepped out of the trail he raised his head, and smiled and nodded, and left me wondering where I had seen him before, smiling in the same cheery, confident way and moving in that same position. I knew it could not have been under the same conditions, and yet he was certainly associated with another time of excitement and rush and heat, and then I remembered him. He had been covered with blood and dirt and perspiration as he was now, only then he wore a canvas jacket and the man he carried on his shoulders was trying to hold him back from a white-washed line." It was Doctor Bob Church, former Princeton football star, and now the blood-soaked assistant surgeon of the Rough Riders.

The sight set Davis pondering the role of football in toughening the sons of privilege. "For the same spirit that once sent these men down a white-washed field against their opponents' rush-line was the spirit that sent Church, Channing, Devereux . . . Goodrich, Greenway . . . and a dozen others through the high hot grass at Guasimas, not shouting, as their friends the cowboys did, but each with his mouth tightly shut, with his eyes on the ball, and moving in obedience to the captain's signals."

Though a reporter, Davis obviously felt a part of this team. After coming across various friends who were badly wounded or dead, he picked up a carbine and blazed away at the enemy position. Edward Marshall also joined in with his own revolver.

Roosevelt, now commanding the left wing of the American line, began to gain confidence; "One learns fast in a fight," he thought. The Rough Riders and the Regulars had advanced to the point where they had wanted to meet, the V of the trails. Hearing cheers on his right, Roosevelt assumed they meant that Wood's troops and the Regulars were assaulting the Spanish positions; he jumped up, shouting to his men to charge the red-tiled *rancho* ahead of them, stooping along the way to pick up three shiny brass Mauser cartridges as souvenirs for his children.

The Spanish began a hasty retreat, and as soon as their line broke, Joseph Wheeler, the old Confederate cavalryman, jumped to his feet crowing, "We've got the damn Yankees on the run! We've got the damn Yankees on the run!" White members of his command found it amusing.

On the battlefield, officers and men were looking at their watches in disbelief, shaking them, holding the still-ticking timepieces to their ear, then squinting at the face again. A battle that had seemed to consume the day had taken up only a little over an hour from start to finish.

But as Roosevelt later remarked, "It was a full hour."

EDWARD MARSHALL HAD been shot in the spine, and now had personal knowledge of the suffering of the wounded. As he lay in the improvised field hospital he heard men in agony all around him. "It was a doleful group. Amputation and death stared its members in their gloomy faces." Suddenly a voice started softly to sing, "My country, 'tis of thee . . ." Other voices joined in, but "There was one voice that did not quite keep up with the others. It was so weak that I did not hear it until all the rest had finished with the line, 'Let Freedom ring.' Then, halting, struggling, faint, it repeated, slowly, 'Land—of—the—Pilgrims'—pride, Let Freedom—' The last word was a woeful cry. One more son had died as died the fathers."

Roosevelt accepted the "iron philosophy" of his hard-bitten men. "As I passed by a couple of tall, lank, Oklahoma cow-punchers, I heard one say, 'Well, some of the boys got it in the neck!' to which the other answered with the grim plains proverb of the South[west]: 'Many a good horse dies.' " And he saw something noble in the way men of such diverse origins had come together, fought heroically, and died for a common purpose. "There could be no more honorable burial than that of these men in a common grave—Indian and cow-boy, miner, packer, and college athlete—the man of unknown ancestry from the lonely Western plains, and the man who carried on his watch the crests of the Stuyvesants and the Fishes, one in the way they had met death, just as during life they had been one in their daring and their loyalty."

Twenty-four hours later the Rough Riders moved forward a couple of miles to camp by a lovely stream running through a marshy meadow. Mosquitos and other insects, terrific downpours of rain, and a lack of proper supplies proved the annoyances for the next few days as they settled into a routine. "At daybreak," Roosevelt wrote, "when the tall palms began to show dimly through the rising mist, the scream of the cavalry trumpets tore the tropic dawn; and in the evening, as the bands of regiment after regiment played the 'Star-Spangled Banner,' all, officers and men alike, stood with heads uncovered, wherever they were, until the last strains of the anthem died away in the hot sunset air."

.   .   .

NEWS OF THE military victory was cause for celebration across the nation. Early reports emphasized the role of the glamorous Rough Riders over army regulars, although more attention was paid to the black cavalrymen than to the white. Theodore Roosevelt was sure he knew why that was so: "Our men behaved very well indeed—white regulars, colored regulars, and Rough Riders alike. The newspaper press failed to do full justice to the white regulars . . . from the simple reason that everybody knew that they would fight, whereas there had been a good deal of question as to how the Rough Riders, who were volunteer troops, and the Tenth Cavalry, who were colored, would behave; so there was a tendency to exalt our deeds at the expense of those of the First Regulars, whose courage and good conduct were taken for granted."

There was a surprisingly heated controversy over whether the Rough Riders had been caught in ambush, as if that would have made them naive victims rather than victors, but that soon died away. In Theodore Roosevelt's native state of New York, the *Times,* which had headlined a long story on Las Guasimas "Rough Riders Prove Heroes," reported on June 28 that a coalition of independent Republicans was preparing to nominate him for governor. Also paying close attention to his achievements was his young distant cousin Franklin Roosevelt, a student at Groton Academy, who had planned to run away and join the navy until an attack of scarlet fever made that impossible.

Not everyone was cheering on the troops. This same month an anti-war meeting was held in Boston—it was roundly condemned by those few newspapers that noticed it. Harvard professor Charles Eliot Norton also urged his students not to join in a war in which "we jettison all that was most precious of our national cargo." The conflict was "a turning-back from the path of civilization to that of barbarism," and instead of saving the Cubans would "inflict worse suffering still."

ONE DEVELOPMENT SURPRISING everyone was the disillusionment Americans felt toward their Cuban allies. Racism played a role, since many of the insurgents were of African blood, but also these ragged and starving peons did not look or act the part of "noble rebels" that the press had been celebrating for years. Their propaganda committees had too successfully presented them as being like the American revolutionaries of George Washington's day. Over the following weeks the disdain grew to real antipathy as cultural differences became more and more obvious. When a bullock was to be killed for meat, the Americans wanted to give it a shot behind the ear, but the Cubans insisted on repeatedly stabbing until it bled to death. Outrage grew especially heated when it was discovered that the insurgents sometimes abused Spanish prisoners.

INEFFICIENCY, THE POOR wagon road, and the coming of heavy rains hindered logistics. The two hundred wagons disassembled and brought from Tampa were slow to be landed and put back together, and there were not enough surviving mules to pack supplies to the divisions camped along the road to Santiago. Once the heavy freight haulers were put en route, the road became almost impassable because of rising streams and mud so gummy it bogged wheels, sucking the wagons down to rest on their axles. Soldiers began to go hungry.

Lack of coffee and, especially, tobacco made the troops even more jumpy and irritated. Here, at least, was one good reason for making friends with the Cubans. When a column of their allies passed up the Camino Real, the British correspondent John Black Atkins wrote, Americans "sat by the wayside and demanded tobacco. 'Tobacco,' 'Tobacco,' they said all along the line. The Cubans might have taken the word as a welcome; smiling, they waved back their salutations, and continued to smoke their cheroots." Men adopted the desperate remedy of smoking a mixture of dried roots and manure.

Charles Post and his outfit were positioned off on one flank as a guard detachment. They too suffered from the rains, and lack of food, but like many others as they settled in, they swapped stories, learning new facts about never-visited regions of their common country and its different ways of life. One member of Post's squad was Jesse Pohalski, who had grown up in an Orthodox Jewish family that had come to America before the Revolution. He joked about eating greasy bacon, but his grandparents were extremely devout and his parents, though more liberal, also followed kosher laws. Post found many parallels between the iron tradition of those grandparents and his own Presbyterian ancestors, including a grandmother who refused to celebrate Christmas because it had originally been a pagan holiday and who never allowed her children to have dolls, since they were graven images and thus forbidden by one of the Ten Commandments.

And so it went in all the units, as the soldiers' shared suffering and stories, and rituals of guard mount and evening retreat, made them even tighter bands of brothers.

EXCEPT FOR A FEW dozen nurses, women were mainly excluded from the war, although popular culture tried to use them as symbols of the country wherever possible. "The American Girl Battle Ship March" was one fashionable tune back home. Newspaper and magazine cartoons depicted American women holding rifles and bayonets, and as being capable of beating the Spaniards themselves, while posters showed them proudly holding the flag protectively over Cuba or the Philippines.

On a more private front, mothers, sisters, and sweethearts tried to share the suffering of their menfolk in the war zones as best they could. In New York, Philadelphia, San Francisco, and in small towns and large, they prayed, wrote letters, ate meals of sowbelly and hardtack, and drank only water; they also set up special rooms, as souvenirs and messages began arriving from the front, that were decorated with canteens, machetes, pictures, letters, and telegrams—places to sit and think about distant loved ones.

WHILE THE SOLDIERS on land, suffering pouring rain through both steamy days and uncomfortably cool nights, cinched their belts tighter against lack of food, smoked manure, swapped tales, and nervously passed time crushing tarantulas, scorpions, and other nameless crawlers of dreadful aspect, Rufus Shafter, still on board ship, was sending misleading assurances to Secretary of War Alger that "There is no necessity for haste, as we are growing stronger and they weaker each day. The health of the command is reported to me by the surgeon as remarkable." In fact the command, especially the senior officers, was already ailing. Joseph Wheeler was suffering from malaria, and the brigadier in command of the Second Brigade of the cavalry division had fallen so ill with fever that he had to be replaced by Leonard Wood, moving Theodore Roosevelt up to full command of the Rough Riders.

Both officers and men were growing restless from discomfort and inactivity. "Well, now, so this is what they call strategy," one sergeant wrote home to Missouri, "and you find it in the books. Well, damn strategy! I've never read about it, but I am getting blooming tired of the demonstration of it. There's Santiago, and the dagoes, and here we are, and the shortest distance between two points is a straight line; which is something everybody knows, and don't have to study strategy to find out. I am in favor of going up there and beating the faces off them dagoes, and then let the war correspondents make up the strategy, as they seem to be the only ones who are worrying about it."

The commanding general shared this disdain for elaborate preparations. Although the Spanish could be seen fortifying Santiago's outer line of defense on San Juan Heights, Shafter bided his time, not ordering systematic reconnaissance or adequate maps, not having work parties cut new approaches through the jungle, not even requesting that naval guns, easily within range, bombard the defensive works. There would be "no attempt at strategy," he later explained, "and no attempt at turning their flanks. It was simply [to be] going straight for them." Luckily for the Americans, General Arsenio Linares did not concentrate his ten thousand troops at the crucial blocking points, but scattered them to cover every possible line of attack. He had, however, ordered thousands of soldiers located in the west, in Manzanillo, to march to join his force in Santiago. When Shafter learned of this impending reinforcement, the need for quick action suddenly became evident even to him, and the great mass of his army began jamming the narrow Camino Real as it struggled to get in position for an assault.

Shafter finally came ashore on June 30, meeting with brigade and divisional commanders to lay out his plans for the next day. The major goal was to break the Spanish line on the San Juan Heights, but he had become distracted by the possible threat to his flank from a small fortified village called El Caney. He decided to split his army and capture El Caney early in the morning of July 1, then attack the Heights. Having held this council of war, Shafter retired to recover from his exertions, feeling, he later wrote, "nauseated and very dizzy," and pained by his gouty ankle.

At a time when the armies of Europe were developing rapid-fire field pieces with fixed charges and sophisticated targeting, the cannon assigned to support American troops used black powder, and were aimed more by guesswork and experience than science. Huge siege guns were still on the transports because of fear that they would bog down in mud, making the roads even worse; sixty other light field pieces had been left in Tampa in the rush to depart. Infantry was going to have little support.

Four guns began their bombardment of El Caney at 6:35 a.m., the infantry assault followed at 7:00. The Americans were confident that El Caney would fall within two hours, allowing these troops to join the attack on San Juan scheduled to begin at 10:00. After the first rifle shot, however, nothing went according to schedule.

The war had proceeded so easily—Dewey's astonishing victory, the Spanish failure to defend Daiquiri, the way they had finally run when charged at Guasimas—that the Americans were sure the Dons would put up only a token defense before taking to their heels. Some soldiers worried, as they marched into position, that when the Spanish detected the advance they would evacuate before they could be surrounded and captured, but one reporter, Caspar Whitney, bitterly admitted, "Later in the day we began to wonder if they were ever going to run."

Regulars made up most of the force at El Caney, but volunteers of the Second Massachusetts now discovered the price of their old Springfield rifles as the clouds of smoke it exhaled at every shot drew fusillades from the smokeless Mausers. Again American soldiers had to search for a hidden enemy while under heavy fire.

As CHARLES POST and his outfit marched toward San Juan along the jammed road, they spotted some celebrities. A tall man dressed all in black except for white socks, a scarlet tie, and a scarlet band on his straw hat sat on a too-small horse under a tree.

"Hey, Willie!"—the cry went through the ranks as the men recognized the ungainly form of William Randolph Hearst.

"Hello, Jimmy!" "Hello, Jimmy!" The famous correspondent James Creelman was hailed as he came riding up to confer with his publisher.

Creelman waved, grinning widely through his black beard, and called out, "Boys, you're going into battle. Good luck!" as the Seventy-first marched past.

The shyer Hearst, after some urging from Creelman, raised his scarlet-banded straw hat and called softly, "Boys, good luck be with you."

As the troops marched closer to the front the black oilcloth covers were stripped from their flags so that Old Glory and the regimental banners floated in brilliant tones against the dark green of the surrounding hills. Now combat seemed certain; this was how their fathers' battles had been fought, charging against the foe behind flying colors. Soon they heard the boom of artillery, then the mysterious whispers in the air that meant they were under fire.

·   ·   ·

THE ROUGH RIDERS were up before dawn on July 1, breakfasting on the usual sowbelly and hardtack. There was a fugue of "uneasy excitement" playing over the camp facing San Juan, and Roosevelt strolled about, "calmly lathering his face, reassuring the many who had woken afraid." The cavalry saber that had proved such an impediment at Las Guasimas was left tied to his baggage, and just a revolver salvaged from the *Maine* was carried at his waist. Though not as intimate a killer as a sword, a pistol was effective only in close combat, making any fight almost as personal as a duel. A Spaniard shot down in such a way would provide particularly satisfying revenge for the shattered battleship.

As the sun rose and the men fell into ranks, Captain Grimes' battery of light field guns went dashing up to the crest of the hill in front of them. "It was a fine sight," the colonel thought, "to see the great horses straining under the lash as they whirled the guns up the hill and into position."

Burr McIntosh, also watching the horses rear and plunge with their effort, agreed: "It was a picture worth the brush of a great artist. It will undoubtedly be justly represented some day, as Frederic Remington stood on the brow of the hill upon its arrival." Remington, who was working as both correspondent and combat artist, hastily sketched the scene.

Cannon fire and the pop-pop-pop of rifles could be heard coming from the attack at El Caney as white smoke drifted into the blue sky. Officers facing San Juan Hill fretted about the delay, but finally the order to start the bombardment was given. Shell after shell was lobbed onto the Heights with pleasing regularity and accuracy, the audience behind the booming guns, some of whom lay on the ground to see under the smoke, applauding particularly good shots. It seemed obvious that the Spanish had no cannon with which to reply, and men began wondering if they would not perhaps be lunching in the shade of the distant blockhouse in a few hours.

That expectation changed as the other side belatedly sent in shot after shot of their own with regularity and precision, but from modern Krupp rapid-fire cannon using smokeless powder.

Chaos resulted, with a general shouting, "Get out of this hell spot!" as everyone but the artillerymen, who coolly returned the fire, tried to do just that. Frederic Remington realized that the Spanish must have long since marked off the range of artillery atop El Pozo. "They had studied it out. For myself, I fled, dragging my horse up the hill. . . . Some as gallant soldiers and some as daring correspondents as it is my pleasure to know did their legs proud there. The tall form of Major John Jacob Astor moved in my front in jack-rabbit bounds. Prussian, English, and Japanese correspondents, artists, all the news, and much high-class art and literature, were flushed, and went straddling up the hill before the first barrel of the Dons."

In the midst of this brief rout, a panicked reporter ran up to Richard Harding Davis, grabbing his arm.

"Isn't this awful?"

"Very disturbing," Davis murmured, disengaging himself and nodding gravely. "Very disturbing."

The Camino Real was also under fire from the Heights and from snipers left behind in the trees. The enemy artillerymen's task was made easier by a huge yellow silk balloon bobbing along just above the road, marking the soldiers' route through the jungle. This was the brain-child of Lieutenant-Colonel Joseph E. Maxfield of the Army Signal Corps, an innovation that would, he believed, provide much-needed reconnaissance intelligence to General Shafter. Rounds began falling among the tightly packed troops below, killing and wounding them by the score before the quivering monster, punctured numerous times, slowly deflated and sank.

Vague orders had been given to troop commanders to position their men at the base of the slope and wait, but now the waiting was turning into a massacre. Charles Post's unit, the Seventy-first New York, had discipline problems in the face of the heavy fire. As the lead battalion began to emerge from the jungle into the grassy open field before the ridge, they met such an intense storm of shells and rifle bullets that they staggered, then fell back into cover. Stories would reach their home town that they had run, or at least disgraced their name. "The regiment did not run away," Richard Harding Davis reported, "but it certainly did not behave well. The fault was entirely that of some of the officers. They funked the fight and . . . refused to leave the bushes, and as a result the men . . . funked it too." Undoubtedly their old-fashioned black-powder Springfield rifles played a role here, as every smoky shot brought a lethal response from the Spanish.

Theodore Roosevelt had taken his Rough Riders to the far right of the line, where, according to the optimistic plan devised by General Shafter, the cavalry was supposed to link up with the troops that would come down from El Caney. But that battle was still being fought, and Roosevelt was losing men even though they were spread apart and crouching behind anything that offered protection. The colonel, who had fixed his blue bandanna to the back of his hat as protection against the burning sun, listened and watched carefully, trying to figure out what they were facing. He noted that many of his troops were already looking exhausted in the intense heat. What was the point of this waiting? They were taking almost as many casualties lying in the grass and jungle as they would in an assault—"man after man in our ranks fell dead or wounded . . ." Roosevelt began sending messengers asking for permission to attack.

Frederic Remington was studying all the sights and sounds as closely as any officer, and he found little of the old romance in them. "These long-range, smokeless bolts are so far-reaching, and there is so little fuss, that a soldier is for hours under fire getting into the battle proper, and he has time to think. That is hard when you consider the seriousness of what he is thinking about. The modern soldier must have moral quality."

AT EL CANEY the advance was pressed harder, in spite of heavy casualties, and Spanish positions began to fall. The reporter James Creelman worked his way into the village, hoping to capture the Spanish flag that had flown over its blockhouse. "I wanted it for my country and I wanted it for my newspaper. . . . It was the thing I had come to get. I wanted it for the *Journal*. The *Journal* had provoked the war, and it was only fair that the *Journal* should have the first flag captured in the greatest land battle of the war." But the red-and-yellow banner had been blown away. After some searching he found it in the dust; then, at the moment of his triumph, Creelman was shot. "I was very weak and in great pain, but I shall never forget the cheer that went up when the soldiers saw my body emerge from the breach, and the next thing I knew the Spanish flag I had taken was thrown over me. I don't know how long I lay on the side of the hill among the wounded, but after a while Mr. Hearst, the proprietor of the *Journal,* came to me, and kneeling in the grass, took down my story from dictation." The publisher, revolver at hip, was still sporting his straw hat with the scarlet band. "I'm sorry you're hurt," he told his reporter, "but wasn't it a splendid fight? We must beat every paper in the world."

ALL ALONG THE LINE at the base of San Juan Heights, officers were chafing with angry impatience as they kept taking casualties without moving. Why hadn't the order to attack been given?

Lieutenant John Miley was Shafter's representative at the San Juan front; in a hurried conference with Samuel Sumner and other senior officers, Sumner urged him to order an attack in the commander's name. Miley knew that "A retreat now would be a disastrous defeat," but he hoped a messenger from Shafter would come to give him the go-ahead.

None arrived. The young lieutenant hesitated, then gave the command on his own authority.

Brigadier-General Hamilton Hawkins, white-haired commander of the Sixth and Sixteenth Infantry regiments, thought as other veterans did that the fire his brigade was suffering was heavier than anything experienced in the Civil War. Wounded and dead were everywhere, and more were coming back from the front in a constant flow. The Sixth Infantry had lost a quarter of its men in ten minutes; another unit had lost three succeeding commanders in the same amount of time, and although an attack had been approved, one of his trio of regiments had been mistakenly diverted down a side trail at the last moment by the interference of another general.

Even more important, where was the artillery? There was no artillery battering the works and blockhouses, suppressing Spanish fire from the Heights. Hawkins, who had been a Union officer at Gettysburg, did not want to be responsible for another Pickett's Charge, having his command slaughtered as they rushed across an open slope against an entrenched and determined foe. Staying in place, however, was almost as deadly.

Lieutenant Jules Garesche Ord, himself the son of a famous Civil War general, was serving as Hawkins' aide. "General," he said, "if you will order a charge, I will lead it."

Hawkins hesitated to give such an order; then suddenly a drumming sound came from the distance, and the two men could see spurts of dust along the Spanish trenches. Lieutenant John Parker had reached the front and put his Gatling guns into action. Their revolving barrels fired thirty-six hundred smokeless rounds a minute, and in the absence of effective artillery support they could make all the difference between victory and disaster.

Ord insisted that he be allowed to volunteer to lead a charge. "We can't stay here, can we?"

Spanish fire died down as the Gatlings did their work, but still Hawkins hesitated.

"I only ask you, General, not to refuse permission."

"I will not ask for volunteers," Hawkins reluctantly said. "I will not give permission and I will not refuse it. God bless you and good luck!"

"Come on—come on, you fellows!" Ord yelled as he ran forward with his saber in one hand and pistol in the other. "Come on—we can't stop here!"

Some followed, some hesitated. "We were in front," one particularly honest soldier later admitted, "and then the Sixteenth, or what was left of it,

came up by rushes just as we did and we were ordered to go up the hill. . . .
All I know is when I looked up that gulch and then up that hill . . . I got cold
all over. I could feel the hair stand up on my scalp and my teeth clattered. I
tried to pray but I couldn't. I didn't think of my mother or anything like that;
I only tried to think of some way to get out of going up that hill."

Richard Harding Davis was in a good position to see the men burst from
the scraggly undergrowth and start up the slope. The charge had none of
the traditional pictorial glory about it, and Davis was too good a reporter to
try to make it pretty. "I think the thing which impressed one the most,
when our men started from cover, was that they were so few. It seemed as
if someone had made an awful and terrible mistake. One's instinct was to
call to them to come back. You felt that someone had blundered and that
these few men were blindly following out some madman's mad order. It
was not heroic then, it seemed merely terribly pathetic. The pity of it, the
folly of such a sacrifice was what held you."

Military attachés watching from El Pozo shared the same sense of
dread. When "a little group of blue figures appeared on the green of the terrible hillside" one of them turned to Stephen Crane and cried out incredu-
lously, "Why, they're trying to take the position."

Crane admitted that it appeared to be so. They were going to take the
hill without supporting artillery fire.

"But they can't do it, you know," the attaché protested vehemently. "It's
impossible." He was angry over such a waste of gallant men. "It's plucky,
you know! By Gawd, it's plucky! But *they can't do it!*" He kept up his tirade
until his voice broke. "It will simply be a hell of a slaughter with no good
coming out of it."

Colonel Roosevelt, like so many of his countrymen, had little patience
with traditional military discipline, and was thinking that he should take
the initiative with his troops and "march toward the guns," when he
received orders to do just that. The Rough Riders were to support the Regulars in their attack on the San Juan Heights by assaulting the hill to their
right flank, crowned with its own red-tiled ranch buildings.

Men who have taken cover under fire hesitate to leave it, each wanting
to be sure that he is not alone in exposing himself, and that the whole outfit is rising to advance. Roosevelt overheard two soldiers speak admiringly
of how General Sumner was promenading about on horseback. "That
made us feel all right," one of them then told him. "If the General could
stand it, we could." So the very moment orders came, Roosevelt leaped
into the saddle of Little Texas and began rallying the Rough Riders, riding

Theodore Roosevelt with his Rough Riders on the San Juan Heights. (*Theodore Roosevelt Collection, Havard College Library*)

along the line rasping out orders to captains and lieutenants, prodding the soldiers to their feet.

"Are you afraid to stand up when I am on horseback?" he jeered at one man who was slow to rise, but just as he spoke the fellow jerked forward onto his face, "a bullet having struck him and gone through him length-wise."

All were soon up and moving, Roosevelt leading them through the Ninth and First Regular Cavalry regiments, whose officers had not yet received orders to attack. Roosevelt outranked the elderly captain present and declared to him, "I give the order to charge." But still the captain hesitated.

"Then let my men through, sir," Roosevelt said, leading his grinning troops through the ranks of the Regulars, many of whom joined the column.

Roosevelt pushed his men into position at the foot of the hill; then, swinging his cowboy hat with its flapping blue bandanna, he gave the order to charge. On his right, the Ninth joined in, as did the First to his left. "The whole line, tired of waiting, and eager to close with the enemy, was straining to go forward; and it seems that different parts slipped the leash at almost the same moment."

Conspicuous as the only mounted figure on the hill, the colonel galloped along the ranks, helping his officers get their troops moving. He then wheeled toward the crest, "passing the shouting, cheering, firing men," the blue bandanna floating out behind him like a battle flag. Knicked in the elbow by a bullet as he led the assault and Little Texas scraped by several more, he was forced to dismount forty yards from the summit by a wire fence, and continued the charge on foot. Most of the enemy had run away, but at the crest a Spanish officer suddenly appeared and Roosevelt shot him dead with his revolver.

The entrenched Spaniards on the next line of hills poured heavy rifle and artillery fire into the newly won position; many men and officers were cut down, including two colonels—one dead, one wounded. Shelter was quickly sought behind a huge iron sugar-refining kettle that now gave the place a name: Kettle Hill.

Suddenly a peculiar drumming sound was heard above the crack of the troopers' carbines, and some men shouted that the Spanish had machine-guns, but Roosevelt, listening carefully, figured out what was happening. "It's the Gatlings, men," he shouted, jumping to his feet and slapping his thigh in delight, "our Gatlings." They had a good view of the infantry charging up the slope toward the San Juan blockhouse, which lay to their left. Roosevelt ordered volleying fire on that strong point to support their attack, then led the cheers as the Americans swept to victory and drove the defenders down the other side of the hill. Lieutenant Ord was shot as he leaped the trench in pursuit, and died instantly.

CHAPTER 9

WAGES OF WAR

Tell the President for Heaven's sake to send us every regiment and above all every battery possible. We have won so far at a heavy cost; but the Spaniards fight very hard and we are within measurable distance of a terrible military disaster.

Theodore Roosevelt to Henry Cabot Lodge

Th' gallant boys iv th' navy was settin' out on th' deck, defindin' their counthry an' dhrawin' three ca-ards apiece, whin th' Spanish admiral con-cluded 'twud be better f'r him to be desthroyed on th' ragin' sea, him bein' a sailor, thin to have his fleet captured be cav'lry. Annyhow, he was willin' to take a chance; an' he says to his sailors: . . .'Lave us go out where we can have a r-run f'r our money,' he says. An' away they wint. I'll say this much f'r him, he's a brave man, a dam brave man. I don't like a Spanyard no more than ye do, Hinnissy. I niver see wan. But, if this here man was a—was a Zulu, I'd say he was a brave man.

Mr. Dooley

THERE WAS CONFUSION on the Heights as intermingled regiments of Americans paused for a moment to catch their breath and study the Spanish dead, most of whom had been shot in the head and lay, as Frederic Remington noted, "in the most curious attitudes," the artist thinking that "life never runs so high in a man as it does when he is charging on the field of battle; death never seems so still and positive." Some of the victors were already feeling the burden of their own still comrades, one weeping young

195

officer embracing Remington, then "pointing to twenty-five big Negro infantrymen sitting near," saying, " 'That's all that is left of the Twenty-fourth Infantry.' "

Officers, mostly lieutenants and captains, quickly regrouped their men, and, Remington reported, with "gestures much the same as a woman makes when she is herding chickens" shooed them over the top in spite of all the metal shrieking through the air. They then charged on, driving the enemy through a string of palm trees and over the next chain of hills, from whose crests the Americans looked down on Santiago. Long-legged men like Lieutenants Greenway and Goodrich again pushed even farther ahead, but the generals promptly sent out orders that the advance be halted before troops became too strung out and the Spanish turned to chew them up in detail. Defensive positions were quickly established along the San Juan crest.

"Ammunition! Ammunition! Ammunition!" went the cry along the front; even the wounded making their way to the rear repeated it to everyone they met. Snipers hidden in the jungle still kept the Camino Real under a deadly crossfire "which made it stretch in either direction to an interminable distance," wrote Richard Harding Davis. "I remember a government teamster driving a Studebaker wagon filled with ammunition coming up at a gallop out of this interminable distance and seeking shelter against the base of the hill. Seated beside him was a small boy, freckled and sunburned, a stowaway from one of the transports. He was grandly happy and excited, and his only fear was that he was not 'under fire.' From our coign of safety, with our backs to the hill, the teamster and I assured him that, on that point, he need feel no morbid doubt. But until a bullet embedded itself in the blue board of the wagon he was not convinced. Then with his jack-knife he dug it out and shouted with pleasure. 'I guess the folks will have to believe I was in a battle now,' he said."

It was a fragile line, overextended and underarmed, that stretched across the San Juan hills. Many officers were dead or wounded, and the soldiers so mixed that there was little unit cohesiveness, strangers often supporting strangers under dangerous and trying circumstances as the Spanish reorganized and devoted all the firepower they had to driving the Americans back. So much steel came flying in, causing so many casualties, that Roosevelt made his men lie flat on their faces in the grass on the back slope of the hill, and very little counter-firing was done.

Under the strain, when the colonel saw some black troopers of the

Tenth Cavalry headed for the rear he assumed they were seeking safety, or some of their own officers. Roosevelt recognized their need for officers they trusted, but he could not allow his line to be weakened. He blocked their way, pulled his revolver, and called out that he appreciated the bravery they had already shown but that he would shoot the first man who tried to leave, ending with, "Now, I shall be very sorry to hurt you, and you don't know whether or not I will keep my word, but my men can tell you that I always do."

The Rough Riders had been following the encounter with rapt attention, and when their colonel had fallen silent, "my cow-punchers, hunters, and miners solemnly nodded their heads and commented in chorus, exactly as if in a comic opera, 'He always does; he always does!' "

The black soldiers grinned at one another, laughed, and there was no more trouble, Roosevelt assuming that they now accepted him as one of their own officers. The real reason was that they had been heading back under orders to bring up entrenching tools; if the colonel didn't want them to, that was fine. Roosevelt, of course, had also taunted his own Rough Riders with charges of cowardice earlier in the day, and saw his role as one of "making" soldiers under his command do their best, just as he had to make himself toe the line. The black soldiers understood. "Everyone who saw the incident knew the Colonel was mistaken about our men trying to shirk duty," one of them wrote, "but . . . no one thought ill of the matter."

Remington came upon a pack train that had just arrived with the much-needed ammunition. Some soldiers lifted a box high, then dropped it on one corner, smashing it open.

"Now we can hold San Juan hill against them garlics—hey, son!" yelled one of the cavalrymen to a "doughboy," or infantryman.

"You bet—until we starve to death."

"Starve nothin'—we'll eat them gun-teams."

"Well, well," the artist thought to himself, "I have no receipt for licking the kind of troops these boys represent. And yet some of the generals wanted to retreat."

That was true. Shafter, still unable to work his way to the front, had begun fearing for the precariousness of the American hold on the crests. Casualties had been extremely high, the artillery was not able to do much, and shortages of ammunition, food, and medical supplies were growing. Perhaps a withdrawal would be necessary. Rumors began to work their insidious way along the fighting line.

But the troops would not accept any thought of retreating. Stephen Crane also encountered some who "seemed to have no idea of a grand historic performance, but they were grimly satisfied with themselves."

"Well, begawd, we done it," he heard them crow, but they hurled questions at him about other sections of the line.

"How are things looking, old man? Everything all right?"

"Yes, everything is all right if you can hold this ridge."

"Aw, hell," was the response, "we'll hold the ridge. Don't you worry about that, son."

No matter that there was no food and little sleep that night; a certain amount of cock-of-the-walk strutting among the Americans, proud of having taken strongly defended fortified positions practically with their bare hands, relegated such details to minor importance. "Ord, Ord, that evening the name ran along the trench that we had captured," remembered Charles Post. "All the Sixth and the Sixteenth knew it; he was the man."

Also feeling very much the man was Theodore Roosevelt. He had avenged the *Maine* by killing an enemy in what amounted to hand-to-hand combat; perhaps he was the only soldier in the whole war who had been close enough to kill with a revolver, he thought (finding out only weeks later that one other cavalryman shared the distinction). When General Wheeler came by to talk about the possibility of retreating to a more defensible position, shortening supply lines, he found the colonel full of confidence to the point of insubordination. "Well, General," Roosevelt said, "I really don't know whether we would obey an order to fall back. We can take that city by a rush, and if we have to move out of here at all I should be inclined to make the rush in the right direction." Lieutenant Jack Greenway, who was standing beside him, "nodded an eager assent."

Although there was good reason for the men to feel they had accomplished something worthy of their fathers, there were also causes for mourning. The American force had been decimated: 205 were killed on July 1, and 1,180 wounded; Spanish losses were 215 killed and 376 wounded. "The magazine rifle!" is how Stephen Crane explained the enormous collective number; Theodore Roosevelt explained the disparity: "It would have been very extraordinary if the reverse was the case, for we did the charging; and to carry earthworks on foot with dismounted cavalry, when these earthworks are held by unbroken infantry armed with the best modern rifles, is a serious task."

A serious task indeed, and the question the British military observer Arthur Lee asked is relevant still. Is it "customary" for Americans, he inquired of one officer, "to assault blockhouses and rifle pits before they had been searched by artillery?"

"Not always," was the laconic reply.

Captain Lee later criticized the action at El Caney more directly. "This was a heavy price to pay for the possession of an outlying post, defended by an inferior force, but it only bore out the well-known military axiom that the attack on a fortified village cannot succeed, without great loss of life, unless the assailants are strong in artillery. . . . That the attack succeeded was entirely due to the magnificent courage and endurance of the infantry officers and men."

Another sobering thought was that, although the Heights had been seized, the real object of the campaign had not. Santiago de Cuba was within sight, but still flew the flame-colored banner of Spain. And a new-found respect for the courage of the Spanish soldier made even more chilling the realization that Americans might still be pushed off these hills bought at such a heavy price in blood.

WILLIAM McKINLEY and Secretary of War Alger were growing anxious. General Shafter had sent a message late in the afternoon of Friday, July 1, informing them that he had been in a very heavy engagement and that, "I regret to say our casualties will be above 400." A few hours later a short telegram announced that he had underestimated his losses, and needed a large hospital ship; then—silence. Newspapers began running dispatches claiming Shafter suffered from serious illness, that Joseph Wheeler, next in command, was also incapacitated, and that the dreaded yellow fever had struck troops in Siboney. The president and his advisers tried to keep their spirits up as they waited, sleepless, through Friday and Saturday night. "But," Alger remembered, "the air was filled with foreboding rumors."

HAD THEY BEEN near the front on those nights, McKinley and Alger would have felt an even stronger bite of foreboding. "Dead men lying along the road," as Caspar Whitney described the scene for *Harper's,* "ghastly in their unstudied positions, men dying, men wounded, passing back to the division hospital, some being carried, some limping, some sitting by the roadside, all strangely silent, bandaged and bloody . . . the road was strewn with parts of clothes, blanket rolls, pieces of bacon, empty cans, cartridges . . . the marks of bullets everywhere—the trees shot through and through."

Frederic Remington found this messy aftermath far more disturbing than combat had been: "The rear of a battle. All the broken spirits, bloody bodies, hopeless, helpless suffering which drags its weary length to the rear are so much more appalling than anything else in the world that words won't mean anything to one who has not seen it. Men half naked, men sitting down on the roadside utterly spent, men hopping on one foot with a rifle for a crutch, men out of their minds from sunstroke, men dead, and men dying. Officers came by white as this paper, carried on rude litters made by their devoted soldiers, or borne on their backs. . . . During the day I had discovered no particular nervousness in myself, quite contrary to my expectations, since I am a nervous man, but there in the comparative quiet of the woods the reaction came. Other fellows felt the same, and we compared notes. Art and literature under Mauser fire is a jerky business; it cannot be properly systematized. I declared that I would in the future paint set pieces for dining-rooms. Dining-rooms are so much more amusing than camps. The novelist allowed that he would be forced to go home and complete 'The Romance of a Quart Bottle.' The explorer declared that his treatise on the 'Flora of Bar Harbor' was promised to his publishers."

The artist, awake since three thirty that morning, and in the midst of action since dawn, arranged himself as comfortably as possible, but was unable to fall asleep. "I could not get the white bodies which lay in the moonlight, with the dark spots on them, out of my mind. Most of the dead on modern battle-fields are half naked, because of the first-aid bandage. They take their shirts off, or their pantaloons, put on the dressing, and die that way."

All Friday night the exhausted soldiers dug trenches and rifle pits to prepare for a counterattack; before dawn the Spanish seemed to launch one. "It was about three o'clock in the morning," wrote Roosevelt, "at which time men's courage is said to be at the lowest ebb; but the cavalry division was certainly free from any weakness in that direction. At the alarm everybody jumped to his feet, and the stiff, shivering, haggard men, their eyes only half-opened, all clutched their rifles and ran forward to the trench on the crest of the hill."

That skirmish soon died away, but an hour later more intense fire poured in, and an artillery shell burst where Roosevelt was meeting with some of his officers, somehow not harming any of them, but killing or wounding five troopers nearby. The colonel decided it was time to get down to serious siege work. Everyone not needed in the trenches was dispersed to safer locations in the valley, while the Colt machine-guns and the dynamite gun were brought up. These, however, proved not as effective as the Gatlings, maintained by army regulars, perhaps because of the devil-may-care attitude toward upkeep by the volunteers.

Richard Harding Davis had come across the dynamite gun as its crew tried to correct "a hitch in its mechanism." An officer on an errand also happened by and "halted his sweating horse and gazed at the strange gun with professional knowledge."

"That must be the dynamite gun I have heard so much about," he shouted, to be heard above the gunfire. "I'd like to see you fire it once."

"In just a moment, sir," the sergeant in charge shouted back, "this shell seems to have jammed a bit."

Davis and the officer, neither of whom had noticed the round stuck in the breech, began losing interest. "With elaborate carelessness I began to edge off down the road," wrote Davis, while the officer "gathered up his reins."

"Wait," the sergeant pleaded, "we'll have it out in a minute." He really wanted this chance to "exhibit his toy" to a famous correspondent and a professional soldier.

"What—what," cried the officer, "is that man doing with that axe?"

"He's helping me get out this shell."

"Good God!" shouted the man on horseback as he and Davis skedaddled down the road.

Far more meticulous were the teams of Western hunters and trackers that Roosevelt assigned to clear the area behind the line of Spanish snipers, "who showed not only courage but wanton cruelty and barbarity. At times they fired upon armed men in bodies, but they much preferred for their victims the unarmed . . . the doctors, the chaplains, the hospital stewards." No quarter was to be shown these men, who were regarded as little better than murderers, and Roosevelt's teams proved "much superior at the guerrillas' own game, killing eleven, while not one of my men was scratched."

GEORGE KENNAN, in his roles as both a reporter for *Outlook* and vice-president of the Red Cross, visited the one prepared field hospital, that of the First Division, during the battle for San Juan Heights; what he saw appalled him. The hospital, which lay a few miles back of the fighting in a small opening surrounded by jungle, was "wretchedly incomplete and inadequate" even before the wounded began arriving in the hundreds. "As the hot tropical day advanced, the numbers constantly and rapidly increased until, at nightfall, long rows of wounded were lying on the grass in front of the operating-tents, without awnings or shelter, awaiting examination and treatment. The small force of field-surgeons worked heroically and with a devotion that I have never seen surpassed; but they were completely overwhelmed by the great bloody wave of human agony that rolled back in ever-increasing volume from the battle-line."

The help of Clara Barton and the Red Cross had been refused when their ship had arrived. "What Dr. Winter's reasons were for declining aid and supplies when both were so urgently needed I do not know," wrote George Kennan. "Possibly he is one of the military surgeons . . . who think that women, even if they are trained nurses, have no business with an army, and should be snubbed, if not browbeaten, until they learn to keep their place." Under the press of casualties, however, the military surgeons learned to overcome their prejudices.

Amidst all these scenes that reminded him of a hell on earth, Kennan was inspired by the "uncomplaining fortitude and heroic self-control" of the men, but thought, "If there was anything more terrible in our Civil War, I am glad that I was not there to see it." As soon as he had a chance, he went to General Shafter's headquarters and used the telephone to summon Clara Barton.

ONCE THE ELATION of victory subsided, cold fear gripped the men and officers as they contemplated the possibility of military disaster; Roosevelt wrote his friend Senator Lodge to be sure that the president hurried reinforcements and artillery to Cuba.

One hundred and thirty-four more men were killed or wounded on July 2 and 3 as shrapnel and rifle and Maxim machine-gun bullets continued to batter American positions. Rain soaked through clothing, filled the trenches, and plagued the fragile supply route so severely that there weren't ever enough blankets, tents, food, or, still most painfully missed, tobacco. And the humid heat weighed on everyone. "My clothes smell so that I can't use them for a pillow . . ." Richard Davis told his mother. For the *New York Herald* he wrote an article saying, "The situation here is now critical—alarming . . ."; then he went on to lay out just how critical in such detail that others would later attack him for giving aid, comfort, and valuable intelligence to the enemy, just as he himself had attacked Poultney Bigelow for writing articles about military unpreparedness in Tampa. This dispatch would be cited later as a reason for enforcing severe censorship on correspondents, but Davis felt it imperative to point out that "Another such victory as that of July 1 and our troops must retreat."

At the higher levels of command there was confusion about what to do next. General Wheeler stopped Shafter from giving back the gains of the day by pointing out that "it would cost us much prestige." He now made a reconnaissance of the Spanish defenses just outside Santiago, and was impressed by the skill with which they had been prepared. "With a very powerful glass I viewed them from every possible point, to accomplish which I selected places from which to view them on all sides of the city. This investigation convinced me, and I so reported, that to take the city by assault would cost us at least three thousand men."

Unthinkable. Shafter had said to his adjutant, Colonel Edward McClernand, as the troops landed in Cuba that the American people were no longer hardened to the heavy casualties that the Civil War had produced, and would no longer tolerate such numbers, yet he had already lost ten percent of his force in just a few days of campaigning. A direct assault would be an act of desperation.

But laying siege presented its own problems: now that the heavy daily rains had started, the already bogged and crowded road was becoming a quagmire, delaying the rush of food and ammunition to the front; more important, the rainy season was disease season; soldiers were still being killed and wounded by enemy fire while even more were falling ill. Shafter himself was too weak to walk; he could not visit the front to evaluate the difficulties facing his troops, and he had to be hauled to conferences with his generals on the only stretcher big enough for his bulk—a door taken off its hinges and carried by six strong enlisted men.

The general sent a message to Admiral Sampson asking him to make an attempt to force the harbor entrance, but the sailor pointed out that electric mines were still in place, and the forts that controlled them still in Spanish hands. Impossible to enter, unless the general returned to the original Navy plan and captured those forts. Wheeler also studied that tactical challenge and told Shafter, "I would like to do it, but the effort would be attended with terrible loss." As the historian G. J. A. O'Toole points out, Shafter was faced with a great dilemma: "Lost prestige was the cost of retreat; three thousand casualties, the cost of advance; sunken battleships the cost of forcing the harbor. And the cost of staying in place—rain, disease, and the arrival of the Spanish relief column."

ANXIETY STILL GRIPPED the White House. Early on Sunday, July 3, Alger irritably cabled: "I waited with the President until 4 o'clock this morning for news from you. . . . Not a word was received . . . I wish hereafter that you would interrupt all messages that are being sent to the Associated Press and others and make report at the close of each day, or during the day if there is anything of special importance, at once."

Shafter did respond at once in a long message, but at least part of what he had to say added to Alger's and McKinley's unease. "We have the town well invested on the north and east, but with a very thin line. Upon approaching it we find it of such a character, and the defences so strong, it will be impossible to carry it by storm with my present force, and I am seriously considering withdrawing about five miles, and taking up a new position. . . ." The president was not about to openly overrule his man on the ground, but a quick appeal was sent: "If . . . you can hold your present position, especially San Juan Heights, the effect upon the country would be much better than falling back."

The commanding general, however, had also decided on a bold stroke; the same morning he so depressed the president and secretary of war with his report, he also sent a note to José Toral, the Spanish general who had replaced the wounded Linares, demanding that he surrender: "I shall be obliged, unless you surrender, to shell Santiago de Cuba. Please inform the citizens of foreign countries and all women and children that they should leave the city before ten o'clock to-morrow morning."

SUNDAY, JULY 3, was sparkling and clear, without even a wisp of cloud to mar the blue morning sky. The American fleet kept its arc of steel three miles off the entrance to Santiago harbor, strength somewhat diminished by the departure of the flagship *New York* for Siboney about 9:00 a.m., carrying Admiral Sampson, who had donned leggings and spurs, to a conference with General Shafter; several other warships had steamed east to Guantánamo to recoal. In the admiral's absence the blockade was under the immediate command of Commodore Schley on board the *Brooklyn*, the fastest of the American vessels. This must have caused Sampson some unease. He lacked confidence in the commodore, who had mishandled an earlier search for Cervera's fleet, but the great need for a resolution to the campaign meant he had no choice but to meet with Shafter and again try to convince him to conduct combined operations with the navy against the forts.

Sailors and officers were in their traditional dress whites for Sunday inspection, the ceremonial reading of the Articles of War, and church services, but the crews were still on full alert. Six pillars of smoke had been sighted rising above the harbor on Saturday afternoon, evidence that Spanish ships had fired their boilers, perhaps to move into position for bombarding American trenches at San Juan or, the American sailors hoped, to come out and fight. Although such columns had been sighted before, Robley Evans of the battleship *Iowa* had signal flags made ready to announce "The enemy is attempting to escape" in case the unlikely happened.

This morning the smoke still rose behind the Spanish forts on the seaside heights, and around 9:30 one sharp-eyed lookout thought he detected the columns tilting, as if ships were moving toward the entrance.

The *Iowa* was positioned to see farther into the harbor than any other vessel, and soon spotted the flagship *Maria Teresa* making the final turn in the channel. Immediately the prepared signal flags were hoisted, and Lieutenant F. K. Hill ran to a six-pounder cannon on the bridge, elevated the barrel to its maximum height and fired toward the emerging Spanish column. The rest of the guns on the *Iowa* and the nearby *Oregon* quickly opened up on the *Maria Teresa,* which was about six thousand yards away, as the other American ships steamed toward the channel mouth.

Though not caught unprepared, many officers and men were surprised that after such a long time the Spanish had decided to sortie, and to make the attempt in broad daylight. The nighttime maneuver of keeping searchlights on the entrance had obviously worked. On board the *Indiana,* the captain saw that his "powder monkeys" were "throwing themselves down the steep ladder in their eagerness to reach their posts, until the ammunition deck was swarming with bruised and bleeding men, staggering to their feet and limping to their stations." A sailor on the *Oregon* recalled the same precipitous excitement: ". . . all of a sudden the Ordly made a dive for the Cabin head first, and told the old man [Captain Charles E. Clark] the Fleet was coming out of the Harbor. The old man jumpt up a standing."

What followed was a running version of the Battle of Manila Bay, for the wooden Spanish ships could not survive the fire of the more modern American fleet. It was as if the nineteenth century were being blown aside by the twentieth; great individual courage and old-fashioned ways going down to defeat in the face of equal courage, better teamwork, and more advanced technology, the supremacy of what Dewey himself had called the crux of the new methods of war: management and efficiency.

Even the Americans, busy at their destructive work, were touched by what was being lost. Robley Evans was struck by the glory of Cervera's flagship, flying colorful new battle streamers, her brasswork polished so that it blazed in the bright sunlight. "It was a magnificent, sad sight," thought Evans, "to see these beautiful ships in their death agonies." A Spanish gunner drew the admiration of an American sailor who thought he was "one of the bravest men I ever had the pleasure to look upon" because of the way he stuck to his post. "That man must have known he was going to a shure Deth, he stood on Deck and cep firing at us all the time, and the last time I seen him he was just going up in the air." As one of the enemy ships was burning, and the victors began cheering, Captain J. W. Philip of the *Texas* called out, "Don't cheer, boys! Those poor devils are dying!"

In less than four hours the fighting was over, and boats were launched to save as many of the enemy as possible. Even those Spanish who had made it safely ashore wanted to be picked up, because they feared for their fate at the hands of the Cuban insurgents. "So long as the enemy showed his flag, they fought like American seamen," Evans wrote of his crew, "but when the flag came down they were as gentle and tender as American women." The victory, like Dewey's, was complete: all six Spanish ships were sunk or run aground. There were 323 Spaniards killed and 151 wounded out of 2,227 men, while only one American lost his life and another was seriously wounded.

THE NATION HAD been stunned by the casualties of July 1 at El Caney and the San Juan Heights, and confused about what, exactly, had been achieved. Here, with the sinking, burning, or beaching of a whole Spanish fleet with little loss to America, was something to celebrate. The war, it seemed to many, was as good as over.

European powers were now convinced of the seriousness of the country's strength and resolve. American newspapers had been giving much space to coverage of European attitudes, seeing England as the staunch friend who had prevented France and especially Germany from aiding the Spanish. Now, however, there were five German warships in Manila Bay, perhaps with imperial ambitions for those islands. But after the victory even German newspapers "joined in the chorus of praise of Santiago," writes the historian Margaret Leech, and "Americans recognized a rush to get on the band wagon, and preened themselves on the unaccustomed compliment of the deference due to power."

THE SUNDAY AFTERNOON of the naval battle, less than twenty-four hours after receiving the telephoned message from George Kennan, Clara Barton, accompanied by two Red Cross doctors and several aides, rode on a supply-filled wagon to the field hospital. She had obtained permission from Shafter to requisition any empty wagon needed. "It seemed strange," she remembered later, "passing strange—that after all this more than a quarter of a century, I should be again taking supplies to the front of an army of the United States of America; that after all these years of Red Cross instruction and endeavor, it was still necessary to promiscuously seize an army wagon to get food to wounded men."

Conditions had not improved for these men, who still lay in the tangled wet grass without shelter from sun or rain. Those who had already been operated on were naked, because once their bloody uniforms had been cut from them, there were no other coverings available. "As we passed, we drew our hats over our eyes, turning our faces away as much as possible for the delicacy of the poor fellows who lay there with no shelter either from the elements or the eyes of the passers-by."

But most of the wounded still conscious had other needs on their minds. "My God, boys," shouted one when he saw her. "It's Clara Barton. Now we'll get something to eat." The whole experience—the sight of hundreds of torn and bloody men, the smell of the smoky fire and simple victuals—disoriented the seventy-six-year-old woman, making her relive youthful scenes of the Civil War. "I had not thought ever to make gruel again over a camp-fire; I cannot say how far it carried me back in the lapse of time or really where or who I felt that I was. I did not seem to be me, and still I seemed to know how to do it."

Once assured food was in the hands of the suffering, Barton began organizing more elaborate aid. First, sheets of unbleached muslin were ripped into strips large enough to cover the naked men; blankets, milk, chocolate, rice, and other supplies were soon brought up from Siboney over the "clayey, muddy, wet and cut to the hub" road. Conditions improved as wounded were taken to Siboney or sent home on ships, but she was angry at the unnecessary suffering that had been caused by lack of planning or even the simplest attempts of preparedness; she "felt it was again the same old story and wondered what gain there had been in the last thirty years. Had anything been worse than this?"

At one point during the first few days, she looked up from her duties to see a figure dressed "in khaki uniform showing hard service" and wearing a cowboy hat with a bandanna dangling from its back to protect his neck from the sun. Word had already reached the front lines that conditions in the field hospital were so terrible that it was best to keep the recent sick and wounded with their outfits, but Theodore Roosevelt had also heard of the new source of supplies, and had come quickly.

"I have some sick men with the regiment who refuse to leave it. They need such delicacies as you have here, which I am ready to pay for out of my own pocket. Can I buy them from the Red Cross?"

"Not for a million dollars," one of the doctors told him.

"But my men need these things," Roosevelt said anxiously. "I think a great deal of my men. I am proud of them."

"And we know they are proud of you, Colonel. But we can't sell Red Cross supplies."

"Then, how can I get them? I must have proper food for my sick men."

"Just ask for them, Colonel."

"Oh." Roosevelt gave the Red Cross staff his extraordinary smile. "Then I do ask for them. Lend me a sack and I'll take them right along." A burlap bag was quickly filled with malted milk, oatmeal, canned fruits, rice, tea, chocolate, beefsteak, and vegetables, then Roosevelt hoisted the ponderous load onto his back, and disappeared into the jungle.

IN AN ACCOUNT for the *Chicago Times-Herald,* the Red Cross nurse Janet Jennings described in great detail the work that went on once the wounded were moved to more comfortable surroundings at Siboney. Like many other observers, she found that suffering for a common cause had dissolved social and racial barriers. Among the badly injured men were "Captain Mills, of the First Cavalry, and William Clark, a colored private in the Twenty-fifth Infantry. . . . Their wounds were very similar—in the head—and of such a character as to require cool applications to the eyes constantly. Ice was scarce and worth its weight in gold for the lives of these men as well as others depended chiefly on cool applications to the eyes, with as uniform temperature as possible." All through the long night she went back and forth between Captain Mills and Private Clark, applying the ice to their eyes. "The courage that faces death on the battlefield or calmly awaits it in the hospital is not a courage of race or color," she informed her Chicago readers. "Two of the bravest men I ever saw were here, almost side by side . . . one white, the other black. They were wounded almost at the same time, and in the same way. The patient suffering and heroism of the black soldier was fully equal to that of the Anglo-Saxon. It was quite the same, the gentleness and appreciation. They were a study, these men so widely apart in life, but here strangely close and alike on the common ground of duty and sacrifice."

Shared achievement on that common ground was widely recognized among the troops, and by the reporters. "I cannot refrain," wrote George Kennan, "from calling particular attention to the splendid behavior of the colored troops. It is the testimony of all who saw them under fire that they fought with the utmost courage, coolness, and determination, and Colonel Roosevelt said to a squad of them in the trenches, in my presence, that he never expected to have, and could not ask to have, better men beside him in a hard fight." When Kennan asked one of the black wounded if any of his comrades had showed fear when the troops went into action, the man replied with a grin, "No, not egzactly; two or three of 'em looked kindo' squandered just at first, but they mighty soon braced up."

Theodore Roosevelt was not the only Rough Rider appreciative of the skill and courage of African-American troops. Admitting that his South-westerners had a "strong color prejudice," he wrote that they "grew to accept [black soldiers] with hearty goodwill as comrades, and were entirely willing, in their own phrase, 'to drink out of the same canteen.' "

Roosevelt went on to laud the white officers of the Ninth and Tenth Cavalry regiments, implying that it was mainly because of their courageous and self-sacrificing leadership (these officers suffered the heaviest casualties of any unit on the field) that their men fought so well, but Captain John Pershing, later known as "Black Jack" because of his service with the Tenth, leaves no doubt of the admiration with which he and his fellows regarded their troopers: "We officers of the Tenth Cavalry could have taken our black heroes in our arms. They had again fought their way into our affections, as they here had fought their way into the hearts of the American people."

Whatever affection did find its way into American hearts came through the widely distributed news stories of black heroism; even readers in the little logging town of Mendocino on the coast of California were told of their heroism in a lengthy article reprinted from the *New York Tribune:* "THE NEGRO SOLDIER HAS WON UNBOUNDED RESPECT IN THE WAR WITH SPAIN," read the headline, although the text made a point of noting that the way they charged showed "that their African nature has not been entirely eliminated by generations of civilization, but was bursting forth in savage yells in that wild rush."

FEARFUL OF THE HEAVY casualties that a direct assault on the Spanish entrenchments would entail, Shafter continued sending messages to the Spanish commander requesting surrender. These were very diplomatic, appealing to his humanitarianism and saluting his sense of honor, but they were refused. Shafter also tried to convince Admiral Sampson to run the risk of the mined entrance to the harbor so his ships could bombard Santiago from just off the waterfront. The navy grew to resent the army's constant demands and its cavalier disregard of how difficult a battleship would be to replace, a resentment that went up through the ranks and ended in a squabble between naval historian Alfred Thayer Mahan and Secretary of War Russell Alger during a meeting with the president, with the naval strategist "sailing into" Alger, telling him that he knew nothing about the American fleet or how it should be used. It was "a very pretty scrimmage," thought John Long. "It rather pleased the President, who, I think, was glad of the rebuke."

AMERICAN SOLDIERS GREW tired of watching the white truce flags as negotiators traveled back and forth between the lines. A temporary cease-fire was established, then extended several times to allow the Spaniards time to consider their situation. "The men had placed their own flags along the entire line of trenches," Richard Harding Davis wrote, "and though they afforded the enemy a perfect target and fixed our position as clearly as buoys mark out a race-course, the men wanted the flags there, and felt better seeing them there, and so there they remained. The trenches formed a horseshoe curve five miles in length, and the entire line was defiantly decorated with our flags. When they fluttered in the wind at full length and the sun kissed their colors, they made one of the most inspiring and beautiful pictures of the war."

The soldiers were happy when they heard that the constant extensions of the ceasefire were to be ended; many felt that the repeated requests for Spanish surrender had become unmanly.

"A drunken man," went a story making the rounds, "once considered himself insulted by John L. Sullivan, and, without recognizing who Sullivan was, gave him three minutes in which to apologize. Sullivan appreciated his opponent's condition and said, 'I don't need three minutes, I apologize now. What more will you have to drink?,' and departed. When he had gone the barkeeper said to the man, 'Do you know who that was you wanted to fight just now?'

"The drunken man said he did not know, nor did he care."

" 'Well, that was John L. Sullivan,' said the barkeeper, 'the champion pugilist of the world. Now what would you have done if he hadn't apologized in three minutes?'

"The drunken man gave the question a few moments' brief consideration. 'I guess I would have extended his time,' he said."

One of the Regulars complained to Richard Harding Davis, "I can't make out this flag-of-truce gag. It reminds me of two kids in a street fight, stopping after every punch to ask the other fellow if he's had enough. Why don't we keep at it until somebody gets hurted?"

Now, as the red, white, and blue banners rustled in the breeze over their rifle pits, the men crouched a bit lower and prepared for whatever came next.

AT FOUR O'CLOCK in the afternoon of July 10 American artillery opened up on the Spanish line, and warships began bombarding Santiago from their stations at sea, firing that continued the following day; but on the night of July 11 the area was hit with such a gale of wind and downpour of rain that tents were swept away, trenches flooded, and, most seriously, the unloading of supplies from the transports was made even slower and more difficult than usual at the unprotected anchorage of Siboney. As a further hindrance to the American effort, doctors reported that yellow fever had definitely made an appearance both at the seaside base and at the front.

General Nelson Miles, who had stopped in Cuba with the invasion force he was taking to Puerto Rico, was horrified at the unsanitary conditions he found everywhere, and terrified at the prospect of a plague of yellow fever sweeping through the American force. He ordered Siboney burned to the ground to rid it of bacilli, and wired President McKinley that he agreed with Shafter that General Toral's request to leave the city with his men and arms should be accepted. But again the thought was rejected; it was to be either unconditional surrender or an assault on the city. However, a concession to help resolve the stalemate was thrown in: if the Spanish did surrender, they would be transported back to Spain at the expense of the United States.

Shafter reopened negotiations, relaying the new offer. Now able to rise from his door-stretcher, though needing help to heave his bulk onto the back of a horse, he personally met with his Spanish counterpart to try to convince him of the course of wisdom, pointing out that every day new transports were arriving from the United States, bringing men, horses, mules, artillery, and supplies.

Back and forth went the white flags of truce again. There were misunderstandings, hopes raised, then dashed; the unwieldy general persisted through these difficult days, ignoring advice that Toral was merely playing for time, that he should call off the negotiations and take the city by storm. Finally his patience won out; his enemy would accept a free trip home, but only after Shafter agreed to the demand that, in the interest of honor, the word "capitulate" be used instead of "surrender."

Bittersweet victory after great sacrifice, but Stephen Crane should have the last word on the end of man-to-man killing at Santiago, even though he left, severely ill, while the surrender negotiations were going on, and there was plenty of death yet to come after the city capitulated. "Lying near one of the enemy's trenches," he had observed, "was a red-headed Spanish corpse. I wonder how many hundreds were cognizant of this red-headed Spanish corpse? It arose to the dignity of a landmark. There were many corpses, but only one with a red head. This red-head. He was always there. Each time I approached that part of the field I prayed that I might find that he had been buried. But he was always there—red-headed. His strong simple countenance was a malignant sneer at the system which was for ever killing the credulous peasants in a sort of black night of politics, where the peasants merely followed whatever somebody had told them was lofty and good. But, nevertheless, the red-headed Spaniard was dead. He was irrevocably dead. And to what purpose? The honour of Spain? Surely the honour of Spain could have existed without the violent death of this poor red-headed peasant? Ah well, he was buried when the heavy firing ceased and men had time for such small things as funerals. The trench was turned over on top of him. It was a fine, honourable, soldierly fate—to be buried in a trench, the trench of the fight and the death. Sleep well, red-headed peasant. You came to another hemisphere to fight because—because you were told to, I suppose. Well, there you are, buried in your trench on San Juan Hill. That is the end of it, your life has been taken—that is a flat, frank fact. And foreigners buried you expeditiously while speaking a strange tongue. Sleep well, red-headed mystery."

CHAPTER 10

A WORLDWIDE VICTORY

Why has it not gone hard with the high and the low in the War Department who have withheld from our soldiers the beds, the shelter, the food, the medicines, and the attendance that it was their duty to provide? . . . It is mean, disgraceful, and it certainly ought to go hard with the man who is responsible for it. His name is ALGER. . . . Hundreds of our men have fallen victims to the sloth and incompetence of ALGER. Their blood is on his head. Why doesn't somebody make it go hard with him?

New York Times editorial, September 2, 1898

WILLIAM McKINLEY WAS, of course, delighted at the victory in southeastern Cuba, but he and his fellow citizens now realized that this was just one theater in a war that was worldwide, a war fought in places sporting peculiar names that they would have been unable to spell or find on a map just a few months before, far-off places that suddenly presented challenges requiring immediate and forceful action.

One problem that had taken up much of his time was the renewed effort to annex Hawaii, which had come under United States influence because of a coup d'état engineered by American immigrants to the island kingdom. The treaty, which had been drawn up in 1897, was still unlikely to gain the two-thirds majority required for Senate ratification, so the president decided to submit it to direct legislation, which required only a majority of each house. Speaker Tom Reed of the House of Representatives was opposed, probably more from a desire to irritate McKinley than from any moral qualms, and he had managed for a while to keep it from consideration. The bill's managers persisted, however, and it passed that chamber in June.

The Senate was a more difficult arena, for here was a strong, and vocal, minority, including some influential Republicans, who suspected annexation was the first step on the road to empire. "Is not this but the opening of a grand avenue of conquest and of power?" asked Senator Donelson Caffery of Louisiana, who may also have feared the competitive effects of Hawaiian sugar on his state. "The Philippines next. Part of Asia next. Where will be the limits? . . . This Hawaiian scheme is but the entering wedge that cleaves a way open for empire."

McKinley, however, was very serious about annexing the islands. "We need Hawaii," he said to George Cortelyou, his trusted secretary, "just as much and a good deal more than we did California. It is manifest destiny." Part of his desire was based on commerce, since Hawaii was gateway to the rich markets of China and Japan, and also the sugar produced there had taken on increasing importance because of the cutoff of supplies from Cuba. But their location as waystation to the Philippines was obvious now, and they would serve as a base to protect approaches both to the West coast of the United States and the proposed canal through central America. In other words, he had begun thinking in terms of, not empire exactly, not yet, but expanding American power and influence, what Henry Cabot Lodge called a "large policy."

The president's seriousness was evident in the effort he put into securing passage of the treaty bill. George F. Hoar, Henry Cabot Lodge's fellow senator from Massachusetts, was one of the most influential of the semi-reluctant, but McKinley talked to him convincingly of the possibility that other nations might seize the archipelago, and end up controlling beautiful and strategic Pearl Harbor. "We cannot let these Islands go to Japan," McKinley told him. "Japan has her eye on them. Her people are crowding in there. I am satisfied they do not go there voluntarily as ordinary immigrants, but that Japan is pressing them in there in order to get possession before anybody can interfere."

Hoar ended up giving an important speech on the floor of the Senate in support of the bill, arguing that this was an invitation "to willing and capable people to share with us our freedom, our self-government, our equality, our education, and the transcendent sweets of civil and religious liberty," which was very different from the European example of expansion "held out to us in the far East and in the West Indies as the result of military conquest." The country wanted no part of such imperialism, "the ruin of the empires and republics of former time," but would welcome new territory only "where we can reasonably expect that the people we acquire will, in due time and on suitable conditions, be annexed to the United States as an equal part of a self-governing Republic." These words would come back to haunt the senator when he later became one of the most outspoken of the anti-imperialists.

A filibuster was attempted, but failed; the president looked ready to call a supplementary session, forcing the senators to remain through the hot, humid District summer to ensure passage. Rumors also made the rounds that even if the legislation was defeated, the chief executive would "proclaim the annexation of Hawaii as a war measure." Finally, on July 6, the resolution passed by a vote of 42 to 21, and the president wasted no time in signing it the next day.

MCKINLEY AND HIS ADVISERS worried about the situation of their admiral in Manila Bay. Although he had destroyed the enemy fleet, there were about twenty-five thousand Spanish troops and fourteen thousand Loyalist native militia scattered throughout the archipelago, with ten thousand in or around the capital. George Dewey had advised Washington that "To retain possession and thus control Philippine Islands would require . . . well-equipped force of 5,000 men . . . ," and, again, he thought of his great mentor. "We had the city under our guns, as Farragut had New Orleans under his. But naval power can reach no further ashore. For tenure of the land you must have the man with a rifle."

Before the destruction of Cervera's fleet there was the possibility that the Spanish might send ships from their home waters to retake the bay, but the victory of July 3 removed that threat, since the enemy now had to fear raids on its own coast. Manila and the islands with their tens of thousands of troops remained uncaptured, however, and Dewey was facing another threateningly powerful force that was already sharing the local waters with him: the German Squadron under Vice-Admiral Otto von Diederichs, which consisted of the cruisers *Irene* and *Prinzess Wilhelm,* the transport *Darmstadt,* carrying fourteen hundred men as relief crews, the flagship *Kaiserin Augusta,* and the battleship *Kaiser.*

Spanish soldiers could do his fleet little direct harm, since he had destroyed their ships and moved his own to Cavite, out of range of their artillery. Emilio Aguinaldo, the Filipino rebel leader of mixed Tagalog and Chinese ancestry, was brought from exile in Hong Kong by the *McCulloch,* returning from one of its dispatch runs. "Obviously," Dewey wrote in his autobiography, "as our purpose was to weaken the Spanish in every legitimate way . . . operations by the insurgents against Spanish oppression in the Philippines under certain restrictions would be welcome. . . . [but] . . . my policy was to avoid any entangling alliance with the insurgents." When Aguinaldo arrived, the two men worked out a vague pact of cooperation that allowed the rebels to begin those operations against their common enemy, Dewey waving at the coast and saying, "Well, now go ashore there; we have got our forces at the arsenal of Cavite, go ashore and start your army." Neither leader understood what the other really expected from their cooperation, which would lead to trouble in the coming weeks.

The Germans seemed to present a more serious and immediate challenge to American control of the bay. Other nations had sent visiting warships, but not in such numbers or of such tonnage, and the British, French, and Japanese had scrupulously followed the rules of blockade: identifying themselves upon entrance into Manila Bay, notifying the American flagship of their planned movements, responding courteously to being hailed or signaled, and, most important, not approaching American ships after dark. As Dewey noted, the "fate of the *Maine* when lying at anchor in a Spanish harbor" was never far from his or his men's minds.

The Germans followed none of these established procedures, displaying a lack of respect that not only personally irritated Dewey, as it had earlier in Hong Kong, but also seemed to him to demonstrate an intent to challenge American power and whatever future territorial claims might be made for the fruits of victory. Dewey met with Diederichs and mentioned that the flotilla he commanded seemed out of scale considering that there was only one German commercial enterprise in Manila.

"I am here by order of the kaiser, sir!" Diederichs snapped back.

"From which I could only infer," wrote Dewey later, "that I had expressed myself in a way that excited his displeasure." The Americans watched as "the Germans, with the industry with which they aim to make their navy efficient, were keeping very busy. I saw that they did not mean to accept my interpretation of the laws of blockade. German officers frequently landed in Manila, where they were on the most cordial terms with the Spaniards, who paid them marked attention; and, the wish fathering the thought, the talk of the town was that the Germans would intervene in favor of Spain."

On July 7, Dewey sent his aide, Lieutenant Thomas Brumby, to call on Admiral von Diederichs with a list of complaints; the German replied

mildly and convincingly to the young man that he had no desire to interfere with the blockade or impede American actions. That same day, however, when the *Raleigh* and *Concord* were sent to Isla Grande in Subic Bay
to investigate charges by Aguinaldo that the Germans were aiding Spanish forces in the area, they found the *Irene* acting suspiciously, slipping
its anchor in order to leave quickly. Although no evidence was found
of German interference, the incident led to further distrust. A few days
later, a German officer, Captain-Lieutenant Paul von Hintze, came to the
Olympia to deliver a formal response to the list of complaints presented by
Brumby on the seventh, and when he argued that the Americans had had
no right to attempt to stop the *Irene* at Subic, there was an explosion from
Dewey.

"Does Admiral von Diederichs think he commands here or do I?" asked
Dewey angrily. "Tell your Admiral if he wants war I am ready."

"Mein Gott!" Hintze said to Lieutenant Brumby. "What is the matter
with your Admiral?"

"Nothing," answered Brumby, "he means every word he says and you
better tell your Admiral exactly what it was."

Exchanges between the two admirals continued over the next week,
with the commander of British forces in the bay, Captain Edward Chiches-
ter, supporting Dewey's interpretation of the international laws of blockade. The admirals managed to define their relationship in a way that
avoided serious trouble, but suspicion of German intentions, based on
their actions not only in the Philippines but also in the Caribbean, Samoa,
and Europe, continued to be strongly held by the American public, providing a basis for support of the British and French in the First World War.

Many of Dewey's worries were relieved when two United States monitors, more naval gun platforms than ships, with ten- and twelve-inch cannon, finally joined him, and the expeditionary force that had been
assembled in San Francisco under the direction of Major-General Wesley
Merritt began arriving, bringing a much-needed resupply of ammunition.

Merritt's Eighth Army Corps came in separate contingents. The van-
guard, consisting of three transports and the protected cruiser *Charleston*,
resupplied at Honolulu and then, under orders from Secretary of the Navy
Long, proceeded to the island of Guam, a strategically located Spanish
possession in the Mariana Islands. Captain Henry Glass of the *Charleston*
fired a few rounds at the harbor fort, as he entered, to determine its range.
Soon two small boats rowed out, and uniformed Spanish officers came
aboard, apologizing. "You will pardon our not immediately replying to your

salute, captain, but we are not accustomed to receiving salutes here, and are not supplied with proper guns for returning them. May I inquire what business brings you to San Luis d'Apra?"

No ship had visited since the declaration of war; Captain Glass quickly brought his guests up to date as he took them into custody, then raised the Stars and Stripes over the island, and, carrying the Spanish troops with him but leaving an occupying force, sailed on. There was some confusion among the volunteers and Regulars on board the transports that was matched back home when news of the acquisition arrived. "What about Guam and where is it anyway," one warrant officer remembered the men asking one another, "and what do we want of it?"

AFTER THE SURRENDER at Santiago, the invasion of Puerto Rico that General Miles had been organizing was given the go-ahead by President McKinley. Miles steamed from Guantánamo on July 21. All these wide-ranging campaigns seemed to be progressing nicely, when bad news from Cuba began pouring in.

By the time Santiago had capitulated, half the Rough Riders were "dead or disabled by wounds and sickness," according to Theodore Roosevelt, and even the Seventy-first New York, which had the smallest sick list in the brigade, had only four hundred of their men fit for duty. There were to be no more wounds, but sickness in the ranks grew apace, and this wasting way to death had nothing of glory about it: fever, vomiting, bloody diarrhea, a weakness that left a warrior as dependent as a babe, then, often, a body found stiff and cold in the tent at dawn.

Theodore Roosevelt wanted his outfit to be ordered out of this pest hole to help General Miles. "We earnestly hope you will send us . . . to Porto Rico," he wrote Secretary of War Russell Alger. Over the next two weeks he spent thousands of dollars of his own money buying the supplies now flowing more easily through the docks of the city of Santiago in an attempt to keep his men as healthy and strong as possible for that campaign, but he had to admit, "The lithe college athletes had lost their spring; the tall, gaunt hunters and cow-punchers lounged listlessly in their dog-tents, which were steaming morasses during the torrential rains, and then ovens when the sun blazed down; but there were no complaints." Even the two robust officers he relied on most, Greenway and Goodrich, succumbed to fever for a few days, and if there were no direct complaints, there were the songs with which the soldiers of the Fifth Corps expressed their feelings:

Snakes as long as Halstead Street,
Flies and skeeters that can't be beat.
Oh, how we want to leave Cuba,
Lord, how we want to go home!

These all contrasted with the favorite line from a stage tune that would be sung to passing newspaper correspondents when conditions were satisfactory:

Just tell them that you saw us,
and that we were doing well.

The colonel himself was in excellent fettle, and when General Fitzhugh Lee, who had recently arrived, invited him to visit Morro Castle, which had guarded the entrance to Santiago Bay, he made the most of the opportunity for a sea bath. Roosevelt quickly stripped and told a reluctant Jack Greenway that it would be fun to swim to the wreck of Hobson's *Merrimac,* which lay several hundred yards off shore.

"We weren't out more than a dozen strokes," the lieutenant later told a friend, "before Lee, who had clambered up on the parapet of Fort Morro, began to yell."

"Can you make out what he's trying to say," the old man asked, punctuating his words with long, overhand strokes.

"Sharks," says I, wishing I were back on shore.

"Sharks," says the colonel, blowing out a mouthful of water, "they" stroke "won't" stroke "bite." Stroke. "I've been" stroke "studying them" stroke "all my life" stroke "and I never" stroke "heard of one" stroke "bothering a swimmer." Stroke. "It's all" stroke "poppy cock."

Just then a big fellow, probably not more than ten or twelve feet long, but looking as big as a battleship to me, showed up alongside us. Then came another, till we had quite a group. The colonel didn't pay the least attention. . . .

Meantime the old general was doing a war dance up on the parapet, shouting and standing first on one foot and then on the other, and working his arms like he was doing something on a bet.

Finally we reached the wreck and I felt better. The colonel, of course, got busy looking things over. I had to pretend I was interested, but I was thinking of the sharks and getting back to shore. I didn't hurry the colonel in his inspection either.

After a while he had seen enough, and we went over the side again. Soon the sharks were all about us again, sort of pacing us in, as they had paced us out, while the old general did the second part of his war dance. He felt a whole lot better when we landed, and so did I.

Roosevelt, in his vibrant good health, became commander of the Second Brigade; every other ranking officer, except Leonard Wood, was ill, and Wood was appointed the governor-general of the city.

Bureaucrats in Washington did not recognize the gravity of the situation, devising various impractical plans to move the regiments periodically to get them away from swamp "vapors" thought to be the sources of disease, but in Cuba concern over the health of the Fifth Corps finally penetrated even to its commanding general. At the end of July, Shafter called a meeting of his senior officers to discuss the crisis.

There was no disagreement; all, volunteer officers and Regulars alike, knew that the corps had to leave the island, and quickly. "It was deemed best," wrote Roosevelt, "to make some record of our opinion, in the shape of a letter or report, which would show that to keep the army in Santiago meant its absolute and objectless ruin, and that it should at once be recalled." Since the Regulars were hesitant to harm their careers by protesting too forcefully, Roosevelt agreed to write a strongly worded letter to the authorities in Washington: "To keep us here, in the opinion of every officer commanding a division or a brigade, will simply involve the destruction of thousands. There is no possible reason for not shipping the entire command North at once." And he concluded, "If we are kept here it will in all human possibility mean an appalling disaster, for the surgeons have estimated that over half the army, if kept here during the sickly season, will die."

A "round-robin" letter, milder though still firm in tone, was also sent, signed by all the troop commanders. Unfortunately, both were leaked to the press, probably by General Shafter, at a sensitive time; the Spanish government had approached President McKinley through the French ambassador, and secret negotiations for an armistice had been started. McKinley, angry and indignant at this insubordination, feared the enemy would take advantage of their knowledge of his army's plight to demand better terms; Alger, who had already decided the force should come home, was furious and decided to do some leaking of his own to hurt the bumptious boy he had so often favored, Theodore Roosevelt.

But, for all the anger their publication caused, the letters worked to hasten the withdrawal of the Fifth Corps; orders were sent immediately for it to be replaced by fresh troops from the "immune" regiments, consisting of men who had already had the diseases. Sick and exhausted veterans began staggering on board the unclean, improperly prepared transports to make their way home, some of them so ill that they had to be supported by healthier comrades; everyone believed it was sure death to be sent to the Corps hospital.

Roosevelt, expecting that the Rough Riders would be used in an attack against Havana in the fall, began planning his regiment's part in the campaign as soon as he boarded ship.

A NUMBER OF NAVAL and military strategists, including Alfred Thayer Mahan, had argued that Puerto Rico should be attacked before Cuba because it was less heavily defended, thinking a victory there and in the Philippines might mean the war could be won without assaulting Spain's strongest colony. Because of the closeness of Florida to Cuba and the need to flush Admiral Cervera out of his refuge at Santiago, this advice was not followed, although General Nelson Miles had also been in favor of it, agreeing that attacks on the edges of the enemy's power could lead to strategic victories won at little cost.

There had been no talk before the outbreak of hostilities of annexing Puerto Rico, only discussion of its strategic value. Once war was declared, Philip C. Hanna, who had been American consul in San Juan, wrote that there should be an early invasion: "10,000 American soldiers landed in Puerto Rico can hold the island forever, because I am convinced, that a large number of Puerto Ricans will arise and shake off the Spanish yoke as soon as they are assured of help."

This proved remarkably prescient advice, and probably should have been followed sooner. Richard Harding Davis was impressed by the campaign, which started with a landing at dawn on July 24, and he was struck by a bit of imperial symbolism a few days later when Ponce was occupied. As General Miles' boat approached the docks of the surrendered city, a soldier stood in the bow waving a heavy silk American flag, a multilingual soldier who, when he had served in the French Foreign Legion, had also been the first man to carry the tricolor ashore when Indo-China had been conquered and added to the French Empire. "When one remembers that there are 25,000 regulars in our army to whom it might have been given, it was a curious coincidence that this particular honor should have fallen to that particular man."

The Americans marched from Ponce into the interior in four columns, driving Spanish forces before them; they found the climate mild, the countryside fertile, the people welcoming and generous, and their own leadership skilled. "The army in Porto Rico advanced with the precision of a set of chessmen," Davis reported. "Its moves were carefully considered and followed to success; its generals . . . never missed a point nor needlessly lost a man, nor retreated from a foot of land over which they had advanced. . . . Every day the four different columns swept the Spaniards before them in a net, capturing town after town and company after company."

Davis did some capturing of his own, as did Stephen Crane, who had returned to the war after a partial recovery from his illness. Each had a town surrender to him. And so went the campaign; the relative ease of this triumphal sweep across Puerto Rico, with its plentiful food, more or less welcoming people, and just enough resistance from Spanish troops to add spice to the tropic air, led to teasing complaints from editors and others at home such as Mr. Dooley, who said, "I'd give five dollars . . . if I was out iv this Sixth Wa-ard to-night, an' down with Gin'ral Miles' gran' picnic and moonlight excursion in Porther Ricky. 'Tis no comfort in bein' a cow'rd whin ye think iv thim br-rave la-ads facin' death be suffication in bokays an' dyin' iv waltzin' with th' pretty girls iv Porther Ricky."

BY THE BEGINNING of August, Major-General Merritt had eighty-five hundred men in front of Manila, consisting chiefly of Western volunteers. Together, with a cooperative attitude missing from the Santiago campaign, the commanding general and the admiral began making plans for a combined assault on the Spanish forces, most of which had been driven into the capital by the insurgents.

Dewey and Merritt made a point of not striking any formal agreements with Aguinaldo; they themselves did not know what decisions would be made about the islands after the fighting was over, but for the moment the rebels had been useful. "I was in the South in the Civil War," Dewey remembered, "and the only friends we had in the South were the negroes, and we made use of them; they assisted us on many occasions. I said these people [the Filipinos] were our friends, and 'we have come here and they will help us just exactly as the negroes helped us in the Civil War.' " The rebel leader did help the Americans in practical ways: "It was found necessary," admitted General Merritt, "to solicit [his] aid in obtaining horses, buffaloes, carts, etc., for the purposes of transportation, for which the native population was disposed to charge exorbitant prices."

But Aguinaldo, who had established himself as "dictator" of a revolutionary government while promising his people that elections and a republic would follow the successful end of the revolution, was beginning to suspect that this recently arrived army would not be willing to leave after capturing Manila. He couldn't take the well-defended city by himself, however, since he lacked artillery.

Americans had their own suspicions of the rebels, believing they were obstructing operations, especially by undisciplined firing on Spanish positions, which might bring on a serious battle before they were ready. There was also fear Aguinaldo might be trying to strike a separate bargain with the Spanish. Dewey cabled Secretary Long: "Merritt's most difficult problem will be how to deal with insurgents under Aguinaldo, who has become aggressive and even threatening toward our army."

Dewey was confident that the Spanish, already suffering from the effects of his blockade, would submit when faced with the full complement of naval and military reinforcements sent from the United States. Once the powerful monitors and the troops arrived the delicate negotiations, conducted through the Belgian consul, made good progress, but the Spanish insisted that at the proper moment some force by the United States be used. The commanding general, recalled Dewey later, "said his honor demanded that. So I had to fire, to kill a few people." The Spaniards also insisted that Filipinos not take part in the fighting. These conditions were followed and the city quickly surrendered.

Almost immediately new troubles began. "After the battle," General Merritt later wrote, "the insurgent forces gathered outside the American lines endeavoring to gain admission to the town, but strong guards were posted and General Aguinaldo was given to understand that no insurgents would be allowed to enter with arms. A few of the houses in the suburbs, whose occupants had taken refuge in the town, were looted by the insurgents in spite of the vigilance of the Americans. Considerable fear was evinced among the Spanish forces inside the city that a massacre would be attempted by the insurgents, and they were very anxious to unite with the Americans against them."

Aguinaldo, who was personally keeping his distance out of fear that the Americans might imprison him, wrote them a bitter reproach: "My troops are forced by yours, by means of threats of violence, to retire from positions taken."

The American victory in the Philippines was one that bore within it a bitter foretaste of troubles to come.

JUST AS THE AMERICAN ships were moving into position in Manila Bay and the troops were girding themselves to charge the enemy's defensive works, a protocol establishing a ceasefire was signed in the United States by Secretary of State William Day and Jules Cambon, the French ambassador acting on behalf of the Spanish. Guns immediately fell silent in Puerto Rico, where American columns had made such progress that Nelson Miles was convinced just four more days would have seen the conquest of the whole island; because of Dewey having severed the Philippine cable, word did not reach Manila until the sixteenth, two days after the city was captured.

Negotiations had been handled masterfully by President McKinley through his representatives, and by the end of July he was able to present, at a full Cabinet meeting, preliminary demands being made on the Spanish government. First, Cuba must be given its freedom, and all Spanish troops withdrawn. Second, instead of a monetary indemnity, the United States would acquire Puerto Rico as well as the other Spanish islands in the Caribbean and one, Guam, from the Marianas group in the Pacific. There was complete agreement among the Cabinet officers on these two conditions, but a split occurred over what to do about the Philippines, the disagreement having to do with how much territory to demand. Should the United States take only the port of Manila for a base or should the whole archipelago be seized?

McKinley adroitly maneuvered these discussions, and the final position was that the United States would control Manila, "pending the conclusion of a peace treaty which should determine the control, possession, and government of the Philippines." Appalled, Ambassador Cambon argued that "They are very hard terms." McKinley made one or two small concessions, but the French ambassador, recognizing that the president would flex no further, recommended that Madrid acquiesce. The Spanish, having lost the war at sea, felt they could resist no longer, and agreed, hoping that when the true peace treaty was drawn up they might retain the Philippines.

IN EARLY AUGUST, as word had leaked out that the war might soon be over, many of the 140,000 federalized militia feared they would be denied the glory of combat; requests, backed by state and local politicians, to be immediately shipped to a war zone like Puerto Rico or the Philippines came flooding in to Secretary Alger. Since he and his War Department were under increasing public, and especially Democratic, criticism for the poor handling of the Santiago campaign and worsening health conditions in the stateside camps, Alger was eager to prove his competence by moving all available volunteer regiments to Puerto Rico to support General Nelson Miles.

President McKinley was not impressed. "Mr. Secretary," he asked, shaking his head, "what do you think the people will say if they believe we unnecessarily and at great expense send these boys out of the country? Is it either necessary or expedient?"

Russell Alger could say little in defense of the idea. "The discussion of the subject," noted the president's secretary, George Cortelyou, "ended abruptly."

ONE VOLUNTEER WHO HAD indeed benefited from the glory of battle returned to the United States on Monday, August 15. So great had the fame of Roosevelt and his Rough Riders grown that there was a horde of well-wishers and reporters waiting for him when his transport docked at Montauk Point, Long Island. As soon as he was spotted on the deck a chant of "Roosevelt! Roosevelt! Hurrah for Teddy and the Rough Riders!" thundered louder than the surf across the sandy beach.

"How are you, Colonel Roosevelt?" called an officer on the pier.

"I am feeling disgracefully well!" came the roaring reply. After a pause so the crowd could study the haggard faces of other Rough Riders on deck, he said, "I feel positively ashamed of my appearance when I see how badly off some of my brave fellows are." Then, to cheers and laughter, "Oh, but we have had a bully fight!"

Once he was ashore, and officially welcomed back to the country, Roosevelt made his way to the reporters.

"Will you be our next governor?" one asked.

"None of that . . . All I'll talk about is the regiment. It's the finest regiment that ever was, and I'm proud to command it."

That regiment, or rather what remained of it, drew the shocked sympathy of the crowd. "My God," one man said, "there are not half of the men there that left."

CAMP WIKOFF, named after an officer who had fallen at San Juan Heights, was established at Montauk because its location at the tip of Long Island would allow units returning from Cuba to be placed in quarantine safely distant from populated areas while still supposedly close enough to obtain good food and care for the sick and wounded. The prevailing wind, too, was an advantage, blowing away, as Edmund Morris points out, "whatever yellow-fever bacilli lingered among the troops—wafting them somewhere in the direction of Spain." It did not take long for the soldiers, and the press, to discover just how inadequate the place was for thousands and thousands of sick, malnourished, and exhausted men.

Charles Post and the Seventy-first New York, after a voyage made bearable only by the joy of going home, hove into view around the same time as the Rough Riders. Most of the men were ill with dysentery and fever, but all wanted to appear able to make it ashore under their own power. "Men fought against sickness," Post noted, "as if sickness were yielding to something effeminate." Even stretcher cases had to be ordered by medical officers to lie down, but, not surprisingly, there were not enough stretchers or ambulances to carry everyone to the hospital detention camp, where the yellow flag flew to indicate quarantine for yellow fever.

"SCANDAL," THAT DREAD word to politicians, was already appearing in newspaper headlines. The "Round Robin" and Roosevelt letter from Santiago sparked a firestorm of criticism of the treatment of the nation's soldiers; then typhoid and dysentery appeared as well in the stateside camps, probably because of the poor sanitary discipline of the volunteer troops. The volunteers had not kept their bad health a secret from their hometowns; parents, local nabobs, and town and country newspapers alerted the big-city papers as they zinged their angry complaints to Washington. At the very moment of victory, the country was as aroused as an angry beehive.

Why were conditions in the camps so bad? How could the complete array of equipment for a two-hundred-bed hospital be lost somewhere in

limbo for weeks? Why had the Tampa embarkation of equipment and supplies been botched? Where had all the other vanished consignments gone?
Why had the government-issued food for soldiers in the field been so ined-
ible? Was that canned beef as poisonous as rumor had it? And there
inevitably followed the questions so spine-chilling for politicians: Who was
responsible? And was their culpability due to incompetence or corruption?
The public's need to personalize these various disasters meant that heads
were going to roll, and everyone started ducking.

NONE OF THIS popular anger, of course, touched Theodore Roosevelt,
although Secretary of War Russell Alger, after publication of the letter
about ill health in the Fifth Corps, had tried to mar Roosevelt's reputation
by slyly releasing his earlier letter requesting transfer of the outfit to Puerto
Rico. It contained some bragging remarks: "the Rough Riders . . . are as
good as any regulars, and three times as good as any State troops."

Disapproval of such a remark coming from a potential state governor
had been heated and loud. As Roosevelt admitted, "The publication of the
extract from my letter was not calculated to help me secure the votes of the
National Guard if I ever became a candidate for office." But Alger soon
apologized to his old friend, and the uproar quickly subsided as a patriotic
and indulgent citizenry recognized that the remarks had sprung from both
his ebullient style and an overweening pride in his outfit; besides, it came
to be argued, hadn't his letter from Santiago forced Alger and the other
uncaring bureaucrats in Washington to withdraw the Fifth Corps, thus
saving it from even worse suffering?

This outspoken warrior found on his return that he had become the
most famous man in America, even, for a while, outdrawing in public
attention the victor of Manila Bay. The New York World reported on August
28 that "Travelling men of all shades and classes declare him more talked
about than any man in the country."

Politicians came calling to his tent at Montauk Point. The first to present himself was John Jay Chapman in his role as a leader of the Independent Party. Chapman was not a practical man in politics or anything else,
but if he could convince his old friend to run for governor on the Independent ticket, then the state Republican boss, Senator Thomas Platt, would
be forced by Roosevelt's popularity to put him at the head of the Republican list as well. This would mean that the public would be presented with
contrasting slates for other offices—upright young reformers of the Inde-

pendents versus the Republican Party hacks under Platt. And given such a clear choice, Chapman was sure, voters would want to send their hero to Albany backed by honest men.

Roosevelt was noncommittal; Chapman gave him a week to think the offer over and left confident of, and dazzled by, his candidate. "I shall never forget the lustre that shone about him . . . at Montauk Point, and my companion accused me of being in love with him, and indeed I was. I never before nor since have felt that glorious touch of hero-worship which solves life's problems by showing you a man. Lo, there, it says, Behold the way! You have only to worship, trust, and support him."

Next day came visiting Lemuel Quigg, trusted associate of the "Easy Boss" of the Republican machine, Tom Platt. Quigg was also trusted by Roosevelt, who'd been grateful for the man's support when running for mayor of New York City in 1894. Quigg and other Party leaders had been pushing Platt, in spite of the boss's intense dislike of the independent-minded fellow, to choose Roosevelt for the nomination. Frank S. Black, the current Republican governor, had been hurt by a financial scandal involving repairs to the Erie Canal, and the party was also split into factions between machine and anti-machine elements. The Easy Boss had been, as he himself put it, "doing a heap of thinking," and was not enthusiastic about the choices facing him: defeat by the Democrats or winning with the untamed Rough Rider. "If he becomes Governor of New York, sooner or later, with his personality, he will have to be President of the United States. . . . I am afraid to start that thing going."

Quigg spent a couple of hours with Roosevelt and his brother-in-law, Douglas Robinson, in the colonel's tent, asking for a "plain statement" from him as to whether or not he wanted the nomination, and whether he would "make war" on Platt and his friends "or whether I would confer with them and with the organization leaders generally," Roosevelt later wrote, "and give fair consideration to their point of view as to party policy and public interest."

Roosevelt said he wanted the nomination, and that he would not "make war on Mr. Platt or anyone else if it could be avoided; that what I wanted was to be Governor and not a faction leader . . . but that while I would try to get on well with the organization, the organization must with equal sincerity strive to do what I regarded as essential for the public good." He would run an open administration, consult with anyone "who might possess real knowledge" of whatever issue was at hand, and would act "as my own judgment and conscience dictated."

None of this surprised Quigg, who carried the tidings to Thomas Platt and the Republican State Committee while Roosevelt, his period of quarantine over, went home to Sagamore Hill at Oyster Bay, Long Island, for a rousing hero's welcome from the local populace, followed by a few days of quiet rest before returning to duty, relaxation made all the more enjoyable by front-page newspaper headlines reading: "RISING TIDE FOR ROOSEVELT."

ANOTHER VETERAN WELCOMED home by his community was Captain Malcolm W. Rafferty of Company K in the Seventy-first New York, and his parade can stand for ritual celebrations of varying sizes and Party inclinations being given all across the country. Rafferty, like Roosevelt, was a genuine hero, validated as such by the testimony of many witnesses, including Charles Post, who had served under him. But here, too, was the touch of an old-fashioned political campaign as his procession started at the Democratic clubhouse and wound through the streets of his home borough of Queens illuminated by bonfires at the street corners. "Shortly after 7 o'clock whistles began to blow, bells to ring, cheers resound and fireworks to fizz." A squad of policemen led, then came a grand marshal, various Democratic politicians either currently in office or with hopes for the fall, members of the soldier's family riding in carriages, the Seventy-first Regiment's Fife and Drum Corps, and all the members of Company K healthy enough to ride in carriages. "They were cheered to the echo. Following them came one hundred men of the North Beach Improvement Company . . . the Astoria Maennerhor Society, four hundred strong, and the Frohsinn and Harmonie Societies with two hundred members. After them followed 300 members of the Queens County Athletic Club. Then came 100 members of the Main Social Club, filling the air with patriotic cheers. All kinds of transparencies were carried. One read:

> Remember the Maine,
> To S— hell Spain.

A dozen bands marched by, and a dozen more fraternal societies, and the Sunswick Democratic Club chanting: "What's the matter with Rafferty—Why Raff? Raff? RAFF?—He's a-l-r-i-g-h-t. He said 'Come on F'; that was Rafferty!"

But the biggest thrill for this partisan crowd of fifty thousand came when Rafferty reached the corner of Fulton Street and Jackson Avenue, where "barrels and boxes were piled thirty feet high. Up on top of them was an old-fashioned rocking chair in which was placed a dummy stuffed with straw, and labeled 'Secretary Alger.' As Capt. Rafferty passed, the wood, which had been saturated with kerosene, was ignited, and quickly lighted up the whole square."

THERE WAS NO HERO'S welcome for a very ill Private Charles Post, who, along with hundreds of his fellows, lay virtually unattended at Camp Wikoff, weltering in his own filth. "Tents were latrines" for men too weak to carry themselves more than a few feet without collapsing, and "the grass between the tented streets was flecked with blood and dysentery." They did receive, however, periodic visits from a Bible-clutching agent of the Lord. "You men—oh, you men!" he would scold them. "Such blasphemy, such taking the Name. You soldiers, who have been so near to death—to use such language! Oh you, you, who have been in the presence of death, who have faced your God! I am praying for you. I am praying for you!"

The men, in "unrestrained secular language," responded that carrying food to them rather than praying over their emaciated bodies would be more helpful, but "He turned the thought aside." A fierce wind and rainstorm blew down the tents, and rumors spread that five men had suffocated under the press of wet canvas; a riot started when an officious cook began striking hungry men with his heavy ladle. "We would have killed him had we been able—and I say *we* thoughtfully, for I would not have shirked the decent instincts and impulses of that moment. These were no tame tabby-cat men."

The next day Russell Alger inspected the camp. Everything had been cleaned and groomed for the visit, and the Secretary of War walked through the streets of tents impeccably dressed in frock coat and silk hat, followed by an equally immaculate staff. "He was a small man, and slight, with a gray mustache and a goatee."

Veterans of El Caney and San Juan Heights were not intimidated by the glittering insignia on the shoulders of his attending officers. Over and over again he was told of the true conditions; Charles Post was one of those who spoke up. "Mr. Secretary . . . We are dying here without attention, without rations or medicines. Five men were picked up yesterday morning, dead. . . . Every effort has been made to make this place nice for your inspection. And it's a lie. We're dying of neglect."

Alger, in his mild, pleasant way, responded soothingly, "There, there, my man. . . . We'll fix everything."

The secretary had been suffering tremendous criticism, some fair, some decidedly not. His name had become the byword for incompetence and corruption in government service; his head was the one that public outrage was demanding, as voters preferred to forget that they themselves had pressured congressmen and senators not to spend money for a well-organized and efficient military establishment until it was too late, and that they had then supported their militias' disdain of rigorous discipline, contributing to camps becoming breeding grounds for typhoid. "The smaller fry can be investigated afterward," one editor wrote now. "Sweep Alger out of the way first. Remove the polluting influence of Michigan politics and the rest will follow as a matter of course. Algerism is at the bottom of the war scandals. Remove Alger and you administer to Algerism its death blow."

Sweep Alger out of the way indeed was what Republican candidates across the country were begging of the president, fearing a debacle in the upcoming elections if he were allowed to remain in his post; the *New York Times* ran a front-page story with a headline quoting the Democratic ex-governor of Ohio as saying, "IF MANY MORE SOLDIERS DIE REPUBLICAN DEFEAT IS CERTAIN," and even Republican newspapers began attacking the secretary of war. William McKinley was too subtle and experienced a politician, however, for a public head-lopping. While announcing that he refused to abandon Alger, the president began distancing himself from the secretary and the War Department. At the same time he paid a well-publicized visit to Montauk Point, his cavalry escort of Rough Riders commanded by Colonel Roosevelt, to show his concern about the citizen-soldiers' condition, then he appointed what became known as the Dodge Commission to investigate the scandals.

Alger refused to resign, but was not able to defend himself very ably against the storm of criticism because his vanity and self-righteousness got in the way. "He made no distinction," writes one historian, "between politically motivated slanders and reasoned criticisms of the conduct of operations, but rejected both as reflections on his personal integrity." The *New York Times* reported in a front-page story that he went so far as to imply that the source of complaints was the softness of American men: "The Secretary added that, in Europe, the people, with their full military training, knew what hardships must be encountered by troops in a campaign . . . [the public] could scarcely fail to gain the impression that the American people are lacking in soldierly qualities."

President William McKinley at an improvised desk during the summer of 1898.
(*Courtesy Library of Congress, photo by Francis Benjamin Johnston*)

Alger was able, however, to argue a crucial point to the few who would listen: "When we think of calling for an army from civil life, gathering it together, arming and equipping it, when there was no equipment for it, fighting battles all the way from Manila to Porto Rico, and closing the whole matter in three months, we realize it is something that has never before been equalled, and I doubt if it ever will be."

Of course, the man's obtuseness did block his understanding of the full picture. Testimony of veterans like Post and his fellows did not impress him. Instead, he took the word of the officials in charge, boasting that "only" 126 men had died at Camp Wikoff out of the thousands processed through, as if that proved every one of them had been adequately cared for.

Even Roosevelt had given up on him, writing Henry Cabot Lodge, "I am very much afraid that with Alger the trouble is congenital. He simply *can't* do better; he *can not* learn by experience. Now I don't want to grumble, and I am doing my best to keep the 'Rough Riders' from grumbling, but we did not have good food on our transport coming back here; we did not have good water; and we were so crowded that if an epidemic had broken out, we should have had literally no place in which to isolate a single patient. . . . I do most earnestly wish that the President would change Alger before election, and change him for some man who would himself begin to uproot the evils in the [War] Department."

PRIVATE POST FAKED being healthy enough to obtain a pass from Camp Wikoff. Bloated with malnutrition, he gorged himself at the train station lunch counter on milk, canned peaches, pie, drinking cup after cup of coffee with milk and heaping spoons of sugar before staggering to the Pullman car clutching his precious sketch books and a bag of emergency provisions for the journey. Buoyed and strengthened by his happiness in escaping the camp, he made it to the city, only to collapse into the arms of a Red Cross man who rushed him to Roosevelt Hospital in an ambulance.

By September the tent city was dismantled row by row as the volunteers were discharged and sent by railroad to their homes, and perhaps to other disappointments. A popular bit of doggerel entitled "Hardships of War" ran:

> At Santiago he had lumbago,
> At Tampa the fever and chills;
> Before El Caney the weather was rainy,
> And there he had other ills.

He reached Camp Alger and got neuralgia
And at Montauk the fever yellow,
But at home was the blow that laid him low,
His girl had another fellow.

Theodore Roosevelt and his Rough Riders enjoyed their time at Camp Wikoff, especially after a week of good food and regular sleep restored their strength. The men left behind at Tampa, who had suffered through the domestic fever epidemic, joined them, suffering now from envy of their combat-tested comrades.

The colonel's duties were light, and he would often gather up Kane, Greenway, Goodrich, and other officers to swim in the surf or go for long rides over the rolling countryside. There were also riding competitions, as his troopers challenged the other cavalry regiments in bronc-busting, taking on any mount around the base that had a bad reputation, or showing off cowboy skills by having horses lie down at command or mounting them while they were running at full speed.

But all this comradeship and fun was drawing to an end, and the colonel was not only sad, but worried. On September 11, at the last Sunday church services before the regiment disbanded, he followed Chaplain Brown's sermon with one of his own "of a rather hortatory character," warning them that although the world would treat them as heroes for a week or so, "after that time they would find they had to get down to hard work just like everyone else, unless they were willing to be regarded as worthless do-nothings." He was, with good reason, particularly concerned that these rough and violent innocents from the Great West would be seduced by the luxurious permissiveness of the Great Metropolis.

Monday night was devoted to a bacchanalia that started tamely enough, Roosevelt remembered: "A former Populist candidate for Attorney-General in Colorado delivered a fervent oration in favor of free silver; a number of the college boys sang; but most of the men gave vent to their feelings by improvised dances. In these the Indians took the lead, pure bloods and half-breeds alike, the cowboys and miners cheerfully joining in and forming part of the howling, grunting rings that went bounding around the great fires they had kindled."

The next afternoon the Rough Riders were mustered out, but not before they had summoned their colonel from his tent to a surprise ceremony of their own. He found the regiment formed in a hollow square, with a blanket-shrouded form on a table in the center. There was a loyal thick-voiced oration by Private Murphy, then the mystery was unveiled and revealed to be a Remington bronze, "The Bronco Buster."

While the ranks of grizzled veterans wept over this bittersweet parting after the most intense 133 days of their lives, Roosevelt, husky-voiced with emotion himself, told them how touched he was that enlisted men instead of just officers had given him such a gift. "This is something I shall hand down to my children, and I shall value it more than the weapons I carried through the campaign."

"Three cheers for the next Governor of New York," one of the soldiers bellowed.

CHAPTER 11

BATTLES AT HOME

What with Indian fights in Minnesota and battles with striking miners in Illinois, we hardly miss the excitements of the late war.

Harper's Weekly

Right here at the exposition are enough people coming every day to put an end to every Indian in the world if they saw fit to do so. Then, besides this, the white men have all . . . of the big guns and they are the ones that count. . . . I am an old man and I want to see my people learn the ways of the whites. I want to see them raise corn and cattle and live in houses and I believe that the president and the big men at Washington will help my people if they will try to help themselves.

Geronimo

As an advertisement of the potential riches of the Trans-Mississippi West, and celebration of American Progress, the fair in Omaha was a solid success. Though hurt by the war, especially by the diversion of railway passenger cars to transport troops instead of tourists, and the slowness of Congress to vote the appropriation for an Indian exhibit, attendance had been good. Now that the armed struggle had ended in victory, newspapers and magazines were writing about the pleasures and edification to be found at the exposition, and people from across the country were responding.

Favored over all else by visiting Westerners was the Electricity Building, decorated with stone cogwheels and other symbols of the industrial machinery its energy drove, and crowned with colossal sculptural groups

depicting men wrestling with wild beasts, symbolizing the way these people saw their own struggle with the still raw frontier. Thomas Alva Edison
had scores of his inventions on display; Nikola Tesla exhibited the latest
developments in wireless telegraphy and models of power development at
Niagara Falls; Professor Elihu Thompson demonstrated his electrical type-
setting machines and the searchlights he had improved and that had been
used so effectively by American warships at Santiago. "In the Electricity
Building," wrote "Thanet" [Alice French], "(which is also the machinery
building and shows machines of every kind from stone-crushers to
watches . . .) sits the wonder-worker of modern life, the chained and harnessed genius from the skies, infinitely more capable than Aladdin's
slave—sits and purrs and fans, and works with equal ease a mortar and a
glove cleaner. There is the apparatus that transmits the living voice thousands of miles; and there is the apparatus that causes to live again on the
ear 'the sound of a voice that is still.' The kindly slave can be studied fighting our battles in one section and tending our kitchen fire in another; while
in a third he is at the service of the surgeon or the dentist. It is a wonderful
building, wonderful and terrible, saying much in its inarticulate way, and
hinting infinitely more. To go through the electricity department is to feel a
thrill of realization of the awful power of man over nature. I have seen men
come out of that grand vestibule silent, solemn, with a touch of awe in
their bearing. It was the unconscious, involuntary homage to the possibilities of the human soul."

Just across the lagoon were the Ionic colonnades of the Mines and Mining Building, which paid homage to the more immediate possibilities of
underground riches that this new form of power could release. Edison was
also one of the inventors displaying wizardry there—in his case a new
method of extracting valuable metals from low-grade ores.

Education was an important purpose of the exposition, and that power
had been placed under the guidance of the Board of Lady Managers. The
women's clubs of Nebraska had decided that, instead of the usual
Woman's Building, they would support a Girl's and Boy's Building, which
not only had exhibits of young people's arts and crafts but also provided
child care, a "crêche" as it was called. A Congress of Women was held in
Omaha, as well as meetings of a number of women's groups, to discuss
important issues having to do with children and education, including society's responsibility to orphans and the desirability of establishing kinder-
gartens.

When arguing for the exposition, one of the local newspapers had written that "We are living in an age of surprises," and that being exposed to the newest developments, as well as to other cultures and races, "is worth more to the next generation than much book learning." Another journal argued that children "are unusually impressionable, and the exposition will be to most of them a revelation of the wonders of the world. They will carry through life the mental picture of the new White City . . . comprehending the whole exposition as typical of the advancement of the human race," and stating that it would be "an invaluable school."

A particularly American form of this education for advancement was laid out in a written set of instructions to mothers from a Mrs. A. Hardy that was published by one of the women's clubs. To really benefit from these displays, the children had to be prepared. "Special, previous, mind culture is the thing that will get it best and quickest." With this special preparation, "The mother can so trend the mind of her boy and girl that, when passing through Machinery Hall, the wonderful engines will mean to them not simply iron and steel and noise; but, beyond all that they will realize a something almost akin to human, which gives to the machine a personality second only to that of its inventor."

Machines were seen as "almost akin to humans" and as symbols of Progress; the Fine Arts Building also supported lessons about the improvement of human society. Its centerpiece was an elaborate fountain made up of sixty "heroic figures" in stone depicting "the progress of civilization." First came trappers, soldiers, and pioneer farmers, followed by inventors, writers, artists, statesmen, and philosophers, then "peering out in wondering amazement from the rear," a visitor wrote, "are the original inhabitants, the Indians."

James Mooney, an anthropologist with the Bureau of American Ethnology at the Smithsonian Institution, had helped organize an Indian Congress that he hoped would be a popular but serious depiction of the native peoples' different ways of life, believing that the exposition directors were interested in "genuine presentations . . . not of the dime museum order." John Wesley Powell, the great explorer of the Colorado River basin and head of the Bureau of American Ethnology, gave his support because it would allow citizens "to understand more clearly the nature and characteristics of savagery and the problem which is present to the Indian department in the endeavor to lift the aboriginal inhabitants of the country into the status of civilization." At the same time, however, emphasis was placed on bringing and exhibiting the most "primitive" ways of life, and while some school-educated Indians were part of the exhibits in Omaha, bringing their printing presses and newspapers, the need to draw tourists with gaudy displays soon overwhelmed any genuine attempt to understand either the old or new ways of life of native peoples.

Congress, because of the war, had been late with its Indian Congress appropriation, and had then cut it back to forty thousand dollars, less than half of what had originally been proposed to aid the tribes in their travel and living expenses. Still, most major tribes sent representatives, including the Dakota (or Sioux), Pueblo, Sauk, Cheyenne, Fox, Potawatomi, Apache, Arapaho, Siksika (or Blackfeet), Winnebago, Mohave, and the Nez Perce. A reporter noted that "the Apaches are about as interesting to the Mesquakies [the Fox] as they are to the whites."

A particularly interesting group to anthropologists was the remnants of the Tonkawa, the only cannibal tribe ever in United States territory, who had been placed on a reservation in 1859. "The other tribes," reported James Mooney, "which hated them for their cannibal habit and for the assistance which they had given the troops in various border campaigns, took advantage of the confusion resulting from the outbreak of the rebellion to settle old scores, and joining forces against the Tonkawa, surprised their camp by a night attack on October 23, 1862, and massacred nearly half the tribe. Since then their decline has been rapid, until there are now but 53 left alive, on lands allotted to them in eastern Oklahoma."

Some famous leaders came: Man-Afraid-of-His-Horse, Rain-in-the-Face, Goes-to-War, Black-Hawk of the Winnebago. The greatest draw of all was Geronimo, whose band of Chiricahua Apache had been run down and captured by Nelson Miles in 1886. Available for interviews, he also made a good income selling autographs for fifty cents and photographs for a dollar, which caused James Mooney to criticize him as "a natural leader of warriors, but withal a most mercenary character."

There were other attendees who received considerable attention. One was Big-Whip, whose name had been Pablino Díaz until he was stolen by the Apache during a raid on his home town when he was eight years old. "He is one of a considerable number of captives still living among these southern tribes," wrote Mooney, "which formerly made Mexico and the Texas frontier their foraging grounds. Unlike most of these unfortunates, Pablino retains the knowledge of his name and his Spanish language, and remembers vividly how he was taken." Another was White-Swan, an Absaroka, or Crow, who was a former army scout and claimed to be sole survivor of Custer's command at the Little Bighorn, where "he was shot and hacked almost to pieces and finally left for dead, but managed to save his life by covering himself with the blanket of a dead Dakota. With his hearing destroyed by blows of the tomahawk, his hands crippled by bullets, and his whole body covered with enduring scars, he is still able to tell the story in fluent sign language."

Just as Westerners were drawn to the displays of electric machines and other signs of progress that could help them in their daily labors, Easterners were most fascinated with the Indian Congress. Under a huge American flag, tipis, wikiups, and wigwams were raised in the cornfields along a bluff overlooking the Missouri River as a "serious ethnological exhibition," Alice French wrote, "not a Wild West show." There visitors could watch Indians as they would "embroider their leggings and deer skin shirts, make birchbark canoes, plait baskets, and weave and dye blankets. The Indian band sits in its rude stand and plays 'There'll be a hot time in the old town to-night,' or 'The Stars and Stripes,' with as good success with its brasses as any village band."

That was not the only music, of course. As French watched painted braves in war bonnets dancing to drums in a cleared area near the tipis she noticed a "handsome young Indian in his smart tweed suit who was holding an umbrella attentively over two Indian maidens in civilized finery . . ."

"Say, Jim," a white man asked him, "why ain't you painted up like them, an' dancing?"

"I wasn't ever painted in my life," the Indian youth replied scornfully, "or danced, neither!"

For Alice French, this was proof of the "doom of the old ways." Part of the interest of Easterners in the Congress sprang from a kind of patronizing nostalgia leavened by guilt over "the blackest and ghastliest chapter of our annals, the story of the red man's wrongs and reprisals." They felt privileged in being able to catch this last display of the "old ways," and took any opportunity they could to apologize for the misdeeds of other Americans. Alice French was impressed with the Indians' good spirits, and the way they seemed interested in everything around them, including the first chance many of them had enjoyed to meet Indians from other tribes.

She bought some red-and-white candy at a stand run by "the much wronged Poncas. The chief proffered me a dignified and sticky hand. After what has passed in the matter of the Poncas, I did not feel that I could decline it, had it been covered with tar." French shook hands with the chief, and then with all the other sticky-handed members of the tribe who were nearby. "Later in the day I discovered that they were not Poncas but Sacs from Iowa. However, our dealings with the Sacs are not impeccable; I do not regret the incident."

For all the sentimentality or sheer silliness underlying much of the interest of such visitors, some like Alice French could at least recognize, in spite of their romantic lamentation over the passing of the world of the buffalo and painted warriors, that native peoples were able to adapt to modern ways when given a chance, and that new relationships were possible. "It cannot," French believed, "whatever the other aspects of the congress, work anything but good for red men and white to have an opportunity of meeting under new conditions."

Although the original intent had been to present a serious study of aboriginal ways of life, the need for carnival showmanship to attract and entertain tourists came to dominate the "Congress." The Improved Order of Redmen, another of those white businessmen's organizations with contrived exotic trappings, proposed that there be an elaborate sham battle with cowboys and friendly Indians (impersonated by the businessmen) fighting "hostiles" played by the visiting tribes.

This was held in August, with almost seven hundred Indian and white performers whooping, yelling, charging back and forth on horses, and firing hundreds of blank cartridges. A whole ritual of conquest and submission took place on the improvised battleground. "Hostile" Indians were led by a renegade white man, "Wyoke Nicyople Tigurebli Acolthy, or Great Man Who Fights Them All," a part played by William A. Mercer, the army captain overseeing the Congress. These warriors were at first victorious; cowboys and soldiers taken prisoner were "scalped or turned over to the squaws who were following in the wake of the savages like so many vultures," reported the *Omaha Bee*. "Hostiles" actually did wave bloody scraps of hair as they rode about, pieces cut from the hides of recently slaughtered cattle.

When the full force of cavalry arrived, they found that their compatriots playing the dead had been mutilated (the appearance of real gore again aided by butchered cattle) and those taken prisoner were screaming from torture at the hands of the women. Enraged, the cavalrymen charged the camp to "wipe out the entire savage outfit." After fierce fighting the white renegade saw that his force had lost, and sued for peace, promising "to quit his roving life and settle down and become [an] Indian agent, if given the chance." Christian mercy gave him the chance, and the show ended with the new agent leading the now-subdued Indians to a reservation.

The event was such a success that it would be repeated to gawking crowds over and over again during the remainder of the exposition—sometimes with the variation of one Indian tribe fighting another. These play battles helped the Trans-Mississippi and International Exposition set an attendance record for such a fair at two and a half million paid visits, the thrills they provided being given extra force by the fact that while they were being staged the last of the real battles, with genuine blood and gore, was being fought between the United States army and Chippewa warriors only a few hundred miles away in Minnesota.

That these displays were playing to the prejudices and stereotypes of the "old days" seems to have bothered only James Mooney to any great degree. The "serious ethnological exhibit," to which he had devoted such effort, even inducing some of the tribes to perform rarely witnessed sacred ceremonies, had "degenerated into a Wild West show with the sole purpose of increasing gate receipts." Disgusted with the "evident purpose to reduce everything to the level of a 'Midway' performance," he withdrew his support.

It is unlikely there was ever much chance of changing popular prejudice, especially through such an easily corrupted medium as an exposition. Probably most onlookers agreed with Mary Alice Harriman, who wrote in the *Overland Monthly* that at Omaha one could witness "the Indian as the Alpha of the alphabet of American history, as the exposition, with its wealth of accumulated inventions, of art, science, and culture, is its Omega." Journalist Fay Fuller stated, "The object lesson of the Congress of American Indians in connection with the Trans-Mississippi Exposition is that of progress. . . . From the primitive, crude wigwams of the aborigines the visitor walks beneath the evening sky, star strewn and blue as Puget Sound, to gaze upon the Royal Court of the Grand Canal, the triumphs of illuminating the masterpiece of the Exposition, and when he remembers that less than half a century ago the same docile Omahas, who are peacefully dozing to-night by their campfires within the Exposition gates, were waging the war of the tomahawk and bow on these very grounds, the heroic march of civilization and the progress of American development is solid."

Nevertheless, many who took pride in the accomplishments of science and technology on display felt that these benefits could also be extended to Native Americans, and all other people of good faith, no matter what their color or previous level of "civilization." William Allen White, however, spoke for those who had doubts. The editor from Emporia, Kansas, celebrated the exposition as an emblem of the triumph of Anglo-Saxon civilization, and argued that the basis of that triumph was in the blood; efforts to educate lesser breeds in the ways of citizenship amounted to a waste of time and resources. "The Indian school exhibit prescribes the boundaries of the power of Democracy. It can work wonders with the men of the north countries of Europe. It can transform a wilderness into a State in the passing of a generation, using Anglo-Saxons, Celts, Teutons, or Slavs. But Democracy cannot civilize the Indian. In barren soil the mustard-seed dies. A man may not become a participant in the blessings of Democracy by education alone. Neither can he change his complexion by proclamation, nor his disposition by legislation. Democracy is a birthright." And not one for Indians, blacks, or even the new immigrants from southern Europe, "men of the Latin race."

This split between people such as Alice French, who saw the technological and moral achievements of modern "Anglo-Saxon" civilization as extendable to everyone, and those who felt, like William Allen White, that these achievements were beyond the understanding of others, ran all through the exposition, just as it did throughout the country.

The Midway was the most exciting educational feature for many. Henry Wysham Lanier, a well-known magazine writer, thought highly of its displays of "Moorish villages and Cairo streets, African savages and Southern darkies, with their cake-walks, songs, and varied old-time plantation activities, Chinese, Japanese, and other Eastern peoples—examples of all these will help the Caucasian to a clearer understanding of the many races and civilizations besides his own." How clear that understanding would be is questionable, given "exhibits" such as the Old Plantation. Billed "as a genuine exhibition of southern Negro character and habits . . . it brings back old memories of the barn yard frolics of the old plantation." Attempts at visual authenticity had certainly been made—five bales of Louisiana tree moss were brought to Omaha, along with two possums that peered out cutely from the draped trees. Also imported were twelve log slave cabins "occupied by genuine darkies, engaged in spinning flax and weaving cotton." And all were grinning, bowing, and scraping, in "genuine" happiness, while buck-and-wing dancers and a "Pickininny quartet" were big hits in the attached theater.

African-American slaves as frolicking denizens of the barnyard—yet also held at the exposition was a conference of the National Colored Persons Liberty League, and August 19 was declared Colored Peoples Day, on the occasion of which Judge D. A. Straker of Detroit gave a speech arguing that "what the Negro needed was equal opportunity . . . more unity and race pride." The judge asked that the supporters of Negro schooling "carefully consider what they were educating the Negro for. . . . Why educate him if, educated and graduated, he could not be taken behind the counter of a grocery?"

And, some citizens were beginning to ask, how could the United States take in more colored people, like the Filipinos and Puerto Ricans, when there was still so much misunderstanding between the races that had known each other for hundreds of years?

"TROOPS BATTLE WITH INDIANS" was the headline in the *New York Times* on October 6, with several large subheads: "Rumored Massacre of One Hundred Soldiers"; "Fierce Fight with Bear Lake Savages in Minnesota"; "GENERAL BACON DEAD?" Word reaching white settlers near the battleground was just as uncertain; rumors swept through the communities of a general uprising of all the nearby Chippewas. Families sought refuge in the larger towns, while loggers and other men began organizing into militia companies. The War Department ordered up relief columns with "the big guns . . . that count," as Geronimo had put it, and authorized Governor Clough to use the Fourteenth Minnesota Volunteers to help suppress the outbreak.

News stories told of "painted savages" on the "war-path" chasing down and killing reporters and soldiers, while a *Times* editorial expressed the shock of the nation. "The fact that the white man is irresistible had seemed to make its way into the minds of the red men. . . . That is what makes the rising so striking. It is a 'bolt out of the blue.' We had all come to consider that the extermination of the Indian as a human being who will not work and hence is out of place in an industrial age and country had advanced so far that there was no danger of an Indian war anywhere within our borders. Upon this comfortable notion descends with a great shock the announcement that a tribe is actually on the warpath within our borders . . . in one of the States, a State furnished 'with all the modern improvements,' with clubs and trolley cars innumerable, and steel-framed sky-scrapers. It is very disconcerting." But those in New York had no doubt of the outcome. "Of course, there can be but one end to this. Civilization will have its way, the white man's law will be enforced, and the white man's power will be vindicated."

.   .   .

A STRONG WIND had risen just before dawn on October 5, kicking up a heavy surf in Leech Lake that delayed the landing, but Brigadier-General John Mosby Bacon, along with troop commander Major Melville C. Wilkinson and his men, were able to finally get ashore on Sugar Point by 8:30 a.m. Bacon headed a mixed force of about a hundred men—soldiers from the Third Infantry, United States marshals, local deputy sheriffs, and some Indian police—who had come to this remote reservation in northern Minnesota with warrants to arrest fugitives of the Pillager band of the Chippewa Indians. Three newspaper correspondents accompanied them.

Friction had started months before over the illegal sale of alcohol. It intensified when fellow tribesmen helped Bug-O-Nay-Ge-Shig escape from the custody of Deputy Marshal Robert Morrison and Inspector of Agencies Colonel Arthur Tinker, who had tried to arrest him for not answering a summons to testify at a trial in Duluth. There were also deeper causes of trouble. In the 1880s a series of dams had been built in these northern lakes to help control the unruly headwaters of the Mississippi so flour millers in Minneapolis could better utilize the river. The dams had backed water over Chippewa villages, drowning wild rice crops and eroding tribal graveyards. More recently, loggers had been crowding the reservation, cutting trees under a new law that allowed access, but the Indians were not receiving the money that was due them from the harvest. There were also rumors that they would be moved from their land to a different reservation, evidently so that even more intensive logging could be carried out. "They are well advanced in civilization," the United States Commissioner of Indian Affairs William A. Jones believed, "many of them wearing citizens' clothes." But although the new reservation supposedly had better land, the band would not willingly leave: "the traditions are strong with them, and they hold with tenacity to their old lands and old associations." Another cause of bitterness was governmental refusal of compensation for houses, barns, and other buildings they would be forced to abandon.

Major Wilkinson quickly marched his men to the nearby cabin of Bug-O-Nay-Ge-Shig, or "Old Bug" as local whites called him. He had refused to answer the summons because on an earlier trip to Duluth for a trial he had been rudely treated and forced, probably because a corrupt Indian agent pocketed his government expense money, to walk the hundred miles back to his reservation. Once home, he had sworn he would never again return to Duluth, nor respond to "the White Man's papers." Since he had called out to his friends to rescue him, Bug-O-Nay-Ge-Shig was regarded as the most important and dangerous of the fugitives.

He was not at the cabin, but an Indian policeman recognized Mah-Quod, one of the twenty-two Pillagers who had freed the wanted man, and tried to arrest him; it finally took four soldiers to wrestle Mah-Quod to the ground. Handcuffed, he was then taken to the small lake steamer *Flora* docked at the lake.

A patrol was sent in a column of twos to search nearby settlements, but by now word had preceded them; Bug-O-Nay-Ge-Shig and his friends were nowhere to be found. Those tribal leaders encountered by the patrol professed friendship and promised to try to persuade the fugitives to surrender. Occasionally, off in the distance, Indian men with rifles were spotted, but they merely watched and made no threatening gestures.

After two and a half hours of frustrating search, the party marched back to the landing spot under a freezing rain, where at Bug-O-Nay-Ge-Shig's house another of the fugitives was recognized and arrested. Both General Bacon and Major Wilkinson were over sixty years old, veterans of the Civil War and many Indian campaigns, and they knew enough to be careful; a squad was sent to search the brush and a nearby stand of timber; nothing suspicious was found.

Almost all of the soldiers were raw recruits, so Major Wilkinson took the opportunity to form them in ranks on the beach and run through drill exercises while lunch was being prepared and the smell of coffee filled the air. Finally the troops were ordered to unload their rifles and rest arms.

At this, a shot rang out. At first the officers thought one of the clumsy recruits had accidently discharged his rifle while unloading it, but then came a second signal shot, followed by a fusillade from the bushes and timber.

Panic swept through the command as six soldiers immediately fell dead or wounded. "You ought to have seen the reporters leg it when the fight began," a soldier later said, "but they were mighty kind to the wounded afterward." Bacon and Wilkinson walked upright among the men, speaking calmly, steadying their nerves, telling them to take cover. The major quickly had his company spread into a skirmish line to return fire, although several had to be shown again how to load their Krag-Jorgensens. Firing was heavy at first, then became a sharpshooting contest with men on both sides waiting for clear targets. The Indians were so well concealed in the brush that only wisps of gunsmoke gave their locations away, and one of them had such a fine Winchester and was so accurate that he seemed to hit a soldier every time he fired; a nearby comrade-in-arms let out a whoop each time that happened. It was this marksman who shot Sergeant William Butler in the head, making three holes in his hat, which his friend Private Godfrey Zeiglar kept as a talisman.

Major Wilkinson stayed erect, encouraging his unseasoned troops, and directing their fire, then he fell, hit in the thigh, calling out to the surgeon, "Ross, I've been wounded, but I won't give up, for it's not bad." A moment later, he was on his feet again, standing behind his prone firing line. "Give it to them, boys, get them going, give it to them; they are cowards and they are going to run." Then he seemed to stagger, and Surgeon Ross ran to him.

Shot in the stomach and dying, Wilkinson raised himself from a pool of blood to shout to Bacon: "Give 'em hell, General! Give 'em hell!"

About an hour into the battle, the Indians began concentrating their fire on the two small steamboats just offshore, bullets splintering the thin planking of the pilothouses, wounding four civilians, one of whom had to have his arm amputated, and driving the boats away to the nearby town of Walker. The last sight of the battle the fleeing passengers had was a line of soldiers and lawmen crouching under the shelter of a low sand bluff near the water.

As MILITIAS BEGAN arming, people talked freely to reporters about their fears and anger. "They say that the savages should be pursued until they are broken in spirit and thoroughly cowed," the *New York Times* reported. "They believed that if the trouble is allowed to drop now it will be but a short time before the malcontents again become defiant. Public opinion upon the subject is that life and property in this region will not be safe until the Indians are exterminated or banished beyond reach of the neighborhood."

Some of the Pillager band evidently attended a meeting held on the Leech Lake reservation, trying to raise support for a bigger rebellion, but Dr. Hart, Indian Agency surgeon, warned the council about the armed civilians who were gathering, who would fight without the restraints of military discipline, saying that if more of the tribe "went on the war-path, there would not be a live Indian on Leech Lake in a week."

Iron plates were fixed strategically to the lake steamers so they could return to Sugar Point the next morning, where they found General Bacon and his men. Seven had been killed, and ten wounded. As they started to evacuate the injured, firing from the woods erupted again, forcing the soldiers back to cover and the boats farther from the shore; it wasn't until

October 7 that General Bacon and his command were able to retreat to Walker, where hundreds of troops from the Third Infantry had by now arrived and were preparing for action.

But there were delays, delays that smacked of federal irresolution to the governor of Minnesota: "I shall pay no more attention to the War Department. If necessary, I shall issue a call for volunteers, arm them with such guns as I can pick up, and let the Government go to the devil. I am tired of doing business with Washington. There is too much red tape about it. Orders are issued one minute and revoked the next. I am not an alarmist, but it is the safe thing to be prepared. It will reassure the settlers and perhaps prevent an outbreak."

Indian Commissioner William A. Jones came up on an express passenger train on October 10, and tried to find a peaceful solution. Many Indian families had fled the reservation and camped just outside of Walker, fearing the retaliation they were sure was coming. One of their leaders, Gay-Gwa-Che-Way-Bimung, was willing to serve as a go-between; sent along with him was a local man named Gus Beaulieu, and Father Aloysius Homanutz, a Catholic priest trusted by everyone. They soon sent word that the "hostiles" were willing to talk, and Commissioner Jones hurried to their camp full of confidence that he would be able to settle the trouble. Soon thereafter he returned, promising that he would be followed by the fugitives the soldiers had originally set out to arrest.

The battle had made headlines across the country and in Europe. A French newspaper, covering the peace talks in Paris between the Spanish and Americans, used the fighting in Minnesota as basis for an editorial against the upstart new power acquiring the Philippines, arguing that Spanish treatment of their Filipino subjects had been better than American treatment of the Indians.

But for all the talk of "extermination" in newspapers and local Minnesota taverns, what was being meant by the phrase in 1898 was cultural, not physical, destruction. Even at the height of the struggle between these different ways of life, the greatest killer of Native Americans had been disease, followed by frontier militia, not the forces of the federal government. Now, with telegraphs and telephones carrying details across the country almost instantly, and trains rushing reporters and photographers to cover the news for big-city papers and sophisticated journals, sympathy, certainly in urban centers, had decidedly shifted to the side of the Indians.

Finley Peter Dunne's Mr. Dooley used satire to explain the situation to

Hennessy and the millions of other Americans who attended his wisdom. "Ye see, Hinnissy, th' Indyun is bound f'r to give way to th' onward march iv white civilization. You an' me, Hinnissy, is th' white civilization. I come along, an' I find ol' Snakes-in-his-Gaiters livin' quite an' dacint in a new frame house. Thinks I, 'Tis a shame f'r to lave this savage man in possession iv this fine abode, an' him not able f'r to vote an' without a frind on th' polis foorce.'

"So says I: 'Snakes . . . get along. . . . I wan ye'er house, an' ye best move out west iv th' thracks, and dig a hole f'r ye'ersilf.'

" 'Divvle th' fut I will step out iv this house,' says Snakes. 'I built it, an' I have th' law on me side. . . . F'r why should I take Mary Ann . . . an' all me little Snakeses, an' rustle out . . . far fr'm th' bones iv me ancestors . . . an beyond th' water-pipe extinsion . . .'

" 'Because . . . I am th' walkin' dilygate iv white civilization,' says I.

" 'I'm jus' as civilized as you,' says Snakes. 'I wear pants . . . an' a plug hat . . .'

" 'Ye might wear tin pair,' says I, 'an' all at wanst . . . an' ye'd still be a savage . . . an' I'd be civilized . . . if I hadn't on so much as a bangle bracelet . . .'

Police are called to evict the man and his family. "Well, me frind Snakes gives him battle, an' knowin' th' premises well, he's able to put up a gr-reat fight; but afther a while they . . . have him in th' pahtrol wagon, with a man settin' on his head."

The lesson? "Th' on'y hope f'r th' Indyun is to put his house on rollers, an' keep a team hitched to it, an', whin he sees a white man, to start f'r th' settin sun. He's rooned whin he has a cellar."

As to the trouble in Minnesota, Mr. Dooley opined that "if we can get in Gatlin' guns enough befure th' winter's snows, we'll tur-rn thim Chippeways into a cimitry branch iv th' Young Men's Christyan Association. We will so."

Although the Gatling guns were ready and waiting, they were not used. General Bacon worked with Indian Commissioner William Jones to ensure a peaceful settlement. The fugitives Bacon, Major Wilkinson, and their command had gone to arrest at Sugar Point did finally surrender, and they served a few months in jail. No charges were ever brought against those who had ambushed the force with such devastating effect; although six Winchesters had been found in the woods after the battle, it was unclear what casualties the attackers had suffered. Commissioner Jones argued that the Chippewa, who had never fought the government before, had been "prompted to their outbreak by the wrongs committed against them" and that the troubles would not recur "if the whites will treat them fairly, which is very likely, as the whites were thoroughly impressed with the stand taken by the Indians."

Bug-O-Nay-Ge-Shig, whose rescue by his fellows had been the immediate cause of the battle, soon returned to his cabin at the point, collected spent shell casings left behind by the soldiers, and made them into a trophy necklace. A small settlement near the battle site was named Wilkinson after the heroic major who lost his life rallying a company of untrained recruits—the last man killed in the last pitched battle of the centuries-long wilderness war between white man and red for control of the continent. The naming was probably of small condolence to his family, who had recently moved out to Redding, California, to start an "orange farm" in advance of his imminent retirement.

THERE WERE TWO other acts of violence that October sharing national headlines with the "uprising" on Leech Lake. One was individual. George Saxton was a renowned "wheelman" in Canton, Ohio, cutting a dashing figure in his bicycle cap and tight-fitting outfit; he was just as locally well known as a "middle-aged Lothario" whose most notorious conquest had been Mrs. Anna George, an attractive local dressmaker who rented shop space in a building he owned. During the height of their passion, he had convinced his mistress to leave her husband and two children, but soon after the divorce was final he grew weary of the relationship and tried to break it off. Anna George, her marriage and reputation ruined, then started a series of lawsuits against him for breach of promise, while her ex-husband, Sample C. George, also sued Saxton for "alienating" the affections of his wife. Anna George subsequently tried to force her way into Saxton's living quarters, telling the police who were called to stop her that he had kept some of her possessions.

Lawsuits and public confrontations had caused embarrassment to George Saxton's brother-in-law William McKinley, who was governor of Ohio when this trouble started, and who must have been grateful that most of the bad publicity had been confined to the state. By October 1898, President McKinley may have thought that the problems were close to being resolved as Sample George, who feared that his recent remarriage might lose him the sympathy of a jury, finally settled his suit for $1,825 instead of the $20,000 he had asked; Anna had earlier received a small amount of damages in hers, but was still bitterly angry, not only obsessed with the

Bug-O-Nay-Ge-Shig wearing the trophy necklace commemorating his victory over the United States army. (*Minnesota Historical Society, photo by James S. Drysdale*)

harm Saxton had done her but also jealous of the attention he was now paying a comely widow named Eva Althouse.

"I'll kill him if he keeps seeing her," she told at least one acquaintance.

"Then you'll hang."

"I don't care."

At six o'clock on the evening of October 7, George Saxton wheeled his way debonairly through the streets of Canton to Eva Althouse's residence. Parking his bicycle, he started up the steps of the terraced lawn. Although Eva had been out of town for several days, she had returned unexpectedly early—or so said a note he had evidently received a short time before. As he climbed the steps, a tall, slender woman clad in black stepped from the bushes, fired two shots at him from a small revolver, then started to walk away.

Saxton, severely wounded, fell, and called faintly for help.

The woman in black turned abruptly, walked back and fired two more shots into his body, then left again, this time running.

Neighbors rushed to him, but George Saxton was dead, still wearing his jaunty bicycle cap; a few hours later Anna George was arrested for murder in the first degree. Refusing to answer any questions, she would say only, "I will talk when the proper time comes." This strategy of dignified silence worked. A jury of twelve chivalrous men, in spite of an impressive array of evidence, later found her innocent of murder.

THE NIGHT OF October 7 William McKinley was hosting a reception at the White House for attendees at the annual convention of the Episcopal Church being held in the capital. It was a distinguished gathering—lay delegates included financier J. P. Morgan, naval strategist A. T. Mahan, and Chief Justice Melville Fuller of the United States Supreme Court—and a self-satisfied one, for the Woman's Auxiliary had just reported raising over eighty thousand dollars for missionary work, twenty-five thousand more than in 1897. In his sermon opening the first session at Epiphany Church, Bishop Tuttle of Missouri had pronounced how the money and Episcopalian influence should be used:

Wide—aye, wide—the work of the Church should be. Extension is in the air for us Americans now. If we fall into line at its bugle blast, some may claim that it will be to our risk and harm, that it is an unwonted call, an out-of-the-way call, an unfit call to such as we are. Be that as it may, the logical course of events is a force not to be counted out, and it may make the sounding of bugle calls and the rolling forward of the chariot wheels of destiny things that we cannot stop if we would.

We who think are startled and subdued and awed at the responsibilities devolved upon the Union now. . . . We ought to be, and want to be, the hammer and the arm driving it to strike hard. Hawaii, Puerto Rico— go forward to possess the land. The Philippines—if the flag we honor and love is to float sovereign there—go ye in there also. And if the forceful logic of events . . . lift the flag into prominence over other regions yet—go there, too, to bide and work and help and save. . . . The Anglo-Saxon race seems harnessed to the twofold work of giving to the world the sweets of personal liberty and the restraints of order, without which liberty cannot be preserved.

No doubt conversation was along these lines of duty, order, and international responsibility as the refined guests circulated, everyone in formal dress. Even the frail invalid Ida McKinley, who usually avoided such occasions, was at her husband's side, wearing "a gown of white satin with a high collar held close to the neck by a circlet of diamonds," as he shook hands with over a thousand of the bishops, rectors, laymen, and their wives, and accepted an invitation to unveil a Peace Cross in the capital.

Halfway through this genteel gathering, a telegram arrived with news of the bloody event in Canton. The president kept it to himself until all his guests had left, then gently informed his wife of the death of her brother, although the sordid detail of it being a murder may have been kept from her. He tried to use the telephone to discover more about what had happened, but the only result seems to have been the crackling of static through the long-distance line.

A Midwestern speaking tour had already been scheduled to start on the ninth of October. William and Ida McKinley attended the funeral in Canton; then he boarded a special presidential train for the Omaha exposition, where, as in Philadelphia, Chicago, and other cities, there were to be celebrations in honor of the hoped-for peace.

The surprising events of the spring, when the reins of government had been pulled from his hands by the popular demand for war, had given the president a great deal to contemplate. The coming fall elections, with widespread outrage over the war scandals, looked very uncertain for Republicans, and his own reelection in 1900 was not assured; McKinley decided he'd better get out on the hustings to take the pulse of the people, especially regarding the question of what to do with the Philippine Islands. A debate about whether to take one or all of them, have the Spanish retain them, or let them go their own way, probably to be snatched up by a European power or the Japanese, was beginning to get heated.

Indiana, Illinois, and Iowa's electoral votes had helped elect McKinley in 1896, while Nebraska and Missouri had narrowly gone to Bryan, so the Midwestern campaign speaking tour had been planned to circle through these states on its way to the Peace Jubilee being held at the Trans-Mississippi Exposition in Omaha. The slaying of George Saxton delayed the schedule only by a couple of days.

Although McKinley was famous for his ability to "read" his people, he had help on this trip; at every station stop a stenographer noted both the intensity and length of applause for different lines he spoke. Some were standard political boilerplate: references to the "valor and intrepidity of our soldiers," others even claiming, "Our achievements on land and sea are without parallel in the world's history." Pointing out that "North and South have been united as they have never before been united," he stated that "there is no part of this glorious country where every citizen may not feel at home," and, perhaps with the bloody fighting in Minnesota and simmering labor troubles in Illinois in mind, made a call for more social and political unity: "We want no differences at home until we have settled our differences abroad; when that is all done, we can have our little differences among ourselves."

Under sunny autumn skies, he pointed out the economic gains made during his administration: "We have gone from industrial depression to industrial activity. We have gone from labor seeking employment to employment seeking labor. We have abundant currency and we have an unsurpassed national credit, better than it has ever been before in our history." And he hinted at the gains that might come from the recent victory: "blessings that are now beyond calculation. It will bring also burdens, but the American people never shirk a responsibility and never unload a burden that carries forward civilization. We accepted war for humanity. We can accept no terms of peace which shall not be in the interest of humanity."

Lines hinting at the "blessings" and "burdens" were the subtle code used to refer to the Philippines, and they received thunderous applause. There was but one direct reference to the benefits of expansion: "We have good money, we have ample revenues, we have unquestioned national credit, but what we want is new markets, and as trade follows the flag it looks very much as if we are going to have new markets."

The president's own popularity was obvious; when his "special" paused for a few minutes in Mount Vernon, Iowa, leaving him time to say only, "Am very glad to meet you all," the cheering was so loud that as he reentered his car he said to Senator William Allison, "That was the best speech I have made yet." At Dixon, a young man climbed from the mass of people jamming the station onto a ledge on the rear platform as the train began to pull out, extending a hand and saying, "Here, McKinley, give us a shake, please." McKinley did, then urged him to jump off quickly before the train picked up too much speed.

"JOURNEY ONE LONG OVATION" headlined the *New York Times*, but the greatest ovation of all was waiting in Omaha, where tens of thousands of people lined the streets as the president, escorted by the mounted Knights of Ak-Sar-Ben, rode through the town in a carriage. He then stood on a platform to review the forty floats parading past, which were accompanied by marching bands and choral groups.

On President's Day, the twelfth of October, almost a hundred thousand visitors paid admission to the exposition. As the naked cherubim, the sculptural groups of men wrestling wild animals, and the gigantic figure of Liberty looked down upon the masses filling the grounds, McKinley used his resonant tenor voice to assure Americans in his indirect way that if the Philippines were kept, there was no need to worry about the Republic: "One of the great laws of life is progress, and nowhere have the principles of this law been so strikingly illustrated as in the United States. . . . Hitherto, in peace and in war, with additions to our territory and slight changes in our laws, we have steadily enforced the spirit of the constitution secured to us by the noble self-sacrifice and far-seeing sagacity of our ancestors . . ."

He asked, "Shall we deny to ourselves what the rest of the world so freely and so justly accords to us?" The audience shouted a thunderous "No!" Enthusiastic applause greeted lines such as, "The war was not more invited by us than were the questions which are laid at our door by its results. Now as then we will do our duty," and "Right action follows right purpose."

The president then toured the grounds, but the exhibition he was most eager to see was the Indian Congress. There he was greeted by a "chorus of yells and chants" as well as the Indian band playing "a martial air." Each tribe was introduced by name, and McKinley "graciously doffed his hat in response to the greetings."

Suddenly Geronimo charged toward the president, startling everyone, but then he reined his horse in, pulled off his buffalo-horned cap, and "bowed with a grim smile to the chief of the white men."

Another sham battle was fought, on this occasion tribe against tribe. There were mock scalpings, burnings at the stake, and mutilations, but the *Omaha Bee* noted that the president "appeared to study rather than to take amusement out of the spectacle." To the *Bee* it was obvious what lessons there were to be learned from such close study:

> Yesterday morning President McKinley received the homage of a hundred thousand representatives of a race that stands at the pinnacle of the greatest civilization of the world's history and of a nation that in the opinion of many statesmen is just commencing to play its great part upon the stage of the universe. In the afternoon the president was rendered honor by a thousand representatives of a passing civilization that was in its way great and of a dying nation that acted within its limitations as magnificent.

ONE OF THE MULTIPLE ironies of the year 1898 was that less than twenty-four hours after the sham Indian battle was mounted for the president, and just a few days after the bodies had been buried from the all-too-real one in Minnesota, an even bloodier struggle was being fought in Virden, Illinois, about four hundred miles east of Omaha.

The United Mine Workers Union had been successfully organizing miners throughout the coal regions, aided by the near-feudal conditions under which workers lived. Company towns had been established with employer-owned houses, schools, churches, and stores, the miners allowed to stay there on sufferance while employed at low wages and paying high prices for their food and rent. The depression of the 1890s had made this hard life harder; there were reports of families eating their dogs to survive, and instances of actual starvation.

Although the economy improved in 1897, wages did not. Miners were often paid less than thirty cents a ton, and their usual ten-hour day of back-breaking labor produced about three tons, so daily earnings averaged less than a dollar. A strike had been called in July of 1897, and by January of

1898 the mine owners were ready to negotiate. Meetings held in Chicago produced a contract that provided for an eight-hour day and improved wages, but this agreement was resisted by twenty large companies in southern Illinois who argued that the increase would make their coal too expensive to sell on the Chicago market. When in August the union asked that workers receive forty cents instead of twenty-eight cents for each ton mined, these companies refused.

Leader of the resistance was Fred W. Lukens of the Chicago-Virden mines, whose works at Virden had "hoisted" 348,000 tons the year before, the largest production of coal by an Illinois company. Four of the operators, including the Chicago-Virden and the Pana Coal Company, appealed to the national executive board of the United Mine Workers, arguing that they could not afford to pay forty cents a ton. They all agreed to abide by the decision of the executive board, but when that decision went against them they vowed to fight by hiring non-union labor.

The Pana Coal Company first tried to find white strikebreakers, but were unsuccessful. Threats were then made to bring in Chinese workers from California before the operators realized it would be easier to go South to find cheap labor. Many of the Illinois miners were immigrants from the British Isles—Irish, Welsh, English, and Scots—who had considered Slavic immigrants, hundreds of thousands of whom had entered the country in the previous ten years, as the biggest menace to their economic success. Now they faced a new threat.

The Afro-American Labor and Protective Association in Birmingham, Alabama, resisted having their people used as strikebreakers, but the companies' agents were able to lure workers by diverse stratagems. One put out circulars:

> Wanted—One hundred and seventy-five good colored miners for Virden, Illinois. Pay in full every two weeks, 30 cents per ton, run of mines. . . . all coal weighed on top. Bring your tools well tied up if you wish to carry them . . ."

The Pana Coal Company had their recruiters lie and say they were hiring because all the white workers had joined the army for two years to fight in the Spanish-American War, and a new mine was being opened. Wages of three to five dollars a day were promised.

At the start of the strike, union men had armed themselves with rifles, shotguns, and revolvers and formally warned the mine owners that they would resist the introduction of scab labor. It has been estimated that in the late nineteenth century three miners were killed in accidents every two days, while thousands more were injured or maimed annually. The fatalism bred by the dangers underground, combined with the miners' determination not to let their families starve or go without a roof, meant their threats should have been taken seriously.

On September 1, the first violence occurred at the Springside coal mine, when strikers "took forcible possession," as the *New York Times* phrased it, of President D. J. Overholt and his brother Louis, owners of the works. They at first threatened to shoot their prisoners, but "after a few hours of exciting uncertainty conservative counsel prevailed." This "conservative counsel" to release the men was provided by local union official John Mitchell, whose cool head and brave actions during the strike later helped him become president of the United Mine Workers.

Republican governor John Tanner was asked by the mine owners to send state militia to the town, but he refused. He was well aware that the general public opposed the owners' attempts to bring in out-of-state workers, and the midterm elections to be held in November were looking questionable for his party because of the growing war scandals. The leader of the state Democrats was the charming and eloquent former Governor John Peter Altgeld, already recognized as a friend of labor because of his pardon of three of the Haymarket rioters in Chicago earlier in the decade. Both parties quickly made clear their support of the miners.

On September 30, 150 strikers stopped a Baltimore and Ohio train that was carrying sixty African-American workers and their families to Pana to labor in the mines, and union representatives convinced some of them to return to Birmingham; the majority went on to the coal company's headquarters. No one was harmed, but the miners were reported to be furious at this importation of scab labor, and more threats were made.

Meanwhile, General Manager Fred W. Lukens of the Chicago-Virden Coal Company made threats of his own. The *Times* quoted him saying that he would keep his operation open in Virden even if he had to do it "at the muzzle of Winchesters." Lukens had an elaborate stockade with towers and barracks erected around the main shaft house of his mine, and brought in fifty guards: twenty-one were former members of the Chicago police force; most of the rest were agents of the Thiel Detective Agency of St. Louis. All were provided with rifles. The general manager then put pressure on the county sheriff, John Davenport, to have them deputized, but the state attorney general informed local authorities that could not legally be done.

When reports reached the union that another group of Alabama strike-breakers would be arriving on October 13, it was decided to try to stop the train and send them back. Hundreds of determined union members began arriving in Virden from Pana, Mount Olive, and other mining towns, where they were organized into paramilitary companies. Four camps were set up around the shaft entrance, and armed patrols watched the yards of the Chicago and Alton Railroad.

Mine operators again demanded state troops to help them open their works, but Governor Tanner again refused; telephone calls and telegrams were exchanged warning that the other would be the guilty party if any violence occurred. "We . . . give you notice that we are going to operate our mines," the owners cabled Tanner, "and we absolutely decline to assume any of the responsibility that the laws of Illinois place upon the Executive. The mob of armed men at Virden are awaiting the arrival of the men who are going to work there with the avowed intention of assault and not defense."

Governer Tanner in turn notified them, "Under the present well-known conditions at Virden, if you bring in this imported labor you do so, according to your own messages, with the full knowledge that you will provoke riot and bloodshed. In my opinion the well matured sentiment of the people of Illinois is largely opposed to the pernicious system of importation of labor, and I repeat that I am not wedded to any policy which is in opposition to the will of the people of Illinois." The governor also gave an interview to the *Illinois State Journal* arguing that "The laboring man's only property is the right to labor, which is as dear to him as the capitalist's millions."

Union spies were watching stations along the line, and probably supporters among the train crews also informed them of the "special's" progress. John Hunter, president of the Illinois District of the United Mine Workers, somehow managed to sneak on board the heavily guarded coaches carrying the African-Americans, evidently in the hope of again convincing some of them not to work as scabs. As the organizer was talking to two of the Alabamans, he was spotted by railroad company guards, who immediately threw him from the moving train. A bypasser found Hunter unconscious and badly injured lying near the track, got him into his buggy, and rushed to a doctor.

In Virden the mood was ugly as strikers waited for strikebreakers. "We tried our best to get [Sheriff Davenport] to stop the train," said a union leader, "and let us have peaceable conferences with the negroes, but he refused all peace overtures and did just as Lukens wanted him to." Scouts waited along the track with instructions to fire ten quick shots in the air when the train was spotted.

It is difficult, from the conflicting stories, to reconstruct exactly what happened next, but the idea of making rifle shots a signal was a poor one. At 11:00 in the morning of October 13, the Chicago and Alton Limited sped through Virden's station an hour late on its way to Chicago, displaying flags on its last car signaling that a Special was following. Word spread fast, and miners came running to line the station platform while another crowd gathered around the stockade gate. At 12:40 the train from Alabama came racing into the station on its way to the shaft head fortifications, and the signal shots were fired. The fifty or sixty armed guards on the train evidently thought they were under attack and poured rifle fire from coach windows into the massed miners, immediately killing or wounding more than a dozen. An Alton and Chicago railroad detective who was guarding the switch then fell dead with a bullet in his brain.

Firing was heavy by the time the train reached the fort. "The miners and the train were enveloped in a cloud of smoke," wrote a reporter, "and the shooting sounded like a continuous volley." One of the detectives in the stockade described the firing as "hotter than San Juan Hill." Locomotive engineer Burt Tigar was hit in the arm and fell to the floor of the cab, but his fireman grabbed the throttle, gave it a hard jerk to get the train back up to speed as fast as possible, and raced off to Springfield. Sharpshooters stationed in the high tower continued firing even after the train left, cutting down more of the miners, forcing them to retreat. Gradually gunfire died away.

Several men in the stockade had been wounded, so at two o'clock they telephoned Superintendent J. F. Eyster, who had been waiting at the Climax Trading Company, the store owned by Chicago-Virden Coal, to bring doctors. Eyster jumped in a delivery wagon, picked up two doctors, and rushed them to the mine. No one interfered with his medical trip, but as he returned to Climax Trading a cry was raised that General Manager Fred Lukens was with him, and a crowd of miners charged the store, firing as they came.

Eyster ran behind the shop counter and grabbed a revolver for each hand; then he fled upstairs, shooting behind him as the miners broke in.

Once on the roof, he took cover behind a chimney, while his attackers ran back into the street to send volley after volley at him, blowing so many chips off his brick shield that he jumped across to the roof of another store, firing into the street below as he went.

Wounded in the side and bleeding, he tried to make his escape, but lost his balance and fell through a glass skylight and into the arms of his enemies. They dragged him outside and beat him until a group of policemen forced them back. Police carried the motionless body to the nearby city square and laid it on the grass. Rumors had swept through the crowd that it was Fred Lukens they had killed, or one of the worst of the company sharpshooters who had murdered so many of their friends; no matter, they thought, he was dead now.

But as the police began to disperse them, the man stirred, and with one hand tried to wipe blood from his face. Several miners ran back and began kicking him, but the police formed a wedge, rescued Eyster again, found a stretcher, and this time carried him to safety at the Buckles Hotel.

Angry strikers began gathering around the stockade that night, taking count of the seven of their fellows killed, and the thirty or so wounded. Word had spread that state troops were on the way, and many of the men began saying that they should storm the fortifications and destroy the mine head before the troops arrived. They were preparing to attack when Edward Cahill, president of the local union, arrived. "He told them," reported the *New York Times,* "that if they precipitated the battle this time they would lose all they had gained. They had attained their object of keeping out the colored miners, though the cost was fearful."

Most of the men were convinced, departing to tend their wounds or mourn their friends, but at least one stayed behind. When, in predawn darkness, the train carrying the Sons of Veterans state militia regiment pulled up before the stockade, Tom Preston, a guard who had been a lieutenant on the Chicago police force, opened the gate and stepped outside. One of the strikers hiding nearby shot him dead.

Fred Lukens claimed to be surprised by the scale of the violence, although Captain Charles Fervier of the Sons of Veterans reported he had seized 125 Springfield rifles and 2,500 rounds of ammunition from the company stockade. "I deplore the matter as much as any one," the general manager announced. "I never supposed such a thing would result when we brought the negroes here." The fact that only two company men had been killed and fewer than six wounded, compared to the heavy losses of the strikers, he could only attribute to a "miracle."

When a reporter asked, "In view of the result, Mr. Lukens, do you expect to import other negroes when the soldiers leave?" all he would say is "I do not feel disposed to answer that question."

Although all of the strikebreakers were to be "colored" or "negroes" from the South, there does not seem to have been any racial overtone aside from that. The African-American miners stayed in Springfield for a while, then were taken to St. Louis before they made their way back to Birmingham. By mid-November the Chicago-Virden Coal Company capitulated, rehiring its former workers and paying them the forty cents-a-ton rate. Problems in Pana took longer to resolve, but in the end operators there gave way as well.

Results for the United Mine Workers were greater than a simple wage increase. Relatively new to organizing, the union built on this victory, going on to success in other mining regions where miners had previously feared joining the union movement. An even more important consequence was the experience union leaders gained in guiding and restraining their members; Illinois was to provide national labor leadership for the next half century.

CHAPTER 12

OPPORTUNITIES

If my worst enemy was given the job of writin' my epitaph when I'm gone, he couldn't do more than write: "George W. Plunkitt. He Seen His Opportunities, and He Took 'Em."

George Washington Plunkitt of Tammany Hall
explaining how he became rich through politics

We've got the Ph'lippeens, Hinnissy; we've got thim the way Casey got the bulldog—be th' teeth. . . . As Hogan an' McKinley both says: "Th' natio's in th' hands iv the Lord, an'll give Him what assistance it can spare fr'm its other jooties." . . . We're a gr-reat civilizein' agent, Hinnissy, an' as Father Kelly says, "so's th' steam roller." An' bein' a quiet man, I'd rather be behind thin in fr-ront when th' shtreet has to be improved.

Mr. Dooley

"IF OLD DEWEY had just sailed away when he smashed that Spanish fleet," William McKinley complained to his friend H. H. Kohlsaat, "what a lot of trouble he would have saved us." The "lot of trouble" was, of course, what to do about the conquered islands. Major American conditions for a peace treaty were obvious with regard to Cuba and Puerto Rico: "It is not compatible," the president believed, "with the assurance of permanent peace on or near our own territory that the Spanish flag should remain on this side of the sea."

It was not so clear that a New World power should become imperial.

Some urged that the United States return the Philippines to Spain, retaining only a naval base and trading station at Manila. But Spanish rule in the Philippines was reported to have been even harsher and more incompetent than in Cuba. Returning them would betray the hopes of the native peoples. Should they, then, be allowed independence, with the United States insisting only on its naval station? Was Aguinaldo capable of turning the former colony into a republic, or would, as one adviser feared, "anarchy and slaughter" result from an American withdrawal? Naval experts argued that properly defending a naval base would mean controlling the entire island of Luzon.

What would the imperial powers do if the United States stepped aside? Both the Japanese and British governments had already said they wanted the islands if the United States did not, and rumors were being printed in American newspapers about Germany, France, and Russia forming alliances to gain the archipelago. It seemed obvious the powers would not allow the islands to remain independent. And witness their already dangerous competition in China and Africa. Would the Philippines become a new provocation for war as the imperialists struggled to dominate world markets?

Or should the United States take the whole archipelago under its protection as a colony? William Day, who resigned as secretary of state to become one of the peace negotiators, feared assuming responsibility for "eight or nine millions of absolutely ignorant and many degraded people," while others, like the Baptist minister Robert Stuart MacArthur, thought "The Philippine Islands . . . should be made the garden of the universe. . . . We will fill them with school houses and missionaries." But would this country be able to remain a republic if it began taking on overseas possessions, especially ones with such a different cultural and racial background?

Some business interests were enthusing over the well-populated markets of the Far East, and Representative Joel P. Heatwole of Minnesota, like a number of other politicians, announced, "On general principles, I believe we should hold fast to all that we can get." McKinley himself managed to combine this sentiment with a higher moral tone. "I think the United States possessed of all of Spain's colonies would do well to act with great magnanimity and show European governments the lofty spirit that guides us. Apart from that idea I favor the general principle of holding on to what we get."

Proponents of expansion found allies in evangelical Protestant church

leaders, who thought that those same heathen multitudes that so frightened William Day could be now brought to enlightenment. Opponents
feared that turning to empire would threaten the republican virtues that
had kept America strong and independent, and many doubted the abilities
of these various non-Anglo-Saxon peoples to benefit from liberty.

The president spent hours pacing to and fro in the White House, trying
to determine his course of action. Always sensitive to public opinion,
McKinley asked the citizenry to help him decide what to do, while he
formed the commission that would negotiate the peace. Letters cascaded
into the White House, including a nationwide "endless chain letter"
started by Edward Lowye of Chicago, published in leading newspapers,
that read:

> Knowing you to be a staunch defender of liberty, and that as a servant of
> all the people you desire to know their will, I would most respectfully ask
> you to do all in your power to keep the Philippine Islands and make them
> free.
>
> I would most earnestly beseech you to heed the agonizing cry of these
> terribly oppressed people for freedom from their relentless oppressions
> of many centuries. And I ask that you instruct your Peace Commission to
> insist on the complete separation of these islands from Spanish control.
> For peace at the price of their continuance in practical slavery, and such
> merciless treatment as they will always receive under Spanish control, is
> worse than war.
>
> Keep the Philippines and thereby make the name of McKinley stand
> out in history, as one who, like the immortal Lincoln, brought freedom
> and enlightenment to millions of poor human beings, who are crying
> aloud for help. I pray you do not fail to heed this call, as an opportunity to
> do so great an act will never come again.

This letter struck the tone of most of the advice sent to McKinley, as
well as his sense of the people's will gained from his October tour of the
Midwest. There seemed no great sense of contradiction in the public mind
between "keeping" the islands and giving them "liberty." After all, wasn't
this the country that had practically invented the idea of freedom? Newspapers and magazines were full of "experts" on the islands stating that the
native peoples were not yet ready for self-government. What better way
could the oppressed and ignorant Filipinos learn how precious liberty was,

as well as the responsibilities that went along with it, than by being apprenticed to America?

THERE WAS PUBLIC unhappiness about the power of political machines in 1898, but nothing approaching the anger that, sparked by Lincoln Steffens and other reporters' "mudraking" exposés, would sweep the country a few years later. Beatrice Webb, who had traveled in 1898 from England with her husband, Sydney, to study the problems of municipal governance, was appalled at the endemic corruption, but felt that the rogues who ran the New York, Philadelphia, Chicago, and other machines also had certain positive qualities. Over and over she was struck by their energy: "these ward politicians have a certain distinction of physiognomy—they are forceful men: a strange combination of organizing capacity, good fellowship, loose living, shrewdness and strong will." These qualities would often be turned to the good of the community. "And as there are only certain occasions in the government of a city in which private gain is possible or practicable, the rest of the city affairs are managed with very fair ability and good conduct; quite as well, if not better, than they would be by honest but inexperienced reformers, without knowledge of men, or experience in the technique they have to direct."

George Washington Plunkitt was one of the leaders of New York City's Tammany Hall during the 1890s, parlaying his influence into a return of a million dollars or so, but also feeling that what he had done was not immoral. "Everybody is talkin' these days about Tammany men growin' rich on graft," he would later complain to a journalist, "but nobody thinks of drawin' the distinction between honest graft and dishonest graft. . . . I've made a big fortune out of the game, and I'm gettin' richer every day, but I've not gone in for dishonest graft—blackmailin' gamblers, saloon-keepers, disorderly people, etc.—and neither has any of the men who have made big fortunes in politics."

Plunkitt gave examples of how honest graft worked. If Tammany is in power in the city, and decides to undertake "a lot of public improvements," insiders are "tipped off" as to where, say, a new park will be built. "I see my opportunity and I take it. I buy up all the land I can in the neighborhood. Then the board of this or that makes its plan public, and there is a rush to get my land, which nobody cared particular for before. Ain't it perfectly honest to charge a good price and make a profit on my investment and foresight? Of course, it is. Well, that's honest graft." In other words, there is no grievance or crime, since no money was taken directly from the public treasury. "Every good man looks after his friends, and any man who doesn't isn't likely to be popular. If I have a good thing to hand out in private life, I give it to a friend. Why shouldn't I do the same in public life?"

To illustrate dishonest graft, Plunkitt turned to Philadelphia, which was ruled by a Republican machine, where the politically appointed superintendent of the poorhouse stole the zinc roof off the building and sold it for junk. "That was carryin' things to excess. There's a limit to everything, and the Philadelphia Republicans go beyond the limit. It seems like they can't be cool and moderate like real politicians. . . . A big city like New York or Philadelphia or Chicago might be compared to a sort of Garden of Eden, from a political point of view. It's an orchard full of beautiful apple-trees. One of them has got a big sign on it, marked: 'Penal Code Tree—Poison.' The other trees have lots of apples on them for all. Yet the fools go to the Penal Code Tree. Why? For the reason, I guess, that a cranky child refuses to eat good food and chews up a box of matches with relish. I never had any temptation. . . . The other apples are good enough for me, and O Lord! how many of them there are in a big city." So many that he could claim he didn't own a dishonest dollar, and that his worst enemy would have to admit: 'George W. Plunkitt. He Seen His Opportunities, and He took Em.' "

Good government reformers, disdainfully referred to as "Goo Goos" by their more worldly critics, had been struggling to raise the level of municipal administration for years, but with only intermittent success. Theodore Roosevelt goes to some length in his *Autobiography* to explain how the political machines succeeded for so long, and why the reformers, whose objection to bosses was often "aesthetic" revulsion at their crude style rather than moral disgust, almost always failed in their attempts to defeat them. Reform leaders were usually those whom Abraham Lincoln had called the "silk stockings," and they "excited almost as much derision among the plain people as the machine itself excited anger or dislike." For candidates they ran "some rather inefficient, well-meaning person, who bathed every day, and didn't steal, but whose only good point was 'respectability.' " In other words, "They had not the slightest understanding of the needs, interests, ways of thought, and convictions of the average small man; and the small man felt this . . . and sensed that they were really not concerned with his welfare, and that they did not offer him anything materially better from his point of view than the machine."

George Washington Plunkitt would have agreed with Roosevelt on this point, explaining that the only way to govern a big city was to understand people and act accordingly. "You can't study human nature in books. Books is a hindrance more than anything else. If you have been to college, so much the worse for you," he warned. To be effective in politics, you had to rid yourself of illusions about human nature, then go into the streets to study the needs of the inhabitants of your ward and city. "I know every man, woman, and child in the Fifteenth District. . . . I know what they like and what they don't like, what they are strong at and what they are weak in, and I reach them by approachin' at the right side."

A young man is proud of his singing voice? He would be invited to visit the Hall and join the organization's Glee Club. "He comes and sings, and he's a follower of Plunkitt for life." A ball player? "I bring him into our baseball club. That fixes him. You'll find him workin' for my ticket at the polls next election day." The same for rowers, dancers, boxers—"I rope them all in by givin' them opportunities to show themselves off. I don't trouble them with political arguments. I just study human nature and act accordin'."

That wise philosopher Mr. Martin Dooley of Archey Road had wide experience with the realities of ward politics, and he also knew those who would improve the system well enough to explain their weaknesses to "Hinnissy." "This is th' way a rayform candydate is ilicted." From the comfort of their club wealthy reformers hear that things in the city aren't going right. Municipal contracts are not going to anyone they know, and once in a while a fellow clubmember, "comin' home a little late an' thryin' to riconcile a pair iv r-round feet with an embroidered sidewalk, meets a sthrong ar-rm boy that pushes in his face an' takes away all his marbles. It begins to be talked that th' time has come f'r good citizens f'r to brace up an' do somethin', an' they agree to nomynate a candydate f'r aldherman."

After arguing about the candidate with the proper social cachet, they decide on Willie Boye, who, after due consideration, decides that, by God, he *will* be the standard bearer of the people, and orders three dozen pairs of new pants.

The reformers don't realize for a time that other candidates are in the race, but there are. The most serious of these is Flannigan, a retail dealer in wines and liquors who lives above his store, and who campaigns tirelessly. "Who was it judged th' cake walk? Flannigan. Who was it carrid th' pall? Flannigan. Who was it sthud up at th' christening? Flannigan. Whose cards did th' grievin' widow, th' blushin' bridegroom, or th' happy father find in th' hack? Flannigan's. Ye bet ye'er life. Ye see Flannigan wasn't out f'r th' good iv th' community. Flannigan was out f'r Flannigan an' th' stuff."

When election day comes, all the eminent friends of good government have special telegraph wires strung into their club, where they sit, waiting for the returns. The first precinct to report shows 28 votes for Willie Boye to 14 for Flannigan.

"That's my precinct," says Willie, wondering who the disloyal fourteen were.

"Coachmen," a friend explains.

Doing some quick addition, Willie Boye determines the enormous margin of his coming victory and orders "a keg iv sherry wine" put on ice, then begins planning all the ways he will relieve the community from "misrule."

But then the results of the sixth precinct, whose exact location is unknown to most of the reformers, come in. Three hundred and eighty-five for Flannigan, and one for Willie Boye. The sherry wine is ordered taken off ice, and the disappointed candidate heads home. "An', as he goes down th' sthreet," Dooley concludes, "he hears a band play an' sees a procission headed be a calceem light; an' in a carredge, with his plug hat in his hand an' his di'mond makin' th' calceem look like a piece iv punk in a smoke-house, is Flannigan, payin' his first visit this side iv th' thracks."

Theodore Roosevelt was no Willie Boye. He had come out of Harvard and Columbia to jump into New York politics with his eyes wide open, learning early that victory always goes to experience over theory. The reality was that there were two machines in New York that had to be dealt with: Richard Croker's "Democracy" of Tammany Hall dominating the great city, and Thomas Platt's Republican organization controlling the state. "The rural districts," noted Beatrice Webb, "are puritanical in spirit, limited in outlook, with agriculture as the chief occupation. New York [City] is metro-politan if not cosmopolitan, with a strong Irish and German element both alike intensely hostile to the puritanical spirit of the native American." It was on this great cultural divide that the two machines based their appeal.

Leaders of the Independent Party thought Roosevelt was their chance to take the governorship, and perhaps other offices if his coattails were long enough. "Now for a State ticket with Roosevelt at the head," John Jay Chapman wrote enthusiastically, "and decent men from both parties behind him, men known to the whole state if possible . . . honest men in any case. . . . He is to be the instrument of the citizen destroying the Boss." But the "instrument" felt no such power. He was again swimming in shark-infested waters, but this time with true predators, whom he'd also studied all his life, not the cowardly sort he and Jack Greenway had challenged off Morro Castle.

When delegations from both the reformers and Senator Platt had come courting at Montauk, he'd resisted committing himself, but as he had time to study the situation it became obvious that the machine offered the most realistic opportunity to govern. If it was necessary to compromise with the Easy Boss, then so be it. Once elected, he could reform.

He did not, however, withdraw his name from consideration by the Independents. He informed Chapman and his allies that he would run officially only as a Republican, but would regard the nomination of the Independent Party as valuable support. The reformers were delighted with this, figuring that Roosevelt would be listed on the ballot by both parties, and their honest candidates, with this additional aid from the Rough Rider's aura, would surely be preferred by the voters over the machine hacks they would be running against.

Thomas Platt obviously feared they might be right, for he quickly demanded that Roosevelt reject the Independents if he wanted the Republican nomination. Roosevelt wasted no time in writing Chapman: "I do not see how I can accept the Independent nomination and keep good faith with the other men on my ticket. It has been a thing that has worried me greatly; not because of its result on the election; but because it seems so difficult for men whom I very heartily respect as I do you, to see the impossible position in which they are putting me."

"They" certainly did not see or admit to it easily. There were exchanges of letters, face-to-face meetings, shouting matches. Tears were supposedly shed by Roosevelt when R. Fulton Cushing, who Chapman thought "one of the most cultivated . . . and aristocratic of the reformers," delivered such a severe tongue-lashing that the apostate "could hardly walk when he left."

Perhaps the emotional *Sturm und Drang* gave the reformers some satisfaction, but it did not drive the candidate back to the fold. "No matter how long Roosevelt lives or what he does," Chapman wrote, "he can never again furnish such a terrible example of the powers of the boss as he did when he refused to allow his fellow-citizens to vote for him except on the Platt ticket."

Roosevelt had already begun campaigning, taking the advice of Lemuel E. Quigg to cultivate a broader image than just that of a reformer: "I think that this invitation of the Brooklyn Sunday School Association would be a first rate one to accept, although it would probably have to be followed by an address to the Brooklyn Association of Amalgamated Liquor Dealers or something of the sort." But just three days before the Republican nominating convention, the energetic and ambitious politician was suddenly accused of being ineligible to run for office.

Although Governor Black was under a cloud because of scandals involving Erie Canal contracts, he continued to cherish hopes of being renominated, and his friends were eager to help. State Superintendent of Insurance Lou Payne managed to discover, probably with the help of Tammany Democrats in the New York City tax bureau, an affidavit signed by Theodore Roosevelt declaring that "I have been and am now a resident of Washington."

Taxes were of such great concern to affluent New York residents in the 1890s that many had moved, even after long careers in the city and state. "Wheeler H. Peckham," reported the New York Times about one lawyer, "has followed the example of a number of other wealthy New Yorkers and transferred his legal residence to another State for the purpose of lightening his burden of taxation." Mr. Peckham, a former New York district attorney who had prosecuted the "Ring" of corrupt political boss William Marcy Tweed and who was the brother of Rufus W. Peckham of the United States Supreme Court, declared, "I am one of the many who have been driven out of this State by the tax laws and have no vote here." Other prominent refugees included Elbridge T. Gerry and Robert Goelet, both of whom asked a Rhode Island judge to grant them certificates of state citizenship after displaying receipts for property taxes paid there. "Some of the men . . . have made the change because of the present tax laws," the Times wrote, "while others have . . . to protect their estates from a possible subjection to the operation of an inheritance tax in the future."

Roosevelt had signed his affidavit six months before, following the unfortunate recommendation of family advisers while under tremendous personal pressure from the illness of his wife and son, and when he was working endless days as assistant secretary of the navy. Now this "bomb," as the newspapers headlined the story, could scuttle his campaign just as it was launched; New York required candidates to have been residents for five years. Astute Republican lawyers such as Joseph Choate and Elihu Root looked closely at the problem, and the closer they peered, the less sanguine they felt. Not only had the war hero claimed residency in Washington, D.C., to avoid taxes in New York City, but he had also earlier claimed residency in the city to avoid taxes on his Oyster Bay estate, although as yet no one knew of that affidavit.

Most of this crisis, ugly enough on the surface, had really been the innocent result of poor counsel and the untimely death of an uncle who was supposed to have put all to rights while the colonel was in Cuba; Roosevelt had actually paid unnecessary double assessments for a time without protest, and letters to family and friends showed that he had never intended to renounce his New York residency, but the scandal loomed so large that the anxious candidate was unable to eat or sleep. Depressed and sure this was the end of his political career, he reportedly called on Platt and offered to withdraw.

"Is the hero of San Juan Hill a coward?" asked the Easy Boss.

"By Gad! I'll run."

But what could be done now? Thomas Platt knew what tack to choose from happy experience with machine politics; he and Benjamin Odell, chairman of the state Republican Party, pointed out that the candidate would probably be elected along with a Republican attorney general, who would be loath to investigate his own governor. Elihu Root devised an obfuscating but plausible argument over the definition of the word "resident" that he presented with great oratorical verve at the Saratoga convention; Roosevelt received the official nomination, and soon after wrote a check for $995.28 to pay the New York taxes he had earlier avoided.

Victory in the general election, however, was far from a sure thing. Scandals over Governor Black's administration and public anger about Republican conduct of the war had eaten away at the Party's support, never particularly strong in New York anyway. As the *Times* noted in an editorial, "This is a Democratic State. The Republicans have never carried it in the last twenty-five years without Democratic help." Winning that help would be difficult given public disgust over state Republican corruption and "Algerism."

The Republican's first speech to a large rally was on the hot, rainy evening of October 5 in an overflowing Carnegie Hall. "It was a brilliant scene," a reporter wrote, "formed by thousands of faces, framed in the profuse drapery of flags." In addition to the many flags, banners, and rosettes visible, women in bright-colored dresses waved their fans and lace handkerchiefs whenever the name of the hero of San Juan was mentioned. It was obviously a monied crowd, with beautifully gowned women escorted by men in evening dress, moving one of the Republican leaders to remark that "It looked like a grand opera night." He lamented that the gathering was an already partisan group with no potential converts. "This is not vote-getting, but it is magnificent."

When Roosevelt entered the hall "all the splendid assemblage" rose and

cheered, stamping their feet, applauding, calling out the detested nickname "Teddy! Teddy!" and receiving the broad toothy grin in return.
Although the purpose of the meeting was to ratify the selections of the
nominating convention in Saratoga, the head of the Republican ticket did
not address state questions such as excise taxes, or supervision of municipal elections, and certainly not the canal scandals, but instead spoke on
"The Duties of a Great Nation":

> There comes a time in the life of a nation, as in the life of an individual,
> when it must face great responsibilities, whether it will or no. We have
> now reached that time. We cannot avoid facing the fact that we occupy a
> new place among the people of the world, and have entered upon a new
> career. . . . We can see, by the fate of China, how idle is the hope of
> courting safety by leading a life of fossilized isolation. If we stand aside
> from that keen rivalry with the other nations of the world . . . we would
> perhaps for a few decades be allowed to busy ourselves unharmed with
> interests which to the world at large seem parochial; but sooner or later,
> as the fate of China teaches us, the safety which springs from the con-
> temptuous forbearance of others, would prove a broken reed. We are yet
> ages from the millennium; and because we believe with all our hearts in
> the mighty mission of the American Republic, we must spare no effort
> and shrink from no toil to make it great.
>
> Greatness means strife for Nation and man alike. A soft, easy life is
> not worth living, if it impairs the fibre of brain and heart and muscle. We
> must dare to be great; and we must realize that greatness is the fruit of
> toil and sacrifice and high courage.
>
> The guns of our warships in the tropic seas of the West and the
> remote East have awakened us to the knowledge of new duties. Our flag
> is a proud flag, and it stands for liberty and civilization. Where it has
> once floated, there must be no return to tyranny or savagery . . .

The speaker, warming to his topic of national destiny and duty, then
went on to claim that the achievement of greatness was dependent on the
Republican Party, that not supporting the McKinley administration, that is,
voting anything but Republican, would be "a repudiation of the war from
which we have just emerged triumphant. It will strengthen the hands of
every hostile power which views with jealousy our victories in the Antilles
and the Philippines; it will mean that the nations that now secretly and
enviously wish to clip the wings of our pride will be emboldened."

This stirring message was enthusiastically received by the loyal thousands inside Carnegie Hall and the other thousands standing in the wet streets outside, but not by John Jay Chapman, who sneered, "He really believes he is the American flag." Republican leaders, such as Senator Platt, who had opposed the war, and party chairman Odell must have thought the speech sounded more like a presidential address on an imperialistic platform rather than one asking for votes in a bid for a state governorship. They decided their candidate should stay out of direct campaigning, so Roosevelt retreated to his estate at Sagamore Hill while others took up his cause.

MARK HANNA, who had so ably directed William McKinley's campaign against William Jennings Bryan, stirred himself to the same degree of effort for the national elections in the fall of 1898. Once more he "milked" big donors, and set about applying the proceeds to the cause of victory. The West was where the greatest effort was directed, for that region had fervently supported the war, and was now most enthusiastic about national expansion, while the silver issue had diminished in importance as the economy began to recover.

The Democrats did not take this opportunity to challenge the Republicans on national and international issues, confining themselves to trying to restir the silver crucible wherever it seemed possible, and basing their campaign on local issues where it did not. Although the newspapers were full of continuing condemnations of "Algerism," the opposition was wary of appearing to attack the president or the victory. The Republican strategy of waving both the flag and the bloody shirt, just as Roosevelt did at Carnegie Hall and their elders had done for decades after the Civil War, was working wonderfully.

But local Republican leaders were not confident. The same voter lethargy that was forcing state politicians across the country to beg for appearances by President McKinley was evident in New York, and, if nothing else, it was obvious that the Rough Rider was a tonic for apathy. Upstate activists besieged Odell in his office at the Fifth Avenue Hotel, begging for the "Hero of San Juan" to "make a brilliant and dashing campaign, sweeping the State from end to end with his fire and fervor." They particularly wanted a "flying trip" or "meteoric flight" by private railway car, where he would make five- and ten-minute speeches from its rear platform at every small town, instead of a few formal set addresses in cities such as

Albany and Rochester. The bosses listened: the candidate went back on the road.

Tammany Boss Richard Croker had selected as Democratic candidate Judge Augustus van Wyck, brother of New York Mayor Robert van Wyck. Though not as well known as his Republican opponent, van Wyck had a reputation for honesty that could be effectively used against the scandal-plagued party of Governor Black; Roosevelt himself admitted that van Wyck was "a respectable man." Betting on the outcome of elections was common in the 1890s, and both Croker and Odell laid large amounts of money on the line to back their people. Edmund Morris records that the bookies of Broadway quickly chose van Wyck as the favorite at odds of three to five, although he also notes, "The only even odds, as some wag remarked, were that the next Governor would be a Dutchman."

Roosevelt stormed into action, accompanied by Rough Riders in uniform, rippling flags, even a bugler, who would summon crowds to the small-town stations by playing the cavalry charge; more important, he had found the issue with which to bludgeon his opponents. Richard Croker had dropped Tammany support from a Democratic state supreme court justice named Joseph F. Daly, who had served on the bench for twenty-eight years, and Croker in his arrogance had even been publicly forthright in giving his reason: the judge was too independent-minded, and had refused to reappoint a machine hack to his staff; Daly had originally won his seat because of their support, and "Tammany Hall has a right to expect proper consideration at his hands."

Roosevelt recognized that the target to strike was not van Wyck but Croker, and he knew how to lure him from cover. "Under my attack, Croker, who was a stalwart fighting man and who would not take an attack tamely . . . came to the front." To help the public understand that the contest was between Croker and himself, Roosevelt presented a dozen or more speeches a day across the state, in cities, towns, and small rural stations. When he addressed conservative farmers he would often downplay the war, but on most other occasions it was his major theme. To what was billed as an "Afro-American mass meeting," he lauded the Ninth and Tenth Cavalry, telling the cheering crowd how their courage had won the respect of the Rough Riders, and promising that he would always live up to "Americanism . . . [which is] that you shall treat a man for what he shows himself to be as a man, neither favoring him nor opposing him for anything unconnected with the qualities he really possesses."

As the campaign went on his voice roughened, then started wearing out.

The dangers of allowing others to speak for him became obvious, however, when "Buck" Taylor, one of his favorite accompanying Rough Riders, helped with an impromptu address at Port Jervis. Roosevelt stood back, listening contentedly until Buck reached his peroration: "I want to talk to you about mah Colonel. He kept ev'y promise he made to us and he will to you. . . . He told us we might meet wounds and death and we done it, but he was thar in the midst of us, and when it came to the great day he led us up San Juan Hill like sheep to the slaughter and so will he lead you." The listening crowd was "delighted" with the speech, Roosevelt later remembered, although it "hardly seemed a tribute to my military skill."

Fervently denying him any military skill or respect were the veterans of the Seventy-first New York, who resented both his reported comments about their poor behavior in front of San Juan Hill and the letter Secretary of War Alger had vengefully released where the colonel argued for the Rough Riders to be sent to Puerto Rico because they were "three times better" than any state regiment. Their dislike was widely quoted, and Tammany built on this by spreading rumors that Roosevelt was just a rich fake who had not even been near San Juan Hill. Roosevelt, who had hoped to be recognized for his valor in Cuba with the Congressional Medal of Honor, redoubled his efforts for the award, arguing he needed it to help counter these slurs, but nothing came of them. More amusing was Tammany Hall's attempt to spread another rumor that he wanted restrictions placed on bicycle-riding because of the dangers it presented to the public, and therefore did not deserve the vote of the state's wheelmen.

Even the *New York Times* weighed in with its own attacks on his character and judgment, criticizing him for making pronouncements on national issues while avoiding discussion of state problems, but also looking beyond the current election to editorialize about what a poor president the man would make, given his "inborn pugnacity and his reputation as a . . . fighting man. . . . will not the sober, conservative voters of New York hesitate a good deal before they cast a vote that may start this Hotspur on his way to a greater office than the one he now seeks, where he will have the power to deliver the counter-check quarrelsome and follow it up with a naval demonstration before the harbor entrances of some power whose reply will be immediate war?"

Young Hotspur, who turned forty on October 27, decided that it would be delightful to deliver a quarrelsome counter-check in the very lair of the Tammany Tiger, the Lower East Side. "The crusade of the Bowery" is what his supporters called the visit of November 5, although many warned him

Orchard Street on the Lower East Side in 1898. (*Museum of the City of New York. The Byron Collection*)

in the morning that it might be best to call the challenge off since a riot was being planned as greeting, with bricks, stones, and the dead cats that local boys called "sun birds" being held in readiness. Even Republican Chairman Benjamin Odell whispered that he should keep the carriage closed and his head inside. Roosevelt laughed.

At 6:10 p.m. the procession set out, with the Rough Rider's first stop at his doctor's to have his throat sprayed: ten speeches were planned. "My voice is going back on me," he told his first audience, "but I don't care as long as Croker's is in good order." Preliminary stops went well; as the line of open carriages circled the outskirts of the Bowery the only impediments were crowds jamming the streets, but when the Lower East Side proper was entered things became more fevered. Hundreds of boys howling his name surrounded Roosevelt's carriage, bringing more people from the houses and tenements to see what was going on.

Roosevelt kept to his speaking schedule, including one at a hall that sported gaudy placards promising an "underwear contest for ladies" later in the evening. Bricks began raining on the parade soon after, along with "sun birds," which, a *Times* man reported, "did not have the odors of Araby." At Grand and Mott Streets a brick hit Roosevelt's driver square in the face, and it was decided to close the carriages; then, at Marion Street, torches and bonfires were spotted just ahead. A dozen burly policemen, nightsticks in hand, surrounded the party and escorted them into a yard with a twenty-four-foot fence. The mob had to be content with banging on the gate and chanting, "Afraid to come out! Afraid to come out!"

Roosevelt responded by climbing onto a balcony, haranguing the crowd as well as his voice allowed. And so the crusade went, everyone, except those hit by bricks or dead cats, having a good, lively time, and Roosevelt was able to claim to the morning newspapers that he "was the first candidate in the history of the State who had ever made such a complete tour of the Bowery."

All his frenetic campaigning was obviously helping. That very day Republican Chairman Odell bet another twenty thousand on his candidate, this time at even odds.

ONE PLACE THE national Democratic Party usually could rely on winning was the Solid South. It was generally believed that few besides grateful blacks in the region voted for the party of Lincoln, and restrictions on their access to the polls in many states had been steadily instituted since the end of Reconstruction twenty years before. In 1894, however, an uneasy alliance of Populists and Republicans had won power in North Carolina, and in 1896 Republican Daniel Russell was elected governor. As reward for their support, African-Americans began receiving a share of both state and federal patronage jobs: postmasterships, aldermen, justices of the peace, with one, John Campbell Dancy, appointed by William McKinley to be collector of customs in Wilmington, North Carolina. During the 1890s four blacks were elected to the United States Congress from North Carolina, and in 1897 five were elected to the state House of Representatives.

The Democratic Party had vowed to reverse these defeats, and in 1898 attempted to split the Populists from the Republicans by claiming that the two parties were responsible for growing "Negro domination" of North Carolina, citing especially the loss of jobs by poor whites to blacks. Democrats in the South did not discuss broader political or economic issues, focusing only on race. A major source of their propaganda was the

Raleigh *News and Observer,* edited by Josephus Daniels, which published a series of anti-Populist, anti-Negro stories starting in August and lasting until the election on November 8, using such headlines as: "Negro Control in Wilmington," "Unbridled Lawlessness on the Streets," "Greenville Negroized," "Arrested By A Negro: He Was Making No Resistance," "Negroes Have Social Equality," "Is A Race Clash Unavoidable?" Sensational cartoons depicted African-Americans lording it over whites and threatening to take even more of their jobs.

The Populists, who were mainly rural and white, wavered before their leaders decided to continue their "fusion" with the Republicans. But in the spring of 1898, the Wilmington *Record,* an African-American newspaper edited by Alexander Manly, had published an article defending black men, or at least light-skinned black men, accused of making unwelcome advances to white women, declaring that "Poor white men are careless in the matter of protecting their women, especially on the farms. They are careless of their conduct toward them and our experience among poor white people in the country teaches us that the women of that race are not any more particular in the matter of clandestine meetings with colored men than the white men with colored women. Meetings of this kind go on for some time until the woman's infatuation or the man's boldness brings attention to them and the man is lynched for rape. Every negro lynched is called 'a Big Burly Black Brute' when in fact many of these who have been thus dealt with had white men for their fathers and were not only 'not black and burly' but were sufficiently attractive for white girls of culture and refinement to fall in love with them as is well known to all."

The Raleigh *News and Observer* republished this piece in August, when it would do the most damage; the Democrats distributed thousands of copies across the state and politicians of all parties came running to protect the reputation of Southern womanhood, although the most vociferous in their condemnation were Democrats, who pointed out that this was exactly the kind of insult that came from allowing Negroes any rights at all. To discourage blacks from voting, a vigilante group calling itself the Red Shirts began a campaign of terror, particularly around Wilmington in the southeastern section of the state, targeting political meetings and rallies. On November 7, Democratic leader Alfred Waddell, who had served as a colonel of Confederate cavalry, told his followers: "Go to the polls tomorrow and if you find the negro out voting, tell him to leave the polls and if he refuses, kill him, shoot him down in his tracks. We shall win tomorrow if we have to do it with guns." The result of all these efforts was an overwhelming victory throughout North Carolina for the Democratic Party on November 8.

But tensions did not dissipate. The train carrying Republican governor Russell back to the capital from his home town was stopped by a mob shouting, "Lynch him! Lynch the fat son of a bitch!" And two days after the election fighting broke out in Wilmington. There had been much bitterness over the way Populists and Republicans had restructured the city's government after winning power in 1897 because the changes seemed to guarantee that they could never be ousted. Many poor whites felt that the only good local jobs, such as brickmasons, carpenters, and mechanics, were reserved for blacks, and they resented the comparative wealth of black businessmen and professionals like John Campbell Dancy, whose position as collector of customs paid $4,000 a year, $1,000 more than the governor made and $1,500 more than state Supreme Court justices. Some of these black families had pianos, servants, lace curtains at their windows, a prosperity that led Democratic orators to ask their audiences, "How many of you white men can afford to have pianos and servants?"

Rumors circulated in both communities that the other was arming and planning trouble. Whites heard that servants were ready to burn their employers' homes if the Republicans lost, while black workers would burn the cotton warehouses. Stories spread that poor whites would drive Negroes from the city and seize their property for their own use.

A committee calling itself the "Secret Nine," led by Alfred Waddell, issued ultimatums to African-American leaders demanding that whites be given a large share of the jobs in the city, and that Alexander Manly, who had published the article on white women willingly meeting with blacks, "leave the city forever" and take his printing press with him. If these demands were not met within twelve hours, force would be used. The Committee of Colored Citizens replied, but either the letter was not delivered in time or it was ignored by Waddell. At 8:00 a.m. on the morning of the tenth, thirty minutes after the deadline, Waddell led his armed followers from the Wilmington Light Infantry Armory, where they had met, straight to the offices of Manly's newspaper and torched the building. Then, having accomplished what they'd planned, they set off a fire alarm so that Saint Luke's Baptist Church, the largest black church in Wilmington, would not be harmed by the spreading flames.

Most of the group marched back to the armory and were starting to disband when they heard that hundreds of Negroes with rifles and pistols were gathering at Sprunt's Cotton Compress loading dock in the port. They immediately rushed there, but found only unarmed workers and their employers. Some of the white men had recently returned from Cuba, and one yelled to his comrades, "You have just been through the war and so you know what should be *done,* so let's get started and be through with it."

Alexander Sprunt was noted for the paternalistic care he took of his black workers. When he saw the mob approaching he jumped up on a pile of cotton bales and told them, "Shoot if you will, but make me the victim." No one took the opportunity. Perhaps they respected the man or saw plain enough that none of the blacks were organized to resist. Or they may have been discouraged by the four guns on Sprunt's yacht, which the crew had trained on them. They left without harming anyone.

But now everybody was arming and chasing through the streets after rumors. A white mob encountered a group of blacks who refused to disperse. After a tense face-off, a shot was fired, killing a white man. So it was later claimed, anyway, and general fighting broke out, which resulted in fourteen black men being killed, along with several whites. Especially targeted were those who had been active in politics or who were armed. No women or children were physically harmed, and Waddell himself guaranteed the personal safety of at least one African-American man. The violence had a specific political goal and that was achieved: the Wilmington city government was taken over in a coup d'état.

Hundreds of black families and white families fled the city, many forever. African-American businesses never recovered, and were replaced by white-owned ones. Alexander Manly, one of the prime targets of white anger, managed to escape because a white friend warned him the day before the trouble started that he might be lynched, giving him the password that was to be used by Red Shirts roaming the countryside, as well as twenty-five dollars to help him on his way. Manly, his brother, and two friends were stopped that night by one of the mounted Red Shirt patrols.

"We are having a necktie party in Wilmington," the leader said, peering into their buggy. "Where are you gentlemen going?"

"We are going after that scoundrel Manly."

"What! With no guns?" And the Red Shirts, who were undoubtedly looking for "a big burly black brute," lent Manly's party, all of whom were fair-skinned enough to pass for white, some guns and waved them on their way.

The new Democratic state administration quickly instituted literacy tests and the other methods of denying African-Americans the right to vote that were being used across the South, but it was the terrible lesson of November 10 that really convinced a once proud and energetic community that there was to be no more power coming to them through the ballot, and no help coming from Washington. A delegation from the National Afro-American Council visited the White House to ask for justice in the Carolina massacre and to plead for the president "to exert his influence in all proper ways to improve the condition of the colored race," but although sympathetic words were spoken, no meaningful action was taken. The Spanish-American conflict had healed the wounds of the Civil War as far as William McKinley and most of his countrymen were concerned, and they were not about to reopen them.

Years later, Josephus Daniels, editor of the race-baiting Raleigh *News and Observer* who went on to be Woodrow Wilson's secretary of the navy, still defended his actions, but with a note of apologetic explanation. "I made enemies and I garnered friends, and my vehemence of denunciation of opponents was not always tempered with charity. . . . But I look back . . . amazed at my own editorial violence at times, even when I understood the circumstances which surrounded it. . . . The poverty of the South, the poverty of my State, and resentment at the Politics of Reconstruction, bred a violence in insecurity which reduced to pure bitterness the contest between men and groups and races."

ELECTIONS PROCEEDED MORE or less peacefully across the rest of the country, although at least six men were killed in individual political quarrels in Texas. Republicans retained control of the House of Representatives, and the new Republican state legislatures that took office meant, in this day before direct election of senators, that they would also increase their majority in the Senate. This was particularly important to McKinley, because it was the upper house that would determine the fate of the peace treaty being negotiated in Paris. Democrats were resisting the acquisition of the Philippines and other islands, but the president could not rest easy even after the election, for there was also a growing reluctance among members of his own party, a reluctance supported by some of their wealthiest backers. Since a two-thirds majority was needed to affirm the agreement, a minority could torpedo it.

The president later claimed that he had not made his final decision about the Philippines until just before the election. Even after his visits to the Midwest and Eastern cities, where the crowds seemed eager to keep the islands, he had still welcomed advice from all quarters, still paced the uneven floor of the White House night after night trying to determine his proper course of action. "I am not ashamed to tell you, gentlemen," he explained later to a group of visiting Methodist bishops, "that I went down on my knees and prayed Almighty God for light and guidance more than one night. And one night late it came to me this way—I don't know how it was, but it came: (1) That we could not give them back to Spain—that would be cowardly and dishonorable; (2) that we could not turn them over to France or Germany—our commercial rivals in the Orient—that would be bad business and discreditable; (3) that we could not leave them to themselves—they were unfit for self-government—and they would soon have anarchy and misrule over there worse than Spain's was; and (4) that there was nothing left for us to do but to take them all, and to educate the Filipinos, and uplift and civilize and Christianize them, and by God's grace do the very best we could by them, as our fellow-men for whom Christ also died. And then I went to bed, and went to sleep, and slept soundly, and the next morning I sent for the chief engineer of the War Department (our map-maker), and I told him to put the Philippines on the map of the United States"—at this moment McKinley pointed to the large map on the wall of his office—"and there they are, and there they will stay while I am President!"

Andrew Carnegie was especially worried that the taking on of imperialist duties would in the long run prove unpopular with the American people, lead to the defeat of the Republican Party, and subsequently allow demagogues like William Jennings Bryan to assume power and destroy the industrial economy that he and his peers had dedicated themselves to building. He called at the White House to warn that the Filipinos would resist being taken as a colony of the United States, even to the point of bloodshed. McKinley evidently just smiled, secure now in the Christian grace of his decision.

Carnegie, the wealthy textile manufacturer Edward Atkinson, Senator George Hoar, Boston lawyer Moorfield Storey, and other influential men met in November 1898 to form the Anti-Imperialist League, its purpose to stop the country from following the European example. "We hold that the policy known as imperialism is hostile to liberty and tends toward militarism," they announced. "We regret that it has become necessary in the land of Washington and Lincoln to reaffirm that all men, of whatever race or color, are entitled to life, liberty, and the pursuit of happiness. We maintain that governments derive their just powers from the consent of the governed. We insist that the subjugation of any people is 'criminal aggression' and open disloyalty to the distinctive principles of our Government."

Intellectuals and writers, such as William James and Mark Twain, also spoke out against an imperialist policy. Twain, who was living in Austria in 1898, had supported the humanitarian impulse behind the Spanish-American struggle. "I have never enjoyed a war," he wrote a friend, "—even in written history—as I am enjoying this one. For this is the worthiest one that was ever fought. . . . It is a worthy thing to fight for one's freedom; it is another sight finer to fight for another man's. And I think this is the first time it has been done." But he angrily turned against the effort to gain territory from victory, now denouncing the whole endeavor as a "wanton war and a robbing expedition."

Carnegie volunteered to spend twenty million dollars (the same amount the United States was to pay to Spain as compensation) to buy the Philippines and set them free. The steel magnate so pestered the administration with warnings and threats ("Your friend personally," he wrote the president, "but the bitterest enemy you have officially") that John Hay, the new secretary of state, thought, "Andrew Carnegie really seems to be off his head."

George Hoar, who had played such an important role in winning Senate approval for annexing Hawaii, was firmly against keeping the Philippines, but he and the president were able to retain their friendship.

"How are you feeling this winter, Mr. Senator?" McKinley had asked as the vote drew near.

"Pretty pugnacious, I confess, Mr. President."

Tears came to McKinley's eyes and, grasping Hoar's hand, he said, "I shall always love you, whatever you do."

Other politicians based their opposition to acquiring foreign possessions on racial grounds. Senator Arthur Gorman of Maryland, who led Democratic opposition, said, "The islands are filled with small darkies, and God alone can take care of them—America ought not to do so. . . . [They are] . . . so small in stature that they could slip between our legs as we went to the polling booths."

The struggle was intense, and came to a head even before the new Senate, with its stronger Republican majority, took office. Fighting broke out between American troops and Filipino insurgents on February 4, 1899. McKinley immediately understood what this meant: "It is always the unexpected that happens, at least in my case. How foolish these people [the insurgents] are. This means ratification of the treaty; the people will insist on its ratification." Within forty-eight hours a patriotic Senate voted the two-thirds majority it had been denying the president, although it was still very close: 61 voting yea and 29 nay. Within two years, after suffering frustration and massacre at the hands of the rebels, the United States army would be guilty of many of the same crimes in the Philippines it had gone to war to save the Cuban people from at the hands of the Spaniards, moving Mark Twain to suggest that skulls instead of stars should adorn the American flag.

THEODORE ROOSEVELT narrowly won his election as governor of New York, costing Tammany Boss Richard Croker tens of thousands of dollars in lost wagers. When a reporter for the *Times* visited the Roosevelt estate at Sagamore Hill the day after the election, he found the exhausted, hoarse-voiced victor reading the congratulatory messages that poured through the Oyster Bay telegraph office in record numbers, and writing his responses until he couldn't stand to be confined any more. Jumping on his bicycle, he took "a spin" along the Sound shore, and when he returned the reporter noted, "his face showed the effects of the exercise, and his eyes had regained some of their brightness." Roosevelt admitted that the last six months had been wearing, and that during the previous three years he had enjoyed little time to himself; now he was going to be "taking it easy" until he was sworn in as governor.

"I have played it with bull luck this summer," he wrote a good friend a short time later. "First, to get into the war; then to get out of it; then to get elected. I have worked hard all my life, and have never been particularly lucky, but this summer I *was* lucky, and I am enjoying it to the full. I know perfectly well that the luck will not continue, and it is not necessary that it should. I am more than contented to be Governor of New York, and shall not care if I never hold another office. . . ."

CHAPTER 13

THE NEW AMERICAN WAY

I know the banker, merchant and railroad king well . . . and they also need education and sound chastisement.

Theodore Roosevelt

Without imagination, no wants. Without wants, no demand to have them supplied. . . . the advertiser's problem . . . may be considered the controlling of other people's imaginations for his own advantage. It is a certain state of mind, and not the real condition of things, which is essential to the advertiser's success.

Katherine Fisher, advertising expert

WILLIAM MOORE and Adolphus Green had been opposing lawyers when the National Biscuit Company was formed in February 1898. Moore, who represented the New York group in the merger, was rewarded for his efforts with millions of dollars in shares, which he was forced to sell to cover his losses in the stock market. He bounced back later in the year, using his expertise in corporate mergers to organize the American Tin Plate Company, the opening maneuver in the national consolidation of the steel industry. Moore's reputation as a swashbuckling speculator and his association with the notorious John "Bet-a-Million" Gates caused serious investors such as Andrew Carnegie and J. P. Morgan to view him with suspicion, but he went on to control two additional steel corporations, building himself a new fortune that grew enormously after those corporations were absorbed in the 1901 formation of the United States Steel Company.

background

Adolphus Green was a very different man from William Moore. Born in Boston in 1843, eleventh and youngest child of a poor bootmaker, he was such a gifted scholar that he entered Harvard at the age of sixteen to follow a classical course of study: Greek, Hebrew, and Latin. After teaching and working as a librarian for five years, he "read law" at the leading Wall Street firm of Evarts, Southmayd & Choate. Green, passing the bar exam in 1873 during another of the severe "panics" that periodically disrupted the American economy, decided that Horace Greeley was right and headed west to start his career, arriving in Chicago as it was rebuilding from the great fire that had destroyed the city two years before.

In this raw, rough, and booming city, Green established himself as a successful trial lawyer who was widely respected in political and legal circles, although sometimes his demanding perfectionism sparked animosity. He also served as a mentor to ambitious young men such as Frank Peters, who had moved to Chicago as a poor Jewish boy from New York and become a messenger in Green's firm. Impressed with the youth's seriousness and intelligence, Green helped pay his way through law school, later forming a new concern, Green, Honore & Peters, with his protégé. Like a proverbial good New Englander, Green applied himself full force to whatever he undertook and lived up to that region's reputation for moral acuity and love of learning.

Local bakers had come to him for help in forming the American Biscuit & Manufacturing Company, and he had done such a good job of managing the competitive battles before the merger that now he became chairman of the board and de facto chief executive of NBC, or Nabisco, as people began calling it. Green established corporate headquarters in the eight-story Home Insurance Company building, the world's first true skyscraper, designed by William LeBaron Jenney with a steel skeleton supporting a curtain wall. His law offices were in the same building, and he may at first have thought that the biscuit company would take only part of his time. Very quickly, however, he became absorbed in every detail of running this sprawling collection of mismatched components.

Like so many other Americans, Adolphus Green was a man with a vision of how to improve life for common people, and like these other visionaries, from Henry Ford to Theodore Roosevelt, he would have to meet and overcome great challenges and criticism. Green was not the only businessman to feel this way; many saw themselves on an adventure for Progress just as great as that of the inventors and idealists. For this scholarly lawyer, the ideal was to build the National Biscuit Company into a force for both profits and good by improving efficiency, eliminating waste, and raising the quality, especially cleanliness and freshness, of baked products available to the public.

The unwieldy size of the new corporation made for inefficient organization and also accentuated the diverse interests and opinions of its agglomeration of independent-minded bakers, so Green immediately trimmed thirty-one bakeries and cut back on the variety of goods sold. Such decisive actions brought protests from the old-school entrepreneurs, who were already suspicious of their new partners. The lawyers and bankers, in turn, regarded these men, used to running their own small businesses, as being too traditional and unscientific to adopt modern corporate structuring and means of production. *marketing*

Green and his allies held to their course, sure that the company should establish its identity with one original and popular product before introducing others nationally. After examining all the goods, from animal cookies to zwieback, that the scattered Nabisco plants made, he decided to feature a version of the common soda cracker that was traditionally sold from a wooden barrel or box in the country store. As a preliminary step in marking their product as an uncommon treat, Green had the corners of the cracker trimmed to reshape it into an octagon. This brought more criticism from the traditionalists, as well as scornful complaints that the new-fangled recipe selected would never work.

Other defining characteristics were necessary. Instead of the anonymous and unsanitary barrel, where broken bits of crackers, dirt, moisture, and cat and rodent hairs gathered, there would be a neat individual package guaranteed to keep the crackers fresh until sold, guaranteed through a readily identifiable trademark and a brand name. Although he wanted to have the product on the market by December of 1898, Green was not discouraged by the fact that there was no existing package that would keep a cracker crisp, and neither the trademark nor the brand name had yet been determined. Critics in the company now began to accuse him of being a dreamer who did not have a firm enough grasp of the fundamentals of baking or practical commercial methods.

Green, who had intellectual interests broader than most lawyers and businessmen, was a book collector. Late one night in the spring, while leafing through a Renaissance volume on printer's emblems, he happened on a cross with two bars surmounting an oval, the mark used by the Society of Printers in Venice during the fifteenth century to symbolize the "triumph of the moral and spiritual over the evil and the material." Feeling that this perfectly represented the social good he hoped to achieve, he chose it as the trademark for National Biscuit.

Harder to discover was an appropriate name for the soda cracker. Brand names were not yet common in American life, nor was most advertising much more sophisticated than the "public notice" displays in newspapers and magazines, such as the small ads Alexander Winton was currently running in trade journals for his automobile. Up until recently, the only merchandise regularly mounting more elaborate campaigns were soaps and patent medicines, concoctions often laced with alcohol or opiates that promised cures for cancer and other horrors before which contemporary medical science was helpless. "I can advertise *dish* water and sell it, just as well as an article of merit," one of these frauds bragged. "It is all in the advertising."

As industrial productivity increased, the railroad transportation network grew, and better packaging was developed, corporations realized they could eliminate the expensive middlemen, or "dealers," who had always performed the local breakdown of their bulk shipments. All that was necessary was to package the goods at the plant, "brand" them with their own name, then make that name so respected that people nationwide would ask for it. This discovery would be as revolutionary to everyday life as assembly line production techniques, and it produced another new player to sit alongside lawyers and bankers in the councils of business: the advertising expert.

The pioneer agency in making brands well known was N. W. Ayer and Son of Philadelphia, which in 1892 had moved beyond the usual function of such a company—to buy space in publications that was then resold to advertisers—and hired a copywriter to compose advertisements in-house. The firm became expert in ways to establish, then build, brand loyalty, providing advice for such new companies as Montgomery Ward, Procter & Gamble Soaps, Burpee Seeds, and Hires Root Beer, while also winning a reputation for ethical business practices by refusing to handle advertising for manufacturers or dealers in alcoholic beverages, patent medicines, or speculative financial promotions.

Green recognized the need for such expertise. Just a few months before National Biscuit was founded, *Harper's Weekly* had pointed out that these more elaborate advertisements were becoming "part of the humanities, a true mirror of life, a sort of fossil history from which the future chronicler, if all other historical monuments were to be lost, might fully and graphically rewrite the history of our time." The writer then went on to emphasize how people's lives were being affected by the change: "Once we skipped [advertisements] unless some want compelled us to read, while now we read to find out what we really want." Advertising had just leaped from information to persuasion.

In the summer of 1898, the Ayer agency sent the experienced Henry McKinney to Chicago to meet with Adolphus Green. McKinney himself had planned (or would later) the advertising campaigns, and frequently devised the name of such products as Karo syrup, Keds shoes, Necco wafers, and Meadow Gold dairy products. The two men respected each other immediately, and agreed on the importance of a strong brand name as well as a distinctive packaging design to foil imitators. Green already had decided to call his cracker a biscuit, because he thought it sounded more dignified and English, thereby bringing some snob appeal. But when he showed McKinney a list of brand names he was considering, the Ayer professional had to diplomatically convince the classically educated chief executive that none of his choices were appropriate for the mass market.

One of the favorites was Pherenice Biscuit, ancient Greek for "thirst," and had the added charm, Green assured McKinney, of being pronounced "very nice." Among other suggestions were Bekos, Greek for bread, and Dandelo, a celebrated Venetian doge. "The name must be simple and easily pronounced," McKinney replied to his client, "and as nearly as possible capable of only one pronunciation. It must also sound well and be easily spoken." Pherenice was "too difficult for the masses. . . . Try a dozen of the medium class and see how few will make it sound anything like 'very nice.' " Similar objections were raised to the others, so the search for a proper name went on.

So did the search for a new type of moisture-proof packaging to protect the biscuit, until a surprise tinkerer managed to design a machine to manufacture it. Frank Peters, the young partner Green had helped through law school, became fascinated with the challenge of finding some way that waxed paper could be mechanically folded around delicate soda crackers without breaking them. For months he spent evenings experimenting at his kitchen table with paper, blocks of wood, and a foot treadle, until finally he found a process that worked, and was awarded a patent for a process the corporation would soon label "In-Er-Seal." Green was so impressed that he declared Peters should become "a scientific baker, something we have not got in the National Biscuit Company."

The discovery of a way to package also led to the discovery of a name. Robert Gair had been an early manufacturer of paper bags, the revolutionary packaging invented by Luther Childs Crowell in the late 1860s that had "sped up" retail sales, particularly the sale of groceries, by eliminating the need for elaborate wrapping in the store. Gair himself had, among other inventions, designed a machine to make inexpensive folding cardboard boxes, which had their own revolutionary effect on commerce.

When Henry McKinney conferred with Gair's son about enclosing Frank Peters' waxed paper-covered biscuits inside a special cardboard package, the son said, "You need a name." Something obviously clicked; "Uneeda" appeared on a list with a number of other suggestions sent to Green, and he underlined it in red ink. Uneeda Biscuit was baptized.

Once that important problem was solved, planning for the campaign proceeded quickly. Green found further inspiration in his library: a border decoration on the hand-tooled binding of a sixteenth-century book provided part of the packaging design. He also specified that purple and white would predominate on the box. Frederic W. Goudy, a young artist who would later become world famous in this field, won a design contest for the type used for "National Biscuit Company." Mottos had become important in marketing in the previous few years. Kodak camera's "You press the button: we do the rest" was very effective, as was Ivory Soap's "It floats," and Dr. Williams' tablets' "Pink pills for pale people." After much experimenting, "Lest you forget, we say it yet, Uneeda Biscuit" was selected.

Green was so determined to make a success of this initial product from Nabisco that he decided to launch the first million-dollar advertising presentation in history, a figure so grand that when this news was released it attracted sensational comment in the press, so providing some free publicity. No promotional opportunity was to be ignored, and Ayer contracted for extensive billboard, newspaper, and magazine space. Associates at National Biscuit protested that his proposed price of five cents would not return enough profit to make such costs worthwhile, arguing for both raising the price and increasing the size of the package. Green, however, recognized that there were different rules in the mass consumer economy that was developing. "Reduction in prices . . . will increase consumption," he explained to stockholders just as the new product appeared on the market, "and in itself enable us to decrease our percentage of profit on sales without diminishing the aggregate volume of our profits."

Less than a year after the corporation was formed, simple two-word ads began appearing in newspapers, on billboards, and in streetcars: "Uneeda Biscuit."

A few days later this was followed by a question: "Do you know Uneeda

Biscuit?" Over the next several weeks these teasers came and went in various forms, while an army of salesmen drummed up business across the country, focusing particularly on crossroads stores, giving out posters for barns, livery stables, fences, and railroad stations. They were also generous with stick pins, watch fobs, and cuff links for store owners, all these promotional items bearing "Uneeda" across their faces. Contestants won even better prizes in biscuit-eating contests held in store windows. A corps of Uneeda cadets followed along in the drummers' wake, checking to ensure that only fresh crackers were being sold. Scores of horses and wagons bearing the logo and brand name had been purchased to make deliveries, and they were soon seen everywhere on the roads and streets, as well as in children's hands, for toys were modeled on them.

A cartoon appeared making fun of the whole effort. An elderly man was shown sitting in a crossroads store, saying, "The idea! Spendin' their money for advertisin'! I tell ye, boys, th' only formula for a rattlin' good grocery bisness is checker games, with plenty o' free crackers." But one of Green's executives saw the company effort as promoting cleanliness and progress: "namely the breaking down of habit and ignorance, the habit of buying from barrels, bins and boxes, and ignorance of what that meant." The traditional cracker barrel that generations had gathered around in country emporiums across the nation was soon to be no more.

Many advertisements targeted women, pointing out that they had more important things to do than bake over a hot stove all day, and stressing how clean and fresh the In-Er-Seal kept the crackers. "Every woman's baking day can now be banished in the limbo of tallow dips and home spinning," went the argument. "Today, there are so many interesting things for every woman to do, that few can say they do not need more time for their families and the world outside their homes as well." Human interest was added by having a young boy as "mascot" of the campaign. This idea seems to have been lifted from the French makers of Lu Biscuits, who had been using a schoolboy in their ads since at least 1897, but it was even more effective in the United States. Pictured during a storm wearing a yellow rain slicker and sou'wester hat while clutching an equally watertight package of the biscuits, this image appeared on posters, banners, cartoon strips, streetcar ads, newspapers, and magazines. The figure was so ubiquitous, so inescapable, that he was adopted by popular culture—children began dressing as the "slicker boy" in parades and at costume parties.

Adults were drawn into the magic of the promotion too, forgetting that this was a commercial product and making it part of their lives. A town in

West Virginia was named Uneeda, and unsolicited testimonials and poems were sent to the corporate office:

> *I am Uneeda, I defy*
> *The roaming dust, the busy fly.*
> *For in my package, sealed and tight*
> *My makers keep me pure and white.*

The whole endeavor proved so overwhelmingly successful that historians consider it the prototype for modern mass distribution. In less than a year, ten million packages of Uneeda Biscuits were being sold a month, while the total annual sales of all other packaged crackers were somewhere around five hundred thousand. Almost immediately there appeared on the market Isagood soup, Uwanta beer, and *Ureada Magazine,* but they disappeared just as quickly.

Green, now being called the "Boss of the Biscuit Business," had a new challenge: fighting for increased efficiency in order to meet demand. Complaining of "enormous waste," he regarded the carelessness of some plant managers as "almost criminal," in that they could barely produce four hundred packages from a barrel of flour while others managed five hundred. He tried to bring order to the widely scattered facilities of National Biscuit, but found that "They look on me as an idealist." In May 1899, the largest bakery ever built was opened in New York City with a parade that included a marching band, mounted police, colorful floats, and 112 horse-drawn delivery wagons. Although it was exclusively dedicated to making Uneedas, even this huge plant was unable to keep up with the orders that continued to pour in.

At the same time Green and his executives were struggling to satisfy the monster they had created, they were already laying the groundwork for the next Nabisco product. This one was made possible by a machine the prolific inventor James Henry Mitchell had designed that surrounded a kind of fruit "pie" or jam with dough, both being extruded from tubes in an endless stream. Since they were first produced in Newton, a suburb of Boston, and most commonly incorporated fig jam, they came to be called Fig Newtons. Their national launching also proved to be a success, and others followed: within a decade the National Biscuit Company had forty-four items on its marketing list.

Some corporations had preceded the Uneeda campaign on a smaller scale, and others soon were spending even larger amounts to establish their brand names. Also being established were what the historian Daniel Boorstin calls "consumer communities," groups of diverse people who did not share religious or political beliefs, but were bound into a common sense of identity by their preferences for specific commercial brands. These proved to be powerful forces for assimilating the millions of immigrants entering the United States during the 1890s and after the turn of the century. "Joining consumption communities became a characteristic American mode of acculturation," argues Boorstin, and a contemporary writer for the advertising trade journal *Printer's Ink* would have agreed with him. The Uneeda Biscuit, and particularly its brilliant public relations launching, was, he declared, "an agent of Americanization."

ROBERT PEARY, ON leave from the navy, was still hoping to become a symbol for American grit and skill by "nailing the Stars and Stripes to the Pole." He had reached Greenland in July 1898 and, after laying in a store of walrus meat, tried to drive his ship, the *Windward,* north through the summer ice. But this year the ice was thicker than usual, and the *Windward,* because of underfunding, lacked sufficient engine power. By the middle of August the expedition was icebound four hundred miles from the place where he had hoped to start his trek. The explorer had taken as his motto a phrase from the Roman philosopher Seneca: *Inveniam viam aut faciam*— "I shall find a way or make one." As soon as the ocean ice became firm enough, he began making one, portaging supplies to sites that could serve as advance depots for his major attempt.

On December 20, 1898, Peary, with Matthew Henson, his African-American assistant and man-of-all-work, plus four Eskimos and dog teams, set out for an earlier expedition's abandoned base, hoping to find that the supplies they had left behind were still usable. He came very close to finding death instead. By December 29 they were struggling through a dark, frozen wilderness. "The moon had left us entirely now, and the ice-foot was utterly impracticable, and we groped and stumbled through the rugged sea ice. . . . we slept a few hours in a burrow in the snow, then started across Lady Franklin Bay. In complete darkness and over a chaos of broken and heaved-up ice, we stumbled and fell and groped for eighteen hours. . . ." Conditions were so bad, with temperatures down to 63 degrees below zero Fahrenheit, that it wasn't until January 6, 1899, that Peary led his team into the shelter of the old camp. It had been a marvelous feat of navigation and endurance that had saved their lives, but for the last stretch of the trek

Peary had been bothered by a suspicious wooden feeling in his feet. Henson later described what he found when he helped remove the expedition leader's *kamiks*. Both legs were "bloodless and white up to the knee, and as I ripped off the undershoes, several toes from each foot clung to the hide and snapped off at the joint." Peary lost parts of seven toes, and suffered weeks of excruciating pain before he was strong enough to be sledged back to the *Windward*.

At the same time he was undergoing this ordeal, his supporters in the United States met and founded the Peary Arctic Club, promising funds that would ensure him continuing financial support. More good news was that the Norwegian expedition he had feared was in competition for the polar prize was not. Though now crippled, he refused to give up his quest, and in the face of further physical punishment Peary persisted, trying again and again, until he was able to announce that he had carried the Stars and Stripes to the Pole on April 6, 1908. It would prove, however, a bitter victory. Dr. Frederick A. Cook, a physician from Brooklyn who had spent 1898 in Antarctica, claimed to have beaten Peary by a year to the geographical "top of the world." A great controversy began that continues to this day, with both men having their passionate advocates. Peary has generally been accepted as the hero, celebrated almost as much for his self-sacrificing discipline and resolution as for his achievement.

WHILE A NEED for physical challenge, excitement, and glory drove some men to seek adventure in polar wastes and tropical battlefields, hazards such as runaway horses, train and trolley wrecks, and unshielded equipment in industrial workplaces contributed a thrill of danger to the regular routine of even the most conventional Americans. Severe weather, unpredictable by the technology of the time, was the greatest of the natural forces that could affect their lives, quickly turning days that began as mundane into a struggle for survival. On the Saturday after Thanksgiving in 1898, a sudden, unexpected storm struck the East Coast and developed into one of the most devastating in the country's history.

The early morning of November 26, 1898, was calm enough, with clear skies and a slight chill in the air, but two powerful weather systems, one traveling from the Gulf of Mexico and the other from the Great Lakes, unexpectedly joined forces over the Mid-Atlantic coast and began moving north. Baltimore, Philadelphia, and New York City were caught by surprise at the suddenness with which temperatures dropped, and the speed at which snow piled into huge drifts. The Baltimore Country Club had invited golfers from one hundred and twenty-five clubs across the country to play in a tournament, but was forced to cancel the event; snow started falling in Philadelphia at 11:00 a.m., and, combined with a fierce wind, quickly brought all transportation to a standstill. A few hours later, New Yorkers also found themselves battling record levels of snow driven by gale-force winds. Temperatures fell to below freezing so quickly that people were caught on streets and roads without the protection of winter clothing; bodies would be pulled from snowdrifts for days afterward. Particularly affected, of course, were the homeless. A mother with three young children was found buried in a bank of snow near Wyckoff Street and Third Avenue in New York City by a passing policeman who heard a child asking, "What shall we do?" and the mother's response, "Stay here and freeze." They were escorted to the warmth of a police station. The *New York Times* reported that a "little boy whose pitiful face was almost blue with cold" walked into the Marlborough Hotel and begged the clerk, "Say, Mister, if you just let me stand before your fire for five minutes I'll sweep the whole of your sidewalk for you."

But for all the misery on land, the largest loss of life and property took place at sea; the next two days saw the greatest destruction of shipping in the long history of the coastal trade in the United States. In 1898 sea routes were still of major importance in carrying freight and passengers, and a huge, varied fleet of commercial vessels existed to carry them: sloops, schooners, brigantines, barkentines, full-rigged ships, and both paddle- and screw-driven steamers. The storm would subsequently take its name from the disappearance of one of the largest of these ships, becoming known as The *Portland* Gale.

Even while heavy snow and wind were battering the Mid-Atlantic coast, New England was enjoying fair skies and a light breeze. By afternoon clouds were moving in, but the wind stayed moderate. At India Wharf in Boston Harbor in the evening of November 26, the 291-foot paddle steamer *Portland* began boarding passengers for the regular run to her namesake city in Maine. Less than ten years old, the ship was fast and strongly built, though she had a tendency to pitch and roll in high seas so that the paddle wheels would alternately lift out of the water. Captain Hollis H. Blanchard had been warned of a storm moving up the coast from New York, but he thought his ship would be able to reach the safety of the dock in Portland before the strong winds would arrive. He had successfully outrun foul weather many times before.

Later, hundreds of people would claim to have been planning to take the steamer, but to have either changed their minds at the last minute or been delayed by a slow trolley. There were, however, at least two people who evidently did decide not to make the voyage after arriving at India Wharf. George Gott was standing in the pre-departure confusion, just preparing to board when he noticed the ship's cat carrying a kitten from the ship to a large nearby shed. He watched as she repeatedly went back to the *Portland* and brought off kitten after kitten until her whole litter was in the building. Disturbed by this feline lack of faith, Gott decided to stay in Boston. Anna Young was already aboard and resting in her stateroom when a message from her mother was delivered. "Mother believed a storm was coming, and she had a premonition that I shouldn't sail. Carrying my child, I ran for the gangplank just as they started to lift it, and they waited for me. When I got ashore I heard the final whistle of the *Portland* as she left the wharf."

When the ship departed India Wharf at seven, there was still no sign of unusually bad conditions. A few hours earlier the small steamer *Kennebec* had set out for Bath, Maine, but her captain had found the seas rough and been bothered by the strange appearance of the sky and light (another mariner of great experience thought it was the "greasiest" evening he ever saw). The *Kennebec* returned to shelter inside the harbor, and whistled a warning to the larger *Portland* as she passed. The whistle was ignored.

When, an hour after leaving the wharf, the *Portland* neared the open sea, the skies began spitting snow and sleet. The tugboat *Channing* passed close by the paddle-wheeler around eight o'clock. Ten or twelve boisterous young men were gathered on the upper deck of the steamer, the tug's mate later remembered, and one of these "young bloods" yelled across to him "to get my old scow out of the way." The mate, who could tell a strong gale was building, shouted back, "You'd better stop that hollering, because I don't think you'll be this smart tomorrow morning." The ship was sighted just a few hours later pitching and rolling in the heavy seas.

Later, men who had been at sea all their lives swore that they had never known a storm to come on so suddenly, or the wind to blow so violently. Gusts of 72 miles per hour were reported after midnight. "It was blowing so hard," one sailor reported, "that I was obliged to kneel down to get my breath." The two weather systems had joined together to create one enormous Northeaster storm of unprecedented strength.

Every captain then at sea was faced with a difficult decision: either make for the shelter of a port, if one was nearby, or work further out to sea to avoid the horrors of a lee shore. For many ships neither course was available, as visibility had been cut to less than a hundred yards while wind and waves continued to mount so that even normally safe harbors offered no refuge. Dozens of vessels had already sunk or been wrecked on beaches from Delaware Bay to Long Island, but the full fury of the storm was unleashed on New England. Over twenty-four vessels were driven onto the island of Martha's Vineyard; twenty-seven vessels suffered the same fate at Provincetown, on Cape Cod, including the pilot schooner *Columbia*, which crashed onto a cottage on Scituate Beach; twenty-five were wrecked at Boston Harbor; twenty-nine at Gloucester. The numbers of ships and lives lost stunned the nation. "CALAMITIES UNPRECEDENTED IN THE HISTORY OF NEW ENGLAND," headlined the *New York Times* once telegraph service was restored and the full scope of the disaster became known, "CAPE COD'S STORY OF DEATH." Every town along the coast was also heavily damaged, with giant waves sweeping through main thoroughfares as the tide reached record heights, while further inland wide swaths of trees were blown down in the forests.

During a brief lull in the storm between nine and eleven o'clock Sunday morning, the *Portland* was sighted off Cape Cod, along with two other ships. But then the wind-driven snow and sleet started flying again, dropping visibility back to a hundred yards. It was the last time she was sighted; twelve hours later debris from the large passenger ship began appearing on the Cape's beaches. First a lifebelt marked STR PORTLAND was found, then nine or ten 40-quart creamery cans, empty but tightly stoppered, floated ashore, followed by doors, mattresses, chairs, and paneling, as well as part of the ship's cargo of coffins. All this wreckage collected along the surf line in piles ten to twelve feet high. Hours later the bodies of passengers began washing up on the sand. Of the almost two hundred men, women, and children on board, only thirty-six bodies were ever recovered. Watches in their pockets had stopped between 9:15 and 9:20, indicating the time that Sunday night that she had sunk.

Around one hundred and fifty ships were wrecked in New England waters alone, most never to be replaced, and over four hundred and fifty people died during the storm. Newspapers were filled with human-interest stories of suffering and heroic rescue, but it was the mysterious disappearance of the *Portland* that most fascinated the public—New England's greatest single loss of life by maritime disaster during the nineteenth century. People were also haunted by the question of how such a large, strong vessel with an experienced and well-respected captain could founder and leave behind only scattered piles of wreckage.

The *Portland* and the gale named for it entered the folklore of the New England coast. One enterprising antiques dealer, who seems to have had a prescient sense of how popular souvenirs of the disaster would be, arrived at the beach early on Monday morning with a large wagon to begin collecting the debris to sell from his shop.

Many theories were devised to explain what might have happened, but it was thought that the true cause of the sinking would never be known. Then, in the early 1940s, more than fifty years after the storm, a boat dragging for scallops off Cape Cod brought up material that was identified as belonging to the *Portland*. Nearby, the captain found the wreck of another ship, probably the ninety-six-foot two-masted schooner *Addie E. Snow* from Chebeague Island, Maine, carrying a load of granite. Edward Rowe Snow, a writer who had spent decades researching the story of the *Portland*, paid for a deep-sea diver to investigate the wreck sites during the summer of 1945. It was Snow's conclusion that the granite schooner collided with the side-wheeler when snow, sleet, and gigantic waves hampered visibility, sending both to the bottom.

LYMAN FRANK BAUM grew up in a wealthy New York family, but had decided while still a teenager against following his father into the oil business. Instead he had been drawn to the theater, and in his early twenties wrote and produced his own plays, *The Maid of Arran* and *The Queen of Killarney,* starring in them with his wife as they toured through the East and Midwest. This was a wonderful creative experience, but less successful as a money-maker. While not completely giving up the theater, he worked as a traveling salesman, and then started an enterprise related to his father's: Baum's Castorine Company, producing an axle grease made from crude oil.

In 1888, at the age of thirty-two, he opened a retail store, Baum's Bazaar, in Aberdeen, South Dakota, where his wife's brother and sisters had homesteaded a farm. A sudden downturn in the local economy put the Bazaar into bankruptcy, but Baum, displaying the optimistic adaptability of the American entrepreneur, then shifted to journalism, not only publishing the *Aberdeen Saturday Pioneer*, but also writing and setting in type almost every word that went onto its pages, both news stories and advertising. "To gain all the meat from the nut of life is the essence of wisdom," he informed the readers of Aberdeen, "therefore, 'eat, drink, and be merry'—for *tomorrow* you die." This emphasis on sensual pleasures must have been somewhat shocking to the conservative farmers of the region, but Baum saw himself as a revolutionary force for changing Americans from pinch-penny savers to consumers of the good things in life. Yes, you might "be forced to borrow a few dollars" in order to afford worldly comforts, but "who will be the gainer when Death calls him to the last account—the man who can say 'I have lived!' or the man who can say 'I have saved'?"

Baum's view of the world had been formed in the wealthy surroundings of his childhood, but he was also influenced by his mother-in-law, Matilda Joslyn Gage, who was a leading feminist and the coauthor, along with Susan B. Anthony and Elizabeth Cady Stanton, of *History of Woman Suffrage*. Gage had found the Protestantism of her own youth too resistant to women's rights, and had instead turned to theosophy, a quirky blend of Eastern mysticism, the paranormal, and a respect for the "objectivity" of science put together by Madame Helena Blavatsky.

One of the New Thought or Mind Cure philosophies that had arisen to fill needs brought about by Darwin's undermining of established religion, theosophy taught that happiness was something to be sought in this world, not postponed until Heaven. There was no Heaven, although theosophists did believe that the "spirits" of dead people were present in another dimension, which could only be reached through mediums and séances. Nor was there a God as traditionally worshipped, but "There is a latent power," one theosophist wrote, "a force of indestructible life, an immortal principle of health, in every individual, which if developed would heal all our wounds." If one developed this latent power, not only good health but money enough to provide comforts and luxuries would result. There was no need to defer happiness.

This made eminent good sense to Baum, but he had a hard time living up to the model in Aberdeen, South Dakota. Continuing bad times sank the *Saturday Pioneer,* and booming, bustling Chicago pulled him to its busy streets, just as it did so many ambitious and penniless young men. He briefly worked as a reporter for the *Chicago Evening News,* then went on the road selling crockery and glassware. Salesmanship was a perfect calling for a man of his optimistic nature, and he was successful enough that soon he, his wife, and four children were able to afford a large house with modern conveniences such as gaslight and a bathroom. But by the late 1890s he grew tired of eating hotel food, traveling endless railroad miles, and being away from his family for long periods of time.

In 1897 he published *Mother Goose in Prose,* illustrated by Maxfield Parrish, and began writing down his own stories, "wonder tales," as he called them. Another avenue, however, offered more immediate financial reward while also allowing him to creatively preach his philosophy of living, and consuming, in the here and now. America had some of the world's largest department stores, jammed full of goods produced by the new industrial order, an abundance that often seemed too much of a good thing. There were challenges in profitably selling such an enormous flow of goods, especially since the retail market not only suffered from labor problems but also was savagely competitive. Baum was confident he could teach department store owners how to move their merchandise more effectively. At the end of 1897 he began publishing a trade journal promulgating his ideas, *The Show Window,* and in February 1898 he organized the National Association of Window Trimmers, whose goal was "the uplifting of mercantile decorating to the level of a profession."

New technological advances helped him develop his concept. Domestic manufacturers had improved the production of plate glass during the decade. Now, instead of importing expensive sheets of glass from France, buildings could be designed with larger, clearer, stronger windows at a much lower price. But owners were slow to understand what this meant until Baum showed them. Customarily goods had been crammed haphazardly in a storefront, but Baum, drawing on his background in drama, merchandising, and writing, designed window displays that enticed pedestrians to stop, study, and be amused and tempted by what was being offered for sale. "It is said," he wrote in his book on the subject, "that people are not as readily deceived by window display, but we all know better than this." Already there was criticism of the intrusive quality of advertising, the way it interfered with the enjoyment of views or street scenes, and to many people this new form of huckstering seemed a step in the wrong direction. But Baum argued that there was "no way to protect people from imposition, even supposing they desired to be protected."

There was some resistance at first. The older generation had been raised to regard gawking at windows as vulgar. To help overcome this reluctance, "window gazers" were hired to stand, stare, and draw a crowd. Baum used his talent and imagination to create the most effective lures: movement, electric light, and color, with revolving stars, mechanical birds and butterflies, vanishing ladies, models of Ferris wheels. "People will always stop to examine anything that moves," he explained, "and will enjoy studying out the mechanics or wondering how the effect has been obtained." He was not shy about stating explicitly how this sense of wonder was to be used: to "arouse in the observer the cupidity and longing to possess the goods." It is no surprise that during 1898 Thorstein Veblen was writing his study of the power of conspicuous consumption, *The Theory of the Leisure Class*.

L. Frank Baum's utopian American fairy tale, *The Wonderful Wizard of Oz*, being written in 1898 but not published until two years later, shared much of the color, excitement, and glorification of abundance visible in his store windows, as well as reflecting the author's fascination with "mind cure" and theosophy.

"Where are you?" Dorothy asks the unseen Wizard in a séance-like setting.

"I am everywhere," answers the Voice, "but to the eyes of common mortals I am invisible. I will now seat myself upon my throne, that you may converse with me."

In both his show windows and Oz books, Baum taught that positive thinking, and consuming, were the American way to happiness. "The time has come for a series of newer 'wonder tales,'" he wrote in the introduction to the original edition, "in which the stereotyped genie, dwarf and fairy are eliminated, together with all the horrible and blood-curdling incidents devised by their authors to point a fearsome moral to each tale. . . . *The Wonderful Wizard of Oz* was written solely to please children of today. It aspires to being a modernized fairy tale, in which the wonderment and joy are retained and the heartaches and nightmares are left out." Two particularly American elements in the resulting series of books were the natural forces depicted—earthquakes and a Kansas cyclone—and mechanical gadgets that could work magic.

As soon as *The Wizard* proved a success, Baum left the retail trade, but his mark remained. Quickly "all glass fronts" became common design elements for department stores, and in a little over a decade the United States was using half the world's window-glass production.

When Mary Antin and her young immigrant girlfriends promenaded the boulevards in 1898 they left "the imprints of our noses and fingers on plate-glass windows ablaze with electric lights and alluring with display." One of her first liberating experiences in the New World occurred when a neighbor led her and her siblings "to a wonderful country called 'uptown,' where in a dazzlingly beautiful palace called a 'department store,' we exchanged our hateful homemade European costumes, which pointed us out as 'greenhorns' to the children on the street, for real American machine-made garments, and issued forth glorified in each other's eyes."

Here was the freedom to remake oneself, to shed one skin for another and thereby be born anew, an emancipation that department store owners believed they were making available to every American through the low prices made possible by their economies of scale. In a democracy each man and woman should be able to define themselves, and increasingly that definition would be through consumption. As with Adolphus Green, Andrew Carnegie, and Thomas Edison, retailers such as John Wanamaker and his New York partner Robert Ogden were sure they were agents of progress. "I have ideals," Ogden wrote in 1898, "at the center of which is the fundamental principal to make money." But he knew he had "added to the sum of human happiness by increasing the power of money to supply the comforts of life." Comforts, identity, and a new way of interacting with the world.

Small-store owners felt the retail giants were sources of discord and destruction rather than liberation, and this year they were at the end of a losing campaign to restrict their growing competitors. Across the nation they had appealed to state legislatures, local governments, and civic groups for help, but with little or only temporary success. Robert Ogden felt the same lack of sympathy for them that Rockefeller and Carnegie had felt for the small-scale producers they had destroyed in their own quests for efficiency and profits. That the small-store owners' livelihood was being ruined was "true to a degree," but the important point was that the department store "conserves opportunities . . . and makes them more abundant. Sympathy for persons who, refusing to recognize existing conditions, have pursued a hopeless venture to a disastrous end is constantly in demand. But the judgment should recognize the fact that the result comes from ignorance or obstinacy, or both. If the suffering individual had simply adapted himself to actual conditions, and had sought his livelihood through some of the large concerns, he would have been in the enjoyment of a fair compensation, and would not appear as a sympathy-seeking mendicant." The giant corporation, in other words, was the way of the future, and if you could not adapt to that, then you would be left either a parasite or a beggar by the side of the road.

Although one purpose of designer windows was to attract customers year 'round and break the economic hold that holidays had over retailers, Christmas became the great season for elaborate displays, and they had never before been so elaborate as in 1898. "The Tide of Prosperity" crowed one of the year-end editorials of the New York Times, "finds all of the creeks and inlets, and visits every land-locked bay, raising the waters everywhere to the level of the brimming sea. From all over the land come stories of its rising flood, topping all previous high-water marks." William Allen White noted the tide's buoyant power in Kansas, where at the beginning of the year farmers' houses across the state had been run down and neglected because of lack of money. Now every one of them seemed to gleam with a new coat of paint.

Crossroads stores, even in the poorest reaches of the South, offered toys and candy for the children. Some had even received their first shipments of Uneeda biscuits. These small rural enterprises, too, had learned to display their wares, although since the dusty roads did not have casual pedestrian traffic they imaginatively used their interiors rather than windows. Toys and Christmas ornaments hung from the ceiling, while there were special arrays of possible gifts for Mom and Dad, such as Martha Washington's Perfume Waters ($1.05) or a Harrington & Richardson pistol ($2.98). Especially popular were firecrackers, black powder, and Roman candles to celebrate the holiday.

But it was in the cities where the flowing tide lifted highest the hopes and spirits of men and women. Streets bowered with green branches and red-and-white decorations were bustling with crowds, most of the men encouragingly sporting a sprig of mistletoe in their buttonholes. Store owners admitted that they had never seen so many shoppers, while reporters commented that everyone seemed more good-natured than usual. "Few got grumpy even under strong provocation. Children seemed the objects of particular consideration, and wherever one of the tots was jammed in the crowd a space was quickly opened for it. In front of the gaudy shop windows the little ones were always given place in the front ranks."

In New York City, the sight of two young African-American boys gazing longingly at some pies in a bakery window so moved a bystander that he staggered inside and bought two, an observer commenting that perhaps he was filled with the season's spirit, but also, to judge by his uncertain gait, "with the spirit that is as ardent in July as in December." When he handed the pies over with a gruff "Merry Christmas," the boys were too astonished to say thank you. One immediately began eating his, but the other held back.

"Waser marrer," the philanthropist asked him, " 'fraid of it?"

"Nope, 'fraid er nuffin'," the lad responded. "I was thinkin' of mommer and Liz." And then he disappeared down a side street to take the gift home.

Such good works were always popular at Christmas, and actually came to be regarded as a spectator sport. During the 1890s, gala events under various sponsors were mounted that allowed benefactors to watch the impoverished enjoying themselves at a bountiful meal. Beginning in 1898, the Salvation Army organized annual dinners at Madison Square Garden, where thousands of poor people were fed at tables set up on the arena floor, under powerful electric lights, while wealthy New Yorkers paid admission to sit in the Garden's boxes and galleries and watch. For one of these displays, the *New York Times* ran a front-page story headlined "THE RICH SAW THEM FEAST." The meal opened with both the wealthy and the destitute singing the hymn "Praise God from Whom All Blessings Flow." This made the reporter feel that "position and fortune [were] forgotten for one brief moment," and to look to the future with optimism: "Neither any Continental city nor even London ever had to do anything approaching this in magnitude. It means the dawning of a new era, the bridging of the gulf between the rich and poor."

The governor-elect was also offering gifts to strangers this Christmas. Mrs. Roosevelt and "Miss Alice," his daughter from his first marriage, accompanied him to the Cove Neck School in Oyster Bay, where his portrait, covered with laurel branches, was on the wall next to those of Washington and Lincoln. Before handing out the presents attached to a Christmas tree, he spoke briefly, mainly addressing the boys, whom he urged to enjoy life. But, he said, if the time to fight should come he expected them "to be on hand." They should do their duty as young Americans, being "brave and manly and gentle to all."

The fact that they might be called to duty some time soon in the future had become more likely now that the United States had leaped into the midst of the world struggle for markets and empire. Disturbing news was appearing daily about threatening troop movements by the Filipino insurgents, but there were also gratifying headlines and subheads, such as those over a story on Christmas Day in the *New York Times:*

EUROPE FEARS AMERICA
This Country the Commanding Power in Finance and Commerce
MANUFACTURERS ARE ALARMED
American Steel Rails in Demand Everywhere
Russia Turns to Us for a Loan

All Europeans were talking about was the "remarkable, aggressive, commercial prosperity" that this country was suddenly displaying, but even more alarming to them was "with what giant's strides America is coming into the first place in the alignment of the powers." A London banker recognized the unexpected shift of strength in his own field, telling an American businessman, "This is the first time in the history of finance that New York has been in a position to dictate money rates to London, Berlin, and Paris." The Eagle had indeed spread its wings and was starting to scream, as Mr. Hennessy and Mr. Dooley recognized.

"We're a gr-reat people," said Mr. Hennessy, earnestly.

"We ar-re," said Mr. Dooley. "We ar-re that. An' th' best iv it is, we know we ar-re."

THEODORE ROOSEVELT was too impatient to wait until January 1 to take his oath of office, being sworn in as governor of the nation's wealthiest and most populous state on the last day of the year. He set to work immediately to "combine both idealism and efficiency" for the good of the people, but he knew there was a delicate task ahead. Thomas Platt was, as he explained in his autobiography, "to all intents and purposes . . . a majority of the Legislature," and he would have to get along with him to accomplish anything worthwhile. But how to do that without being tarred by the brush of the Republican machine? "I made up my mind that the only way I could beat the bosses . . . was . . . by making my appeal as directly and as emphatically as I knew how to the mass of voters . . . to the men who if waked up would be able to impose their will on their representatives." He would use his skill at public relations to go over the bosses' heads to the people themselves, while he would set an example of what a public servant could be through energy, sterling honesty, and independence.

An opportunity came quickly, when Chauncey Depew, political power broker and head of the New York Central Railroad, sent Roosevelt the free pass that was always given to the governor of the state. It was returned with a note: "How I wish I *wasn't* a reformer. . . . But I suppose I must live up to my part. . . ." Shortly thereafter Thomas Platt arrogantly "suggested" who should be appointed superintendent of public works, and at the same time handed the new governor a telegram of acceptance from the man. Roosevelt turned him down. "This produced an explosion, but I declined to lose my temper, merely repeating that I must decline to accept any man chosen for me, and that I must choose the man myself."

Roosevelt began speaking out on the unhealthy alliance between corporations and politicians, an alliance that led to special privileges for both, and then to abuse of those privileges. To his surprise, he came under attack from those who usually posed as reformers. "Newspaper editors, college presidents, corporation lawyers, and big business men, all alike, had denounced the bosses and had taken part in reform movements against them so long as these reforms dealt only with things that were superficial. . . . But the majority of these men turned to the support of the bosses when the great new movement began . . . as one against privilege in business no less than against privilege in politics, as one for social and industrial no less than for political righteousness and fair dealing."

Much of the strength of this new movement was in the future, but Roosevelt began as governor to try to awaken the people to their peril. The "rush toward industrial monopoly" was proceeding apace, and every year saw more and larger industrial mergers. In 1898 there had been $900,000,000 of capital incorporated, a record that was broken in the first two months of 1899. How was this wealth and power, so often irresponsibly used, to be contained? Roosevelt started using the machinery of state government to regulate the machinery of corporations.

Thomas Platt and the corporate executives of New York were enraged by this, and wanted him out of the state house, a feeling that grew in intensity when they began suspecting that he had radical plans to protect New York's natural resources. But Roosevelt's popularity presented them with a difficulty: when the governor's first two-year term was over, he would most likely be elected to another. Roosevelt also recognized a problem. He wanted to be president with all his heart, but could not challenge McKinley in 1900. If he was reelected as governor, he would be out of office in 1902, which meant he would have no base or pulpit from which to fight the nomination battle for the next presidential election. Popular now, yes, but "I have never known a hurrah to endure for five years."

Then, in November 1899, Vice-President Garret A. Hobart died, and a solution seemed to present itself to Platt. With some resistance, Roosevelt, who feared the position was meaningless, allowed himself to be drafted to run with William McKinley in 1900. Mark Hanna, corporate millionaire and one of the architects of the alliance between business and government, had resisted the choice with ferocious energy, shouting, "Don't any of you realize that there's only one life between this madman and the White House?"

The race was against William Jennings Bryan, who did not realize that silver coinage was no longer an issue, and his vice-presidential candidate, Adlai Stevenson of Illinois, who had been vice-president under Cleveland and was namesake and grandfather of a future presidential hopeful. It was Roosevelt who bore the burden of the fight, traveling thousands of miles by train, speaking at every opportunity of the need to defeat the enemies of progress, until his voice failed again and he felt like "a football man who has gone stale." The result was an overwhelming victory for the Republicans.

Less than a year later, on September 6, 1901, President McKinley was shot twice by the anarchist Leon Czolgosz. He lingered in great pain for eight days, Ida at his bedside, her heart breaking for the last time. Two daughters, her brother, and now her husband, had died before their time, leaving her to face life alone.

Theodore Roosevelt was, as his generation had expected, the first "modern" president—the first to confront the ways the United States had changed in the decades after the Civil War, with the emergence of giant corporations, the need to compete with foreign empires, and a widening gap between rich and poor. It was in 1898 that he became famous across the land and was elected to executive office, but the year had brought him more. The experience of serving so intimately with working-class men, sharing their suffering and fears, listening to their stories, had revealed the burdens of their lives in a way he had never known before, and gave strength to his fight for reform.

John Long, his chief at the Navy Department, had written in his diary the day Roosevelt resigned to join the Rough Riders: "His heart is right, and he means well, but it is one of those cases of aberration—desertion—vainglory; of which he is utterly unaware. He thinks he is following his highest ideal, whereas, in fact, as without exception every one of his friends advises him, he is acting like a fool." Now he took that volume out again and wrote across the page, "Roosevelt was right. . . . His going . . . led straight to the Presidency."

EPILOGUE

The change that . . . overshadows and even controls all others is the indus-
trial one, the application of science resulting in the great inventions that
have utilized the forces of nature on a vast . . . scale: the growth of a world-
wide market as the object of production, of vast manufacturing centres to
supply this market, of cheap and rapid means of communication and distri-
bution between all its parts. . . . One can hardly believe there has been a rev-
olution in all history so rapid, so extensive, so complete. Through it the face
of the earth is making over, even as to its physical forms; political boundaries
are wiped out and moved about, as if they were indeed only lines on a paper
map; population is hurriedly gathered into cities from the ends of the earth;
habits of living are altered with startling abruptness and thoroughness; the
search for the truths of nature is infinitely stimulated and facilitated, and
their application to life made not only practicable, but commercially neces-
sary. Even our moral and religious ideas and interests, the most conservative
because the deepest-lying things in our nature, are profoundly affected.

John Dewey in *The School and Society,* 1899

PROPER DEFINITION of a gentleman was important in 1898, and a number
of writers tried to formulate one that would catch the spirit of the times. As
S. M. Crothers pointed out in the May issue of the *Atlantic Monthly,*
"though the average man would not be insulted if you were to say, 'You are
no saint,' it would not be safe to say, 'You are no gentleman.'" Crothers
traced the origins of the ideal back to ancient times, comparing Abraham,
Confucius, and Plutarch's Romans. His examples differed in details of

behavior and dress, but all were admirable in their sincerity, sense of personal dignity, and confidence. The Romans particularly impressed Crothers, and undoubtedly his readers, with their "masculine" virtue. "No wonder that men who thus learned how to conquer themselves conquered the world."

Gentlemen had evolved over the ages, being especially improved by medieval chivalry. Launcelot, of King Arthur's court, was the paragon: "he was the prototype of those mighty men who were the makers of the modern world." And what of this modern world? Crothers made an effort to differentiate the evolution of the true gentleman from the man of fashion and other weak imitations, and he ended by asking the question, "What becomes of the gentleman in an age of democratic equality?"

The English gentleman, an even greater empire builder than the Romans, had generally been held up as the contemporary exemplar of the type, but most Americans felt there was a particular lack of charm in English class snobbery, with its emphasis on privileged birth. "What is his family?" was the question that would determine a man's status, no matter how sterling his other qualities. The journalist Julian Ralph exposed these prejudices in *McClure's Magazine* at the end of 1898 in an article entitled "What Is a Gentleman: Some English Definitions and Views," and in the same issue John Brisben Walker argued that the American ideal was altogether finer and more appropriate for the modern world, writing that if he "were asked to point out a distinguishing characteristic of the American gentleman, after his natural refinement in thought, speech and action, it is that he has nothing of that caddish tendency which causes so many Englishmen to bow down to the rank and station of those above them—nothing of that willingness to wound the feelings of others in order that he himself may attain some advantage or assume some air of superiority. He is fearless in his beliefs. . . . He is interested in all his fellow men, and never shrinks from meeting and knowing them, in whatever station of life. . . . He kowtows to none, curries favor with none, fears none . . . is ready to respect the rights of all equally with his own, and pity equally with his own the misfortunes of those less favored than himself." In America the ideal was not to be based on privilege, but on character.

This was the self-congratulatory consensus view, and it was expected that the spread of such openness and sensitivity, such tolerance and interest in the workings of the world, combined with patriotism and love of the republic, would be a way of bridging the chasms of American life. But how to continue to produce men and women with these qualities of independent character in an age of concentrated economic power? How could an individual sense of personal dignity and worth be encouraged in a mass society? Or fortitude and self-denial in an age beginning to glorify comfort and consumption? Mothers, it was expected, would continue to properly train their children, and men like Theodore Roosevelt and Richard Harding Davis would provide chivalric examples, but for the larger society, with its growing numbers of immigrants carrying strange customs from around the world, a stronger force was needed.

Americans had long regarded "education" as being able to work miracles of transformation. "It was a secular form of grace," wrote the historian Page Smith, "a sacred institution, the alchemist's stone that might be depended on to change immigrants into 100 percent Americans . . .; freed slaves into middle-class Americans with incidentally black skins; Indians ditto; racially prejudiced Southern (and Northern) whites into champions of black equality; drunkards into teetotalers, and so on, virtually *ad infinitum*." The number of public school children had increased from fewer than nine million in 1876 to almost fifteen million a generation later, but only around five hundred thousand pupils attended high school. The national rate of illiteracy had dropped sharply, and now there began to be a great interest in education for responsible democratic citizenship.

But how to instruct in intellectual and vocational skills while building character? One traditional method particularly needed to be jettisoned: rote learning had dominated American education from its beginnings, but new conditions demanded new approaches. John Dewey, a philosopher at the University of Chicago who later moved to Columbia, became the foremost advocate of modern pedagogy. In the spring of 1898, he spoke on his ideas at the Farmington School of Ethics, then in 1899 published his first important book, *The School and Society.* "The obvious fact is that our social life has undergone a thorough and radical change," he wrote. "If our education is to have any meaning for life, it must pass through an equally complete transformation."

Education, like so much else in an industrial economy, needed organization for "promotion and efficiency" so that waste would be eliminated, freeing more resources to prepare the child to become a full member of society. The school should be the agent of social progress and reform as well as learning, where children could develop all their talents and learn to be confident participants in a democracy. There would be task-oriented and cooperative learning of both manual (cooking exercises, for example) and intellectual skills, and also the development of proper moral character through taking part in the daily experience of the school. "The great thing to keep in mind . . . regarding the introduction into the school of various forms of active occupation, is that through them the entire spirit of the school is renewed. It has a chance to affiliate itself with life, to become the child's habitat, where he learns through directed living, instead of being only a place to learn lessons having an abstract and remote reference to some possible living to be done in the future. It gets a chance to be a miniature community, an embryonic society."

Dewey was optimistic about America's ability to shape the goodness of human nature residing in the "common man and woman," sure that students could be taught to value high intellectual and moral standards in an age of democratic leveling, while also valuing their fellow citizens in all their diversity of thought, feeling, and ability. His theories provided the basis of "progressive education" in the early part of the twentieth century. Unfortunately, his ideas, when taken up by sentimental enthusiasts stressing the "child-centered" part of his message while forgetting his promotion of the mind, increasingly led to classrooms and school systems that graduated students bereft of the mathematical and writing skills needed for success in modern life.

GERMANY AND JAPAN were feared and envied by turn-of-the-century Americans, not only for their aggressive energy, undoubted talents, and great ambitions, but also because each was thought to gain strength through tight internal ethnic bonds, a sense that each nation consisted of people who shared close racial and cultural traits, giving them a sense of identity and purpose, and who were guided by firm leadership in their kaiser and emperor. How could a land of great contrasts and differences, such as the United States, stand up to such challenges?

Those differences, more often than not, turned out to be a fertile source of strength. A further, and undoubted, economic blessing was the existence of one huge domestic market, free of tariffs or customs duties. "We find here," wrote the Englishman James Muirhead in his 1898 book *America: The Land of Contrasts,* "a huge section of the world's surface, 3,000 miles long and 1,500 miles wide . . . containing seventy millions of inhabitants, producing a very large proportion of all the necessities and many of the luxuries of life, and all enjoying the freest of free trade with each other. . . . Collectively they contain nearly half the railway mileage of the globe, besides an incomparable series of inland waterways. . . . The internal commerce of the United States makes it the most wonderful market on the globe." This market, which was shielded from foreign competition by heavy tariffs, allowed industrialists to develop technology, improve productivity, and build giant and irresistible corporations before they entered into international trade.

An example of the process is the way the bicycle prepared a path for the automobile. Technological innovations necessary to produce a light, safe "wheel" acceptable for a mass market were quickly adapted for early horseless carriage production, as were the machine tools developed for their manufacture. Bicycle mechanics became so skilled that they were pioneers in the development of both automobiles and airplanes, while large bicycle manufacturers, who had made their first fortunes in the giant protected domestic market, were some of the earliest automobile producers. They used the lessons they had learned from selling "wheels" to promote their new machine.

By 1899 there were 30 companies producing 2,500 motor vehicles; within a decade there were almost 500 companies competing for a share of the market. The huge distances of the country and its numerous widely scattered communities meant that the automobile was quickly seen as a necessity, and by 1913 the United States was manufacturing almost 500,000 of the world's total production of 600,000. Savage competition soon reduced the number of firms while increasing productive efficiency through the assembly line, and by 1929 85 percent of the world's automobiles were produced in the United States, most by Ford, General Motors, and Chrysler, while a good portion of the remaining 15 percent came from foreign subsidiaries of Ford and General Motors.

Americans were now deriving their sense of identity at least partly from their technological superiority. Thomas Edison, Henry Ford, and scientific-management expert Frederick Taylor were recognized as international heroes of progress. But there were still tremendous social and economic problems in the country. John Dewey had hoped that education could help tame the nation's "economic evils," or at least help raise the consciousness of those who labored hardest. "How many of the employed are today mere appendages to the machine which they operate! This may be due in part to the machine itself, or the *regime* which lays so much stress upon the products of the machine; but it is certainly due in large part to the fact that the worker has had no opportunity to develop his imagination and his sympathetic insight as to the social and scientific values found in his work."

Industrial workers, struggling for union recognition and the right of collective bargaining, held more hard-headed goals, such as decent wages, an eight-hour day, and the strength to have some say in their labor.

SOON AFTER THE TURN of the century, Americans lost whatever desire they had ever felt for the adventure of empire-building. Rudyard Kipling had welcomed the "American cousins" to the duties of imperialism in February 1899 with a poem called "The White Man's Burden," its subtitle "The United States and the Philippine Islands":

> *Take up the White Man's burden—*
> *Send forth the best ye breed—*
> *Go bind your sons to exile*
> *To serve your captives' need;*
> *To wait in heavy harness*
> *On fluttered folk and wild—*
> *Your new-caught, sullen peoples,*
> *Half devil and half child.*

The struggle in the Philippines had been relatively brief, and the islands were more or less subdued by 1902, but it had been an ugly experience that few wanted to repeat. One newspaper poet responded to Kipling:

> *We've taken up the white man's burden*
> *of ebony and brown;*
> *Now will you tell us, Rudyard,*
> *how we may put it down?*

Even Theodore Roosevelt saw the disadvantages by 1907, when a still-critical Andrew Carnegie, claiming the effort had pulled the country into "the vortex of international militarism," called on him at the White House.

"If you wish to see the two men in the United States who are the most anxious to get out of the Philippines, here they are," the president said, pointing to Secretary of War William Howard Taft and himself.

"Then why don't you?" Carnegie replied. "The American people would be glad indeed."

Roosevelt and Taft both said that duty required the United States to stay and fulfill its responsibility to prepare the Filipinos for self-government. As it was, the Philippines would not receive full independence, which was

The first step towards lightening

The White Man's Burden

is through teaching the virtues of cleanliness.

Pears' Soap

is a potent factor in brightening the dark corners of the earth as
civilization advances, while amongst the cultured of all nations
it holds the highest place—it is the ideal toilet soap.

The image of Admiral George Dewey, the victor of Manila Bay, used to sell soap.
(*Vermont Historical Society*)

delayed by the Second World War, until 1946. But there is no question that the men were sincere about their desire to be rid of the burden of empire. War threatened with Japan in 1907, and Roosevelt had suddenly realized that the possession, so vulnerable and so far from the mainland, was, as he called it, the nation's "Achilles' heel."

Goaded by the intense criticism of bungling in the Spanish war, the government had reformed the structure of the standing army and increased its size, but true military preparedness was still inadequate compared to the other Great Powers. Few Americans seemed to care, even after Europeans began fighting in 1914. There was some hope that Woodrow Wilson and his secretary of state, William Jennings Bryan, would be able to keep the nation out of what quickly became a global war, although that desire proved impossible, only postponing engagement for three years.

The United States had irrevocably entered the world in 1898, and although strong isolationist movements would intermittently rise throughout the century, there could be no turning back to the country's earlier policy of avoiding foreign entanglements. In 1917, however, just as in 1898, moral argument was the galvanizing force used to arouse the people, and President Wilson had to legitimize and glorify involvement in the war as being necessary to save democracy.

The Spanish-American struggle was over so quickly that lessons about tactical and logistical mishandling were not really absorbed. American soldiers marched into Belleau Wood and Château-Thierry almost as naively sure of themselves and poorly trained as they had been on their approach to San Juan Heights. This lack of preparation, due to a combination of congressional tightfistedness, overconfidence, and a sense that America was protected by an invincible armament of spirit and idealism, would be a problem until well after World War II, when the country entered the seemingly endless cold war.

The conflict with Spain had not only propelled the United States onto the world stage but also launched the presidency on its way to becoming the dominant branch of American government in the twentieth century. This desire for strong, efficient executives at every political level was already much in the air at the beginning of 1898. Early in her visit that year, the British observer Beatrice Webb noted that "one point was evident: the constant and increasing distrust of the American—whether he be a superior person or the man in the street—of an assembly of representatives. Any device to escape being ruled by a representative assembly seems acceptable: a referendum, a nominated body, or a dictator, a closely knit

syndicate ruled by a boss, even Tammany itself—so long as you escape government by representative institutions."

In October 1897, Judge Simeon E. Baldwin had written an article for the
Yale Law Journal on presidential power, proclaiming "Proudly and safely
rides the ship of state into the opening harbor of the twentieth century;
prouder and safer because one hand, and one hand only, is on the wheel."
This piece was widely distributed, with long sections appearing in newspapers across the country, including Mendocino, the remote logging town on
the northern California coast. Arthur Schlesinger notes in his study *The
Imperial Presidency* that congressional influence began to erode "when it
forced a cautious President into war with Spain in 1898, inadvertently
[conspiring] against its own authority. . . . And the Spanish-American War,
by projecting the United States . . . into the world of great powers,
strengthened the executive not just for the duration but for a long time
thereafter."

How one felt about this development seemed to depend on whose hand
was guiding the ship of state. If it was your man, well and good—if the
other fellow, then throw the rascal out. It wouldn't be until later in the century that philosophical and constitutional criticism grew loud. Some presidents, such as Herbert Hoover, would resist the new prerogatives, but
Theodore Roosevelt bluntly stated his own position: "I believe in a strong
Executive," he said. "I believe in power." And he used that power in ways
never before seen in the country: to help labor, as in the great United Mine
Workers strike of 1902, as well as in the broader battles to control corporations, defend natural resources (though more along Gifford Pinchot's line
than John Muir's), and conduct an aggressive foreign policy.

Democratic President Woodrow Wilson thought that "without the
watchful interference, the resolute interference, of the government there
can be no fair play," and even so conservative a Republican as Calvin
Coolidge understood how important the new executive strength was to
ensure justice and progress for everyone: "It is because in their hours of
timidity the Congress becomes subservient to the importunities of organized minorities that the President comes more and more to stand as the
champion of the rights of the whole country."

Franklin Delano Roosevelt used executive power even more assertively
than had his distant cousin Theodore. During the Great Depression of the
1930s, so severe that it made the collapse of the 1890s appear a mere dip on
the economic charts, and the dangerous struggle of the Second World War,
FDR established policies that fundamentally changed American society. It

was under his shield that labor finally gained collective-bargaining rights, and the government took responsibility for stimulating the economy as well as ameliorating the worst effects of poverty and deprivation. Here was the institution, thought many, that could ensure fairness—producing community, trust, brotherhood, and an equal chance in life for every American.

They were wrong, of course. There was no one magic solution to such problems, although at times a temporary stability of competing ideas and programs was achieved, as after the victory over Japan and Germany in 1945. The search went on as people of good will sought to balance the contrasting needs and ambitions of disparate groups across the nation, searching for some formula by which race, gender, class, and culture could blend into a particularly American identity. No matter what else they desired—profits or power or religious grace—some good and thoughtful men and women had in 1898 tried to bind up the differences of their country, aspiring to bring together a nation undergoing unprecedented and highly disruptive change.

This is what patriots hoped a secular religion of the nation and flag would bring about; it is what Theodore Roosevelt sought with his mix of classes, races, and cultures in the Rough Riders; what Thomas Edison and Henry Ford predicted would result from their technological innovations (the "bringing together" that President McKinley said the telephone was accomplishing); what Booker T. Washington tried to promote by the raising of his people from the degradation of slavery; what W. E. B. Du Bois thought his sociological studies might lead to; what John Dewey philosophized about; what Clara Barton went to Cuba to promote; what Jane Addams wished for at Hull House, what Frederick Winslow Taylor was confident his improvements in productivity could bring, and what the lords of the palatial department stores were certain they were offering the American public at bargain prices.

Balance, identity, perception of a common destiny—one hundred years later, with the United States again confronted with dimly understood technologies, demands for increased efficiency to better compete in international markets, growing disparities of wealth, bitter racial divisions, and washed anew by huge waves of immigration—we search for those qualities still.

Notes

The shortened citations in the Notes refer to books by the author's last name. Articles are indicated by quotes around the title. They are fully cited in the Bibliography, which begins on page 341.

PROLOGUE

PAGE

3   *"Ode to Greater New York"*: See the *New York Journal* of December 26, 1897, for the full text. Americans loving songs as much as they did doggerel, the "ode" was also set to music.

      All quotes in this description of the New Year festivities are from the January 1, 1898, edition of the *New York Times,* unless otherwise noted. Description and background of New York in this Prologue are based on editions of the *New York Times, Journal,* and *Tribune* running from December 26, 1897, to January 7, 1898, and from the *Philadelphia Press* on the same dates.

7   *"Putting out a newspaper"*: Swanberg, 193.

8   *"The bosses"*: *New York Times,* January 2, 1898.

      "bringing us all": Linderman, 9.

9   *"You say you were"*: *New York Times,* January 3, 1898.

10   *"The dead woman's feet"*: Ibid.

12   *"The disastrous war of competition"*: May, 201–2.

      White House: For a brilliant description of one of these New Year receptions, see Prologue in Morris, *The Rise of Theodore Roosevelt.*

13   *"In honoring your mother"*: Leech, 47.

      McKinley shaving: Margaret Leech believed that this technique indicated "a kind of careless optimism." Leech, 25.

16   *"One of the finest"*: Weems, 42.
      "torpedo" explodes: *New York Times,* January 2, 1898.

CHAPTER ONE
LAND OF CONTRASTS

17   *"[The] United States stands"*: All quotes from Muirhead are from *The Land of*
      Contrasts: A Briton's View of His American Kin, unless otherwise noted.
18   *the "lendemain," or future*: Bourget, 5.
      "More than any one": Smith, 549.
19   *"Hanna has advertised"*: Morison, I: 394.
20   *"My father being a poor man"*: *Harper's Weekly,* October 8, 1898.
21   *"My husband came"*: Smith, 425.
      Thomas Jefferson: Ibid., 425–6.
22   *"Applied science"*: *Agricultural Almanac* for 1898, published in Lancaster, Pa.
      My thanks to Christina Scornavaca and Tania Lee for providing this issue.
      "A new drygoods store": All William Allen White quotes are from his *Autobiog-*
      raphy unless otherwise noted.
24   *"Twenty floats"*: Rydell, "The Trans-Mississippi . . .," 591.
      "no . . . class lines": White, "An Appreciation of the West," 579.
25   *"It seems to me"*: Rydell, "The Trans-Mississippi . . .," 591.
      "We shall not always": Thanet [Alice French], "The Trans-Mississippi . . .,"
      600.
      "We are living": Beam, "The Last Victorian Fair," 10.
      Promoters had a powerful ally: Rydell, "The Trans-Mississippi . . .," 591.
26   *"This grand ethnological"*: Mooney, "The Indian Congress . . .," 592.
27   *"Now and then"*: Holt, 33.
28   *"New York astonished me"*: Ibid., 44.
      Lew Chew: All Lew Chew quotes are from ibid., 174–85.
29   *"I got down to business"*: Ibid., 46–7.
      "The only hope": 344.
      "I accepted ill-usage": All quotes from Mary Antin are from her autobiogra-
      phy, *The Promised Land.*
30   *Saloons*: See Schlereth's exceedingly valuable book for insight into saloons
      and other details of American life, 226.
31   *"Men drank their whiskey straight"*: Schlereth, 227.
32   *"The work is not hard"*: *Mendocino Beacon,* January 8, 1898.
33   *"Are we animals"*: Du Bois, *Dusk of Dawn,* 58–59.
      "might have been said": Du Bois, *Philadelphia Negro,* 35, note.
      "It is the . . . development": Ibid., 120.
34   *"Our object"*: Ibid, 130, note.
      "The wisest among my race": Smith, 623–4.
36   *"He told me"*: Dana, 68.
      "The vaudeville theatre": Schlereth, 230.

36   *"when Bessie Finklestein"*: Antin, 260–1.

37   *No despair*: See Ziff, 133, and Kazin, "American Fin-de-Siecle."
        "This life's a hollow bubble": Sullivan, 289.

CHAPTER TWO
THE ADVENTURE OF PROGRESS

39   All Mr. Dooley quotes are from F. P. Dunne, *Mr. Dooley in Peace and War.*
40   *"When I got to"*: Frost, 31.
        "a minor invention": Millard, 6.
41   *"I don't care"*: Smith, 117–18.
        Garrett P. Serviss: The story was first published in the *New York Evening
        Journal,* then reprinted as a book in 1947.
42   *"a bird that can sing"*: Boorstin, 363.
        tripling the output of machine shops: Flink, 46.
43   *Taylor's plan*: Boorstin, 365.
        "140 men": Ibid., 366.
44   *"Of course I have"*: Cahn, 19–20.
47   *"When the company"*: Ibid., 59–60.
        "Well, I'm going to": Wachhorst, 117.
48   *Muir and Pinchot*: For detailed discussions of this controversy, see Hayes,
        Nash, and Strong.
49   *"The first is profitable"*: Pinchot, *Biltmore Forest,* 44–5.
        "We were all made slaves": All Muir quotes are from his autobiography, *The
        Story of My Boyhood and Youth,* unless otherwise noted.
50   *Muir's inventions*: Some of these marvelous machines are on view at the
        University of Wisconsin.
51   *"Muir was a storyteller"*: All Pinchot quotes, unless otherwise noted, are from
        his *Breaking New Ground.*
52   *"I don't want"*: Wolfe, 275–6.
        "Thousands of tired": These articles and others were later reprinted in Muir,
        Our National Parks.
53   *The usual pattern*: Kaempffert, ed., 141.
        "On the bicycle": Harmond, "Progress and Flight: An Interpretation of the
        American Cycle Craze of the 1890s," 244.
54   *Theodore Roosevelt's bicycle squad*: Roosevelt details many of their adventures
        in his autobiography, 201–3.
55   *"A pleasing prospect"*: *The Horseless Age,* November 1895, 8. William Allen
        White records the general disbelief that there would really be a "displace-
        ment" of animal power. "We stood one day in the door of the bookstore, at
        the turn of the century, and watched, in a parade that was passing, a buggy
        drawn by two mules, with a great sign over it 'Horseless Carriage,' and we
        laughed with the others." White, *Autobiography,* 302.
56   *"advertising novelties"*: Clymer, 12.

57　　"*You'll never get*": Editors of *Automobile Quarterly,* 60.
　　　"*developed more all-round*": Flink, 10.
　　　"*George, you are crazy*": Barber, 17.

58　　"*We often wondered*": Nevins, 156.
　　　"*the peculiar sensation*": Ibid., 160.
　　　"*Finally, I had to*": Ford, 33.

59　　"*It seemed as if*": Nevins, 155.
　　　"*My gas-engine experiments*": Ford, 33.

60　　"*Young man*": Nevins, 167.

61　　"*Machinery is accomplishing*": *New York Times,* January 1, 1929.
　　　"*The example of the bird*": *The Independent,* October 22, 1903.
　　　"*The machine has worked*": Morison, vol. 2, 799 and 806. See also Morris, 608
　　　and 840, note 76.

62　　"*They did it*": Bilstein, 12.

CHAPTER THREE
YOUTH AND NEW IDEAS

63　　"*I had let career*": Walker, 14.
　　　"*To be young*": Dana, 88.

64　　*Lancaster, Pennsylvania*: D'Emilio and Freedman, 181.
　　　"*Even in the daytime*": Dana, 118.

65　　"*War, when you are at it*": Howe, ed., *The Occasional . . . ,* 80.

66　　"*The roughness with which*": Bourget, 330.

67　　"*I wished to return*": Walker, 14.
　　　"*Speaking of American art*": *Harper's Weekly,* October 8, 1898.

68　　"*a short thick-set, bullet-headed man*": Shannon, ed., 14.

69　　"*I had never known such a man as he*": White, *Autobiography,* 297.
　　　"*I was nervous and timid*": Roosevelt, *Autobiography,* 61.

70　　"*You have the mind*": Pringle, 17.
　　　"*Take care of your morals*": McCullough, 165.
　　　"*The* caveat emptor *side of the law*": Roosevelt, *Autobiography,* 61.
　　　"*the defective moral quality*": Ibid., 64.
　　　"*if conscientiously done*": Pringle, 49.

71　　"*wanted to put an end*": Chessman, 42.
　　　"*The atmosphere of change*": Dana, 4.

73　　"*mental activity was considered*": Ibid., 50.
　　　"*She is acknowledged*": *The New York Times,* October 8, 1898. The majority of
　　　such articles were negative, not only in the *Times* but in other papers; but
　　　this same issue also included stories about successful businesswomen.

75　　"*Jane Austen renaissance*": *New York Times,* November 5, 1898.
　　　"*Wagner's operas*": Dana, 123.
　　　Mark Twain: Geismer, 415.

76   *National Institute of Arts and Letters:* See Ziff, 345–6.
      "although her death": Dana, 79.
      "The object of the Gideons": Spears, 166.

77   *Edward Bellamy: Looking Backward* sold over two hundred thousand copies
      within two years of its publication in 1888, sparking this wave of utopianism.
      "the utmost attainable advance": Gilman, *The Living of . . .*, 165.
      "an experimental effort to aid": Addams, 90.

79   *"brutal, barbarous, and an outrage upon the age":* Chadwick, *Diplomacy,* 320.
      "one who preached the need of dying": Foner, I: 8.

80   *"The chains of Cuba":* Ibid., 21.

81   *"not only cheap but bright":* Brown, 12.

82   *a contemporary researcher estimated:* Wilcox, "The American Newspaper . . ."
      "the war news factories": Rea, 23.

84   *"The time of the Great Editor":* Brown, 21.

85   *"Five hundred dollars":* R. H. Davis to Charles Belmont Davis. Original letter
      in the Barrett Collection at the University of Virginia; reprinted in Charles
      Belmont Davis, ed., 172.

86   *"DOES OUR FLAG PROTECT WOMEN?":* New York Journal, *February 12, 1897.*
      Pulitzer's World *investigated:* See "Tale of a Fair Exile," *New York World,*
      February 15, 1897. The *New York Times* interviewed another woman who was
      searched and who supported Clemencia Arango's story. See "Cuban Women
      Ill Treated," *The New York Times,* March 2, 1897.
      "where there should have been": Richard Harding Davis, *Cuba in War Time,*
      127.

CHAPTER FOUR
HUMANITY AND SELF-INTEREST

87   *"I would regard a war with Spain":* Pringle, 176.
      "Ah! Capitaine": In a book by Alfred T. Mahan, quoted in Spector, 23.
      "Gentlemen—it's very good of you": Quoted in Kipling, 1981 ed., 44.

88   *"Why? . . . It is because":* Foreign Relations, 1895.

90   *"It is on board":* Tuchman, 153.
      "Whether they will or no": Mahan, *The Interest of . . .*, 18.
      "I hope he has no preconceived plans": Lodge, I: 240.
      "I want peace": Morris, 555.
      "If he becomes": Ibid., 560.
      "Best man for the job": Morgan, 588.

91   *"What is the need":* Long, 156.

92   *"the qualities of entire manliness":* Roosevelt, *The Rough Riders,* 7.
      "We both felt": Ibid., 9.

93   *Even the granting of autonomy:* See Carr, 59.

94   *"I doubt if those Spaniards":* Morison, I: 747.

94   *"Germany shows a tendency"*: Ibid., 662.
     "It was a political demonstration": Pepper, 93.

95   *"Uncertainty exists"*: Millis, 94. Millis, whose account of the war is distorted by his cheap cynicism, somehow reads the events and Lee's actions as reflecting the consul's incompetence.
     "The funny part of it all is": Morris, 594.
     "I feel, sir": Morison, II: 759–64.

97   *German naval vessels*: O'Toole makes an interesting case for the German factor, 115–23.
     "Ship quietly arrived": Sigsbee, 23.

98   *"I see that we have only good news"*: Leech, 165.

99   *"The jingo members of Congress"*: May, 138.
     "Death to the Americans!": The circular is reproduced, and translated, in Sigsbee, 35–7.

100 *"We are masters of the situation"*: Trask, 25–6.
     "Captain Sigsbee's launch": Epler, 286.

101 *He felt . . . a quick surge of pride*: Meriwether, "Remembering the *Maine*."

102 *"We're well protected here"*: Weems, 69.
     "I laid down my pen": Unless otherwise noted, all quotations and reminiscences by Sigsbee are from his book.
     "I instantly turned my head": Unless otherwise noted, the description of the sinking of the *Maine* is based on Weems, Sigsbee, Samuels, and the record of the Naval Court of Inquiry.

103 *"the great glass door"*: Epler, 286–7.
     "The city shook": Meriwether, "Remembering the *Maine*."

104 *"The colonel beat one"*: Rea, "The Night of the Explosion . . ."

105 *"They bent their oars"*: Brown, 116.

106 *"Captain Sigsbee bears the calamity"*: Ibid., 117.

CHAPTER FIVE
WAR FEVER

107 *"There are many things worse than war"*: May, 141.
     "I have been through one war": Hagedorn, I: 141.
     "It was almost impossible": *The American-Spanish War,* 341–2.

108 *"The* Maine *blown up!"*: Millis, 102.
     Scovel's cable: Brown, 120–1.
     "There is not": Hearst, 59.

109 *"the public would know"*: Mayo, 162–3, and Brown, 122.
     "I don't propose": Leech, 168.
     "The Maine *was sunk"*: Morison, 775.
     "Some men, at cost": Roosevelt, *Autobiography,* 241.

110 *Charles R. Flint*: Morris, 605–6.

111   *"during my short absence"*: Ibid., 601–3.

     "the newspaper men cluster": Mayo, 165–6.

     They had started with headlines: See Brown, 123.

112   *"came to this country too late"*: Ibid., 127.

     an enormous leap in circulation: Millis, 108 and 110.

     "Men that I took by the hand": Walter Scott Meriwether, "Remembering the Maine."

113   *Sol Bloom:* Half the profits from the song were donated to the fund established for families of the dead. Bloom, 160.

     "I myself doubt": Morison, II: 779–80.

     "Other nations would be": Trask, 30.

114   *Many Protestant, Jewish, and Catholic religious leaders:* All quotes from May, 140.

     "everything is war talk": Ibid., 141–2.

     "To break in pieces the oppressor": Trask, 58.

115   *"no more backbone"*: Leech, 169.

     "If we wer in Spaines place": May, 122.

     Woodford wrote the president: Both quotes, Trask, 32.

116   *"It has not excited"*: Foreign Relations, 1898, 681–5.

     "Who knows where this war": May, 147.

     Senator Proctor's speech: See Dallek, 129–41.

117   *"converted a great many"*: May, 145.

     "Proctor's position": Dunn, 234.

118   *"Teddy Roosevelt"*: Morris, 601.

     "Vultures now hover": Brown, 125.

119   *They declared it an accident:* There has never been any final answer as to the cause of the disaster. A second court of inquiry held in 1911, when the battleship was raised from Havana harbor, decided that the external explosion probably took place a bit more toward the stern than the 1898 court had found, but it essentially confirmed the findings of the earlier investigators. The *Maine* was then towed out to sea and sunk with full military honors. In 1976, Admiral Hyman Rickover had some of his engineering experts do a quick study of the sinking based on old photographs and court testimony. They concluded that an internal explosion had caused the disaster. More recently, the authors Peggy and Harold Samuels, feeling that Rickover's crew did not do a serious and creditable job of research, reopened the case yet again, and decided that an external explosion was likely. Certainly the Spanish government had no reason to attack the ship, but either Ultra-Loyalists or the Cuban revolutionaries may have thought they would gain from blowing it up.

     "Full self-government": Trask, 40.

120   *"Shall we other monarchs"*: May, 196.

     "almost as prejudicial": Ibid., 204.

     "He appeared to me careworn": Leech, 173.

120   *"His face had grown seamed and haggard"*: Ibid., 181–2.
       "I have been through": Kohlsaat, 66. Also see Leech, 629.
121   *"don't your President know"*: Leech, 184.
       "Dissuade them!": Ibid., 185.
       "I sympathize with McKinley": May, 152.
       McKinley's message to Congress is reprinted in Dallek, 203–12.
122   *Teller amendment*: See Foner, I: 270.
       "I hope they": Trask, 56.
       "The scene upon the floor": Millis, 143.
       Senate vote: See Dallek, 214.
       "Everyone here expects": Trask, 57.
123   *"The interests of the country changed"*: White, "When Johnny . . ."
       "Alger has no force whatsoever": Morris, 611.
       "in the intoxication of such a success": Howe, *Portrait* . . ., 195.
125   *Roosevelt was both amused and outraged*: All Roosevelt quotes are from his
       Autobiography, 234–6.
       "I am going to college!": Hobbs, 14.
126   *"I have put my whole life"*: Wright, 6 and 64.

CHAPTER SIX
THE GLORIOUS FIRST OF MAY

127   *"Success always makes success"*: All Dewey quotes, unless otherwise noted,
       are from his autobiography.
       "I've looked in his eyes": Healy and Kutner, 140.
       Roosevelt had decided he wanted Dewey: Roosevelt, *Autobiography,* 231.
       He unsuccessfully asked: Morison, I, 691–2.
128   *"I want you to go"*: Dewey, 168.
       "Here, write it down": Healy and Kutner, 137.
130   *"Affairs are very unsettled"*: Spector, 41.
       "Things look decidedly": Ibid., 42.
131   *A story making the rounds*: Rodman, 238–40.
132   *"We do not wish to annex Cuba"*: Dewey, 185. He does not mention the cigars
       and wine, while they are featured in Healy and Kutner, 103.
       "we need only a bay": Dewey, 185. He goes on to say, "It did not then occur to
       me that we should be taking Manila Bay permanently."
133   *"Two or more spies watch me"*: Spector, 45.
134   *"War exists"*: Trask, 397.
       "Daily the cry arises": Spector, 47.
135   *"A fine set of fellows"*: Dewey, 192.
       The squadron must leave: The letter is reprinted in Healy and Kutner, 167.
       The governor wrote across the bottom of the page, "God knows, my dear
       Commodore, that it breaks my heart to send you this notification."

135   *"I should be delighted"*: Ibid., 168.
         Dewey spent the next two days: Healy and Kuttner give the details, 168. Dewey says 12:15, but that may have been when the cable was received in Hong Kong.
136   *Harden was less responsible:* Brown, 189.
137   *"There'll Be a Hot"*: Rodman, 243–4.
         "No, don't wash": Fiske, 251.
         Chinese "showed no fear": The American-Spanish War.
138   *"Our fleet"*: Healy and Kutner, 192.
         "I could not have told": Kohlsaat, 68.
139   *"One wore a blue"*: Brown, 184.
         The informal contest: See Sullivan, 319–21.
140   *"sigh of relief"*: Brown, 198.
         "All the children": Spector, 64.
         "all lived in the marvelous Land of Oz!": Baum and MacFall, 107–10.
         Blackton: See Adair, 8.
141   *honorary degrees:* Halstead, 354.
         Senator Proctor is quoted in Dewey, 228.
         "to be composed exclusively": Morris, 613.
142   *"I was wise enough"*: All Roosevelt quotes are from his book *The Rough Riders,* unless otherwise noted.
         "Oh, dear! I had this": Roosevelt, *Autobiography,* 247–8.
         "One fine old fellow": Ibid., 246–7.
143   *Roosevelt making a terrible mistake:* Morris, 612.
         "He has been of great use": Long, 223–4.
144   *"I know perfectly well"*: Morison, II: 817.
         "the one case": Morris, 586.
         Appointment of Joseph "Fighting Joe" Wheeler: Jones, 18–19.
146   *"There is hardly a man on this floor"*: Millis, 157.
         "One of the reasons": Ibid., 155.
         "precede the fire company": White, "When Johnny . . ."
147   *"Every man had at least"*: All quotes of Charles Post are from his book.
         Roosevelt complaining: The *New York Times* article was printed on April 30, 1898.
150   *"The men can go in and drink"*: Pringle, 186.
         "Nectar never tasted as good": Morris, 843, note 31.
         Wood's ideas about discipline: Ibid., 623.
         "I wish to say": Hagedorn, I: 154.
         "he was polite": Morris, 623.
         "Wood often asked advice": Ibid.
151   *"I was in the Franco-Prussian War"*: Pringle, 187–8.
         "If we don't get them to Cuba": Hagedorn, I: 149.
         "hugging each other": Morris, 624.
152   *Even their popularity:* See Morris, 625.

CHAPTER SEVEN
WAITING FOR ORDERS

154   *"I knew that I was doing right"*: New York Times, May 25, 1898.
155   *"Everybody thinks of war"*: Beam, "The Last Victorian Fair."
       "The war with Spain": Thanet [Alice French], "The Trans-Mississippi Expo-
       sition."
       "worthy country dame": Ibid.
156   *"had it not been"*: Beam, "The Last Victorian Fair."
       "would of itself crowd": Thanet [Alice French], "The Trans-Mississippi Expo-
       sition."
       "an odor of naphtha": Ibid.
157   *"any dance of an immoral character"*: Beam, "The Last Victorian Fair."
       "We saw the Casino": Ibid.
       "go wild at first": Thanet [Alice French], "The Trans-Mississippi Exposition."
       Alice French (1850–1934) was educated at Abbott Academy in Andover,
       Massachusetts, but lived for most of her later life in Arkansas.
       "The temples that stand": White, "An Appreciation of the West."
158   *"the idea of drinking and eating off of coffins"*: Beam, "The Last Victorian Fair."
       "rocking chair period of the war": All R. H. Davis quotes, unless otherwise
       noted, are from his book *The Cuban and Porto Rican Campaigns.*
       "A city composed of derelict houses": Jones, 51.
159   *"No words can paint the confusion"*: Morris, 627.
       "couldn't walk two miles": Cosmas, 189.
160   *"The men of the regular army"*: Brown, 209.
       "Oh, well . . . they'll learn": R. H. Davis to Charles, May 29 [1898], Barrett
       Collection, University of Virginia, reprinted in Charles Belmont Davis, ed.,
       Adventures and Letters . . ., 242.
161   *"I am pretty tired"*: Ibid., 246.
       "I cannot decide": Ibid., 242.
       In spite of his qualms: See R. H. Davis, "Serious Defects of Our Volunteer
       Regiments," New York Herald, June 5, 1898.
       "That some official action": See "Davis Replies to Bigelow," New York Herald,
       June 6, 1898.
       "There's lots to be written": R. H. Davis to Family, June 9, 1898, Barrett Col-
       lection, University of Virginia. This passage was edited from the letter when
       it was published in Charles Belmont Davis, ed., *Adventures and Letters . . .*,
       244.
162   *"Every beautiful newspaperwoman"*: Brisbane, "The Modern Newspaper in
       War Time," Cosmopolitan, September 1898.
       For the story of Watkins and Benjamin, see Brown, 209–12.
163   *"bitten by mosquitoes"*: Ibid., 211.
164   *"Well, d'ya ever have niggra"*: Post, 56.

165   *"If 10,000 men were here"*: Alger, 71.
166   *"Sampson says"*: Trask, 180.
       "There came a waving and halloing": Post, 82.
167   *The Rough Riders and the* Yucatan: See Brown, 274, and Roosevelt, *The Rough Riders.*
       Roosevelt's "zeal for publicity": Albert Smith, 57.
168   *"At the best it was stringy"*: Roosevelt, *The Rough Riders,* 62.
       Riot in Tampa: See Gatewood, *Black Americans . . .,* 52–5.
169   *Charles Post and the Seventy-first*: Post, 18, 21, 98.
170   *"Perhaps no nation but Spain"*: Brown, 279.
       "Today we are steaming": Morison, II: 843.
       "Evidently the plan": Bonsal, 70.

CHAPTER EIGHT
THE REAL THING

171   *"But to get the real thing"*: All Crane quotes are from *Wounds in the Rain* unless otherwise noted.
       "We hoped, and we feared": All quotes from Charles Post are from his book, unless otherwise noted.
       "All men who feel any power": Morris, 654.
       "first a mast": Slocum, 210.
172   *"He was an artist from crown to heel"*: Werthein and Sorrentino, 310–11.
173   *Elliot later commended him*: Stallman, 369.
174   *"one of the most impressive"*: McIntosh, 56.
175   *"We did the landing"*: All Roosevelt quotes, unless otherwise noted, are from *The Rough Riders.*
       "Somehow everything seems": Jones, 91.
176   *"A quarter of an hour of whistle shrieks"*: Brown, 308; Freidel, 89.
       "The fight lasted": Freidel, 91.
178   *"The jungle had a kind of hot"*: Morris, 642.
       "I know nothing about war": Stallman and Hagemann, 155.
179   *"Wouldn't a glass of cold beer"*: Marshall, "A Wounded Correspondent's . . ."
       "from hillock to hillock": Stallman and Hagemann, 156.
       Roosevelt noticed: Marshall, *The Story . . .,* 99–100.
       "Every one went down": Marshall, "A Wounded Correspondent's . . ."
       "It was most confusing country": Roosevelt, *Autobiography,* 256–7.
180   *"Stop that swearing"*: Marshall, "A Wounded Correspondent's . . ."
       "A tall gaunt young man": All Davis quotes are from his book *The Cuban and Porto Rican Campaigns,* unless otherwise noted.
181   *"One learns fast in a fight"*: Roosevelt, *Autobiography,* 257.
       "We've got the damn Yankees": Dierks, 92; Freidel, 106.
182   *"It was a doleful group"*: Marshall, "A Wounded Correspondent's . . ."
183   *"we jettison all"*: Beisner, 80, 150.

184   "*sat by the wayside*": Freidel, 91.

185   "*There is no necessity for haste*": Alger, 125.

        "*Well, now, so this is what*": Trask, 227–8.

186   "*no attempt at strategy*": See Miley, 101–6, and both Shafter articles.

        "*nauseated and very dizzy*": Ibid.

187   "*Later in the day*": All observations from Caspar Whitney are from his
        Harper's Weekly or *Harper's Monthly* pieces.

        As Charles Post: Unless otherwise noted, all quotes and descriptions involv-
        ing Charles Post are from his book.

188   "*uneasy excitement*": See Roosevelt, *The Rough Riders,* and Morris, 650.

        "*It was a picture*": McIntosh, 119–20.

        "*They had studied it out*": Allen, 84. All Remington quotes are from this book.

189   "*Isn't this awful?*": Christy, "The Story of the War."

190   *The reporter James Creelman*: This is based on all three Creelman sources.

        "*I'm sorry you're hurt*": Swanberg, 184–5.

        "*A retreat now would be a disastrous defeat*": Trask, 241, and Brown, 358. Miley
        glides over this decision rather quickly in his own book. See Miley, 110.

191   *Lieutenant Jules Garesche Ord and General Hawkins*: Charles Post met the
        general some years later and got the story, and the dialogue, from him. Post,
        181–5.

        "*We were in front*": Stone, 122.

192   "*a little group of blue figures*": Crane, *Wounds in the Rain.*

194   *Roosevelt shot him dead*: Roosevelt later remembered this as occurring on the
        second line of hills, but I agree with Morris that it took place here.

CHAPTER NINE
WAGES OF WAR

195   "*Tell the President*": Morison, 846.

        " '*I guess the folks*' ": Davis, *Notes . . . ,* 123.

197   "*Everyone who saw*": Roosevelt was obviously much excited and under strain.
        He mistakenly writes that they were soldiers of the Ninth Infantry, but Gate-
        wood in *Smoked Yankees* does a good job of relating the incident.

        Rumors began: See Roosevelt's *The Rough Riders,* 145–6. When two Regular
        officers of the Third Cavalry told him about the rumors, "I cordially agreed
        with them that it would be far worse than a blunder to abandon our position."

198   "*Well, General*": Roosevelt, *Autobiography,* 265.

199   "*This is a heavy*": Lee, "The Regulars . . ."

        "*I regret to say*": Alger, 172.

        Alger remembered: Ibid.

        "*Dead men*": Whitney, "The Santiago Campaign."

200   "*I could not*": Allen, 114–16.

        "*It was about*": All Roosevelt quotes, unless otherwise noted, are from *The
        Rough Riders.*

201   *Dynamite gun:* Davis, *Notes . . .,* 123–4.

        George Kennan: All Kennan quotes are from his *Campaigning in Cuba.*

202   *"My clothes smell":* Richard Harding Davis to mother, July 9 [1898], Barrett
        Collection at the University of Virginia.

        "The situation here": The article was written on July 3, but not published for
        several days. "Our Brave Men Defy Hardships," *New York Herald,* July 7,
        1898, 11. See also his defense in *The Cuban and Porto Rican Campaigns,* 251,
        where he says "It was stated that my despatch . . . had been recabled to the
        Paris *Herald,* that from Paris it was forwarded to Madrid, and that on the
        next day, July 8th, the authorities in Madrid communicated its contents to
        General Toral—so giving the garrison in Santiago increased confidence and
        hope, and encouraging it to hold out longer against us."

203   *"With a very powerful":* Wheeler, 286–7.

        "I would like": Ibid., 277.

        "Lost prestige": O'Toole, 325.

204   *"I waited":* Alger, 173–4.

        "We have the": Alger, 174–5.

        "If . . . you can": Ibid., 177.

        "I shall be obliged": Ibid., 182.

205   *"throwing themselves":* Trask, 262–3.

        "all of a sudden": Ibid.

206   *"It was a magnificent":* All Robley Evans quotes are from his book.

        "That man": Trask, 263–4.

        "Don't cheer, boys!": Captain Philip was such a pious man that his chaplain
        later argued that he must have said "fellows" not "devils." Freidel, 224. After
        the battle he assembled his whole crew to offer thanks to God for bringing
        them through safely.

207   *"joined in the chorus":* Leech, 260.

        "As we passed": Epler, 297.

        "My God, boys": Ross, 216.

        "I had not": Ibid.

208   *"felt it was": Ibid.*

        "I have some": Epler, 299–300, and Ross, 217–18.

        Janet Jennings: Janet Jennings' article is reprinted in Epler, 300–6.

209   *John Pershing:* See Pershing, *Under Fire with the Tenth Cavalry,* 210.

        black heroism: Mendocino Beacon, October 22, 1898.

210   *"pretty scrimmage":* Mayo, 203–4.

211   *"A drunken man":* Davis, *The Cuban and Porto Rican Campaigns,* 261.

CHAPTER TEN
A WORLDWIDE VICTORY

214   *Tom Reed's desire to irritate McKinley:* So Margaret Leech argues, 212–13.

215   *"Is not this":* Pratt, 324.

215   *"We need Hawaii"*: Leech, 213.

        "large policy": Lodge, I: 300.

        "We cannot": Hoar, II: 307–8.

        "to willing and capable": Pratt, 325.

216   *Rumors*: Leech, 213.

        "To retain possession": Trask, 370.

        "We had the City": Dewey, 240. Unless otherwise noted, all Dewey quotes are from his autobiography.

217   *"Well, now go"*: Trask, 403.

        Dewey and von Diederichs: Ibid., 380. Dewey in his autobiography admits merely, "I made use of the occasion by using him as a third person to state candidly and firmly my attitude in a verbal message which he conveyed to his superior so successfully that Vice Admiral von Diedrichs [sic] was able to understand my point of view."

218   *"You will pardon"*: O'Toole, 252.

219   *"What about Guam"*: Trask, 385.

        "We earnestly hope": Morison, II: 859.

        "The lithe college": Roosevelt, *The Rough Riders*, 197.

220   *"Snakes"*: Trask, 327.

        "We weren't out": Morris, 658–9.

221   *"It was deemed"*: Roosevelt, *The Rough Riders*, 205–6.

        "To keep us": Morison, II: 864–5.

222   *Attacks on the edges*: As David Trask points out, later strategists such as Basil H. Liddell Hart called this "the indirect approach." Trask, 341.

        "10, American": Ibid., 340.

223   *"When one remembers"*: All Richard Harding Davis quotes, unless otherwise noted, are from his *Cuban and Porto Rican Campaigns*.

        "I was in the South": Trask, 404.

224   *"It was found"*: *The American-Spanish War*, 266.

        "Merritt's most difficult": Trask, 412.

        "said his honor": Ibid., 415.

        "After the battle": *The American-Spanish War*, 277.

225   *"My troops"*: Trask, 419–20.

        "pending the conclusion": Leech, 286.

226   *"The discussion"*: Ibid., 281.

        "How are you": Morris, 663–4.

        "Will you be": *New York Times*, August 16, 1898.

227   *"whatever yellow-fever"*: Morris, 662.

228   *"the Rough Riders"*: Morison, II: 859.

        "The publication": Roosevelt, *Autobiography*, 278.

        John Jay Chapman: See Morris, 665–8.

229   *"I shall never"*: Howe, *John Jay Chapman . . .*, 142.

        "doing a heap": Pringle, 201.

        "If he becomes": Morison, II: 1475.

229   *"plain statement"*: All Roosevelt quotes are from his *Autobiography* unless otherwise noted.

230   *"RISING TIDE"*: See, for example, the *New York Times, September 3, 1898.*
       Rafferty parade: All quotes about the parade are from the *New York Times,* September 2, 1898.

232   *"The smaller fry"*: Cosmas, 282.
       "IF MANY MORE": New York Times, *September 3, 1898.*
       "He made no": Cosmas, 282–3.
       "The Secretary": New York Times, September 1, 1898.

234   *"When we think"*: Cosmas, 282.
       Alger boasting: Alger, 438.
       "I am very much": Morison, II: 871.
       "At Santiago": Trask, 334–5.

235   *"A former Populist"*: Roosevelt, *The Rough Riders,* 221.

236   *"Three Cheers"*: Morris, 674.

CHAPTER ELEVEN
BATTLES AT HOME

237   *"What with Indian"*: Harper's Weekly, October 22, 1898.
       "Right here": Rydell, "The Trans-Mississippi . . ."

238   *"In the electricity"*: Thanet, "The Trans-Mississippi . . ."

239   *"We are living"*: Beam, "The Last Victorian Fair."
       Children: Rydell, "The Trans-Mississippi . . ."
       "Special, previous": Ibid.
       "heroic figures": Beam, "The Last Victorian Fair."
       Powell: Rydell, "The Trans-Mississippi . . ."

240   *A reporter noted:* Beam, "The Last Victorian Fair."
       "The other tribes": Mooney, "The Indian Congress . . ."
       "He is one": Ibid.
       White-Swan: Ibid.

241   *"serious ethnological exhibition"*: Thanet, "The Trans-Mississippi . . ."

242   *"It cannot"*: Ibid.
       "scalped or turned over": Rydell, "The Trans-Mississippi."
       "to quit his roving": Ibid.

243   *"increasing gate receipts"*: Ibid.
       "evident purpose": Mooney, "The Indian Congress."
       "the Indian as the Alpha": Harriman, "Congress of American Aborigines."
       "The object lesson": Rydell, "The Trans-Mississippi . . ."

244   *"The Indian school"*: White, "Appreciation of the West."
       Lanier: Beam, "The Last Victorian Fair."
       "what the Negro": Ibid.

245   *"TROOPS BATTLE"*: New York Times, October 6, 1898.

245   *"The fact that"*: Ibid., October 7, 1898.

246   *"They are well"*: Ibid., October 6, 1898.

"Old Bug": See Pinckney, "Old Bug's Necklace," for more details. Bug-O-Nay-Ge-Shig translates as "Hole-in-The-Day."

247   *"You ought"*: *New York Times,* October 8, 1898.

248   *"Give 'em hell"*: Ibid., October 7 and 8, 1898.

"They say that": Ibid., October 8, 1898.

"went on the war-path": Ibid., October 7, 1898.

249   *"I shall pay"*: Ibid., October 9, 1898.

French newspaper: Ibid., October 8, 1898.

250   *"prompted to"*: Pinckney, "Old Bug's Necklace," 75.

251   *George Saxton*: Leech, 114. This account is based on Leech, 451–5, and the *New York Times* editions of October 8 and 9, 1898.

253   *"I'll kill him"*: There were many witnesses to such threats. See Leech and the *New York Times,* October 9, 1898.

"I will talk": *New York Times,* October 8, 1898.

"Wide": Ibid., October 6, 1898.

254   *"a gown of white"*: Leech, 451.

255   *"We want no differences"*: See May and Leech for accounts of the trip and his speeches, and the *New York Times,* October 9 and 10, 1898, for quotes.

257   *"bowed with a grim smile"*: *Harper's Weekly,* October 22, 1898.

"appeared to study": Rydell, "The Trans-Mississippi . . ."

258   *Circular*: Hicken, "The Virden and Pana Mine Wars of 1898."

Wages: Ibid.

259   *Miners killed*: Schlereth, 50.

"after a few hours": *New York Times,* October 13, 1898.

"at the muzzle": Ibid., October 11, 1898.

260   *"We . . . give you notice"*: Ibid., October 13, 1898.

"Under the": Ibid.

"The laboring man's": Hicken, "The Virden and Pana Mine Wars of 1898."

261   *"We tried"*: *New York Times,* October 14, 1898.

"The miners and the train": Ibid., October 13, 1898.

"hotter than San Juan Hill": Hicken, "The Virden and Pana Mine Wars of 1898."

262   *"He told them"*: *New York Times,* October 14, 1898.

a "miracle": Hicken records five guards wounded and four killed.

263   *"I do not feel"*: *New York Times,* October 14, 1898.

Illinois was to provide: Hicken, "The Virden and Pana Mine Wars of 1898." 278.

CHAPTER TWELVE
OPPORTUNITIES

264   *"If old Dewey"*: Kohlsaat, 68.

"It is not compatible": Trask, 441.

265   *"anarchy and slaughter"*: May, 246.

        rumors: For example, see the *New York Herald,* July 3, 1898.

        "The Philippine": May, 248–50.

        "On general principles": Ibid., 245.

        "I think": Ibid., 249–50.

266   *"Knowing you to be"*: New York Times, September 2, 1898.

267   *"These ward politicians"*: Shannon, ed., 44–5.

        "Everybody is talkin' ": All quotes from George Washington Plunkitt come from Riordan, 3–10, 46–61.

268   *"excited almost as much"*: Roosevelt, *Autobiography,* 302.

270   *"The rural districts"*: Shannon, ed., 11.

        "Now for a State": Mark Howe, ed., *Chapman,* 142.

271   *"I do not see"*: See the *New York Times,* September 20, 1898, and Morison, II: 876.

        "could hardly walk": Mark Howe, ed., *Chapman,* 143.

        "I think that this": Pringle, 203.

272   *"I have been"*: See the *New York Times* for September 24, 28, and 29, 1898.

        "Wheeler H. Peckham": Ibid., October 9, 1898.

        Roosevelt tax problems: A very good brief explanation of the controversy is in Morris, 853–4, note 75. For fuller treatment see G. Wallace Chessman's "Theodore Roosevelt's Personal Tax Difficulty," *New York History,* 34:54–63.

273   *"Is the hero"*: Morris, 678.

        "This is a Democratic State": New York Times, October 8, 1898.

        "It was a brilliant": Ibid., October 6, 1898.

275   *"He really believes"*: Mark Howe, ed., *Chapman,* 470.

        "make a brilliant": New York Times, October 8, 1898.

276   *"a respectable man"*: Roosevelt, *Autobiography,* 297.

        "The only even odds": Morris, 680.

        "Tammany Hall has a right": Pringle, 207. Judge Daly lost the election.

        "Under my attack": Roosevelt, *Autobiography,* 296.

        "Afro-American": New York Times, October 15, 1898.

277   *"I want to talk to you"*: New York Sun, October 25, 1898, in Morris, 685. Roosevelt has a shorter version in his *Autobiography,* 138.

        "inborn pugnacity": New York Times, October 17, 1898.

278   *"sun birds"*: Ibid., November 6, 1898.

279   he *"was the first"*: Ibid.

280   *"Poor white men"*: Edmonds, 147.

        "Go to the polls": Hofstadter and Wallace, 230.

281   *"Lynch him"*: Prather, 103–4.

        Salaries: Ibid., 23.

        "How many of you": Edmonds, 164.

282   *"You have just"*: Prather, 118.

        "We are having a necktie": Ibid., 97–8.

283   *"to exert his influence"*: New York Times, January 1, 1899.

        "I made enemies": Edmonds, 5.

284   *"I am not ashamed"*: This story was first told in *The Christian Advocate* of January 22, 1903, and reprinted many times. See selection in Ginger, 279–84.
Carnegie's visit: Leech, 355.
"We hold that the policy": Commager, II: 11–12.

285   *"I have never enjoyed"*: Long and LeMaster, 182.
"wanton war": Ibid.
"Your friend": Thayer, II: 199.
"How are you": Trask, 469.
"The islands are filled": *New York Times*, November 5, 1898.
"It is always": Trask, 470.
Senate vote: See Leach, 353–9.

286   *"His face showed"*: *New York Times*, November 10, 1898.
"I have played it": Morison, II: 888.

CHAPTER THIRTEEN
THE NEW AMERICAN WAY

287   *"I know the banker"*: Pringle, 251.
"Without imagination": Leach, 37 and 403, note 97.

289   *"triumph of the moral and spiritual"*: Cahn, 82.

290   *"I can advertise"*: Pope, 14.
"part of the humanities": Ibid., 3.

291   *"The name must be"*: Cahn, 71.
"a scientific baker": Ibid.

292   *"You need a name"*: See Boorstin, 439. Cahn, on page 72, simply includes it on a list along with other suggestions, such as "Taka Craker" and "Usa Cracker."
"Reduction in prices": Cahn, 86.

293   *"breaking down of habit"*: Ibid., 91.

294   *"I am Uneeda"*: See Schlereth, 145–6; Cahn, 92.
"They look on me": Cahn, 97.

295   *"an agent of Americanization"*: Boorstin, 147; Cahn, 93.
"The moon had left us": Wright, 65.

296   *"bloodless and white"*: Ibid., 66.

297   *"What shall we do?"*: *New York Times*, November 28, 1898. This account of the storm is based on coverage in the *New York Times*, the *Philadelphia Inquirer*, and the books of E. R. Snow.
"little boy whose pitiful face": Ibid.

298   *Claims of missing the* Portland: E. R. Snow, who spent years studying the fate of the *Portland*, was convinced of the truth of these two stories. See Snow, *Strange Tales*, 176.
"young bloods": Snow, *Vengeful Sea*, 239.
"It was blowing so hard": Snow, *Great Storms . . .*, 292.

299   "CALAMITIES UNPRECEDENTED": *New York Times,* November 30, 1898.
       Around one hundred and fifty ships: The numbers of ships and lives lost were
       hard to determine. Ships like the *Portland* took their passenger lists to sea
       with them, so the names were lost when the ship went down. These particu-
       lar figures are taken from E. R. Snow's in *Great Storms . . . ,* 285.

300   *Lyman Frank Baum:* This portrait of Baum is based mainly on William
       Leach, *Land of Desire,* and Baum and MacFall, *To Please a Child.*
       "To gain all the meat": Leach, 247.

301   *"There is a latent power":* Ibid., 229.

302   *"the uplifting of mercantile":* Leach, 59.
       "no way to protect": Baum, *The Art of Decorating . . . ,* 7.
       "arouse in the observer": Ibid., 128. Baum describes some of his effects in this
       book.

303   *"The time has come":* Leach, 251. See Leach's incisive commentary on Baum
       and his classic, 246–60.
       "the imprints of our noses": Antin, 187, 261.

304   *"I have ideals":* Leach, 51.
       "true to a degree": Ibid., 29–30.
       "The Tide of Prosperity": *New York Times,* December 29, 1898.

305   *Crossroads stores:* See Schlereth, 144.
       "Few got grumpy": *New York Times,* December 25, 1898.
       "with the spirit that is as ardent": Ibid.

306   *"THE RICH SAW THEM":* Nissenbaum, 252. Nissenbaum discusses charity as
       spectator sport.
       The governer-elect offering gifts: *New York Times,* December 25, 1898.

307   *"combine both idealism":* All Roosevelt quotes, unless otherwise noted, are
       from his *Autobiography.*
       "How I wish": Pringle, 208.

308   *In 1898 there had been:* See Morris, 694.
       "I have never known": Morison, II: 1023.

309   *"a football man":* Pringle, 226.
       The experience of serving: See Morris, 723.
       "His heart is right": Long, 162.

EPILOGUE

311   *"were asked to point out":* *McClure's Magazine,* December 1898.

312   *"It was a secular":* Smith, 589.

313   *"We find here":* Muirhead, 12–13.

314   *"How many of the employed":* John Dewey, 16.

315   *"We've taken up":* Morgan, 111.
       "If you wish to see": Carnegie, 365.

317   *"one point was evident"*: Shannon, ed., 9.
318   *"Proudly and safely"*: See *Mendocino Beacon,* January 15, 1898.
      "when it forced": Schlesinger, 82.
      "I believe in a strong": Linderman, 177.
      "without the watchful": Schlesinger, 404.
      "It is because in their hours": Ibid., 405.

Bibliography

BOOKS

Adair, Gilbert. *Flickers*. London, 1995.

Addams, Jane. *Twenty Years at Hull House*. 1910. Reprint. New York, 1960.

Alger, Russell A. *The Spanish-American War*. New York, 1901.

Allen, Douglas. *Frederic Remington and the Spanish-American War*. New York, 1971.

The American-Spanish War. Norwich, Conn., 1899.

Antin, Mary. *The Promised Land*. Boston, 1912.

Editors of *Automobile Quarterly. The American Car Since 1775*. New York, 1971.

Banta, Martha. *Imaging American Women: Idea and Ideals in Cultural History*. New York, 1987.

Barber, H. L. *The Story of the Automobile*. Chicago, 1917.

Baum, L. Frank. *The Art of Decorating Dry Goods Windows and Interiors*. Chicago, 1900.

Baum, Frank and MacFall, Russell. *To Please a Child: A Biography of L. Frank Baum, Royal Historian of Oz*. Chicago, 1951.

Beisner, R. L. *Twelve Against Empire: The Anti-Imperialists, 1898–1900*. New York, 1968.

Bilstein, Roger E. *Flight in America*. Rev. edn. Baltimore, 1994.

Bloom, Sol. *The Autobiography of Sol Bloom*. New York, 1948.

Bonsal, Stephen. *The Fight for Santiago*. New York, 1899.

Boorstin, Daniel J. *The Americans: The Democratic Experience*. New York, 1973.

Bourget, Paul. *Outre-Mer: Impressions of America*. New York, 1895.

Brands, H. W. *The Reckless Decade: America in the 1890s*. New York, 1995.

Brown, Charles H. *The Correspondent's War: Journalists in the Spanish-American War*. New York, 1967.

Cahn, William. *Out of the Cracker Barrel: The Nabisco Story from Animal Crackers to Zuzus*. New York, 1973.

Carnegie, Andrew. *The Autobiography of Andrew Carnegie*. Boston and New York, 1920.

Carr, Raymond. *Spain 1808–1975*. Oxford, 1982.

Chadwick, French Ensor. *The Relations of the United States and Spain: Diplomacy*. New York, 1909.

———. *The Relations of the United States and Spain: The Spanish-American War*. 2 vols. New York, 1911.

Chessman, G. Wallace. *Theodore Roosevelt and the Politics of Power*. Boston, 1969.

Clymer, Floyd. *Treasury of Early American Automobiles: 1877–1925*. New York, 1950.

Commager, Henry Steele. *Documents of American History*. 2 vols. New York, 1968.

Cosmas, Graham A. *An Army for Empire: The United States Army in the Spanish-American War*. Shippenburg, Pa., 1994.

Crane, Stephen. *Wounds in the Rain*. New York, 1923.

Creelman, James. *On the Great Highway*. Boston, 1901.

Dallek, Robert. *1898: McKinley's Decision*. New York, 1969.

Dana, Nathalie. *Young in New York: A Memoir of a Victorian Girlhood*. Garden City, N.Y., 1963.

Davis, Charles Belmont. *Adventures and Letters of Richard Harding Davis*. New York, 1917.

Davis, Richard Harding. *The Cuban and Porto Rican Campaigns*. New York, 1898.

———. *Cuba in War Time*. New York, 1897.

———. *The Notes of a War Correspondent*. New York, 1911.

D'Emilio, John, and Freedman, Estelle B. *Intimate Matters: A History of Sexuality in America*. New York, 1988.

Dewey, George. *Autobiography of George Dewey: Admiral of the Navy*. Written with the help of Frederick Palmer. New York, 1913.

Dewey, John. *The Middle Works: 1899–1924*. Carbondale, Ill., 1976.

Dierks, Jack Cameron. *A Leap to Arms: The Cuban Campaign of 1898*. Philadelphia and New York, 1970.

Du Bois, W. E. B. *Dusk of Dawn: An Essay Toward an Autobiography of a Race Concept*. 1940. Reprint. New York, 1968.

———. *The Philadelphia Negro*. 1899. Reprint. Philadelphia, 1996.

Dunn, Arthur Wallace. *From Harrison to Harding: A Personal Narrative, Covering a Third of a Century, 1888–1921*. New York and London, 1922.

Dunne, F. P. *Mr. Dooley in Peace and War*. 1898. Reprint. Chicago, 1968.

Edmonds, Helen G. *The Negro and Fusion Politics in North Carolina: 1894–1901*. Chapel Hill, N.C., 1951.

Epler, Percy H. *The Life of Clara Barton*. New York, 1937.

Evans, Robley. *A Sailor's Log: Recollections of Forty Years of Naval Life*. New York, 1901.

Fiske, Bradley A. *From Midshipman to Rear-Admiral*. New York, 1919.

Flink, James J. *The Automobile Age*. Cambridge, Mass., 1988.

Foner, Philip S. *The Spanish-American War and the Birth of American Imperialism*. 2 vols. New York, 1972.

Ford, Henry. *My Life and Work*. Garden City, N.Y., 1922.

Freidel, Frank. *The Splendid Little War*. New York, 1958.

Frost, Lawrence A. *The Edison Album*. Seattle, 1969.

Furnas, J. C. *The Americans: A Social History of the United States.* New York, 1969.

Gatewood, Willard B., Jr. *Black Americans and the White Man's Burden, 1898–1903.* Urbana, Ill., 1975.

———. *"Smoked Yankees" and the Struggle for Empire: Letters from Negro Soldiers, 1898–1902.* Urbana, Ill., 1971.

Geismer, Maxwell. *Mark Twain, An American Prophet.* Boston, 1970.

Gilman, Charlotte Perkins. *The Living of Charlotte Perkins Gilman.* New York, 1935.

———. *Women and Economics: The Economic Relation Between Men and Women as a Factor in Social Evolution.* New York, 1898.

Ginger, Ray, ed. *The Nationalizing of American Life.* New York, 1965.

Hagedorn, Hermann. *Leonard Wood: A Biography.* 2 vols. New York, 1931.

Halstead, Murat. *The Life and Achievements of Admiral Dewey.* Chicago, 1899.

Hammack, David C. *Power and Society: Greater New York at the Turn of the Century.* New York, 1982.

Hayes, Samuel P. *Conservation and the Gospel of Efficiency.* Cambridge, Mass., 1959.

Healy, Laurin Hall, and Luis Kutner. *The Admiral.* New York, 1944.

Hearst, William Randolph. *William Randolph Hearst: A Portrait in His Own Words.* New York, 1952.

Hoar, George F. *Autobiography of Seventy Years.* 2 vols. London, 1904.

Hobbs, William Herbert. *Peary.* New York, 1936.

Hofstadter, Richard, and Wallace, Michael. *American Violence: A Documentary History.* New York, 1971.

Holt, Hamilton, ed. *The Life Stories of Undistinguished Americans as Told by Themselves.* Reprint. New York, 1990.

Howe, Mark A. DeWolfe. *Portrait of an Independent: Moorfield Storey, 1845–1929.* Boston and New York, 1932.

Howe, Mark A. DeWolfe, ed. *John Jay Chapman and his Letters.* Boston and New York, 1937.

———. *The Occasional Speeches of Justice Oliver Wendell Holmes.* Cambridge, Mass., 1962.

Johnson, Walter. *William Allen White's America.* New York, 1947.

Jones, Virgil Carrington. *Roosevelt's Rough Riders.* Garden City, N.Y., 1971.

Kaempffert, Waldemar, ed. *A Popular History of American Invention.* 2 vols. New York, 1924.

Kennan, George. *Campaigning in Cuba.* New York, 1899.

Kipling, Rudyard. *American Notes.* Norman, Okla., 1981 ed.

Kohlsaat, H. H. *From McKinley to Harding: Personal Recollections of the Presidents.* New York and London, 1923.

Leech, Margaret. *In the Days of McKinley.* New York, 1959.

Leach, William. *Land of Desire: Merchants, Power, and the Rise of a New American Culture.* New York, 1993.

Linderman, Gerald F. *The Mirror of War: American Society and the Spanish-American War.* Ann Arbor, Mich., 1974.

Lodge, Henry Cabot. *Selections from the Correspondence of Theodore Roosevelt and Henry Cabot Lodge, 1884–1918.* 2 vols. New York, 1925.

Long, E. Hudson, and LeMaster, J. R. *The New Mark Twain Handbook*. New York, 1985.

Long, Margaret. *The Journal of John D. Long*. Rindge, N.H., 1956.

Mahan, Alfred Thayer. *The Influence of Sea Power upon History, 1660–1783*. 2 vols. Boston, 1890.

———. *The Interest of America in Sea Power, Present and Future*. Boston, 1897.

———. *Lessons of the War with Spain*. New York, 1899.

Marshall, Edward. *The Story of the Rough Riders*. New York, 1899.

May, Ernest R. *Imperial Democracy*. New York, 1961.

Mayo, Lawrence S. *America of Yesterday as Reflected in the Journal of John Davis Long*. Boston, 1923.

McCullough, David. *Mornings on Horseback*. New York, 1981.

McIntosh, Burr. *The Little I Saw of Cuba*. London and New York, 1899.

Miley, John D. *In Cuba with Shafter*. New York, 1899.

Millard, André. *Edison and the Business of Innovation*. Baltimore, 1990.

Millis, Walter. *The Martial Spirit: A Study of Our War with Spain*. Boston and New York, 1931.

Milton, Joyce. *The Yellow Kids: Foreign Correspondents in the Heyday of Yellow Journalism*. New York, 1989.

Morgan, H. Wayne. *America's Road to Empire: The War with Spain and Overseas Expansion*. New York, 1965.

Morris, Edmund. *The Rise of Theodore Roosevelt*. New York, 1979.

Morison, Elting E., and John Blum, eds. *The Letters of Theodore Roosevelt*. 8 vols. Cambridge, Mass., 1951–4.

Muir, John. *The Mountains of California*. London, 1894.

———. *Our National Parks*. Boston, 1901.

———. *The Story of My Boyhood and Youth*. Boston, 1912.

Muirhead, James F. *America: The Land of Contrasts: A Briton's View of His American Kin*. London and New York, 1902 (3rd ed.).

Nash, Roderick. *Wilderness and the American Mind*. New Haven, 1973.

Nevins, Allen. *Ford: The Times, The Man, The Company*. New York, 1954.

Nissenbaum, Stephen. *The Battle for Christmas*. New York, 1996.

O'Toole, G. J. A. *The Spanish War: An American Epic, 1898*. New York, 1984.

Papers Relating to the Foreign Relations of the United States, 1895. Washington, D.C., 1896.

Pepper, Charles. *Tomorrow in Cuba*. New York, 1910.

Pershing, John J. "The Campaign for Santiago," in *Under Fire with the Tenth Cavalry*. Chicago, 1902.

Pinchot, Gifford. *Biltmore Forest*. Chicago, 1893.

———. *Breaking New Ground*. New York, 1947.

Pope, Daniel A. *The Making of Modern Advertising*. New York, 1983.

Post, Charles. *The Little War of Private Post*. Boston, 1960.

Prather, H. Leon, Sr. *We Have Taken a City: Wilmington Racial Massacre and Coup of 1898*. Cranbury, N.J., 1984.

Pratt, Julius W. *Expansionists of 1898: The Acquisition of Hawaii and the Spanish Islands.* Baltimore, 1936.

Pringle, Henry F. *Theodore Roosevelt: A Biography.* New York, 1931.

Rea, George Bronson. *Facts and Fakes About Cuba.* New York, 1897.

Rice, Wallace, ed. *Heroic Deeds in Our War with Spain: An Episodic History of the Fighting in 1898 on Sea and Shore.* Chicago, 1898.

Rickover, H. G. *How the Battleship Maine Was Destroyed.* 1976. Reprint. Annapolis, Md., 1995.

Riordan, William L., ed. *Plunkitt of Tammany Hall.* New York, 1905.

Rodman, Hugh. *Years of a Kentucky Admiral.* Indianapolis, 1928.

Roosevelt, Theodore. *An Autobiography.* New York, 1919.

Roosevelt, Theodore. *The Rough Riders.* New York, 1910.

Ross, Ishbel. *Angel of the Battlefield.* New York, 1956.

Samuels, Peggy and Harold. *Frederic Remington: A Biography.* Garden City, N.Y., 1982.

———. *Remembering the Maine.* Washington, D.C., and London, 1995.

Schlereth, Thomas J. *Victorian America: Transformations in Everyday Life.* 1991. Reprint. New York, 1992.

Schlesinger, Arthur M. *The Imperial Presidency.* Boston, 1973.

Shannon, David A., ed. *Beatrice Webb's American Diary: 1898.* Madison, Wisc., 1963.

Sigsbee, Charles D. *The "Maine": An Account of Her Destruction in Havana Harbor.* New York, 1899.

Slocum, Joshua. *Sailing Alone Around the World.* 1900. Reprint. Sheridan House, 1985.

Smith, Albert. *Two Reels and a Crank.* New York, 1952.

Smith, Page. *The Rise of Industrial America: A People's History of the Post-Reconstruction Era.* New York, 1984.

Snow, Edward Rowe. *Great Storms and Famous Shipwrecks of the New England Coast.* Boston, 1943.

———. *Strange Tales: Nova Scotia to Cape Hatteras.* New York, 1949.

———. *The Vengeful Sea.* New York, 1956.

Spears, Tomothy B. *100 Years on the Road: The Traveling Salesman in American Culture.* New Haven and London, 1995.

Spector, Ronald. *Admiral of the New Empire: The Life and Career of George Dewey.* Baton Rouge, La., 1974.

Stallman, Ralph W. *Stephen Crane: A Biography.* New York, 1968.

Stallman, Ralph W., and Hageman, E. R., eds. *The War Dispatches of Stephen Crane.* New York, 1964.

Stone, Herbert S., and Co. *The Events of the War as Described by Eyewitnesses.* Chicago and New York, 1899.

Stickney, Joseph L. *Life and Glorious Deeds of Admiral Dewey.* Chicago, 1898.

Strong, Douglas H. *The Conservationists.* New York, 1971.

Sullivan, Mark. *The Turn of the Century.* New York, 1927.

Swanberg, W. A. *Citizen Hearst.* New York, 1961.

Thayer, William Roscoe. *Life and Letters of John Hay.* 2 vols. Boston, 1915.

Trask, David F. *The War with Spain in 1898.* New York, 1981.

Tuchman, Barbara. *The Proud Tower.* New York, 1966.

Veblen, Thorstein. *The Theory of the Leisure Class.* New York, 1899.

Wachhorst, Wyn. *Thomas Alva Edison: An American Myth.* Cambridge, Mass., 1981.

Walker, Franklin. *Jack London & the Klondike.* San Marino, Cal., 1966.

Weems, John Edward. *The Fate of the Maine.* New York, 1958.

Wertheim, Stanley, and Sorrentino, Paul. *The Crane Log: A Documentary Life of Stephen Crane, 1871–1900.* New York, 1994.

Wheeler, Joseph. *The Santiago Campaign.* 1898. Reprint. Port Washington, N.Y., 1971.

White, William Allen. *The Autobiography of William Allen White.* New York, 1946.

Wolfe, Linnie Marsh. *Son of the Wilderness: The Life of John Muir.* New York, 1945.

Wright, Theon. *The Big Nail: The Story of the Cook-Peary Feud.* New York, 1970.

Ziff, Larzer. *The American 1890s: Life and Times of a Lost Generation.* New York, 1966.

ARTICLES

Archibald, James F. J. "The Day of the Surrender of Santiago." *Scribner's Magazine,* September 1898.

———. "What I Saw of the War." *Leslie's,* February 2, 1899.

Axeen, David. " 'Heroes of the Engine Room': American 'Civilization' and the War with Spain." *American Quarterly,* Fall 1984.

Beam, Patrice Kay. "The Last Victorian Fair: The Trans-Mississippi International Exposition." *Journal of the West,* January 1994.

Brisbane, Arthur. "The Modern Newspaper in War Time." *Cosmopolitan,* September 1898.

Christy, Howard Chandler. "An Artist at El Poso." *Scribner's,* October 1898.

———. "The Story of the War." *Leslie's,* August 4, 1898.

Creelman, James. "Hearst." *Pearson's Magazine,* September, 1906.

———. "My Experiences at Santiago." *Review of Reviews,* October 1898.

Harmond, Richard. "Progress and Flight: An Interpretation of the American Cycle Craze of the 1890s." *Journal of Social History,* Winter 1974.

Harriman, Mary Alice. "The Congress of American Aborigines at the Omaha Exposition." *Overland Monthly,* June 1898.

Hicken, Victor. "The Virden and Pana Mine Wars of 1898." *Journal of the Illinois State Historical Society,* Summer 1959.

Kazin, Alfred. "American Fin-de-Siècle." *The Saturday Review of Literature,* February 3, 1940.

Lanier, Henry Wysham. "The Great Fair at Omaha: The Trans-Mississippi and International Exposition, June 1 to November 1, 1898." *American Monthly Review of Reviews,* July 18, 1898.

Lee, Arthur H. "The Regulars at El Caney." *Scribner's,* September 1898.

Marshall, Edward. "A Wounded Correspondent's Recollections of Guasimas." *Scribner's,* September 1898.

Meriwether, Walter Scott. "Remembering the *Maine.*" *United States Naval Institute Proceedings,* May 1948.

Mooney, James. "The Indian Congress at Omaha." *American Anthropologist,* January 1899.

Pinckney, Roger. "Old Bug's Necklace." *American History,* December 1994.

Rea, George Bronson. "The Night of the Explosion in Havana." *Harper's Weekly,* March 5, 1898.

Rydell, Robert W. "The Trans-Mississippi and International Exposition: 'To Work Out the Problem of Universal Civilization.' " *American Quarterly* 33 (1981).

Shafter, W. R. "Capture of Santiago." *Century* 57 (February 1899).

———. "The Land Fight at Santiago." In *The Great Republic.* Vol. 4. New York, 1901.

Stickney, Joseph L. "With Dewey at Manila." *Harper's Monthly,* February 1899.

Thanet, Octave [Alice French]. "The Trans-Mississippi Exposition." *Cosmopolitan,* October 1898.

White, William Allen. "An Appreciation of the West: Apropos of the Omaha Exposition." *McClure's,* October 1898.

———. "A Typical Kansas Community." *Atlantic Monthly* 80 (1897).

———. "When Johnny Went Marching Out." *McClure's,* June 1898.

Whitney, Caspar. Articles in *Harper's Weekly.* June 11, June 18, July 9, 1898.

———. "The Santiago Campaign." *Harper's Monthly,* October 1898.

Wilcox, Delos F. "The American Newspaper: A Study in Social Psychology." *Annals of the American Academy of Political and Social Science,* July 1900.

Index

Numbers in italics refer to pages that contain illustrations.

A NOTE ON THE TYPE

This book was set in Fairfield, the first typeface from the hand of the distinguished American artist and engraver Rudolph Ruzicka (1883–1978). In its structure Fairfield displays the sober and sane qualities of the master craftsman whose talent has long been dedicated to clarity. It is this trait that accounts for the trim grace and vigor, the spirited design and sensitive balance, of this original typeface.

Rudolph Ruzicka was born in Bohemia and came to America in 1894. He set up his own shop, devoted to wood engraving and printing, in New York in 1913 after a varied career working as a wood engraver, in photoengraving and banknote printing plants, and as an art director and freelance artist. He designed and illustrated many books, and was the creator of a considerable list of individual prints—wood engravings, line engravings on copper, and aquatints.

Composed by ComCom, an R. R. Donnelley & Sons Company,
Allentown, Pennsylvania
Printed and bound by Quebecor Printing, Martinsburg, West Virginia
Designed by Robert C. Olsson